Applied Behavioral Economics Research and Trends

Rodica Ianole
University of Bucharest, Romania

A volume in the Advances in Finance, Accounting, and Economics (AFAE) Book Series

IGI GLOBAL
DISSEMINATOR OF KNOWLEDGE

www.igi-global.com

Published in the United States of America by
IGI Global
Business Science Reference (an imprint of IGI Global)
701 E. Chocolate Avenue
Hershey PA, USA 17033
Tel: 717-533-8845
Fax: 717-533-8661
E-mail: cust@igi-global.com
Web site: http://www.igi-global.com

Library of Congress Cataloging-in-Publication Data

Names: Ianole, Rodica, 1986- editor.
Title: Applied behavioral economics research and trends / Rodica Ianole, editor.
Description: Hershey, PA : Business Science Reference, [2017]
Identifiers: LCCN 2016045669| ISBN 9781522518266 (hardcover) | ISBN 9781522518273 (ebook)
Subjects: LCSH: Economics--Psychological aspects.
Classification: LCC HB74.P8 A664 2017 | DDC 302.3/5--dc23 LC record available at https://lccn.loc.gov/2016045669

This book is published in the IGI Global book series Advances in Finance, Accounting, and Economics (AFAE) (ISSN: 2327-5677; eISSN: 2327-5685)

British Cataloguing in Publication Data
A Cataloguing in Publication record for this book is available from the British Library.

Advances in Finance, Accounting, and Economics (AFAE) Book Series

Ahmed Driouchi
Al Akhawayn University, Morocco

ISSN:2327-5677
EISSN:2327-5685

MISSION

In our changing economic and business environment, it is important to consider the financial changes occurring internationally as well as within individual organizations and business environments. Understanding these changes as well as the factors that influence them is crucial in preparing for our financial future and ensuring economic sustainability and growth.

The **Advances in Finance, Accounting, and Economics (AFAE)** book series aims to publish comprehensive and informative titles in all areas of economics and economic theory, finance, and accounting to assist in advancing the available knowledge and providing for further research development in these dynamic fields.

COVERAGE

- Internet Banking
- International Economics
- E-Accounting
- Economic Indices and Quantitative Economic Methods
- Field Research
- Economics of Agriculture and Biotechnology
- Managerial Accounting
- Evidence-Based Studies
- Public Finance
- Microfinance

IGI Global is currently accepting manuscripts for publication within this series. To submit a proposal for a volume in this series, please contact our Acquisition Editors at Acquisitions@igi-global.com or visit: http://www.igi-global.com/publish/.

The Advances in Finance, Accounting, and Economics (AFAE) Book Series (ISSN 2327-5677) is published by IGI Global, 701 E. Chocolate Avenue, Hershey, PA 17033-1240, USA, www.igi-global.com. This series is composed of titles available for purchase individually; each title is edited to be contextually exclusive from any other title within the series. For pricing and ordering information please visit http://www.igi-global.com/book-series/advances-finance-accounting-economics/73685. Postmaster: Send all address changes to above address.

Titles in this Series

For a list of additional titles in this series, please visit: www.igi-global.com

Tools and Techniques for Economic Decision Analysis
Jelena Stanković (University of Niš, Serbia) Pavlos Delias (Eastern Macedonia and Thrace Institute of Technology, Greece) Srđan Marinković (University of Niš, Serbia) and Sylvie Rochhia (Université Côte d'Azur, CNRS, GREDEG, France)
Business Science Reference • copyright 2017 • 305pp • H/C (ISBN: 9781522509592) • US $205.00 (our price)

Corporate Espionage, Geopolitics, and Diplomacy Issues in International Business
Bryan Christiansen (PryMarke, LLC, USA) and Fatmanur Kasarcı (PryMarke Business Academy, Turkey)
Business Science Reference • copyright 2017 • 374pp • H/C (ISBN: 9781522510314) • US $210.00 (our price)

Handbook of Research on Globalization and the International Political Economy
Abdulkadir Isik (Namik Kemal University, Turkey)
Business Science Reference • copyright 2017 • 397pp • H/C (ISBN: 9781522508526) • US $265.00 (our price)

Handbook of Research on Global Indicators of Economic and Political Convergence
Ramesh Chandra Das (Katwa College, India)
Business Science Reference • copyright 2016 • 616pp • H/C (ISBN: 9781522502159) • US $345.00 (our price)

Global Perspectives on Trade Integration and Economies in Transition
Vasily Erokhin (Moscow University of Finance and Law, Russia)
Business Science Reference • copyright 2016 • 407pp • H/C (ISBN: 9781522504511) • US $210.00 (our price)

Handbook of Research on Social Entrepreneurship and Solidarity Economics
José Manuel Saiz-Álvarez (Tecnológico de Monterrey, Mexico)
Business Science Reference • copyright 2016 • 606pp • H/C (ISBN: 9781522500971) • US $230.00 (our price)

Economic Modeling, Analysis, and Policy for Sustainability
Anandajit Goswami (The Energy and Resources Institute (TERI), India) and Arabinda Mishra (ICIMOD, Nepal)
Business Science Reference • copyright 2016 • 388pp • H/C (ISBN: 9781522500940) • US $210.00 (our price)

Financial Market Regulations and Legal Challenges in South Asia
Amit K. Kashyap (Nirma University, India) and Anjani Singh Tomar (Gujarat National Law University, India)
Business Science Reference • copyright 2016 • 346pp • H/C (ISBN: 9781522500049) • US $200.00 (our price)

IGI GLOBAL
DISSEMINATOR OF KNOWLEDGE
www.igi-global.com

701 E. Chocolate Ave., Hershey, PA 17033
Order online at www.igi-global.com or call 717-533-8845 x100
To place a standing order for titles released in this series, contact: cust@igi-global.com
Mon-Fri 8:00 am - 5:00 pm (est) or fax 24 hours a day 717-533-8661

Table of Contents

Detailed Table of Contents

This work is a position paper discussing alternative viewpoints on factors that may influence the values of certain crucial healthcare efficiency indicators. We draw attention to the latest research in the area of behavioral economics, and make obvious certain inefficiencies in base healthcare packages, which are in close connection with human behavior. We begin with an analysis of healthcare expenses, first in absolute terms and then compare them with the Euro zone as well as former communist countries from Eastern Europe. The purpose is to offer multiple perspectives in relation to the widespread idea that medical care in Romania does not have the financial backing enjoyed in other places. We continue with the presentation of several healthcare variables and the attempt to find possible alternative explanations for their values and dynamics. Finally, we sum up with an emphasis on certain human behaviors that might underlie inefficiencies in healthcare packages and examine the corresponding experimental results, which offer some simple solutions to correct them.

Inter-temporal choices have been an important aspect of Behavioral Economics, as they deal with time-dependent decision-making of people in various situations. This chapter discusses hyperbolic time-discounting, which has gained significant recognition and has become an important part of public-policy and economic studies in last few years. It also highlights the importance of this concept from a real-life perspective, by showing its relevance in credit-behavior of individuals. This is shown by highlighting the unstable preferences of individuals using credit-cards, which exploit time-inconsistent behavior. Despite the paucity of current research, understanding impulsive-behavior has gained popularity recently because of the relevance of wellbeing and happiness in the global scenario. As is evident, credit debt does hamper people's quality of life, and so it becomes important for researchers and policymakers to reduce impulsivity and self-control issues, by making consumers use costly commitment-devices and other behavioral options to help them make rational and justified choices.

It is generally believed that self-employment offers ample opportunities for tax evasion. Therefore, this paper examines whether attitudes toward tax evasion has any influence on the choice of self-employment. Our analysis, based on a random sample of Americans, indicates that an individual who believes that tax evasion is "not wrong and a bit wrong" is more likely to be self-employed as compared to an individual who believes that tax evasion is "wrong and seriously wrong." This decision is not affected by gender. In addition, our analysis finds that a self-employed person earns more income than a person who works for someone else. However, an individual who believes that tax evasion is "wrong and seriously wrong" earns more than an individual who believes that tax evasion is "not and a bit wrong". Moreover, a self-employed person who believes that tax evasion is "not and a bit wrong" earns less than all other people, with all other parameters being the same.

The authors analyze three social choice rules (plurality voting, approval voting and Borda count) from a behavioral economics perspective aiming three objectives: 1) if it is a viable solution to use these procedures during mass elections; 2) why individuals prefer a specific social choice rule and not another; 3) how status quo bias and framing effect influence the preference of individuals for a certain social choice rule. The research is conducted with 87 participants to a lab experiment and data suggest that for using approval voting and Borda count during mass elections is necessary to increase the people level of information about their benefits. When making a decision in a political or economic context seem that people tend to prefer simple plurality rule do to its availability and maybe because of its strong reliance with status quo bias.

The aim of the agent-based model presented in this chapter is to explain the determinants of inflation and to forecast the inflation rate in the Eurozone for the next five years. The behaviors of agents and their expectations are interrelated and explained by macroeconomic models applied to heterogeneous agents of three classes: individuals, companies and financial institutions. In addition, the behavior of public sector and central bank is also modeled with a single agent of each kind. Once the quantitative easing policy is implemented, the quantitative theory of money expects higher inflation rates in the long run. Inflation should remain low taking into account the Phillips-Curve. Last, according to the Aggregated Supply and Demand as well as to the Money Market equilibrium, the behaviors modeled allow forecasting low inflation. However, an external shock, as it would be an increase in the price of important commodities, can alter the inflation rate to a great extent.

Current behavioral economics/game theory and social psychology literature have been captivated by the idea of altruism and egoism. In large part, these two disciplines have tried to determine the foundation of selfish and selfless behavior, without much result. The current chapter examines the root issues associated with this inquiry and argues for a shift in attention towards factors associated with cooperation. As such, empirical research from both disciplines is presented to show the advancements in relation to identification of these factors. Additionally, the authors offer a possible solution to the fractured literature in an effort to merge findings from both disciplines in an attempt progress this line of research.

This chapter seeks to understand the multidimensionality of urban consumption and the nature and the levels of consumer–retail structure interrelations. A holistic conceptual framework of urban consumption is proposed. It views the needs, wants, and desires as the motivating forces for consumer behavior, and conceptualizes the dimensions of consumption space and the forms that consumption takes within these dimensions (the platforms of consumption). Qualitative data (respondent-generated photographs and written explanations) is used to exemplify the forms of consumption within the proposed platforms.

The effects of global warming are becoming apparent through- out the world. Europe has begun to experience more severe winters and increased rain. Massive flooding in South Eastern Europe has devastated communities and repeatedly strains the economy of these regions resulting in mass trauma to the residents of multiple countries. Intergenerational effects of trauma have been noted to be an increasing world-wide concern. These traumatic effects are not only psychologically based but result in structural and functional changes within the brain and body. This chapter explores the application of decision making and Relational Dynamics to mass victims of floods by creating healing sites of sustainable energy and rural tourism to assist mass victims of natural disaster flooding.

Preface

Since the publication of the first issue of the *International Journal of Applied Behavioral Economics*, in 2012, the field of Behavioral Economics has grown enormously and on many different levels. Its primary scope and mission "to increase the explanatory power of economics by providing it with more realistic psychological foundations" (Camerer & Loewenstein, 2004, p. 3) has been gradually and consistently implemented in economic theories and practices, creating a sophisticated community of academics and sympathizers around the world. Moreover, what we can immediately observe at a simple glance is the high boost in the popularity of Behavioral Economics ideas. This was mainly achieved through the spread of some great behavioral science books for the general public (Daniel Kahneman's *Thinking, Fast and Slow*, Richard Thaler's *Misbehaving: The Making of Behavioral Economics*, seconding the bestseller *Nudge*, or Sendhil Mullainathan and Eldar Shafir's *Scarcity: The New Science of Having Less and How It Defines Our Lives*, just to give a couple of examples), but also in what concerns a certain level of academic attractiveness expressed in multiple new conferences and workshops (besides the "classical" ones organized by SABE – Society for the Advancement of Behavioral Economics – and IAREP – International Association for Research in Economic Psychology), along with the creation of more dedicated graduate programs around the world (both master and doctoral specializations). There is even an on-line Behavioral Economics guide, reaching a third edition in 2016 (and translations in multiple languages), with a very comprehensive approach on the current perspectives, practicalities and available resources in the field.

Secondly, from a more detailed and content-oriented point of view, it is important to highlight that the methodological realm of experiments and other research techniques specific to behavioral science has clearly undergone a profound refinement. Topics like replicability and generalizability have created a lot of awareness in terms of real-life implications of research results, fueling up more attention in the media. It is very important that, more than talk and reflection, there are also concrete initiatives like the report of Colin Camerer and his team, recently published in *Science* (2016), which summarizes the replication of 18 studies from the *American Economic Review* and the *Quarterly Journal of Economics* (appeared between 2011 and 2014). Their conclusions point to the fact that, on average, the replicated effect size consists of 66% of the original. In a similar vein, the syntagm of "weirdest people in the world," proposed by Joseph Heinrich, Steven Heine and Ara Norenzayan (2010) has consistently drawn attention to the nature of the samples used in many experimental studies – mostly individuals from Western, Educated, Industrialized, Rich, and Democratic (WEIRD) societies (with the additional comments of the authors that it's not just the subjects – there are too many WEIRD researchers). This has sparkled more interest for the idea of cross-cultural variability (Falk, Becker, Dohmen, Enke, Sunde, & Huffman, 2015) when measuring different behavioral constructs: risk and time preferences, social norms, trust, etc.

Thirdly, but not last, the practical applications of Behavioral Economics have also multiplied, sometimes in such a multi and interdisciplinary frenzy that it is almost impossible to track the conceptual influence of one field or the other (and mostly facing different types of interaction effects). Nudges are still top of the list (despite the ongoing philosophical debate about the lack of rationality that justifies libertarian paternalism), benefiting in general by a high degree of adherence from the public. For example, a recent study by Lucia Reisch and Cass Sunstein (2016), "Do Europeans Like Nudges?," signals a strong majority support for nudges (being already adopted or just under consideration) in democratic nations. However, they have also found two exceptions – Hungary and Denmark – without providing any mediating explanatory framework, at least for now.

Within this very generous and dynamic context, to offer a comprehensive perspective on the current research in Behavioral Economics is an extremely challenging task to be solved in one book. Thus, the main purpose of the volume is to acknowledge this difficulty by bringing forward a diverse spectrum of applications and research designs. From a reflection exercise proposed in the position paper, to core studies for the field, discussing inter-temporal and social choice or attitudes and perceptions in consumer behavior, and finally to the integration of new areas like agent based modeling, the volume hopes to gradually develop into an informative and interdisciplinary walk along the current landscape of Behavioral Economics. This endeavor is intricately related to the fact that the *International Journal of Applied Behavioral Economics* has entered into his fifth year of existence – an age we can consider appropriate to generate a collection of works exponential for its mission: to bring a significant contribution to the understanding of complex economic behavior, its triggers, and its practical implications. The present volume comprises ten chapters, among which four are extended versions of previously published articles in IJABE, and the rest of them are new, original works. While their selection was not by far similar to a type of random walk process, it is worth to mention that we are completely aware that we have probably omitted some good visionary articles that may be soon defining the new trends in Behavioral Economics. Working in a bounded rationality paradigm and under the auspices of the availability heuristic, we do hope that this aspect will not turn out into a flaw but into one more argument stating the complexity and fascinating dynamics of Behavioral Economics as a field. The critics stating the exact opposite – the fact that Behavioral Economics does not follow the characteristics of a grand unified theory – are missing a very subtle distinction: a macro-result is generated by micro-behaviors, ideas and tools in this particular case. Their aggregation takes time, particular rules and no centralized authority. This edited positions itself as a witness of the emergence of a phenomenon from a decentralized process, with the single intervention of capturing some of the multiple transformations into a printed snapshot.

The first chapter, "How Behavioral Economics Can Help When You Think You Don't Have Enough Money: A Glimpse into the Romanian Healthcare System," is actually a position paper underlying the link between Health and Behavioral Economics for the case of Romania. While both these two important fields have already entered into the mainstream economic discourse (especially Health Economics), they are still marginally known in Romania, and in consequence their theories and empirical findings are far from being implemented either in the public or the private sector. In this light, the importance of the paper lays mostly in its signaling force towards embracing new paradigms for solving crucial socio-economics problems. The specific purpose is to offer multiple perspectives in relation to the widespread (and correct) idea that medical care in Romania does not have the financial backing enjoyed in other places. While obtaining more money for health can be viewed as an all-time desiderate, more attention to sometimes unconventional research showing the possibility of obtaining better performance without increasing costs is clearly the optimal choice.

The second chapter tackles one of the most popular topics in the decision-making literature: how do people choose over time and how much they acknowledge the explicit trade-offs that come with this type of choice. This is of course a framework that applies to most of our decisions, but this particular paper streamlines through the literature and discusses its relevance for consumer credit behavior, also connecting it to consumer wellbeing. The core problem underlined by the author consists in the increasing debt from credit-accumulation, an issue present not only in the developed economies but also a growing feature of many transition societies and other developing countries. The "buy now and pay later" option has gradually surpassed its functionality and has deepened our present focused bias, with negative implication both for individuals and societies.

The approach of the third chapter revolves on another facet of individual behavior: its relationship with labor and the associated responsibility in the form of paying taxes. More precisely, the author is interested in the very narrow link between attitudes toward tax evasion and the choice of self-employment. Again, this is a pervasive and growing problem in most countries. For behavioral economics, this is a standard case of decision making under uncertainty, bringing into discussion concepts like reference-dependent preferences, loss aversion and the entire arsenal of cumulative prospect theory. The empirical results point out that, for the US case, an individual with the attitudes of "not wrong and a bit wrong" is more likely to go for self-employment compared to an individual with the attitudes of "wrong and seriously wrong". This generates a very unexpected and troublesome new attribute for this type of labor regime, so frequently associated with entrepreneurship.

The fourth chapter switches the focus towards collective decision-making, opening up the floor to questions aimed to identify how do people determine the social choice rules that best aggregate individual preferences into collective decisions. This is definitely a multilayered scope, structured on items dealing with the reasons that lead individuals to prefer a social choice rule over another, with the analysis of the context-dependence of the preference for a specific social choice rule and finally with a greater discussion on these implications for the voting process. The theoretical perimeter is complemented by an extensive experimental procedure that employs three of the common voting procedures (plurality rule, approval voting and Borda rule), with the purpose of seeing whether using them in mass elections would be feasible. Along the way, there are multiple emphases on why one rule is preferred to another, and the manner in which status quo bias and framing effects influence these particular preferences.

The fifth chapter brings along a new unconventional research methodology – agent-based modeling. At first glance, this may seem a strange choice given the theme of the present chapter since ABM models are usually applied to finance and macroeconomic forecasting. However, a closer look to the emerging field of Complexity Economics will quickly reveal the fact that ABM models require high amounts of information about agents in terms of micro data and behavioral rules. Therefore, there is enough common ground and signs for good collaboration premises with Behavioral Economics, as Rosser and Rosser (2015) emphasize in a very elegant and straightforward manner: "Complexity provides an ultimate foundation for bounded rationality and hence the need to use behavioral economics in a broader array of contexts than most economists have thought appropriate." With this mind we can note that while the scope of the chapter remains a macro one – to forecast the inflation rate – the underlying mechanism are highlighting the importance of correctly examining how behavioral rules impact the level of prices. The author's strong belief is that by doing so we can improve predictions and make models more realistic in terms of decision-making processes and agents' learning.

The next chapter has a more social psychology flavor, aimed at deciphering one of the most debated hypothesis in standard economics (but also in philosophy, biology, sociology, etc.): the selfish versus the altruistic attribute. Since the multi-disciplinary literature behind the subject in truly huge, the paper proceeds in a very operational manner by firstly providing a list of key terms and their definitions, mapping thus the conceptual territory for consistent and inconsistent results. Furthermore, the focus is narrowed to social psychology and behavioral economics, outlining factors that influence selfish, non-cooperative vs. selfless, cooperative behavior. The generous overview is crystalized by a dual process model, and finally implications are drawn for business management, politics, and social issues.

The seventh chapter is dedicated to consumer behavior in urban contexts, with the purpose to explore and conceptualize the consumer – retail structure interrelations. A comprehensive perspective is depicted for the consumption process and space, both described in a multilayered fashion: from a perceptive state of sensing and thinking, to the dynamic nature of doing, embedded in social relations, interactions and emotional experiences. A qualitative methodology was employed for a sample of Finnish university students, with to objective of inquiring how young consumers (as a homogeneous consumer group in Finland) are related to at different levels to the prevailing retail structure, and second, what the visual and textual material tells about their behavioral patterns with regard to these levels.

The eight chapter introduces the novel concept of relational dynamics as a structured mindset for better understanding the interplay between the drives for dominance and acceptance in a specific interaction, along with the potential shift from non-cooperation to cooperation, and of course the reverse. Within this theoretical framework strongly embedded in game theory and psychology, the author further expands its practical demeanor by building up a study case on rural tourism and sustainable green energy as a means of healing mass trauma, but also will improve living conditions and the economics for a region or country. The strong feature of this research is easily traced to its pragmatic and humanitarian objective: to expand the current knowledge of trauma theory by pairing it up with the relational dynamics approach and by finally offering an effective healing alternative for mass interventions in different areas of the world.

The ninth chapter brings forwards another interesting application, this time for the construction industry and its distinctive attribute, as indicated by the authors: the complex business of establishing contractual relationships with a wide range of parties. The main focus of the paper lays on examining the perception of engineers, both Greek and foreign individuals, regarding the performance of a certain product of their activity – highway projects Contract Types (CTs) – against selection criteria. The central takeaway is that these perceptions change relatively to the profile of the decision maker, with nationality and experience ranking as the most relevant factors. The other type of influences – scope and process uncertainty, contractual difficulties and claims, value for money, criticality of schedule – tend to cluster together, irrespective of the particular contract in discussion and the profile of the decision-maker. These findings are further useful especially in order to set a common ground and facilitate contract negotiations among the project stakeholders.

The last chapter closes the volume in the same technical area, with a slight, but important, switch towards innovation: the rise of green technologies for the transportation sector. The authors are particularly interested in the study of the diffusion of Plug-In Hybrid Electric Vehicles (PHEV) among consumers. The major line of interest is to examine the potential impact trend of learning on consumer's decision towards hybrid technology adoption. To this purpose, the paper points out to the set of factors relevant for PHEVs adoption by carefully taking into account both important features of the product and the degree of ambiguity about quality and learning for this sustainable technology.

Summing up, one conclusion after assembling this collection of papers one salient conclusion remains the fact that while it is extremely difficulty to sum up the current trends in Behavioral Economics, it is a fascinating and inspiring endeavor for the editors, authors and hopefully for the readers also. We trust that this somewhat eclectic volume will serve as a significant reference book both for some of the main application areas covered in the first part – health, consumer credit behavior, tax behavior, and social choices – and also for generating insight, motivation and new collaboration practices in the light of the themes addressed in the second part - integration with new research methodologies like agent-based modeling, along with creative applications to trauma treatments, the construction industry or the diffusion of new transportation technologies.

Rodica Ianole
University of Bucharest, Romania

REFERENCES

Camerer, C. F., Dreber, A., Forsell, E., Ho, T. H., Huber, J., Johannesson, M., & Heikensten, E. et al. (2016). Evaluating replicability of laboratory experiments in economics. *Science*, *351*(6280), 1433–1436. doi:10.1126/science.aaf0918 PMID:26940865

Camerer, C. F., & Lowenstein, G. (2004). Behavioral economics: Past, present, future. In Advances in Behavioral Economics, (pp. 3-51). Academic Press.

Falk, A., Becker, A., Dohmen, T., Enke, B., Sunde, U., & Huffman, D. (2015). *The nature of human preferences: Global evidence*. Working Paper.

Henrich, J., Heine, S. J., & Norenzayan, A. (2010). The weirdest people in the world? *Behavioral and Brain Sciences*, *33*(2-3), 61–83. doi:10.1017/S0140525X0999152X PMID:20550733

Reisch, L. A., & Sunstein, C. R. (2016). *Do Europeans like nudges?*. Available at SSRN 2739118.

Rosser, J. B. Jr, & Rosser, M. V. (2015). Complexity and behavioral economics. *Nonlinear Dynamics Psychology and Life Sciences*, *19*(2), 201–226. PMID:25783044

Chapter 1
How Behavioral Economics Can Help When You Think You Don't Have Enough Money:
A Glimpse into the Romanian Healthcare System

Elena Druică
University of Bucharest, Romania

Rodica Ianole
University of Bucharest, Romania

ABSTRACT

This work is a position paper discussing alternative viewpoints on factors that may influence the values of certain crucial healthcare efficiency indicators. We draw attention to the latest research in the area of behavioral economics, and make obvious certain inefficiencies in base healthcare packages, which are in close connection with human behavior. We begin with an analysis of healthcare expenses, first in absolute terms and then compare them with the Euro zone as well as former communist countries from Eastern Europe. The purpose is to offer multiple perspectives in relation to the widespread idea that medical care in Romania does not have the financial backing enjoyed in other places. We continue with the presentation of several healthcare variables and the attempt to find possible alternative explanations for their values and dynamics. Finally, we sum up with an emphasis on certain human behaviors that might underlie inefficiencies in healthcare packages and examine the corresponding experimental results, which offer some simple solutions to correct them.

DOI: 10.4018/978-1-5225-1826-6.ch001

INTRODUCTION

The year 1981 brought to the forefront of scientific research one of the most important results in behavioral economics (Tversky & Kahneman, 1981), specifically that our decisions are influenced by many different subjective elements. The way in which information is *framed* plays a crucial role in the decision making process. The famous example of the Asian disease, discussed in the aforementioned paper, presents the choice between two alternatives, formulated in slightly different ways, as seen below.

We are presented with the (obviously hypothetical) situation in which the US is preparing to deal with an Asian disease that will, most likely, kill 600 people. There are two alternatives that may be chosen, programs A and B. The two options are as follows:

Option 1:

- If Program A is adopted, 200 people will be saved.
- If Program B is adopted, there is 1/3 probability that 600 people will be saved, and 2/3 probability that no people will be saved.

Option 2:

- If Program A is adopted 400 people will die.
- If Program B is adopted there is 1/3 probability that nobody will die, and 2/3 probability that 600 people will die.

It is easy to notice that, objectively, the two options are equivalent: to say that 200 people would be saved by Program A is the same as saying that 400 would die as a result of the same decision. Furthermore, a 1/3 chance that all 600 would survive is the same as saying that there is a 1/3 probability that nobody would die. Finally, a 2/3 chance that nobody would be saved, as per option 1, is identical to the 2/3 likelihood that all 600 would die. Therefore, the only difference between the two options is, what the authors call, the framing of the decision: positive (in terms of "survival") in the first case and negative (in terms of "number of dead") in the second one. The results obtained by Amos Tversky and Daniel Kahneman indicate that people choose differently when the information is presented to them with another framing: option 1 shows that 72% prefer Program A, as opposed to only 28% for Program B, manifesting what is known in the literature as certainty bias when it comes to gaining something: the positive framing in option 1 triggered a preference for saving 200 people. The second options shows that only 22% would choose Program A, the majority of 78% would rather negotiate the loss of 600, instead of coming to terms with 400 people dying.

In the summary of the paper, the two authors tell us how "the psychological principles that govern the perception of decision problems and the evaluation of probabilities and outcomes produce predictable shifts of preference when the same problem is framed in different ways" (Tversky & Kahneman, 1981). In other words, this is the birth statement of the powerful framing effect, with such a simple mechanics and such a great impact on decision-making and different types of behaviors, economic and non-economic ones. Changing preferences for certain alternatives goes beyond the hypothetical and is responsible for different choices which are made in real life, a fact which is explored in further detail in the fifth section.

A second stream of arguments standing for analyzing health care in light of behavioral economics can be generously traced to the more methodological camp of causal relationships and subjective, hidden relationships. The Freakonomics example of Steven D. Levitt and Stephen J. Dubner (Levitt & Dubner, 2005) is still among the most convincing one. The beginning of the 1990s was, in the United States of America, an era in which the state was fighting a losing battle with a decades long growing crime rate. The period before 1995 was characterized by inefficient efforts on the part of the state in order to lower crime rates by: increasing the number of police, improving street lights, gun control and other similar policies. At the time, there were experts predicting that the crime rate would be expected to rise by 15% in the coming decade.

However, starting with 1995, suddenly and without explanation, the crime rate started to go down, reaching, in the years after 2000, the lowest percentage in 35 years and prompting experts in different fields to offer justifications for this change. The explanations ranged from the increased performance of the US's economy to the idea that all the policies implemented in the past started to have effect. The factor which contributed massively to this change came from an unexpected source: the year 1973 marked the legalization of abortions in the US and so, many of the children, who would have been born in an environment which favored criminal behavior, were never born. But, as the two authors point out, none of the criminal experts mentioned legalized abortion as a possible cause for a lower crime rate in the US.

The examples above focus on two aspects which are essential to the positioning of this paper:

1. The framing of information matters.
2. Not all the variables which one would take into consideration actually explain or are the most relevant to the studied phenomenon.

Starting from these observations and from the fact that, most of the time, the public discourse in relation to the Romanian healthcare system is one which focuses on the lack of funding as well as the conviction that an underfinanced system cannot be efficient, our objective is to investigate other possible framings for the same objective situations and possible unexpected factors which might contribute to improving efficiency of the healthcare system, without increasing current expenses. This attempt is based on prior experimental results obtained in healthcare behavioral economics and, while we are not at a stage where we can guarantee that each alternative perspective is actually relevant, the overall argument cannot be denied.

The paper is structured as follows: we will begin with an analysis of healthcare expenses, first in absolute terms and then compare them with the Euro zone as well as former communist countries from Eastern Europe. The purpose is to offer multiple points of view in relation to the widespread idea that medical care in Romania does not have the financial backing enjoyed in other places. This is be followed by a presentation of several healthcare efficiency indicators, as recognized by the literature and the attempt to find possible alternative explanations for their values. In the third part we will present certain human behaviors which might underlie inefficiencies in healthcare packages and examine a few experiments which offer some simple solutions to correct them.

Speaking of Money: Simple Analyses and Unorthodox Explanations

The almost universal opinion, as found in public statistics and reports as well as the opinions of average people, is that there isn't enough money for the Romanian healthcare system. Without having a very clear understanding on what "enough" is supposed to mean, we started out from the idea that it suggests a comparison with something (be that the European average, or what happens in Germany, a very common assessment found not just in the financial assessments of the system) or a result which ought to be achieved (such as a certain performance). Following the same steps as those of the majority opinion, we analyzed some data as follows. We started by comparing healthcare expenses per capita with the evolution of the GDP per capita and found, as can be seen from Figure 1, that Romania is not much different from the Euro zone. The difference between GDP per capita and healthcare expenses is greater in the Euro zone, which would suggest that, despite the common criticism, Romania tried to achieve better results with limited funding even before 2000, when the graph shows a significant increase in GDP.

The major consideration which needs to be taken into account when analyzing Romania and the Euro zone, for example, is the discrepancy in the purchasing power parity enjoyed by the institutions in each country. If they are all represented under the same exact conditions, it is easy to notice that Romania barely shows up on the chart when compared to other Euro countries. This is a fact that must be taken into consideration every time when stating that expenses in Romania are "way below those in more advanced countries". This fact goes hand in hand with another one which is just as important, and can be found in Figure 2.

Without going into too much detail, a simple analysis of the graph (a) above shows that in 1990 Romania (represented in green) was only above Bulgaria in terms of GDP per capita, when compared to the rest of the Eastern European former communist bloc countries. Furthermore, at the time, Romania was one of the poorest countries in Europe, only above Albania and Bulgaria. Sadly, the situation has not changed since then. Each one of these economies has improved since then; however, their order has not changed. This is an objective aspect which must be considered so as to point out that while significant efforts have been made, the historic, economic, cultural and social truth cannot be ignored.

Figure 2b makes the injustice of comparing with developed countries even more obvious. We can notice that, when comparing the *entire* eastern bloc with benchmarks of the free economy, such as the UK or Germany, the lag remains the same, not just for Romania but for all of these countries, in relation to the benchmarks. These are fundamental truths which cannot be avoided when attempting to compare our national performance with other reference points which, historically, are not like us.

Another idea which is commonly found in the literature is that "out of the entire European Union we allocate to healthcare expenses the smallest percentage of the GDP" and the numbers cannot be contradicted. Figure 3 presents the percentage of the GDP allocated to healthcare in the US and Canada. It

Figure 1. Comparison between healthcare expenses per capita and GDP per capita Romania and Euro zone
Source: Worldbank. Graphs created by the authors using R.

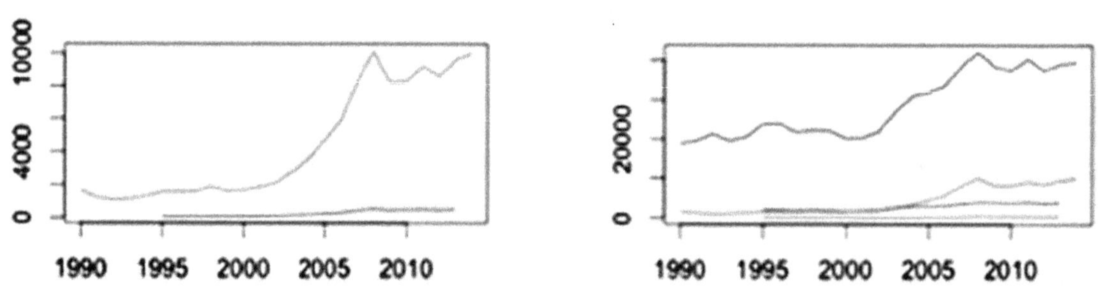

(a) GDP/capita & Health Expenses/capita - Romania **(b) Romania (red), EURO zone (blue)**

**For a more accurate representation of this figure, please see the electronic version.*

Figure 2. The evolution of GDP per capita: Romania and the rest of the eastern European former communist bloc countries and compared with Germany and the UK
Source: Worldbank. Graphs created by the authors using R.

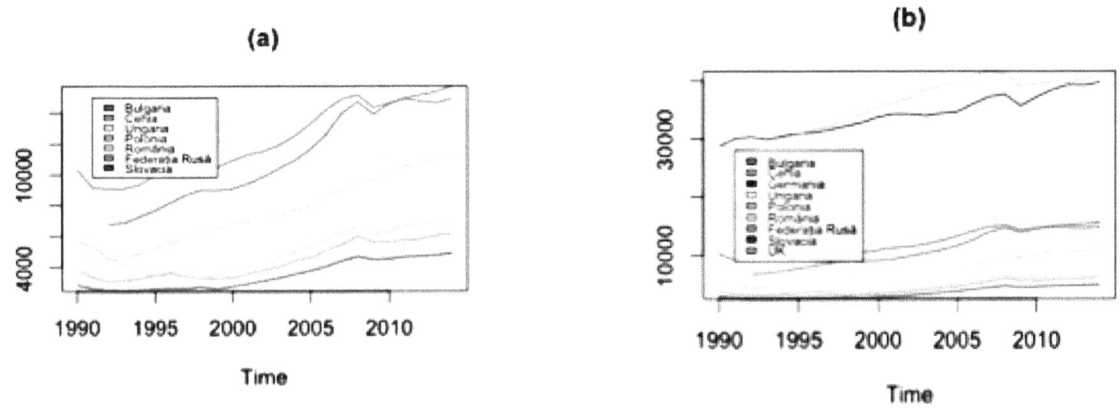

Bulgaria – blue, Czech Republic – red, Hungary – yellow
Poland – pink, Romania – green, Russia – grey
Slovakia – dark red, Germany –black, UK - orange

*For a more accurate representation of this figure, please see the electronic version.

Figure 3. Healthcare expenses in the USA (red) and Canada (blue) between 1995 and 2014
Source: Worldbank. Graph created by the authors using R.

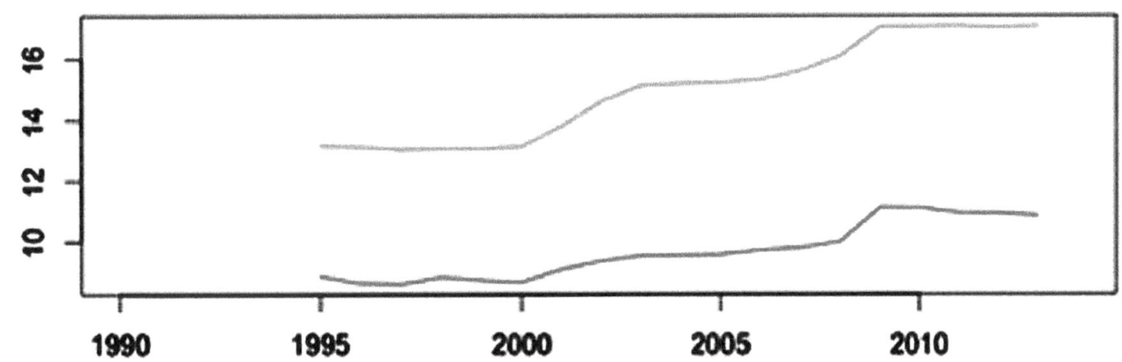

*For a more accurate representation of this figure, please see the electronic version.

can be noticed that the US's northern neighbors allocate only 2/3 of the American expenses, however, the opinion across the board is that "the healthcare industry in the US is strange, we allocate 18% of the GDP for healthcare and yet, other countries seem to obtain better results – and we don't know why" (Hough, 2013).

The discrepancy between expenses in the US and the lack of adequate results has been the focus of study for a multitude of papers. Without investigating all the explanations which have already been brought forward by others, we will point out that, in line with our paper, the thesis that more money will guarantee better results cannot be generalized. And yet, the fact that an underfinanced system cannot be efficient is unanimously accepted. Foregoing the annoying fact that we have yet to establish what *adequate* financing actually means, we will focus on efficiency in healthcare. In order to measure efficiency, while staying in line with the purpose of the paper, we will focus on two, generally accepted, indicators: average life expectancy and probability of death between the ages of 30 and 70. We will study these two from an ordinary statistical perspective as well as some less than usual points of view.

Money or... Something Else?

Figure 4 shows the evolution of the average life expectancy in Romania (red) and the European Union (blue) between 1990 and 2013. The 6 year difference between the two lines is obvious, a fact which can be recorded as (yet) another failure on the part of the Romanian healthcare system when it comes to taking care of its citizens, this being the result of inadequate funding.

This paper does not deny the basic premise that more funding can lead to better healthcare conditions and, as a consequence, improvements in the average life expectancy. However, it posits that other less obvious factors exist and that they can be just as important. Such an example is a study conducted by Yale University (Levy et al., 2002) which focused on the attitude towards aging. The sample was formed of middle aged participants who were observed for a period of 20 years. The final data showed that those people who had a positive outlook towards aging had, on average, a life expectancy greater by 7.6 years than the rest. The authors found this result to be very surprising because other factors which are better known to contribute to improved average life expectancy – such as not smoking, regular exercise, an appropriate level of cholesterol and blood pressure – contribute only by 4 years on average.

The idea that "just" having a positive attitude will have an impact twice as large on the average life expectancy as living a life as recommended and monitored by the official healthcare system in Romania is not only interesting, but also quite appealing for those people who wish to let go of the pressure that they cannot control what happens around them. Speculating on this result, one can say that this is of little use when the general attitude is that "you cannot have a positive attitude when the system does not help you make one".

The likelihood of death between the ages of 30 and 70 is another efficiency indicator which we will analyze in this paper as being relevant to our purposes. Figure 5 shows that, in Romania, the risk that a person will die between 30 and 70 is 21%. Evidently, there is a very close correlation between healthcare expenses and the value of this indicator and the difference, when compared to Germany (a country with which we seem to insist on comparing ourselves and which chosen for unclear reasons), is clear and very

Figure 4. Average life expectancy in Romania (red) and the Euro zone (blue) between 1990 and 2014
Source: World Health Organization. Graph created by the authors using R.

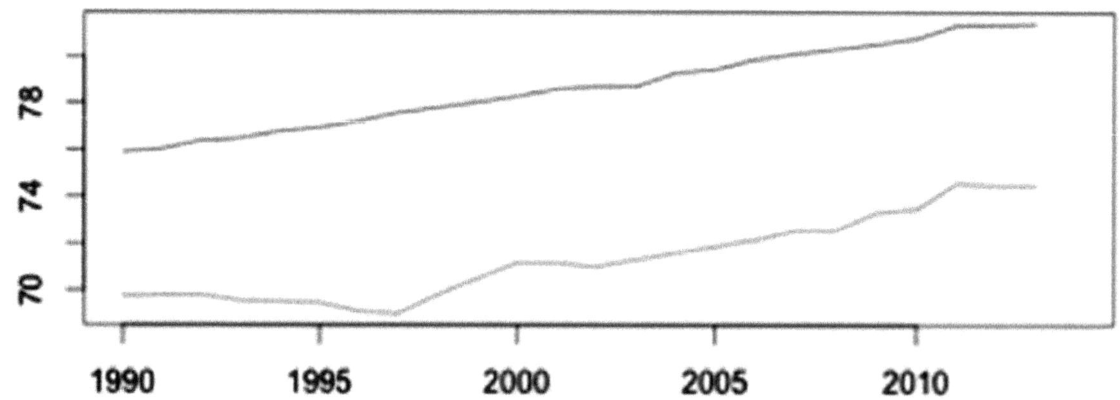

**For a more accurate representation of this figure, please see the electronic version.*

Figure 5. The likelihood of death between the ages of 30 and 70, in the year 2012, for 6 former communist countries in Eastern Europe
Source: World Health Organization. Graph created by the authors using R. The most recent available data was for 2012.

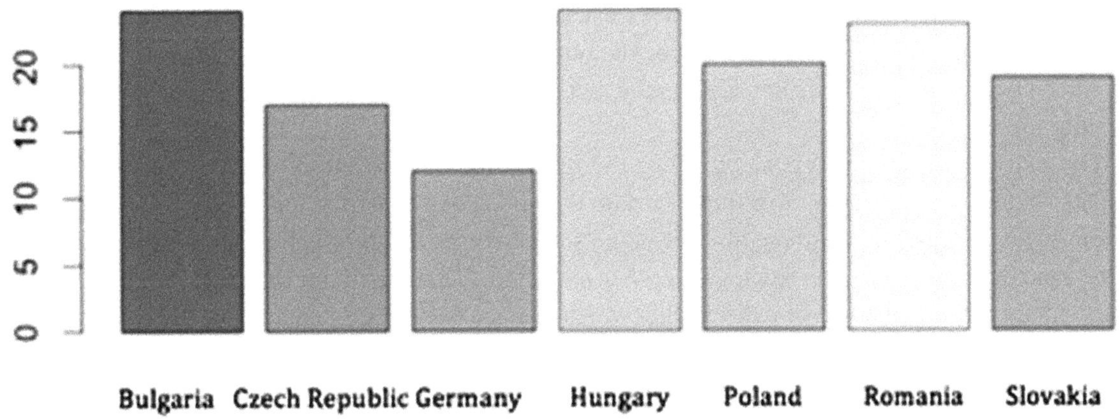

obvious. However, an interesting and immediate observation is that the situation in Romania is similar to that in Bulgaria and Hungary, three countries in the same geographical area. As such, while financing plays a significant role, we cannot ignore other aspects which ought to be investigated.

A study worth taking into consideration in this context was conducted by Duke University (McGonigal, 2015, p.xiv) and it involved a sample of adults over the age of 55, which were monitored for a period of 15 years. At the end of this period what was found was that 60% of the people who believe other people to be trustworthy were alive, as opposed to those who did not consider other people to be trustworthy of which 60% were not alive. This result, which can be summed up simply by saying that "those people who trust other people tend to live longer" is relevant because it draws attention to one of the most important features of Romanians, specifically the lower level of trust which they have not just in institutions but also other people (Mitruț et.al, 2013). This is a possible side-effect of the more than 42 years spent under communism (Vâlsan et.al, 2015), or maybe an inherently Romanian trait (Zamfirescu, 2008), whatever the exact reason behind it, it might point us towards less obvious (but just as important) causes for the high likelihood of death between 30 and 70 and the low average life expectancy.

In this last part of this section we would like to draw attention to a well-known aspect, recognized by national and international forums, that an increase in the average lifespan will be associated inevitably with an increase in the number of people who suffer from chronic disease, in the number of deaths by chronic disease and the percentage of medical services dedicated to different age groups. As such, an increase in average life expectancy needs to be accompanied by improved *quality* of life, so that the risk of disease and death in a certain age intervals will be lowered. On the other hand, there is evidence that, beyond outside interventions, we too can also help ourselves.

A 1998 study, conducted in the USA, researched the effect of stress on the risk of dying (McGonigal, 2015). Initially, 30.000 people were asked

1. How much stress were they subjected to in the last year,
2. Whether they believe that stress is dangerous.

Eight years later, the results showed that high levels of stress were associated with a 43% increase in the risk of death. The surprising part was that this result was true only for those who answered that stress is dangerous. The researchers came to the sad conclusion that, over the course of those 8 years, while the results were not known, 180.000 Americans had died because they were convinced that stress is affecting them. What is going on, as per the quoted author, is that a single factor need not impact the health of a person, or their life expectancy, but a combination of that factor and the belief that it is harmful may influence it.

The purpose of this section was to show the reader that beyond those objective factors which we consider relevant when trying to explain certain dynamics or values for some indicators, and most of the time this is rightfully so, there also are some subjective elements which influence the expected results – and their impact can be much greater than expected. Detecting them and quantifying their impact can be done through the use of experiments which are not easy to implement, are expensive, or there are ethical limitations which need to be considered. On the other hand, we believe that continuing such investigations will lead to unexpected benefits in any healthcare system, not just the Romanian one, by helping the patient, or potential patient, reach a mental state which can be of a very real use in preventive care and recovery.

The Good and the Bad of Basic Packages

On the 1st of June 2014, a new basic healthcare package was introduced in Romania, along with the relevant legal framework. The information sources at the time (http://www.hotnews.ro/stiri-esential-17398547-pachetul-servicii-medicale-baza-contractul-cadru-intra-vigoare-1-iunie.htm) explained the differences between the previous design and the reason for which they were implemented. We can glean from these descriptions the desire to improve the efficiency from a functional perspective (by eliminating some of the bureaucracy), but also on the provided services: more types of services and improved access. An important aspect of this new package involved a different type of improvement in efficiency, related to reduced costs (in as much as that is possible) and a redistribution of resources in support of other initiatives; to be more precise, a more careful decision making process when it comes to admitting someone in the hospital for care, with the high costs for hospital treatment being well known, and a focus on preventive care which, in the medium and long term, ought to lead to a natural reduction in expenses at the level of the entire healthcare system.

In 2013 the first basic healthcare package was implemented in Romania. It was the result of more than six years of high-level talks among Romanian authorities (http://www.hotnews.ro/stiri-esential-15707508-cum-schimbat-ersul-doctor-pachetul-baza-romanii-vor-invata-numere-consultatiile.htm), and it lasted for only one year before it was modified. Far from being a sign of inadequacy in relation to the assumed objectives, the desire to change the package after one year is, in our opinion, a result-orientation focus which is in line with the experience of other countries: there is no such thing as an optimum package to be applied (see Wong&Bitran, 1999).

The limited experience of Romania in this area of expertise is a reality which we cannot and should not deny and it is expected that the structure and implementation of the basic healthcare package will be adjusted as more knowledge is gained. However, from the available information, the trend seems to be that of optimizing what is already offered, in the detriment of other components for which there is no available data.

The literature available from countries with more experience in this area is awash with explanations and examples related to the discrepancies between what is offered and what is actually received or used when it comes to a basic healthcare package. The parties involved in the development of such a package – the government, the service providers, the people who is actually in need of healthcare services and sometimes, when the payment is not done by the state, the financier – have very different interests and priorities and, most of the time, the result of their deliberations is an adequate response only for the needs of some and less so for others, so that the (sometimes perceived) needs of the population are not always in alignment with the services covered by the basic package. Once more, the argument brought up, for why the population does not receive what it wants, is inadequate funding, with money being the most obvious signal for the quality of the expected result. The following section will show that there still are significant factors which have yet to be adequately considered, such as the fact that we have too little information concerning people who, for subjective reasons, are not following their treatment, even if it is covered.

In order to understand what exactly we are referring to when we mention unavailable information, let us take a look at Figure 6 which shows the number of deaths caused by heart disease in Romania and in other former communist countries.

We can notice that Romania is in second to last place, just above Bulgaria, which would lead us to believe that the care provided to those who suffer from heart disease needs to be improved. Without contesting this idea, but staying in line with the same reasoning as up until now, we must admit that there is no statistical data on whether these people were registered as suffering from heart disease, whether they were under some kind of treatment for it, or whether the information was obtained simply by taking into account the information from the death certificate. Without access to more data – named "silent data" by statisticians – it is very hard, if not impossible, to establish a direct link between an indicator and the efficiency, or inefficiency, of the healthcare system.

Another aspect which needs to be taken into consideration when discussing the accuracy of the information underlying the decision, irrespective of the area of interest, can be illustrated by the press releases, issued by the National Institute of Statistics, concerning the percentage of the population which, for financial reasons, did not have access to medical services. The annual data for the period 2007-2013, divided by sex and age group, can be found in Figures 7 and 8.

Figure 6. Number of deaths caused by heart disease, in 2012, for 6 former communist countries in Eastern Europe

Source: World Health Organization. Graph created by the authors using R. The most recent available data was for 2012.

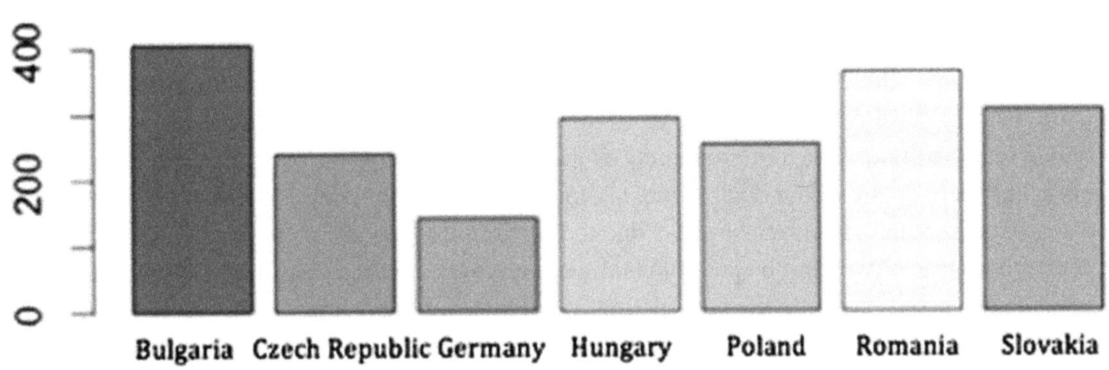

Figure 7. The percentage of the population, by sex, which did not seek medical attention for financial reasons. The data is for 2007-2013
Source: National Institute of Statistics. Graph created by the authors using R.

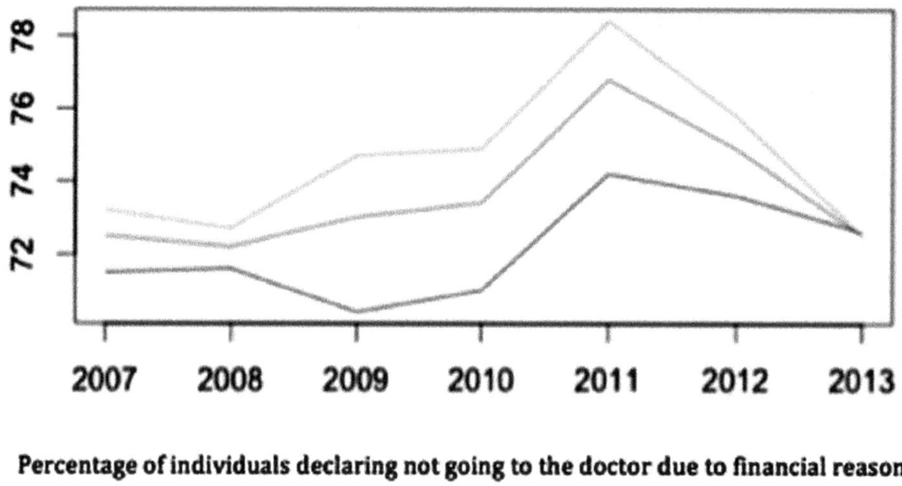

*For a more accurate representation of this figure, please see the electronic version.

Figure 8. The percentage of the population, by age group, which did not seek medical attention for financial reasons. The data is for 2007-2013
Source: National Institute of Statistics. Graph created by the authors using R.

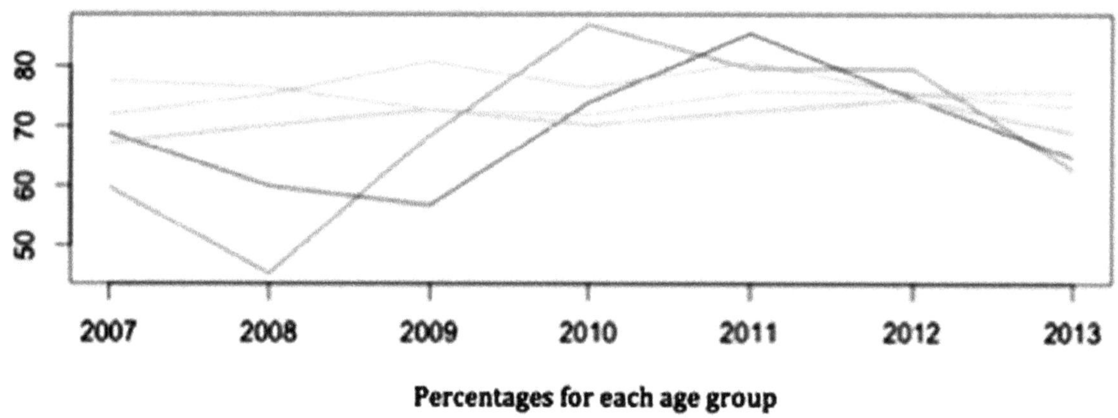

*For a more accurate representation of this figure, please see the electronic version.

From Figure 7 we can see that the percentages are rather large, greater than 70% when talking about the population as a whole, which might lead us to believing that, in Romania, the financial aspect is the main reason for which people do not go to the doctor. On the other hand however, we cannot help but notice that the group which offers money as the main reason for not going to the doctor is the one composed of men, about whom doctors already know that they only come in for a consultation when the disease has reached an advanced phase due to the fact that they are more fearful than women. Are the percentages true or would it be possible that these answers are only *substitutes* for the real reasons? This will be discussed further in the next section. What is surprising is that the age group does not seem to have an important impact (and we are referring here to large differences and not just *statistically significant*) on the percentage of those who do not go to the doctor for financial reasons.

Judging from an economic perspective, Figure 8 is hard to interpret for a European country. Intuition would tell us that a working age person has a lower probability of reporting financial difficulties when they require medical attention, in comparison to a retired person for whom income is drastically reduced.

Figure 9 might signal the fact that the year 2013, when the basic healthcare package was introduced, was one in which people's access to medical services was limited due to financial constraints and the initiative came just in time. According to data from the National Institute of Statistics, the 50 to 64 years age group is the one most affected by financial constraints, with a percentage of 75,6%, greater even than the 75 and above group, which reported "only" 73.7%.

At the same time, taking a more moderate perspective on these results forces us to point out that, while we can find explanations based on objective factors for each one of these graphs (the effects of the crisis on income levels, unemployment for the 25-34 years old age group, the difficulty in finding employment between the ages of 50 and 64 etc.) we cannot help but compare them with the same data from Eurostat and notice that, for the same indicators, they provide much lower values. Furthermore, we cannot help but notice that the distribution of the data in Figure 9 is almost uniform, which contradicts the assumed income distribution for different age groups as well as demand for healthcare services in accordance with age. It is true that the National Health Institute explicitly states that this is based on self-reported data, meaning that it contains the reasons considered most important for not going to the doctor from the perspective of the respondent and are influenced by societal expectations, but the information itself casts doubt on the validity of using this type of statistical data when basing a decision.

Most likely the differences between the two are the result of how the information was obtained. The National Institute of Statistics reported, most likely, the percentages when compared to the total number of people who required healthcare services but were not able to obtain them, whereas Eurostat got the percentage by comparing those who did not seek medical attention due to financial constraints out of the total interviewed population, which also included 80% of the respondents who did not need to seek medical attention. Despite the fact that there are explanations for the numerical differences themselves, in the absence of more careful studies, it is not possible to know whether or not we can rely on these

Figure 9. The percentage of the population, by age group, which did not seek medical attention for financial reasons. The data is for 2013
Source: National Institute of Statistics. Graph created by the authors using R.

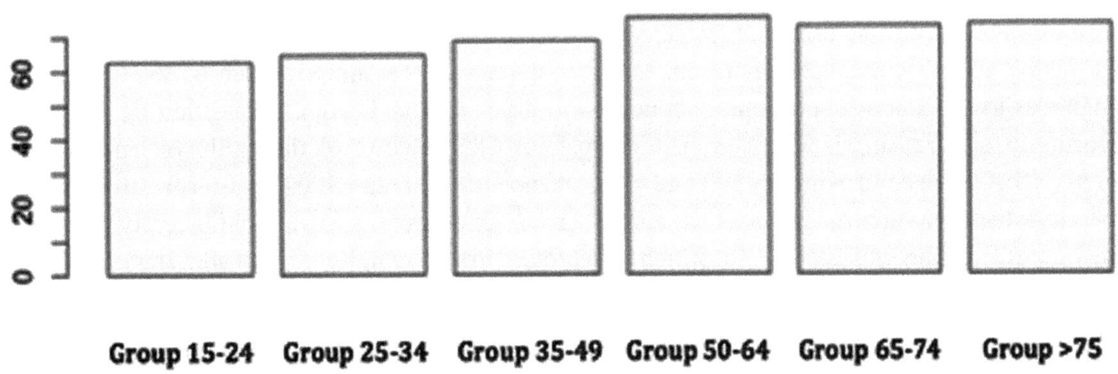

percentages when trying to decide what are the real reasons for which people did not seek a consultation or medical care.

If the subjective reasons for which Romanians do not go to the doctor are hard to identify and will remain, most likely, an area for future study, other countries – with more available resources, such as the United States, for example – are confronted with a slightly different problem: the moral hazard of those who are in the care of a doctor, are offered services and medication, and yet they do not abide with the treatment program. We do not know whether this is the case for Romania as well because here too there aren't any available data. However, because basic healthcare packages are still in their infant stages, we believe that it may be useful to learn from the experience of other countries in terms of patient behavior and to what degree does it align with the purpose of the healthcare package.

On the Behavioral Economics of Health

Many of the choices we are confronted with, either in general of related to health, have an inter-temporal dimension: the costs and associated benefits are placed at different moment in time. For example, when making the decision to exercise daily we are taking into consideration some immediate costs (such as the time it takes, the gym membership costs or the physical effort) and a series of benefits which we hope will manifest in the future (better physical condition, improved heart rate etc.) Similarly, we are confronted with decision in which the benefits are immediate, such as enjoying a dessert and the cost are deferred to the future.

A "perfectly rational" analysis, that is one in which everyone does as they are supposed to, ought to compare, in a similar fashion, the costs and benefits, without allowing for significant differences in the evaluation process. Nevertheless, a more realistic approach, beyond this idea, points out the fact that accepting immediate costs is, in itself, a more difficult process than accepting immediate benefits, given the large number of temptations around us and our imperfect self-control (Thaler & Shefrin, 1981). Therefore, it is no surprise that a large number of behaviors, economic and non-economic, stray from the recommendations of the cost-benefit analysis.

Patient behavior, specifically the lack of total adherence to different treatment plans, usually follows this trajectory. A research team at the University of Pennsylvania, Center for Health Incentives and Behavioral Economics, lead by Kevin Volpp (2008), investigated this troublesome situation on a group of patients who were in recovery following a heart attack. The reference benchmark is given by statistics which show a very low level of adherence to the prescribed medication, usually warfarin, in the year following the heart attack, That is, despite the significant benefits of the treatment, 40% of subjects do not take 20% or more of the recommended medication (Kimmel et al., 2007).

The study involved the use of a "smart" vial, built with the ability to monitor and transmit wireless information about the medications taken. In the first stage, the assumption behind the experimental design was to introduce supplementary benefits for taking the medication in question by creating the opportunity to win cash prizes for conscientious patients (those who took their pills) by using a lottery: there is a 10% chance of winning $20 and a 1% chance of winning $100. This formed the treatment group. For the other group, known as the control group, there were no additional incentives for taking drugs, apart from the intrinsic benefit, which is to protect from the high risk of death. The level of adhesion increased, but not to the expected level or that predicted by standard economic though, which says that financial incentives are one of the most powerful influences when it comes to changing behavior.

These results led to a second experiment, structured in an almost identical way to the first. The only difference was the fact that all the patients, regardless of their behavior towards their treatment were included in the lottery, so theoretically had the opportunity to win a cash prize. The difference appeared after the lottery winner was determined. The way it worked is that they announced the winner if the patient had adhered to the treatment or the patient was told what they *could have won if they have taken their medication.* The structural difference in the experiment illustrates the concept of loss aversion (Kahneman & Tversky, 1984) and is a significant factor when determining human behavior, in this case generating a level of adhesion of almost 100%.

One of the most popular ways for making use of loss aversion is by integrating it in the framing effect of a decision problem. The study conducted by McNeil et al (1982) shows this effect by analyzing the preferences of individuals for two medical treatments. Specifically, subjects were given statistical data concerning the results of tow treatments for lung cancer: surgery or radiation therapy. Survival rates for five years favor surgery, but in the short term it is a riskier option than radiation treatment.

Half of the participants read statistics on the survival rates and the other half were given information concerning mortality rates. Following that, they had to choose the treatment that they preferred:

Scenario 1: The survival rate after surgery is 90% in the first month.
Scenario 2: The mortality rate after surgery is 10% in the first month.

Although it is easy to see that the two propositions are equivalent from a logical perspective, the results of the experiment showed that the surgery was a much more popular option in the first framing, being chosen by 84% of the subjects. In the second framing only 50% chose surgery, thus pointing to a loss aversion behavior. The framing effect (the way in which the information is presented) is emotional: survival is good (90% is an encouraging percentage), but mortality is frightening (even at a 10% level).

Another important characteristic of this study is that it was conducted on different types of subject. What is remarkable is the fact that the group formed entirely of doctors was found to be just as sensitive towards the framing effect as the non-medical groups, one being formed from the patients in a hospital and another one from graduates of economic studies. Therefore, medical studies need to be supplemented by knowledge concerning the way in which people perceive, understand and process the different types of information available, especially statistical information.

This same type of significant results, which are not influenced by the analyzed population, are found when discussing the placebo effect. Although when compared to the other phenomena analyzed in this sections – loss aversion and framing effects – it has been know for much longer, its implementation in an experimental design, which constitutes the replica of a well-known situation, continues to yield surprising results.

In a study conducted at Duke University, Dan Ariely (2008) showed that a painkiller which cost 10 cents did not combat pain as well as one which cost $2.5, given that both of them were in fact the same placebo. The experiment was done on 82 subjects; each one being administered a standard protocol of electric shocks to their wrist, in order to get a subjective evaluation of the pain they felt. The test was conducted both before and after the placebo was administered. The difference between them was that half of the participants received a leaflet which described the pill as a newly approved painkiller which cost $2.5, whereas the other half received a leaflet saying that the pill cost 10 cents, without any further explanations. The results showed that 85% of the members of the first group (price of $2.5) reported a reduction in pain and only 61% of the second group (price of 10 cents) reported a reduction.

Therefore, even if money is the justification brought up for different behaviors, this type of empirical evidence ought to draw more attention to the fact that this belief is only in our mind and that, in reality, the true reason is something completely different.

Being aware of the general tendency towards maintaining the status-quo, especially when it comes to ideas so deeply entrenched in the collective mind, we do not expect for the general perspective to change in a very short period of time. This is also due to the fact that there are situations in which the available statistics show that money matters, but this is significantly easier to remember than the follow-up interpretation for them: it matters, but not as much as one would expect. In this spirit, General Electric conducted a very interesting experiment with the purpose of promoting giving up smoking, with the possibility of getting a reward for it (Volpp et al., 2009). The study was done following the random assignment of the subjects to either the control group, which did not receive any type of stimulant, and the treatment group, where individuals were offered $250 if they abstained from smoking for a period of 6 months or $400 for 12 months.

The results showed significant differences between the groups, the success rate being three times larger for the "financial treatment" group. However, a closer look at the results shows very low success rates (14.7% in the treatment group, compared to 5% for the control for a period of 12 months, and 9.4% compared to 3.6% for a period of 18 months). The statistical difference is important on a theoretical level; however the numbers show that money has a much lower importance than what we would be tempted to believe.

This impact proves to be non-existent, especially when the changes are expressed with a lower level of precision. For example, in a study, conducted in Northern Ireland, aimed at encouraging a healthier lifestyle in the workplace (Hunter et al., 2013), the researchers worked in a manner similar to the quitting smoking experiment: the subjects in the treatment group were monitored, for a period of 12 weeks with a follow-up after 6 months, in order to record the level of physical activity and, in return, they received a card which they could use afterwards in order to get different rewards. On the other hand, the subjects in the control group went through the same monitoring procedures without receiving any type of reward for it. In this case, the final data showed no significant difference between the two groups with respect to physical activity, suggesting the need to implement a different type of stimulant, either separate or along with a financial one.

Besides these examples which clearly show a lack of total efficiency, if not low or completely non-existent, of these financial stimulants, the market approach which includes them raises, in the case of healthcare, a number of structural concerns. First of all, these interventions can easily lead to moral hazard issues in the sense of encouraging a total lack of individual responsibility towards personal health. If we were to consider the financing source for these programs, the perception being much more acute when discussing public funds, but the situation is the same for private sources as well, the negative arguments can take on a type of lack of correctness or fairness towards less fortunate individuals who are sicker due to reasons independent of them, or without the possibility of establishing a strong link such as in the case of smoking of lack of physical activity. And finally, the basic argument, that shows up repeatedly, which is that maintaining a good level of health relies on changing personal attitudes, and this is something which cannot be done, in a sustainable and realistic manner, through monetary payments.

CONCLUSION

Despite the bold title, the purpose of this paper was not to question the utility or the need of basic healthcare packages. What we wanted to point out is that too often we rely on causes beyond our control simply because we have come to consider them as being obvious. The system needs better financing, optimization and somebody will have to do this one day. However, by focusing only on this perspective we risk externalizing authority and accentuating our lack of control and powerlessness. There are moments when the simple option, which we can use at any time, such as access to medical services, makes us postpone using them and so amplifying both the costs and the associated pain.

Let us not forget that, just because something is available, it does not mean that it is actually being used. And it is up to us to do better. Many healthcare systems are confronted with the same problems, indifferent of the amounts that are invested, the infrastructure that is used or the medical personnel that they have access to. These problems are generated by human nature, by our lack of rationality manifested in areas which do not offer a benefit.

This paper underlines a few of the problems which might show up when individual behavior contradicts (most of the time unintentionally and unknowingly) the general objectives of governmental intervention and explains a few of the ways in which simple and non-expensive changes in choice architecture can correct these inefficiencies. Furthermore, we wanted to show that, even if the financial elements are the most obvious signs of involvement and are considered sufficient motivation to change the behavior of a person, when it comes to levels of patient adhesion to different treatment plans they do not go up – at least not as much as one would expect – simply because they received some type of reward.

Of course the studies brought up can be surprising and the results, which have been presented, can create the impression that they are counterintuitive. Until similar studies are conducted in Romania it is impossible to know whether there are differences in our behavior when compared to developed countries. However, until behavioral economics in the area of healthcare becomes an area of active research in Romania, we will close by saying that small changes in our day to day behavior can lead to improvements which will have a significant and long term impact on our level of health.

ACKNOWLEDGMENT

The paper was funded by the project 'Intelligence in health', coordinated by the 'Chronically ill patients alliance in Romania' (contract number 7/17.12.2015).

REFERENCES

Hough, D. (2013). *Irrationality in Health Care*. Palo Alto, CA: Stanford University Press.

Hunter. (2013). Physical activity loyalty cards for behavior change: a quasi-experimental study. *American Journal of Preventative Medicine*.

Kahneman, D., & Tversky, A. (1984). Choices, values, and frames. *The American Psychologist*, *39*(4), 341–350. doi:10.1037/0003-066X.39.4.341

Kimmel, S. E., Chen, Z., Price, M., Parker, C. S., Metlay, J. P., Christie, J. D., & Gross, R. et al. (2007). The influence of patient adherence on anticoagulation control with warfarin: Results from the International Normalized Ratio Adherence and Genetics (IN-RANGE) study. *Archives of Internal Medicine*, *167*(3), 229–235.

Levitt, S., & Dubner, S. (2005). *Freakonomics. A Rogue Economist Explores the Hidden Side of Everything*. New York, NY: William Morrow & Co.

Levy, B. R., Slade, M. D., Kunkel, S. R., & Kasl, S. V. (2002). Longevity increased by positive self-perceptions of aging. *Journal of Personality and Social Psychology*, *83*(2), 261–270. doi:10.1037/0022-3514.83.2.261 PMID:12150226

McNeil, B. J., Pauker, S. G., Sox, H. C. Jr, & Tversky, A. (1982). On the elicitation of preferences for alternative therapies. *The New England Journal of Medicine*, *306*(21), 1259–1262. doi:10.1056/NEJM198205273062103 PMID:7070445

Mitrut, C., Serban, D., & Vasilache, S. (2013). Indicators of Social Trust in Romania – A Quantitative Analysis. *Economic Computation and Economic Cybernetics Studies and Research*, *47*(1), 27–40.

Thaler, R. H., & Shefrin, H. M. (1981). An economic theory of self-control. *Journal of Political Economy*, *89*(2), 392–406. doi:10.1086/260971

Tversky, A., & Kahneman, D. (1981, January30). The framing of decisions and the psychology of choice, *Science. New Series*, *211*(4481), 453–458.

Tversky, A., & Kahneman, D. (1989). *Rational choice and the framing of decisions*. Berlin: Springer. doi:10.1007/978-3-642-74919-3_4

Vâlsan, C., Druică, E., & Ianole, R. (2015). Social Capital, Sustainability, and a History of Transitions in Romania: From Communism to Free Markets. In O. Schwarz-Herion & A. Omran (Eds.), *Strategies towards the New Sustainability Paradigm: Finding the Balance between Global Anarchy and Global Dictatorship* (pp. 35–48). Springer International Publishing.

Volpp, , Troxel, A. B., Pauly, M. V., Glick, H. A., Puig, A., Asch, D. A., & Audrain-McGovern, J. et al. (2009). A randomized, controlled trial of financial incentives for smoking cessation. *The New England Journal of Medicine*, *360*(7), 699–709. doi:10.1056/NEJMsa0806819 PMID:19213683

Volpp, K. G., Loewenstein, G., Troxel, A. B., Doshi, J., Price, M., Laskin, M., & Kimmel, S. E. (2008). A test of financial incentives to improve warfarin adherence. *BMC Health Services Research*, *8*(1), 272. doi:10.1186/1472-6963-8-272 PMID:19102784

Waber, R. L., Shiv, B., Carmon, Z., & Ariely, D. (2008). Commercial features of placebo and therapeutic. *Journal of the American Medical Association*, *299*(9), 1016–1017. doi:10.1001/jama.299.9.1016 PMID:18319411

Wong, H., & Bitran, R. (1999). Designing a benefits package. Prepared for the flagship course on Health Sector Reform and sustainable financing. World Bank Institute.

Zamfirescu, D. (2008). *Nevroză balcanică*. Editura Trei.

Chapter 2
Inter-Temporal Choice and Its Relevance in Consumer's Credit Behavior

Shruti Surachita
XLRI, India

ABSTRACT

Inter-temporal choices have been an important aspect of Behavioral Economics, as they deal with time-dependent decision-making of people in various situations. This chapter discusses hyperbolic time-discounting, which has gained significant recognition and has become an important part of public-policy and economic studies in last few years. It also highlights the importance of this concept from a real-life perspective, by showing its relevance in credit-behavior of individuals. This is shown by highlighting the unstable preferences of individuals using credit-cards, which exploit time-inconsistent behavior. Despite the paucity of current research, understanding impulsive-behavior has gained popularity recently because of the relevance of wellbeing and happiness in the global scenario. As is evident, credit debt does hamper people's quality of life, and so it becomes important for researchers and policymakers to reduce impulsivity and self-control issues, by making consumers use costly commitment-devices and other behavioral options to help them make rational and justified choices.

INTRODUCTION

Historically, it was assumed that people were rational decision-makers, having an ability to calculate the trade-offs between benefits and costs, even in the face of uncertainty and still make choices that would maximize their present and future utilities. However, over time, research in Economics has realized that people's real behavioral patterns deviate from the rational models, as they sometimes tend to make irrational choices despite having all the necessary knowledge required to make optimal decisions. Thus, to understand such anomalies, a new branch in Economics called Behavioral Economics has developed that integrates theories from Economics, Psychology and Neuroscience to evaluate the facets of human judgment and decision-making. Research in this area comprises of three important stages – firstly, the

DOI: 10.4018/978-1-5225-1826-6.ch002

study builds on experimental evidence where a latent variable ignored in standard economic analysis is considered to be relevant. Secondly, it welcomes the observed violations of traditional economic models by incorporating the observed biases into the behavior of a person. This in turn leads to the third stage where an analysis of the psychological sources of such observed biases becomes essential (Pesendorfer, 2006). Thus observed real behavior in behavioral experiments represents the decision-making skills of an individual, showing how a person thinks and decides a choice, in a particular situation. There have been various contributions by Behavioral economists to help improve standard economic theories to make them more realistic, the most relevant being the Prospect Theory, the Endowment Effect, Inter-temporal choice and Social Preferences.

The objective of the present chapter is to focus on people inter-temporal decisions and time-dependent preferences because most human decisions revolve around the dimension of time for evaluating the subjective value of a given choice. Here, consumer-credit in general and credit card in particular has been studied from this perspective, concerning self-control issues to evaluate peoples' borrowing and repayment behaviour realistically. Credit-cards have become popular because they make use of the strategy of 'buy now and pay later' which allows consumers to make impulsive purchase—decisions. Infact by 2001, 76.2% of American households had atleast one all-purpose credit card and also such payment cards accounted for almost 20% of all American personal consumption expenditures. This is because consumer's propensity to consume on current consumption increases as the liquidity of the available funds increases (Shefrin & Thaler, 1988). When consumers are given such financing tools such as credit cards, their spending gets enhanced, as such cards remove any liquidity constraint (Ausubel, 1991; Liabson, 1997). Therefore, this is a relevant field of research for various stake-holders such as policy-makers, social analysts, and researchers, as debt from credit-accumulation has become a major cause of concern as it impacts peoples' happiness and wellbeing negatively.

The chapter is structured into six sections—it starts with a background section, which talks about the origin and evolution of the theory of inter-temporal choices- the Discounted Utility Model (DU). In the second section, it highlights the drawbacks of the DU model and discusses the emergence of the Hyperbolic Discounting model (HDM), whose details are given the next section. The fourth section discusses the applicability of inter-temporal choices in consumer-credit behavior, stressing on its impact on credit-card users. The fifth section provides some suggestions and future recommendations via. Nudge techniques and the chapter ends with a conclusion in the sixth section.

Background and Evolution of Discounted Utility

Inter-temporal choices involve trade-off between costs and rewards happening at distinct times. (Frederick, Loewenstein & O' Donoghue, 2002; Urminsky & Zauberman, 2015). Such choices are extremely important for decision-making as they directly impact people's health, wealth and overall wellbeing. Infact, Adam Smith argued that these inter-temporal choices have the ability to influence the economic prosperity of various economies. The historical evolution of the theory of inter-temporal choices was mostly governed by John Rae, Eugen von Bohm-Baverk, Irving Fisher and Paul Samuelson, who formulated the theory mostly through introspection and personal observation. It got widely accepted in Normative Economics because of its simplicity and its familiarity to the basic compound interest formula, and not because of any empirical validity. Such choices became an established and relevant topic in traditional economic theory in 1834, when the Scottish economist John Rae published, "The Sociological Theory of Capital", which focused on the sociological and psychological determinants of such choices. He believed that such behavior was actually the joint product of various determinants which either improved or lessened the 'effective desire of accumulation' (EDA) - the driving force of such preferences. Infact the two main determinants which improved the EDA were the bequest motive and the propensity to exercise self-restraint. On the other hand, factors that lessened the EDA were the uncertainty of human life, the happiness produced by the prospect of immediate consumption and also the accompanying discomfort of ignoring such available gratifications.

In 1937, Paul Samuelson introduced the first structured model describing inter-temporal choice, called the Discounted Utility Model (DU), which was accepted and popularized immediately, not only as a valid standard for public policies, but also as an extremely accurate representation of human behavior in decision-making. This model was intended to offer a generalized idea of inter-temporal choices, which would be valid for multiple time-periods and it also gave an impression that representation of such trade-offs necessitated a cardinal measure of utility. Moreover, in the model, all the psychological factors discussed in the previous eras were condensed into a single parameter called the 'discount rate'. In understanding the models pertaining to inter-temporal choices, it is important to understand the key notions of time-discounting and time-preference. Time-discounting envelops all kinds of reasons for bothering less about a future event or consequence, involving factors that lessen the expected utility created by a future event such as uncertainty or even variable tastes. On the other hand, time-preference refers to the "preference for immediate utility over delayed utility" (Frederick, Loewenstein & O' Donoghue, 2002, p.352). The DU model advocated by Samuelson, mentioned a decision-maker's inter-temporal preference over his/her various consumption profiles. Under the general assumptions of consumer behavior- completeness, transitivity and continuity, such preferences could be defined by an inter-temporal utility function $U^t\left(C_t,\dots,C_T\right)$. The mathematical formulation of DU model could be written as

$$U^t\left(C_t,\dots,C_T\right)=\sum_{k=0}^{T-t}D\left(k\right)\cdot u\left(C_{t+k}\right),$$

where $D\left(k\right)=\left(\frac{1}{1+\rho}\right)^k$.

Here $u\left(C_{t+k}\right)$ is considered as the individual's cardinal instantaneous utility function or wellbeing in time $\left(t+k\right)$ and $D\left(k\right)$ is explained as the individual's discount function, ρ shows the individual's rate of time-preference or discount rate, which reflects the ' psychological considerations' underlying such choices.

Hyperbolic Discounting and Its Implications

The DU model remained popular for many decades due to its characteristic assumptions such as utility independence, stationary instantaneous utility, consumption independence, constant discounting and time-consistency, diminishing marginal utility and positive time-preference, all of which were in sync with the traditional economic assumptions of consumer behavior (Frederick, Loewenstein & O' Donoghue, 2002). Moreover, the advantage of the discounted utility model was in its simplicity and applicability as all such choices could be evaluated using this model. However, in last few years, economists have observed various empirical inadequacies in the DU model. In recent years, with the help of research in Behavioral Economics and Neuroscience, it has been found that people discount the future consequences in a non-exponential manner. In fact discounting behavior is hyperbolic, which states that delayed rewards are inversely proportional to delay. Such discount functions corrode at an extremely rapid rate in the short run than in the long run and so people are more impatient while making short-run choices than long-run future choices.

Several empirical evidences, in the last few decades, have been interpreted as hyperbolic discounted behavior. Firstly, when subjects in an empirical session were asked to compare between a smaller but quicker reward and a bigger but later reward, the implicit rate of discount over longer time frames was lower than shorter time frames (Thaler, 1981). Similar observations have been found in more recent studies, which prove that hyperbolic time-discounting represents human behavior more accurately than exponential time-discounting. (Thaler, 1981; Benzion, Rapoport & Yagil, 1989; Chapman, 1996; Chapman & Elstein, 1995; Pender, 1996; Redelmeier & Heller, 1993). Secondly, when mathematical functions were made to fit such data pertaining to inter-temporal choices, a hyperbolic functional form fitted the data more accurately than an exponential functional form; i.e. declining discount rates were more representative of behavioral data than constant discount rates.(Kirby, 1997; Kirby & Maraković 1995; Myerson & Green, 1995; Rachlin, Raineri & Cross, 1991) Thirdly, behavioral scientists have observed that, owing to such time-inconsistent behavior, preferences between two distinct delayed rewards, sometimes reverses, in favor of the more proximate one, as time to obtain both the reward falls. These kinds of preference-reversal attitudes have been observed in people as well as in pigeons.(Green, Fristoe & Myerson, 1994; Millar & Navarick, 1984; Solnick et al, 1980; Ainslie & Herrnstein, 1981; Green et al, 1981) Moreover, for a certain delay, such discount rates change across different types of inter-temporal choices: for instance, gains are generally discounted more heavily than losses, small amounts are also discounted much more than larger amounts and finally certain explicit series of multiple outcomes are always discounted differently than single individual outcomes. Apart from time-discounting, there are several other dimensions of inter-temporal choices such as anticipation, self-control, and representation which have not been properly represented in the DU model (Berns, Laibson & Loewenstein, 2007).

Strotz (1955) was the first to look for alternatives to the exponential discounting model stating that "there is no reason why an individual should have such special discount function" (p. 173). Additionally, he observed that for any non-exponential discounting function, preferences would inevitably be time-inconsistent. According to him, people made two important strategies while making such inter-temporal choices, namely using a pre-commitment device and using the notion of strategic planning. Motivated by Strotz and other researchers in this field, Phelps and Pollak (1968) introduced a functional form of hyperbolic discounting model (HDM), which was applied to individual decision-making by Elster (1979). The mathematical form of this model could be represented as follows:

$$D(k) = \begin{cases} 1 & if\ k = 0 \\ B \cdot \delta^k & if\ k > 0 \end{cases}$$

The model presupposes that the per-period rate of discount between now and the next time-period was $\frac{1-B\delta}{B\delta}$ and the per-period rate of discount between any two future time-periods was $\frac{1-\delta}{\delta} < \frac{1-B\delta}{B\delta}$.

Here, the two parameters $(B,\ \delta)$ consider a declining discount rate between this period and next period but a constant discount rate after that.

This model of inter-temporal choice has been used by economists to study various kinds of consumer's economic behavior. For instance, Laibson (1997) studied that illiquid assets such as housing assets worked as great commitment devices, thereby helping consumers to limit over-consumption, by diverting income in such assets. In fact many researchers have corrected various consumption-saving models using both exponential discounting and hyperbolic discounting and have observed that the latter represents empirical observations better. (Angeletos et al; 2001). They further explain how hyperbolic discounting could account for the co-existence of high 'pre-retirement wealth, low liquid asset holdings and high credit-card debt. Moreover, such declining discount rates have also been shown to explain procrastination and self-control problems, thereby helping to realize the relevance of pre-commitment strategies such as deadlines to minimize such behavior. (Fischer, 2001; O' Donoghue and Rabin, 1999, 2001). Additionally, by incorporating hyperbolic- discounting model into procrastination problems, O' Donoghue and Rabin (2001), have not only explored when an individual should complete a task, but also which task to complete. They point out that people never undertake a very easy or very good option, because they continuously plan to undertake an even better and difficult option. Apart from procrastination, hyperbolic-discounting model has also been used to study addiction in people (O' Donoghue & Rabin, 1999, 2000; Gruber & Koszegi, 2000; Carrillo, 1998). The results of various experiments show that such declining discount rates make people over-consume harmful drugs and evaluate the harm caused by such disastrous over-consumption. Finally research has been conducted to observe how inconsistent preferences affect an individual's decision to obtain information. According to studies, hyperbolic discounting leads to "strategic ignorance" in people i.e. an individual with such inconsistent preferences, being scared about withdrawing from a profitable action when the costs begin to show, might choose not to acquire free information, if by doing so, increases the risk of opting out. (Carrillo & Mariotti, 2000; Benabou & Tirole, 2000)

Characteristics of HDM

When evaluating trade-offs between two future options, people having present-biased preferences give more weight to the earlier option as it gets closer. But to evaluate such preferences, the type of choice, the degree of biasness and self-awareness about future behaviour becomes extremely relevant. To evaluate such trade-offs, two distinctions need to be made clear, viz., firstly, choices with immediate costs, where cost of the action is immediate and reward is delayed and/or choices with immediate rewards where reward of the action is immediate and the cost is delayed. Secondly, Strotz (1955) and Pollack (1968) stated that individuals with time-inconsistent preferences fall under two extreme alternatives. At one extreme, a person is completely unaware of his inconsistent preferences and believes that all the future preferences will be similar to the current ones. Such an individual is considered to be naïve. At the other extreme, a person could be completely aware of his inconsistent preferences and make accurate predictions about his future behavior. Such an individual is considered to be sophisticated. In recent years, there has been a concept of partial naiveté, where an individual may be aware of future inconsistent preferences, but be unaware of the magnitude of such choices. (O' Donoghue & Rabin, 2001). With such people, severe procrastination can never occur, however, they do exhibit certain naïve characteristics, due to which they show mild procrastination.

When present-biased preferences influence people's behavior, it is called the *present-biased effect.* When there are choices involving immediate costs, individuals have a tendency to procrastinate, and when there are choices involving immediate rewards, people tend to expedite. With immediate costs, they wait for time-periods, when they should do it, so as to avoid such costs. Likewise with immediate rewards, they do the action in time periods, when they should wait because, they require the reward now. Based on empirical evidence, it has been observed that naïves are easily affected by the present-bias effect, as they always procrastinate and expedite for immediate costs and immediate rewards respectively. On the other hand, the behavior pattern of sophisticates is more complex because of an additional effect controlling their behavior, which is called the 'sophistication effect' (O' Donoghue & Rabin, 1999) where sophisticates are fully aware of their time-inconsistent preferences, which in turn influences the present behavior. Compared to naïves, these people remain more pessimistic about their future behavior and thus perform actions much earlier in time, irrespective of whether the actions involve immediate costs or immediate rewards.

Secondly, though sophisticates perform actions before naïves do, their actions vary slightly with immediate costs and immediate rewards due to the sophistication effect. For immediate costs, sophisticates perform the action much earlier than naïves, because the sophistication effect helps reduce the tendency to procrastinate. On the other hand, when there are immediate rewards, such people have a stronger tendency to expedite, because then the sophistication effect aggravates the self-control problem. Basing on these two observations, empirical evidence shows that such time-inconsistent preferences can lead to severe welfare losses in individuals. For instance, the idea of a Pareto optimal criterion from savings literature (Goldman, 1979, 1980) observes the difference in behavior and welfare losses (long-term utilities) in sophisticates and naïves. Since sophisticates never procrastinate like naïves do, they get differences in utilities only when sophisticates anticipate costly procrastination. In case of immediate costs, naïves exponentially increase their self-control problems, by procrastinating repeatedly, hoping to perform the action in the next period. Every time they procrastinate in a certain period, they suffer a small welfare loss in terms of long-run utilities, and as this behavior repeats itself in subsequent time-periods, the welfare loss becomes severe in the long run. On the other hand sophisticates rarely procrastinate with immediate costs, and even if they do, they know exactly, when they would perform the task if they would wait, and so the delay will be a single decision to procrastinate. This in turn, will lead to much lower welfare loss in the long run. Thus, with immediate costs sophisticates generally obtain a Pareto optimal strategy, but naïves fail in doing so.

On the other hand, with immediate rewards, sophisticates reduce their welfare, in an unwinding mechanism- in the end, such people, will surely expedite, and since they understand this, they expedite a little earlier and this process goes on with each passing time period. For each period, loss in welfare is small, but because of repeated behavior, over multiple time frames, the total welfare loss increases drastically. In contrast, naïves perform a single decision to expedite with immediate rewards, and so their welfare loss is minimum. In this case, naïves undertake a Pareto-optimal decision, while sophisticates do not (O' Donoghue & Rabin, 1999).

There has been more research done in this area to observe if any other external criteria could modulate behavior patterns related to procrastination. A recent study by O' Donoghue and Rabin (2001) found two important results in this direction. Firstly, by giving additional options to people, the tendency to procrastinate increased. This is because, if the new added option had sufficient high long-run net advantage, an individual would plan to choose this new option as opposed to what he would have otherwise done. However, if the new option incurred large cost relative to immediate reward, then an individual would procrastinate. For instance, an employee might immediately invest his savings in the company's shares if there would be a single simple option. However, if there are multiple options given, then the employee would have to constantly plan and figure out the best option among them, and thus that would lead to procrastination. Secondly, they observed that people had a tendency to procrastinate more with important goals than with unimportant goals. This is because, as the goal became more vital, an individual became more ambitious in planning to achieve the goal. This led to higher effort level, which was more than necessary, leading to procrastination.

Neuroeconomics research has also provided scholars with startling evidences to evaluate the mechanisms of inter-temporal choices. At one end, empirical evidence seems to show that inter-temporal choices share valuation and decision structures with other forms of choices (Benzion, Rapoport, & Yagil, 1989; Green & Myerson, 1996). This could be explained by the reasoning that temporal delay would be one of the many determinants that adds on to the representation of value for a choice option. Another set of evidence show that fundamental differences lie between inter-temporal choices and other choices, from which one could infer that such choices represent the working of another different neural system for reward valuation. (Chapman & Weber, 2006; Prelec & Loewenstein, 1991). Under such a mechanism, a delayed option's subjective value would only be compared with another option's value at the last step before response selection. Combining both kinds of evidences, researchers at present, with functional magnetic resonance imaging (fMRI) studies infer that there lies an intermediate prospect- the primary form of such valuation reflect neural functioning which is different from other forms of choice, but the associated value signals are eventually described within a common reward system. (Carter, Meyer & Huettel, 2010).

INTER-TEMPORAL CHOICE AND CREDIT-BEHAVIOUR

General Framework

There has been considerable research in understanding inter-temporal choices, because they explain consumer behavior in many ways (Fomotor & Paradi-Dolgos, 2015). The most important phenomenon explained through such time-inconsistent behavior has been in consumer-credit, which has a direct relationship with consumer-wellbeing. People mainly make two types of decisions regarding their credit behavior. Firstly, how much to borrow today from their income sources in the future, for instance, a person should decide whether or not to buy a product, and once it is bought, he should decide whether to pay immediately or to pay it over time. Secondly, people must decide as to how and when to pay off their debts, i.e. deciding or not to pay bills with accompanying risks of future punishments. As both these decisions revolve around inter-temporal substitution, considering dynamic preferences, which change over time, becomes a critical part of decision-making. It is expected theoretically, that people who are relatively impatient and thus discount time exponentially, will borrow more in the present. Moreover, as they also tend to have a low present value, as far as borrowing is concerned regarding a future option, they are more likely to fail at repaying credit. However recent research in consumer-credit behavior proves otherwise-- people do not discount time exponentially, but rather hyperbolically, with declining discount rates over time, and are thus, present-biased. (Frederick, Loewenstein & O' Donoghue, 2002). Additionally, such people also have different degrees of present-bias tendencies (Coller, Harrison & Rutström, 2005).

Present-biased preference is also considered as dynamic- inconsistent behavior, when people dictate a smaller discount-factor between the present and the future than between two sequential time-periods in the future. This leads to self-control issues in decisions regarding credit-consumption and repayment. As previously stated, the hyperbolic-discounting model in inter-temporal choice considers two parameters namely, β representing present-bias and δ, signifying the long-run discount factor. Such parameters actually help to explain consumer-credit behavior – intuitively, a lower β and δ should lead to high borrowing and low repayment levels. Firstly, present-biased individuals borrow more than optimal level with the given reasoning – two individuals with exactly identical δ should ideally borrow a similar amount of credit, given all conditions equal. However, if one of them is time-inconsistent and has present-bias preferences, then he tends to discount all future periods more heavily than the future discounting made by the other time-consistent individual. As a result of such excessive future discounting, the present-biased individual's present consumption's relative value increases, while the value of the financial cost that would be realized in the future decreases (Meier & Sprenger, 2007). Thus tempting future funding provisions and a desire for instant consumption and satisfaction, in such present-biased people leads to excessive credit- borrowing behavior (Liabson, Repetto & Tobacman, 2003; O' Donoghue & Rabin, 2005).Similar intuition follows for low levels of repayment in such consumers—the chances of non-payment of future financial costs are correlated with present-biased preferences as both β and δ make a time-inconsistent person procrastinate, when faced with a repayment obligation. Moreover, such an individual realizes that he would over-borrow in the near future and thus tries to limit further consumption by means of defaulting, hoping that such a technique would work as a commitment device. Thus, looking at both the perspectives of consumer-credit behavior, one realizes that β plays a significant role in evaluating people's borrowing and repayment actions.

Another point of consideration is that such inter-temporal choices are modeled as the interaction between two distinct cognitive decision-making systems – the affective system which provides a high subjective value for instant satisfaction from consumption and discounts the future time-periods quite sharply, and the deliberative system, which evaluates long-term actions and exhibits high discount factors (McClure et.al 2004). Thus, for present-biased individuals the affective system has higher control over decision-making than the deliberative system as is evident by the relevance of β in such scenario (Meier & Sprenger, 2007). In fact, marketers design techniques which stimulate the affective system in both choice environments – credit borrowing and repayment. They make use of the dynamic inconsistency by encouraging consumers to focus on 'instant fulfillment' while borrowing and spending credit. Credit cards have been the most influential payment method in this respect as immediate rewards and future costs are much more attractive than other methods of payment, such as cash, to present-biased individuals (Bar-Gill, 2004; Prelec & Lowenstein, 1998). However, the behavior regarding credit- repayment is very different from initial credit-borrowing both from the consumer as well as the marketer's viewpoint. Consumers are never encouraged by marketers to repay back credit on time. Infact credit-granting organizations prefer customers to make the exact minimum payment, but not less than the required amount. But marketers play no role in influencing the affective system, leading to a situation where consumers would willingly repay back credit just the way they borrowed it initially. Moreover, sometimes the context in which the repayment action is made may not stimulate the affective system at all, thereby not influencing repayment behavior.

Dynamic-Inconsistency in Credit-Card Users

Credit-card use has become an integral part of consumer-consumption in USA. According to data in 2008, there were approximately 177 million credit cardholders, portraying about 80% of the adult population. Moreover, the average consumer has around 3.5 credit-cards (Foster, Meijer, Schuh & Zabek, 2010). In 2009, 20.2 billion credit transactions were made with credit-cards alone, representing a purchase volume of $1.76 trillion. However, inspite of rampant usage of such cards, consumers still end up mismanaging their credit balances and face rising debt issues. Most consumers make impulsive purchases, which along with high interest-rates and late fees, accelerate the debt problem. It has been observed that when people purchase products using credit cards, they end up spending more credit than when using cash in a similar purchase situation (Feinberg, 1986; Prelec & Simester, 2001). Consumers also have a poorer retrospection of the purchases made on a credit card and also have a lower level of psychic loss associated with such spending(Soman, 2001), which in turn encourages more spending in the future. Additionally, when consumers have a higher credit limit on their cards, it makes them feel richer, independent of their actual income levels, and they end up buying beyond their financial limits (Soman & Cheema, 2002). Even when repaying back bills, people anchor on their minimum amount due instead of clearing out the entire outstanding balance leading to future debts (Stewart, 2009). Such type of attitudes leads to other issues such as increased anxiety (Drentea, 2000) and bad health and wellbeing (Drentea & Lavrakas, 2000). When credit-card users have an outstanding credit balance after the last monthly payment, they are referred to as 'revolving credit card-users' (Bird et.al, 1997). With passing time, such credit card revolvers and credit-debt has vastly increased (Bird et.al, 1997; Canner & Cyrnak, 1985; Lindley, Rudolph & Selby, 1989; Yoo, 1998). According to the 1998 Survey of Consumer Finances, about 44% of families had an outstanding credit-card balance (Kennickell, Starr-McCluer & Surette, 2000). Such issues of rising debt could result in years of financial struggle for households of varying economic positions, leading to lower levels of wellbeing and happiness. Thus, understanding the root-cause of such a phenomenon and ways to overcome such attitudes in consumers have become the focus of study in Social Sciences in recent years.

When an individual has limited liquid assets, he faces two choices regarding purchasing a product – buying the product later with saved income or buying it immediately with borrowed credit. If he would save his income, he would have to forgo his present consumption for the sake of future purchases. But if he would buy the product now on credit, he would have to sacrifice his future consumption for the current purchase as he would have to pay a higher price with added interest. This trade-off between present and future purchase decision would involve an inter-temporal choice (Fischer, 1930). Here, an individual's long term desires conflict with his short-term ones which sometimes leads to irrational choices. Though, initially such choices were viewed from the point of standard discounted utility model, following an exponential discount-rate, research in Behavioural Economics studies suggest that discount rates actually decrease with the passage of time and so inter-temporal choices reflect hyperbolic discount rates (Ainslie, 2001; Chung & Herrnstein, 1967). This is why credit card users are dynamically-inconsistent and thus change their preferences over time. Infact experimental evidence on the response of delay on such inter-temporal choices prove that such delayed outcomes are devaluated hyperbolically (Green & Myerson, 2004; Mazur, 1987), as represented by the following function:

$$V = \frac{A}{\left(1 + kD\right)}$$

where

V = subjective value of the delayed item;
A= amount of the delayed item;
D= delay and
k= free parameter reflecting the discount rate.

Credit card users are generally conflicted regarding their spending and borrowing decisions due to the inter-temporal choices. For instance, consider a situation where a new mobile phone is launched in the market and a consumer becomes extremely interested in buying the phone. However, he has liquidity constraints and so he comes across two choices – either to save up money to buy the phone at a later future date or to immediately purchase it with a credit card. Though he may be skeptical regarding credit card use initially, he would still estimate the relative benefits of both the options—the saving option would look attractive economically as he would pay less money with cash than with interest-laden credit card but the use of credit card would be fascinating as well due to the option of immediate purchase. A point to be considered here is if the saving option does not take a lot of time, it would not be discounted much, and whatever discounted subjective value it would have, its value would be higher than the credit card option. On the other hand, if saving and buying the product would take a lot of time in the future, its subjective value would be more sharply discounted and that would lead to an increased value for the credit-card option. Thus, depending on the time-gap between today and the future as well as the time-gap among the future time-periods, a consumer would decide whether or not to make purchases with credit card (Fagerstrom & Hantula, 2013). Today a number of research papers show that such time-inconsistent preferences and present-biased attitudes lead to borrowing and spending decisions with credit-cards (Laibson, 1997; Fehr, 2002; Heidhues & Koszegi, 2008). Present-biased individuals look for instant gratification and since credit cards fulfill such desires, it leads to increased borrowing as well as debt issues. Apart from dynamic-inconsistency many other factors have also been considered the cause of credit-borrowing and debt—for instance cumulative cost neglect which refers to high borrowing resulting from small purchases, extending over a long time-frame could be a potential cause of such a problem. Here consumers, who would not opt to obtain, say $20,000 worth of revolving debt in a single large purchase with a high rate of interest would anyway have the same debt value by borrowing a small amount of credit over a longer duration. Moreover, naïve individuals procrastinate while repaying back loans and also have unrealistically high optimism about having to pay back their future credit obligations. However, all these determinants could actually be considered to be resulting from time-inconsistent preferences and thus go hand-in-hand with hyperbolic discount rates. Additionally, empirical evidences also prove that present-biased individuals are between 15-20% points more likely to borrow money using credit-cards than people with time-consistent preferences. They also have around 25% more debt than dynamically-consistent individuals even after controlling for demographics, credit-access and credit-limit constraints and a proxy for rates of interest (Meir & Sprenger, 2010)

Credit-Debt and Consumer Wellbeing

Happiness or overall wellbeing is considered to be the ultimate goal in people's lives. It is a general pre-requisite for proper survival and functioning of people, communities and societies. (Diener, 2009; Huppert et.al, 2005; Huppert, 2009; Seligman, 2011). Psychologists consider an individual's subjective wellbeing to be composed of two parts—an affective part which is considered to be happiness and another cognitive part usually referred to as life-satisfaction (Vitterso et.al, 2005; Baumeister et.al, 2013). Though the idea of happiness has always been considered to be a necessary aspect of human existence---the notion of achieving happiness being considered as one of the three unalienable rights for all men (Jefferson, 1776)—there had not been much research in understanding the theory of wellbeing. In the recent years, as many social scientists and economists have started studying the notion of happiness and its impact on people's lives (Diener, 2009; Diener & Seligman, 2004; Dolan & White, 2007; Huppert & Willoughby, 2010; Michaelson et.al, 2009), they have realized that credit-card debt has become a major cause of concern, as it directly impacts happiness levels.

Although dynamic-inconsistency is a major reason of debt accumulation, several other factors have also been observed to cause debt issues. For instance, attitudinal factors, income levels, home-ownership and family size were all positively correlated with rising debt on credit cards (Livingstone & Lunt, 1992). Furthermore, studies also reveal that credit constraints could occasionally lead to unexpected results, with 75% higher debt levels than predicted (Cox & Jappelli, 1993; Jappelli, 1990). A point to be noted here is that financial knowledge and consumer attitudes are generally different between debtors and non-debtors, though more studies need to be done in this regard. For instance, empirical evidence suggests that students with no previous debts would normally underestimate the time-length it would to take for interest laden loan repayment, thought this behavior could be improved with further studies (Lewis & van Venrooij, 1995; Seaward & Kemp, 2000). This kind of under-estimation arises from not being able to see the repercussions of acquiring debt. On the other hand, students who over-estimate their future income were more prone to acquire debt (Seaward & Kemp, 2000). Thus people who go into debt do not normally understand the consequences of their credit- spending actions, while those who already are in debt rate their skills at managing money pretty poorly (Lea, Webley & Walker, 1995), proving that people are normally aware of their borrowing actions and their implications.

As far as attitude is concerned, those individuals with more liberal attitudes regarding credit are more likely to acquire debt, than those with stricter attitudes. (Livingstone & Lunt, 1992). Additionally, students become more tolerable with debt, as debt begins to accrue (Davies & Lea, 1995), which indicates that there could be a cyclic link between pro-debt attitudes and debt level. Sometimes, the presence of a credit card is sufficient to lead to excessive consumer purchases, irrespective of debt-tolerant attitudes. For instance, in an experimental study it was observed that people with credit cards made more impulsive purchases and spent more money that others, suggesting that credit cards accelerate consumer-spending and since most people procrastinate while repaying back, the credit spirals exponentially over time leading to higher debt level(Feinberg,1986).

Today, credit cards have become so necessary that households at some point of time are bound to face credit-debt due to the above-stated reasons, which, consequently would lead to financial stress and lower levels of wellbeing. Recent research (Brown, Taylor, Price, 2005) shows that there exists a strong statistical relation between financial constraints and severe psychological issues, for example, rising depression cases among British civil servants (Weich & Lewis, 1998). Moreover, other studies reflect that students with credit debts are more prone to psychological distress, than other groups of people in the general population (Roberts, Golding & Towell, 1998). Indebted students have a decreased sense of capability to manage their money and a lower level of self-esteem (Lange & Byrd, 1998). They also show a lower level of financial wellbeing and a higher level of stress and anxiety (Norvilitis et.al, 2003). Additionally, students who had to drop out of college due to financial constraints were observed to have weaker mental health as well as poor social functioning (Roberts et.al, 1999). A point to be noted here was that not all students that owed credit cards had debt issues—some of them had realistic attitudes and expectations regarding borrowed money and repaid them back in due time, showing a high degree of sophisticated behavior.(Warwick & Mansfield, 2000). However, this group of individuals represents a very small section in the overall population of consumers owing credit cards. Infact, critics in the credit-card industry have claimed that consumer-bankruptcy is at all-time high since the last hundred years and that consumers would be benefited if their access to credit would be limited. (Loewenstein & O' Donoghue, 2006). They propound that such bankruptcy is higher with time-inconsistent behaviour and thus, individuals would be better off when the credit-debt arising from such a mode of payment is addressed realistically. (Warren, 1998; Brown & Plache, 2006).

RECOMMENDATIONS AND FUTURE RESEARCH

Behavioural Economics models of hyperbolic-discounting reflecting inter-temporal choices and time-inconsistent preferences have actually helped to explain consumer's credit-behavior realistically. The recent findings from consumer credit-card research proves that reasons of debt-accumulation such as impulsive over-spending and procrastinating while repaying back debt could be understood from the viewpoint of dynamic-inconsistency in human decision-making (Meir & Sprenger, 2010; Fagerstrøm, & Hantula 2013; Brown & Plache 2006). This helps social analysts and policy-makers not only to better recognize the cause of self-control and procrastination issues, but also to make judicious strategies and policies to keep a check on such behavioral patterns. At present, effective strategies to 'debias' individual biases remain debatable in consumer decision-making research (Larrick, 2004). Some suggest that consumers should be well-trained in following rational decision-making rules such as understanding the law of large numbers and avoiding sunken costs (Nisbett, 1992), while others recommend modifying the decision environment to ameliorate reasoning skills (Klayman & Brown, 1993). The latter strategy has gained significant focus in the last few years and has earned an attractive label called '*Nudge*' (Thaler & Sunstein, 2008; Johnson et.al, 2012). For instance, policy makers have strongly focused on nudging people to make savings the default option so that employees could save better for retirement period (Thaler & Benartzi, 2004).

Incorporating inter-temporal choices into the credit-behaviour of consumers has been a recent development in this area of research, and so very few nudge techniques have been formulated until now. Relevant nudge techniques have been highlighted here, since they are easy to apply in the real world by researchers and policy-makers, without manipulating the decision-making skills of consumers in any way. Firstly, as was stated by Wärneryd (1999), "habit formation affects the utility obtained from current consumption" (pp. 266). A habit means that a consumer will tend to follow a repetitive and routine behavior. Thus, loan repayment habits could be implemented at a macro-level, so that debt-accumulation due to delayed repayment could be minimized. Moreover, such a habit would keep the consumers well-informed about their purchases, leading to a reduction in impulsive buying, as consumers would think more about the costs as opposed to the benefits (Kim & DeVaney, 2001). Secondly, consumers may be aware of their financial situation, yet end up accumulating debt. Thus, didactic education, which is considered to encourage rational credit-use would definitely not be effective in the real world (Norvilitis & MacLean, 2010; Robb & Sharpe, 2009). Likewise, looking for certain personality traits that would improve or worsen credit behavior will be a failure, as the link between such behavior and personality remains ambiguous. Instead, policy-makers and researchers should focus on using pre-commitment devices to reduce impulsive buying and improve loan-repayment behavior. Thirdly, consumer credit-card usage exploits a certain rule-governed behavior—"behavior that is controlled by the description of relations between responses and verbal stimuli, rather than actual exposure to these contingencies." (Skinner, 1969, p.52). People normally make impulsive purchases on their credit cards in the presence of attractive verbal stimuli, such as "Purchase the mobile phone on credit and get it by tomorrow". According to studies, there are three important functional units of a consumer's rule-governed behavior, namely, augmenting, tracking and pliance (Zettle & & Hayes, 1982). Moreover, augmentals are associated with people's motivation to buy on credit and so they would be able to help to better understand how and why people buy on credit, despite the interest and cost on future consumption (Fagerstrom, Foxall & Arntzen, 2010). Infact, verbal stimuli could be used by credit lenders to encourage lenders to repay back debts, which in turn would be beneficial for both the lenders as well as the consumers.

Though research on inter-temporal choices and people's credit behavior have given support to Behavioural economic models of time-inconsistent preferences in consumer choices, a lot of avenues still remain for further research. Firstly, though current research shows the correlation between present-bias and credit-card borrowing, more studies need to focus on the causal association that exist between these two variables to provide a stronger validation. (Meir & Sprenger, 2010). Secondly, more research needs to be done to observe whether such correlation between dynamic-inconsistency and borrowing could be extended to other forms of debt, such as installment loans and mortgages. This is because credit-card debt is psychologically very different from other debt-forms and so future work should investigate whether the above stated correlation could be generalized across all forms of debt. (Prelec & Simester, 2001).Thirdly, as far as considering the impact of credit-card debt on wellbeing is concerned, present studies have evaluated only the population of college students, implying the need to extend this behaviour across all kinds of consumers. (Fagerstrom & Hantula, 2013, Norvilitis et.al, 2006). Additionally, more information could be gathered to observe how peoples' discounting functions vary as a function of the cost and nature of the products bought, present interest-rates and predictable future interest-rates (Fagerstrom & Hantula, 2013). Furthermore, there is still uncertainty regarding where heterogeneity in consumer time-preferences arises. Impatient attitudes are generally stable over a time-frame and sometimes in very early childhood, heterogeneity in impatient attitudes helps foresee future behavior (Eigsti et.al, 2006; Mischel, Shoda & Rodriquez, 1989). However, researchers still doubt whether parts of consumer preferences are evolved endogenously (Becker & Mulligan, 1997). External shocks, such as credit problems and bankruptcy could also impact people's preferences and so future research should probe whether negative credit experiences could actually affect consumer's preferences and decision-making.

CONCLUSION

Inter-temporal choices, which involve decisions that are spread over time, are an important aspect of Behavioural Economics. Choices in consumption, investments, crime, education, relationships etc. consist of such inter-temporal adjustments. The first model in this regard—the Discounted Utility (DU) model was quite popular for some time, until it was accepted that it lacked descriptive realism and empirical support. It was observed that people in reality had declining discount rates as opposed to the constant discount rates proposed by the DU model. This anomaly gave rise to the hyperbolic discounting model (HDM), which reflected people's time-inconsistent preferences over such choices. Over time, researchers have tried to incorporate the concept of time-inconsistent preference across all areas of life such as consumer credit-behavior, employee productivity, diet and exercise, addiction problems and so on.

Consumer credit-behavior which has been the focus here revolves around two relevant decisions, namely, borrowing and repaying back credit. Both the aspects involve self-control issues and procrastination that are the broad facets of inter-temporal choices. The most relevant studies to understand this relation has been in the field of credit cards, because credit-card consumers do not have time-consistent and stable preferences and fall prey to hyperbolic-discounting. Such individuals mostly consider short-term benefits of such payment-cards but tend to ignore their long-term costs, thereby accumulating more debt, paying higher rate of interest, eventually leading a lower quality of life. Thus, this chapter discusses how consumer-research is trying to understand the mechanism of such time-inconsistent behaviour in the consumer-credit market and emphasizes on certain commitment devices, which could curb the potential problem of debt, thereby improving people's wellbeing level. The chapter also highlights the explicit need for future research in this area and spells out some specific recommendations to lower people's debt in the consumer credit-market, which will improve their happiness in the long-run.

REFERENCES

Ainslie, G. (2001). *Breakdown of will.* Cambridge, UK: Cambridge University Press. doi:10.1017/CBO9781139164191

Ainslie, G., & Herrnstein, R. J. (1981). Preference reversal and delayed reinforcement. *Animal Learning & Behavior*, *9*(4), 476–482. doi:10.3758/BF03209777

Angeletos, G. M., Laibson, D., Repetto, A., Tobacman, J., & Weinberg, S. (2001). The hyperbolic consumption model: Calibration, simulation, and empirical evaluation. *The Journal of Economic Perspectives*, *15*(3), 47–68. doi:10.1257/jep.15.3.47

Ausubel, L. M. (1991). The failure of competition in the credit card market. *The American Economic Review*, *81*(1), 50–81.

Bar-Gill, O. (2004). Seduction by Plastic. *Northwestern University Law Review*, *98*(4), 1373–1434.

Baumeister, R. F., Vohs, K. D., Aaker, J. L., & Garbinsky, E. N. (2013). Some key differences between a happy life and a meaningful life. *The Journal of Positive Psychology*, *8*(6), 505–516. doi:10.1080/17439760.2013.830764

Becker, G. S., & Mulligan, C. B. (1997). The endogenous determination of time preference. *The Quarterly Journal of Economics*, *112*(3), 729–758. doi:10.1162/003355397555334

Benabou, R., & Tirole, J. (2000). *Self-confidence: Intrapersonal strategies* (No. 209). Woodrow Wilson School Working Paper. Princeton University Press

Benzion, U., Rapoport, A., & Yagil, J. (1989). Discount rates inferred from decisions: An experimental study. *Management Science*, *35*(3), 270–284. doi:10.1287/mnsc.35.3.270

Berns, G. S., Laibson, D., & Loewenstein, G. (2007). Intertemporal choice–toward an integrative framework. *Trends in Cognitive Sciences*, *11*(11), 482–488. doi:10.1016/j.tics.2007.08.011 PMID:17980645

Bird, E. J., Hagstrom, P. A., & Wild, R. (1997). *Credit cards and the poor (1148-97)*. University of Wisconsin-Madison: Institute for Research on Poverty.

Brown, S., Taylor, K., & Price, S. W. (2005). Debt and distress: Evaluating the psychological cost of credit. *Journal of Economic Psychology*, *26*(5), 642–663. doi:10.1016/j.joep.2005.01.002

Brown, T., & Plache, L. (2006). Paying with plastic: Maybe not so crazy. *The University of Chicago Law Review. University of Chicago. Law School*, *73*, 63–86.

Canner, G. B., & Cyrnak, A. W. (1985). Recent developments in credit card holding and use patterns among US families. *Journal of Retail Banking*, *7*(3), 63–74.

Carrillo, J. D. (1998). *Self-control, moderate consumption and craving*. CEPR Discuss Paper.

Carrillo, J. D., & Mariotti, T. (2000). Strategic ignorance as a self-disciplining device. *The Review of Economic Studies*, *67*(3), 529–544. doi:10.1111/1467-937X.00142

Carter, R. M., Meyer, J. R., & Huettel, S. A. (2010). Functional neuroimaging of intertemporal choice models: A review. *Journal of Neuroscience, Psychology, and Economics*, *3*(1), 27–45. doi:10.1037/a0018046

Chapman, G. B. (1996). Temporal discounting and utility for health and money. *Journal of Experimental Psychology. Learning, Memory, and Cognition*, *22*(3), 771–791. doi:10.1037/0278-7393.22.3.771 PMID:8656156

Chapman, G. B., & Elstein, A. S. (1995). Valuing the future temporal discounting of health and money. *Medical Decision Making*, *15*(4), 373–386. doi:10.1177/0272989X9501500408 PMID:8544681

Chapman, G. B., & Weber, B. J. (2006). Decision biases in intertemporal choice and choice under uncertainty: Testing a common account. *Memory & Cognition*, *34*(3), 589–602. doi:10.3758/BF03193582 PMID:16933768

Chung, S. H., & Herrnstein, R. J. (1967). Choice and delay of reinforcement1. *Journal of the Experimental Analysis of Behavior*, *10*(1), 67–74. doi:10.1901/jeab.1967.10-67 PMID:16811307

Coller, M., Harrison, G. W., & Rutström, E. E. (2005). *Does Everyone Have Quasi-Hyperbolic Preferences*? University of Central Florida Department of Economics, Working Paper.

Cox, D., & Jappelli, T. (1993). The effect of borrowing constraints on consumer liabilities. *Journal of Money, Credit and Banking*, *25*(2), 197–213. doi:10.2307/2077836

Davies, E., & Lea, S. E. (1995). Student attitudes to student debt. *Journal of Economic Psychology*, *16*(4), 663–679. doi:10.1016/0167-4870(96)80014-6

Diener, E. (2009). The science of well-being: The collected works of Ed Diener. Champaign, IL: Springer Science & Business Media.

Diener, E., & Seligman, M. E. (2004). Beyond money toward an economy of well-being. *Psychological Science in the Public Interest*, *5*(1), 1–31. doi:10.1111/j.0963-7214.2004.00501001.x PMID:26158992

Dolan, P., & White, M. P. (2007). How can measures of subjective well-being be used to inform public policy? *Perspectives on Psychological Science*, *2*(1), 71–85. doi:10.1111/j.1745-6916.2007.00030.x PMID:26151920

Donoghue, O, T., & Rabin, M. (2005). Optimal taxes for sin goods. *Swedish Economic Policy Review*, *12*(2), 7.

Drentea, P. (2000). Age, debt and anxiety. *Journal of Health and Social Behavior*, *41*(4), 437–450. doi:10.2307/2676296 PMID:11198567

Drentea, P., & Lavrakas, P. J. (2000). Over the limit: The association among health, race and debt. *Social Science & Medicine*, *50*(4), 517–529. doi:10.1016/S0277-9536(99)00298-1 PMID:10641804

Eigsti, I. M., Zayas, V., Mischel, W., Shoda, Y., Ayduk, O., Dadlani, M. B., & Casey, B. J. (2006). Predicting cognitive control from preschool to late adolescence and young adulthood. *Psychological Science*, *17*(6), 478–484. doi:10.1111/j.1467-9280.2006.01732.x PMID:16771797

Elster, J. (1979). *Ulysses and the Sirens: Studies in Rationality and Irrationality*. Cambridge, UK: Cambridge University Press.

Fagerstrøm, A., Foxall, G. R., & Arntzen, E. (2010). Implications of motivating operations for the functional analysis of consumer choice. *Journal of Organizational Behavior Management*, *30*(2), 110–126. doi:10.1080/01608061003756331

Fagerstrøm, A., & Hantula, D. A. (2013). Buy it now and pay for it later: An experimental study of student credit card use. *The Psychological Record*, *63*(2), 323–332. doi:10.11133/j.tpr.2013.63.2.007

Fehr, E. (2002). Behavioural science: The economics of impatience. *Nature*, *415*(6869), 269–272. doi:10.1038/415269a PMID:11796988

Feinberg, R. A. (1986). Credit cards as spending facilitating stimuli: A conditioning interpretation. *The Journal of Consumer Research*, *13*(3), 348–356. doi:10.1086/209074

Fischer, C. (2001). Read this paper later: Procrastination with time-consistent preferences. *Journal of Economic Behavior & Organization*, *46*(3), 249–269. doi:10.1016/S0167-2681(01)00160-3

Fisher, I. (1930). *The theory of interest*. New York: The Macmillan Company.

Fomotor, B., & Paradi-Dolgos, A. (2015). The Possible Effects of Inter-temporal Choice Models on Consumer Loan Agreements. *Regional and Business Studies*, *7*(1), 9–17.

Foster, K., Meijer, E., Schuh, S., & Zabek, M. A. (2010). The 2008 Survey of Consumer Payment Choice (Paper No. 09-10). Boston: Federal Reserve Bank of Boston.

Frederick, S., Loewenstein, G., & ODonoghue, T. (2002). Time discounting and time preference: A critical review. *Journal of Economic Literature*, *40*(2), 351–401. doi:10.1257/jel.40.2.351

Goldman, S. M. (1979). Intertemporally inconsistent preferences and the rate of consumption. *Econometrica*, *47*(3), 621–626. doi:10.2307/1910409

Goldman, S. M. (1980). Consistent plans. *The Review of Economic Studies*, *47*(3), 533–537. doi:10.2307/2297304

Green, L., Fisher, E. B., Perlow, S., & Sherman, L. (1981). Preference reversal and self-control: Choice as a function of reward amount and delay. *Behaviour Analysis Letters*, *12*(1), 43-51.

Green, L., Fristoe, N., & Myerson, J. (1994). Temporal discounting and preference reversals in choice between delayed outcomes. *Psychonomic Bulletin & Review*, *1*(3), 383–389. doi:10.3758/BF03213979 PMID:24203522

Green, L., & Myerson, J. (1996). Exponential versus hyperbolic discounting of delayed outcomes: Risk and waiting time. *American Zoologist*, *36*(4), 496–505. doi:10.1093/icb/36.4.496

Green, L., & Myerson, J. (2004). A discounting framework for choice with delayed and probabilistic rewards. *Psychological Bulletin*, *130*(5), 769–792. doi:10.1037/0033-2909.130.5.769 PMID:15367080

Gruber, J., & Koszegi, B. (2001). Is addiction "rational"? Theory and evidence. *The Quarterly Journal of Economics*, *116*(4), 1261–1303. doi:10.1162/003355301753265570

Heidhues, P., & Kőszegi, B. (2008). Competition and price variation when consumers are loss averse. *The American Economic Review*, *98*(4), 1245–1268. doi:10.1257/aer.98.4.1245

Huppert, F. A. (2009). Psychological well-being: Evidence regarding its causes and consequences. *Applied Psychology: Health and Well-being*, *1*(2), 137–164.

Huppert, F. A., Baylis, N., & Keverne, B. (2005). *The Science of Well-being*. Oxford, UK: Oxford Press. doi:10.1093/acprof:oso/9780198567523.001.0001

Huppert, F. A., & Willoughby, A. (2010). *The big flourishing society.* Government Briefing document.

Jappelli, T. (1990). Who is credit constrained in the US economy? *The Quarterly Journal of Economics*, *105*(1), 219–234. doi:10.2307/2937826

Jefferson, T. (1776). *The unanimous Declaration of the thirteen united States of America*. Washington, DC: United States Congress, National Archives and Records Administration.

Johnson, E. J., Shu, S. B., Dellaert, B. G., Fox, C., Goldstein, D. G., Häubl, G., & Wansink, B. et al. (2012). Beyond nudges: Tools of a choice architecture. *Marketing Letters*, *23*(2), 487–504. doi:10.1007/s11002-012-9186-1

Kennickell, A. B., Starr-McCluer, M., & Surette, B. J. (2000). Recent changes in US family finances: Results from the 1998 Survey of Consumer Finances. *Federal. Reserve Bulletin,* (83), 1-24

Kim, H., & DeVaney, S. A. (2001). The determinants of outstanding balances among credit card revolvers. *Journal of Financial Counseling and Planning*, *12*(1), 67.

Kirby, K. N. (1997). Bidding on the future: Evidence against normative discounting of delayed rewards. *Journal of Experimental Psychology. General*, *126*(1), 54–70. doi:10.1037/0096-3445.126.1.54

Kirby, K. N., & Maraković, N. N. (1995). Modeling myopic decisions: Evidence for hyperbolic delay-discounting within subjects and amounts. *Organizational Behavior and Human Decision Processes*, *64*(1), 22–30. doi:10.1006/obhd.1995.1086

Klayman, J., & Brown, K. (1993). Debias the environment instead of the judge: An alternative approach to reducing error in diagnostic (and other) judgment. *Cognition*, *49*(1), 97–122. doi:10.1016/0010-0277(93)90037-V PMID:8287676

Laibson, D. (1997). Golden eggs and hyperbolic discounting. *The Quarterly Journal of Economics*, *112*(2), 443–477. doi:10.1162/003355397555253

Laibson, D., Repetto, A., & Tobacman, J. (2003). A Debt Puzzle. In P. Aghion, R. Frydman, J. Stiglitz, & M. Woodford (Eds.), Knowledge, Information and Expectations in Modern Economics: In Honor of Edmund S. Phelps (pp. 228–266). Princeton, NJ: Princeton University Press.

Lange, C., & Byrd, M. (1998). The relationship between perceptions of financial distress and feelings of psychological well-being in New Zealand university students. *International Journal of Adolescence and Youth*, *7*(3), 193–209. doi:10.1080/02673843.1998.9747824

Larrick, R. P. (2004). Debiasing. In D. J. Koehler & N. Harvey (Eds.), *Blackwell Handbook of Judgment and Decision Making*. Malden, MA: Blackwell. doi:10.1002/9780470752937.ch16

Lea, S. E., Webley, P., & Walker, C. M. (1995). Psychological factors in consumer debt: Money management, economic socialization, and credit use. *Journal of Economic Psychology*, *16*(4), 681–701. doi:10.1016/0167-4870(95)00013-4

Lewis, A., & van Venrooij, M. (1995). A note on the perceptions of loan duration and repayment. *Journal of Economic Psychology*, *16*(1), 161–168. doi:10.1016/0167-4870(95)00002-6

Lindley, J. T., Rudolph, P., & Selby, E. B. Jr. (1989). Credit card possession and use: Changes over time. *Journal of Economics and Business*, *41*(2), 127–142. doi:10.1016/0148-6195(89)90012-X

Livingstone, S. M., & Lunt, P. K. (1992). Predicting personal debt and debt repayment: Psychological, social and economic determinants. *Journal of Economic Psychology*, *13*(1), 111–134. doi:10.1016/0167-4870(92)90055-C

Loewenstein, G., & O'Donoghue, T. (2006). We can do this the easy way or the hard way: Negative emotions, self-regulation, and the law. *The University of Chicago Law Review. University of Chicago. Law School*, *73*(1), 183–206.

Loewenstein, G., & Prelec, D. (1992). Anomalies in intertemporal choice: Evidence and an interpretation. *The Quarterly Journal of Economics*, *107*(2), 573–597. doi:10.2307/2118482

Mazur, J. E. (1987). An adjusting procedure for studying delayed reinforcement. In M. L. Commons, J. E. Mazur, J. A. Nevin, & H. Rachlin (Eds.), Quantitative analysis of behavior: The effect of delay and of intervening events on reinforcement value (vol. 5, pp. 55–73). Hillsdale, NJ: Erlbaum.

McClure, S. M., Laibson, D. I., Loewenstein, G., & Cohen, J. D. (2004). Separate neural systems value immediate and delayed monetary rewards. *Science*, *306*(5695), 503–507. doi:10.1126/science.1100907 PMID:15486304

Meier, S., & Sprenger, C. (2007). *Impatience and credit behavior: evidence from a field experiment (No 07-3)*. Boston: Federal Reserve Bank of Boston.

Meier, S., & Sprenger, C. (2010). Present-biased preferences and credit card borrowing. *American Economic Journal. Applied Economics*, *2*(1), 193–210. doi:10.1257/app.2.1.193

Michaelson, J., Abdallah, S., Steuer, N., Thompson, S., & Marks, N. (2009). *National accounts of well-being: Bringing real wealth onto the balance sheet*. London, UK: New Economics Foundation.

Millar, A., & Navarick, D. J. (1984). Self-control and choice in humans: Effects of video game playing as a positive reinforcer. *Learning and Motivation*, *15*(2), 203–218. doi:10.1016/0023-9690(84)90030-4

Mischel, W., Shoda, Y., & Rodriguez, M. I. (1989). Delay of gratification in children. *Science*, *244*(4907), 933–938. doi:10.1126/science.2658056 PMID:2658056

Myerson, J., & Green, L. (1995). Discounting of delayed rewards: Models of individual choice. *Journal of the Experimental Analysis of Behavior*, *64*(3), 263–276. doi:10.1901/jeab.1995.64-263 PMID:16812772

Nisbett, R. E. (1992). *Rules for reasoning*. Hillsdale, NJ: Lawrence Erlbaum.

Norvilitis, J. M., & MacLean, M. G. (2010). The role of parents in college students financial behaviors and attitudes. *Journal of Economic Psychology*, *31*(1), 55–63. doi:10.1016/j.joep.2009.10.003

Norvilitis, J. M., Merwin, M. M., Osberg, T. M., Roehling, P. V., Young, P., & Kamas, M. M. (2006). Personality factors, money attitudes, financial knowledge, and credit-card debt in college students1. *Journal of Applied Social Psychology*, *36*(6), 1395–1413. doi:10.1111/j.0021-9029.2006.00065.x

Norvilitis, J. M., Szablicki, P. B., & Wilson, S. D. (2003). Factors Influencing Levels of Credit-Card Debt in College Students1. *Journal of Applied Social Psychology*, *33*(5), 935–947. doi:10.1111/j.1559-1816.2003.tb01932.x

ODonoghue, T., & Rabin, M. (1999). Doing it now or later. *The American Economic Review*, *89*(1), 103–124. doi:10.1257/aer.89.1.103

ODonoghue, T., & Rabin, M. (2000). The economics of immediate gratification. *Journal of Behavioral Decision Making*, *13*(2), 233–250. doi:10.1002/(SICI)1099-0771(200004/06)13:2<233::AID-BDM325>3.0.CO;2-U

ODonoghue, T., & Rabin, M. (2001). Choice and procrastination. *The Quarterly Journal of Economics*, *116*(1), 121–160. doi:10.1162/003355301556365

Pender, J. L. (1996). Discount rates and credit markets: Theory and evidence from rural India. *Journal of Development Economics*, *50*(2), 257–296. doi:10.1016/S0304-3878(96)00400-2

Pesendorfer, W. (2006). Behavioral economics comes of age: A review essay on advances in behavioral economics. *Journal of Economic Literature*, *44*(3), 712–721. doi:10.1257/jel.44.3.712

Phelps, E. S., & Pollak, R. A. (1968). On second-best national saving and game-equilibrium growth. *The Review of Economic Studies*, *35*(2), 185–199. doi:10.2307/2296547

Pollak, R. A. (1968). Consistent planning. *The Review of Economic Studies*, *35*(2), 201–208. doi:10.2307/2296548

Prelec, D., & Loewenstein, G. (1991). Decision making over time and under uncertainty: A common approach. *Management Science*, *37*(7), 770–786. doi:10.1287/mnsc.37.7.770

Prelec, D., & Loewenstein, G. (1998). The red and the black: Mental accounting of savings and debt. *Marketing Science*, *17*(1), 4–28. doi:10.1287/mksc.17.1.4

Prelec, D., & Simester, D. (2001). Always leave home without it: A further investigation of the credit-card effect on willingness to pay. *Marketing Letters*, *12*(1), 5–12. doi:10.1023/A:1008196717017

Rachlin, H., Raineri, A., & Cross, D. (1991). Subjective probability and delay. *Journal of the Experimental Analysis of Behavior*, *55*(2), 233–244. doi:10.1901/jeab.1991.55-233 PMID:2037827

Redelmeier, D. A., & Heller, D. N. (1993). Time preference in medical decision making and cost-effectiveness analysis. *Medical Decision Making*, *13*(3), 212–217. doi:10.1177/0272989X9301300306 PMID:8412549

Robb, C. A., & Sharpe, D. L. (2009). Effect of personal financial knowledge on college students' credit card behavior. *Journal of Financial Counseling and Planning*, *20*(1), 25–43.

Roberts, R., Golding, J., & Towell, T. (1998). Student finance and mental health. *The Psychologist*, *11*, 481–491.

Roberts, R., Golding, J., Towell, T., & Weinreb, I. (1999). The effects of economic circumstances on British students mental and physical health. *Journal of American College Health*, *48*(3), 103–109. doi:10.1080/07448489909595681 PMID:10584444

Samuelson, P. A. (1937). A note on measurement of utility. *The Review of Economic Studies*, *4*(2), 155–161. doi:10.2307/2967612

Seaward, H. G., & Kemp, S. (2000). Optimism bias and student debt. *New Zealand Journal of Psychology*, *29*(1), 17.

Seligman, M. (2011). *Flourish*. New York: Nicholas Brealey Publishing.

Shefrin, H. M., & Thaler, R. H. (1988). The behavioral life-cycle hypothesis. *Economic Inquiry*, *26*(4), 609–643. doi:10.1111/j.1465-7295.1988.tb01520.x

Skinner, B. F. (1969). *Contingencies of Reinforcement: A Theoretical Analysis*. New York, NY: Appleton-Century-Crofts.

Solnick, J. V., Kannenberg, C. H., Eckerman, D. A., & Waller, M. B. (1980). An experimental analysis of impulsivity and impulse control in humans. *Learning and Motivation*, *11*(1), 61–77. doi:10.1016/0023-9690(80)90021-1

Soman, D. (2001). Effects of payment mechanism on spending behavior: The role of rehearsal and immediacy of payments. *The Journal of Consumer Research*, *27*(4), 460–474. doi:10.1086/319621

Soman, D., & Cheema, A. (2002). The effect of credit on spending decisions: The role of the credit limit and credibility. *Marketing Science*, *21*(1), 32–53. doi:10.1287/mksc.21.1.32.155

Stewart, N. (2009). The cost of anchoring on credit-card minimum repayments. *Psychological Science*, *20*(1), 39–41. doi:10.1111/j.1467-9280.2008.02255.x PMID:19152539

Strotz, R. H. (1955). Myopia and inconsistency in dynamic utility maximization. *The Review of Economic Studies*, *23*(3), 165–180. doi:10.2307/2295722

Thaler, R. H. (1981). Some Empirical Evidence on Dynamic Inconsistency. *Quasi Rational Economics*, *8*(3), 127–136.

Thaler, R. H., & Benartzi, S. (2004). Save more tomorrow™: Using behavioral economics to increase employee saving. *Journal of Political Economy*, *112*(S1), S164–S187. doi:10.1086/380085

Thaler, R. H., & Sunstein, C. R. (2008). *Nudge: Improving decisions about health, wealth, and happiness*. New Haven, CT: Yale University Press.

Urminsky, O., & Zauberman, G. (2015). The Psychology of Intertemporal Preferences. In G. Keren & G. Wu (Eds.), The Wiley Blackwell Handbook of Judgment and Decision-making (pp. 1-50). West Sussex, UK: Blackwell Publishing. doi:10.1002/9781118468333.ch5

Vittersø, J., Biswas-Diener, R., & Diener, E. (2005). The divergent meanings of life satisfaction: Item response modeling of the satisfaction with life scale in Greenland and Norway. *Social Indicators Research*, *74*(2), 327–348. doi:10.1007/s11205-004-4644-7

Wärneryd, K. E. (1999). *The Psychology of Saving: A Study on Economic Psychology*. Cheltenham, UK: Edward Elgar Publishing.

Warren, E. (1998). The Bankruptcy Crisis. *Indiana Law Journal (Indianapolis, Ind.)*, *73*(4), 1079–1110.

Warwick, J., & Mansfield, P. (2000). Credit card consumers: College students knowledge and attitude. *Journal of Consumer Marketing*, *17*(7), 617–626. doi:10.1108/07363760010357813

Weich, S., & Lewis, G. (1998). Material standard of living, social class, and the prevalence of the common mental disorders in Great Britain. *Journal of Epidemiology and Community Health*, *52*(1), 8–14. doi:10.1136/jech.52.1.8 PMID:9604035

Yoo, P. S. (1998, January). Still charging: The growth of credit card debt between 1992 and 1995. *Federal Reserve Bank of St. Louis Review*, 19-27.

Zettle, R. D., & Hayes, S. C. (1982). Rule governed behavior: A potential theoretical framework for cognitive behavior therapy. In P. C. Kendall (Ed.), Advances in cognitive behavioral research and therapy (pp. 73-118). New York, NY: Academic Press. doi:10.1016/B978-0-12-010601-1.50008-5

KEY TERMS AND DEFINITIONS

Behavioural Economics: A new branch of Economics, dealing with consumer-behaviour, judgment and decision-making.

Commitment Devices: Strategies used by decision-makers, based on their past experiences and expected future behaviour, to overcome self-control problems.

Consumer Credit-Behavior: An individual's behavior mostly pertaining to credit-borrowing and credit-repayment.

Dynamically-Inconsistent: An unstable behavioral-pattern observed with time-dependent decision-making.

Neuroeconomics: A recent area of research, which uses neural techniques to validate standard behavioral economic theories.

Nudge: A technique used in Behavioral Economics to modulate people's behavior by changing the context of the real-world problem, helping them make better choices.

Wellbeing: An overall state of a person's cognitive and affective evaluations of life.

Chapter 3
Attitudes toward Tax Evasion and the Choice of Self-Employment

Vasanthakumar N. Bhat
Pace University, USA

ABSTRACT

It is generally believed that self-employment offers ample opportunities for tax evasion. Therefore, this paper examines whether attitudes toward tax evasion has any influence on the choice of self-employment. Our analysis, based on a random sample of Americans, indicates that an individual who believes that tax evasion is "not wrong and a bit wrong" is more likely to be self-employed as compared to an individual who believes that tax evasion is "wrong and seriously wrong." This decision is not affected by gender. In addition, our analysis finds that a self-employed person earns more income than a person who works for someone else. However, an individual who believes that tax evasion is "wrong and seriously wrong" earns more than an individual who believes that tax evasion is "not and a bit wrong". Moreover, a self-employed person who believes that tax evasion is "not and a bit wrong" earns less than all other people, with all other parameters being the same.

INTRODUCTION

The purpose of this paper is to investigate the link between attitudes toward tax evasion and the choice of self-employment. Tax evasion involves falsification of the true state of affairs to tax authorities with a view to reduce taxes. Taxes evaded can be both direct taxes such as income tax and indirect taxes such as excise duties and sales tax. Falsifications typically include understating incomes and profits or gains and overstating deductions. Other forms of tax evasions include transfer of assets or incomes to others, recording personal expenses as business expenses, paying employees off-the-books, farming out work to small firms, or paying the self-employed or illegal immigrant to do the work for below-minimum wages. Tax evasion is pervasive as long as taxes exist. It is a growing problem in most countries (Torgler, 2002). It is an important problem to investigate for several reasons. Tax evasion can reduce governments'

DOI: 10.4018/978-1-5225-1826-6.ch003

revenue forcing them to consider other forms of proceeds. It can also increase tax burden of the people who comply with the tax laws. Furthermore, it can also increase the cost of tax collection. Tax evasion has significant economic impacts. For example, tax evasion can lead to misallocation of resources by encouraging individuals to invest in activities that have tax evasion opportunities. Since individuals generally make decisions based on after-tax returns, tax evasion can cause unacceptable behavioral changes. For example, people will prefer to work off-the-books if they can get higher wages

People are attracted to self-employment because of many conveniences it provides to the self-employed. However, self-employment also involves considerable risks. For example, wage and salary employment provides certain income whereas self-employment income is uncertain.

The taxation of wage incomes is different from taxation of self-employment income in the U.S.

As a result, tax rates have significant impact on the decision whether to go for self-employment. In addition, self-employment provides ample opportunities for tax evasion. The purpose of this paper is to examine the relationship between attitudes towards tax evasion and decisions to work as self-employed.

This paper is organized into five sections. We provide a brief review of literature in the next section followed by a set of hypothesis. We then provide the methodology and results of our analysis. This paper is closed with discussions and conclusions.

LITERATURE REVIEW

Tax Evasion

The tax evasion problem in economics is modeled as a problem of decision making under uncertainty. A person who cheats on taxes gains because of lower taxes. However, if he is caught, he loses because of penalty and other sanctions. One of the earliest economic analyses of crimes that include tax evasion developed as a decision making problem under uncertainty is by Becker(1968). His model minimizes the sum of losses due to damages of crimes and costs of catching, convicting and punishing for crimes. Allingham and Sandmo(1972) provide a theoretical model based on Becker(1968)'s analysis. Theoretical models, including those by Yitzhaki(1974), Graetz and Wilde (1985), and Pestieau and Possen (1991), indicate that reported income is positively related to income, detection rate, and penalties. In addition, if penalty structure is based on the amount of taxes underreported, then lower tax rates will lead to more evasion.

Taxes and evasion have been subjects of extensive research. Morality, justice, fairness, and a variety of factors have been used to justify and attack taxes and tax evasion. People have always protested against taxes. They have used revolts (Edwards & Mitchell, 2008), demanded tax reforms (Schlaes, 1999), proposed new tax system such as flat tax or consumption tax (Boortz & Linder, 2005; Hall & Rabushka, 1985; Hultberg, 1996) and used other means to mitigate the impact of taxation. There is also extensive research questioning whether the tax burden is shared equitably by different income groups. Most of these analyses focus on whether higher income people should pay a higher share of their income and whether they are paying a fair share or not (see for example Thorndike and Ventry, 2002; McGee, 2012). Blum & Kalven (1953) challenge whether progressive taxation is desirable as it is detrimental unless diminishing marginal utility of money can be proved. Some have even questioned taxes on legal grounds. On the other hand, many scholars have come up with creative arguments in favor of taxes and their compliance. For example, Greenwood (2007) asserts that tax evasion is an attack on our civilization as payment of taxes is everyone's duty.

Tax evasion has been examined from a variety of perspectives. A comprehensive review of tax fraud can be found in Torgler (2008). According to Adams (1993) and Weber and Wildavasky (1986), tax evasion has been pervasive from the time people were subjected to taxes. People have used creative arguments to justify tax evasion. For example, Morales (1998) claims that Mexican immigrant street vendors are more loyal to their families than the government and sometimes it is more important to feed the family than to pay taxes. According to McGee(2006), tax evasion can be never, always, or sometimes ethical. Sometimes, there can be affirmative duty to evade taxes. According to Pennock (1998), tax evasion is ethical if the country collecting taxes is involved in an unjust war. Gregory (1998) asserts that tax evasion is permissible in certain circumstances based on Catholic religious literature. Other perspectives of tax evasion include cultural factors (Alm & Torgler, 2006); psychological issues (Alm, Martinez-Vazquez & Torgler, 2010) and religious reasons (Torgler, 2006).

It is difficult to estimate the extent of tax evasion, as it is a behavior that a perpetuator is trying to hide. Therefore, direct as well as indirect methods are used to approximate the degree of tax evasion. One method is to use results from systematic audits of tax returns. Taxpayer Compliance Measurement Program (TCMP) and National Research Program (NPR) used by the U.S. Internal Revenue Service (IRS) are examples of such surveys. Currency ratio models are most common indirect method for estimating the extent of tax evasion (Feige, 1989). This model assumes that increase in monetary notes in circulation or increased demand for cash reflects increased economic activity in informal sector. Another method to estimate the size of informal sector is to use income expenditure discrepancy method. This method assumes that even though people are likely to misrepresent their income, they will not misrepresent their expenditures when interviewed. However, according to Frey & Pommerehne (1982), the discrepancy method suffers from three shortcomings that include errors in both estimates of aggregate income; errors due to differences in the statistical coverage; and missing of incomes in tax records as well as the national income data.

Tax Evasion in the U.S.

The incomes of wage earners and the self-employed in the U.S are subject to both income tax and employment tax consisting of social security and Medicare taxes. Even though incomes of employees and the self-employed are subject to the same rate of income tax, their employment tax rates are different. The employment tax of an employee is shared by both employee and the employer whereas the self-employed is responsible for the whole portion of the employment taxes. In addition, employers are required to withhold income and employment taxes from wages of their employees and make quarterly payments along with the employer's share of the employment taxes to the government. On the other hand, no third party withholds taxes of the self-employed. They are required to pay income and social security and the Medicare taxes themselves.

In the U.S., an individual tax return consists of the 1040 form or some variations of it and several schedules. Incomes or losses from businesses or professions as a sole proprietor need to be reported using Schedule C. If a person is involved in a business, the goal is to generate income or profit with continuity and regularity. A self-employed individual is required to pay employment taxes each quarter. Since these taxes are imposed on the same income, a self-employed individual who underreports incomes not only reduces income tax liability but also employment taxes as well which can be as high as 16 percent up to a certain income.

Tax evasion reduces tax revenue government collects diminishing its ability to provide public services and increasing public debt. Tax evasion is a crime in the U.S. Therefore, it is very difficult to estimate the extent of tax evasion. Slemrod (2007) provides a comprehensive review of the estimate of tax evasion in the U.S. Most estimates about tax evasion are done by the IRS. Starting 1979, IRS estimated what is known as "tax gap" based on information it gains from its random intensive audits under the Taxpayer Compliance Measurement Program (TCMP). The TCMP data consists of information tax payer reported and information that examiner concluded is being true. However, the TCMP was cancelled in 1995. In its place, the National Research Program (NRP) was started in 2001 (U.S. Department of the Treasury, 2005a & 2005b). The NRP is based on randomly selected 46,000 returns with oversamples of high-income returns and returns that include Scheduled C sole proprietorship income. Even though, only 6 percent of taxpayers file schedule C sole proprietorship income, 46 percent of the NRP sample represented schedule C sole proprietorship income. The sampled returns are then manually reviewed by experienced auditors and categorized into returns that are accepted based on supporting information reported by third parties; returns with at most three items that need to be corroborated and returns that require in-person audit. Auditors are also provided freedom to do additional review of suspicious items of returns subjected to in-person audit.

According to the IRS, the taxes evaded in 2006 amount to about $450 Billion. The taxes evaded include underreported taxes on tax returns, underpayment of taxes due based on filed returns and noncompliance altogether. Taxes evaded include individual income, corporate income, employment, estate, and excise taxes (U.S. GAO, 2012). Individual income tax represents about two-thirds of the taxes evaded. Individuals have opportunities to underreport their both business and nonbusiness incomes. According to the IRS estimate, about 40 percent of tax evasion is by underreporting business income tax and also self-employment tax. There are a variety of ways to underreport business income tax. Sole proprietors, for example, represent a predominant group of major taxpayers who misreport business income by understating receipts or overstating expenses. One major reason for such underreporting by the sole proprietors is because their incomes are not subject to withholding and only a fraction of their incomes are subject to information reporting to IRS by third parties. Wages and salaries are subject to withholding and extensive third party reporting. As a result, it is very difficult to misreport wages and salaries. On the other hand, self-employed income including rents and royalties, farm income, and proprietor income are subject to very little withholding and third party reporting. As a result, self-employed taxpayers estimated to have misreported 56 percent of their income in 2006 (U.S. GAO, 2012 p.6).

Self-Employment

Many people prefer to be self-employed because of many benefits afforded by self-employment. Flexible and convenient work schedule, opportunity to work without a boss and potential increased income are some attractive features of self-employment. However, self-employment is not without drawbacks. A person can make losses in self-employment and lose all assets. Self-employment also has much higher stress level. Policy makers frequently consider self-employment as a route out of poverty. Self-employment encourages inventions and innovations and also creates new jobs as well as new firms. These firms can increase competition and also provide more varieties of products and services to consumers. However, there is very little evidence that self-employment brings about these benefits in practice. According to Birch(1979, 1981), 66% of all net new jobs in the U.S. between 1969 and 1975 were created by firms with 20 or fewer employees and 81.5 employees by firms with 100 or few employees. Birch(1987) subsequently claimed that firms with fewer than 20 employees generated more than 82 percent of employment growth through expansion and contraction of exiting firms and over 88.1 per cent of overall employment growth during 1981-1985. However, Davis (1996a, 1996b) challenges the Birch's conclusions saying that Birch's methodology is flawed and data used is unsuitable for such analysis. Davis also finds no systematic relationship between manufacturing plant size and employment growth. A recent analysis by Neumark et al.(2011) find that small firms and establishments create more jobs. Furthermore, they find a negative relationship between establishment size and net job creation for both the manufacturing and services sectors.

A variety of factors influence self-employment. Lack of capital can be a significant impediment for starting businesses. According to Evan & Leighton(1989) and Evans & Jovanovic (1989), people with more wealth are likely to go for self-employment provided all other factors remain equal. This is based on the analysis of the National Longitudinal Survey of Young Men for 1966-1981 and the Current Population Surveys for 1968-1987. According to Douhan (2009), greater years of education positively influence the likelihood of choosing entrepreneurship. Blanchflower (2000) finds that age is positively related with self-employment in the U.S. He also finds that self-employment in the U.S. is higher among men than women and higher among whites as compared to blacks.

Hypotheses

In this section, we develop several hypotheses for analysis. It is evident that tax evasion opportunities can distort decision making relating to career choice. For example, according to Boeri & Garibaldi (2002), workers in the informal sectors are predominantly with lower levels of skills. Availability of jobs in informal sectors and tax evasion opportunities can reduce returns from education and can encourage people not to pursue higher education (Kolm & Birthe, 2003). It has been generally believed that tax evasion by the self employed is much higher than by taxpayers whose predominant sources of incomes are wages and salaries. Since there are no third-party reports of incomes of the self-employed, the self-employed person has opportunities to misreport income. However, theoretical models of human behavior do not provide any clue about the extent of tax evasion and the extent of tax evasion depends on risk attitudes of the self-employed. Empirical studies done by Joulfian & Rider (1998) find a positive relationship between marginal tax rates and evasion among the self-employed. According to Slemrod et al.(2001), voluntary tax compliance is 99.5 percent for wages and salaries. However, it is only 41.4 percent for the self-employed who file Schedule C. Therefore, we can presume that people who feel that tax evasion is not wrong may prefer to be self-employed rather than work for someone else. So our first hypothesis is:

H1: People with attitudes that tax evasion is less wrong are likely to be self-employed as compared to people with attitudes that tax evasion is more wrong.

In spite of several advantages of going for self-employment, self-employment is subjected to risks. Income of an employee is certain whereas income from self-employment is uncertain. Therefore, a person will have to receive higher income to be self-employed unless advantages of self-employment exceed disadvantages of uncertain income. Therefore our hypothesis relating to the incomes of the self-employed is as follows:

H2: The average income of self-employed persons is likely to be higher than the average income of employees working for employers.

Even though, income tax rates for wage income and income from self-employment are the same, the self-employed are required to pay substantially higher employment taxes. Therefore, if the self-employed underreports incomes to reduce income tax, it also reduces employment tax liabilities. Therefore, a person who feels that tax evasion is less wrong will be satisfied if the income is higher than after tax income of the wage earners. Therefore, the person going for self-employment with the opinion that tax evasion is less wrong is likely to earn less than self-employed person with attitudes of tax evasion being more wrong and everyone else. Therefore, our hypothesis 3 will be:

H3: A self-employed person with attitudes that tax evasion is less wrong is likely to earn less than a self-employed person with attitudes that tax evasion is more wrong and a person who works for others.

Methodology

We use the General Social Survey of the year 2004. (Davis et al. 2005). This survey, conducted every two years, by the National Opinion Research Center, is one of the largest surveys in the United States. This survey, based on a random sample of Americans, contains a variety of demographic information including whether a person is self-employed and response to the question, "Do you feel it is wrong or not wrong if a taxpayer does not report all of his income in order to pay less income taxes." This survey also contains weights for each response that help us to estimate results that are valid for the whole country.

We first perform univariate analysis to examine the association between attitudes toward tax evasion and self-employment by various demographic variables. We use logistic regression analysis to examine the influence of various factors in choosing self-employment. We use self-employment/work for someone else as a dependent variable and gender, race, age, education, hours worked per week, and attitude toward tax evasion as independent variables. In order to analyze the annual income, we use Tobit regression analysis as annual income data is censored from above. We use gender, race, age, education, hours worked per week, and attitude toward tax evasion as independent variables.

ANALYSIS OF RESULTS

Univariate Analysis

Our goal is to evaluate the association between attitudes toward tax evasion and self-employment. We use the answer to the question in the General Social Survey, "Do you feel it is wrong or not wrong if a taxpayer does not report all of his income in order to pay less income taxes" as a proxy for attitudes toward tax evasion. The answers are: not wrong, a bit wrong, wrong and serious wrong. Of 43.3 percent of responders who answered to this question, 2 percent considered tax evasion as "not wrong", 4.5 percent "a bit wrong", 22 percent "wrong" and 13.6 percent "seriously wrong". For the purpose of analysis, we classify the responses into two categories - "not wrong and a bit wrong" and "wrong and seriously wrong".

In Table 1, we present attitudes toward tax evasion and self-employment by race, gender and age group. Even though, there is not much difference in the self-employment rates among whites, and black and others, the percent of self-employment among whites with attitude of "not wrong and a bit wrong" toward tax evasion is considerably higher than percent of self-employment among whites with "wrong and seriously wrong". The self-employment rates among women is only 8.1 percent as compared to 13.7 percent among men. The percent of self-employment among men and women with attitudes toward tax evasion of "not wrong and a bit wrong" is higher than percent self-employment with attitudes of "wrong and seriously wrong". Clearly, both men and women with attitudes of "not wrong and a bit wrong" are more likely to go for self-employment as compared men and women with attitudes of "wrong and seriously wrong". The self-employment rates increase with age. For all age-categories, the self-employment rates are higher for people with attitudes of "not wrong and a bit wrong" than people for attitudes of "wrong and seriously wrong". However, the difference is much less for people over 65 years of age.

In Table 2, self-employment and attitudes toward tax evasion are examined by the highest degree attained by an individual and number hours worked per week. The self-employment rates increase with the highest education attained. People with less than high school, high school and graduate degrees with attitudes of "not wrong and a bit wrong" are more likely to go for self-employment compared to people with "wrong and seriously wrong" attitudes. However, for people with junior college, people with "not-wrong and a bit wrong" attitudes are less likely to go self-employment as compared to those with "wrong and seriously wrong" attitudes. One in five persons who worked for less than 20 hours and who worked over 55 hours per week went for self-employment. Among those people who worked between 21 to 55 hours per week, the self-employment rates are between 7.9 and 10.3 percent. In other words, people who want to work relatively short hours and long hours are likely to go for self-employment at higher rates. When it came to people with "not wrong and a bit wrong" attitudes toward tax evasion. people who worked for 21 to 40 hours are two times more likely to go for self-employment compared to people with "wrong and seriously wrong" attitude. However, there was not much difference among groups working 41 to 55 hours. In addition, roughly one in three persons who worked for less than 20 hours and more than 55 hours with attitudes toward tax evasion "not wrong and a bit wrong" was for self-employment. However, this percentage is between 11,4 to 13 for persons who worked between 21 to 40 hours with the attitudes toward tax evasion of "wrong and seriously wrong".

Mutivariate Analysis

Self-Employment

The univariate analysis considers influence of one variable at a time. So we conduct multivariate analysis of both likelihood of self-employment and annual income. In Table 3, we present the influence of various variables on the likelihood of self-employment. We perform a logistic regression analysis with self-employment (=1 and 0 otherwise) as a dependent variable. We present two specifications with and without male with "not wrong and a bit wrong" attitudes toward tax evasion.

Since both specifications give similar results, we will discuss the results of the specification that includes male with "not wrong and a bit wrong" attitude toward tax evasion as an independent variable. Since the coefficient for men is positive, men are more likely to go for self-employment as compared to women. According to the odds ratio, men are 1.94 times more likely to go for self-employment than women, all else remaining the same. Even though coefficient for race is positive, it is not statistically

Table 1. Attitude toward tax evasion and self-employment by race, gender, and age groups

			Occupational Status		Total
			Self-Employed	Work for Someone Else	
Race	White (81.7%)	Not wrong & a bit wrong	18.10%	81.90%	15.10%
		Wrong & seriously wrong	9.60%	90.40%	84.90%
		Total White	10.90%	89.10%	100.00%
	Black & Others (18.3%)	Not wrong & a bit wrong	2.60%	97.40%	19.10%
		Wrong & seriously wrong	11.50%	88.50%	80.90%
		Total Black & Others	9.80%	90.20%	100.00%
Gender	Male (46.2%)	Not wrong & a bit wrong	17.90%	82.10%	18.30%
		Wrong & seriously wrong	12.80%	87.20%	81.70%
		Total Male	13.70%	86.30%	100.00%
	Female (53.8%)	Not wrong & a bit wrong	11.00%	89.00%	13.6.0%
		Wrong & seriously wrong	7.70%	92.30%	86.4.0%
		Total Female	8.10%	91.90%	100.00%
Age group	18-34 (47.5%)	Not wrong & a bit wrong	9.50%	90.50%	24.70%
		Wrong & seriously wrong	4.30%	95.70%	75.30%
		Total	5.60%	94.40%	100.00%
	35-64 (42.9%)	Not wrong & a bit wrong	19.70%	80.30%	12.40%
		Wrong & seriously wrong	11.20%	88.80%	87.60%
		Total	12.30%	87.70%	100.00%
	over 65 (9.8%)	Not wrong & a bit wrong	17.60%	82.40%	10.90%
		Wrong & seriously wrong	15.20%	84.80%	89.90%
		Total	15.50%	84.50%	100.00%

significant at the 0.05 level. So there is no statistically significant difference in choosing self-employment among whites, and black and others. The age is statistically significant at the 0.05 level. The odds ratios relating to age categories are with respect to people over 65. The odds ratio of 0.07 for age group 18-34 years signifies that people over 65 are 14.3 more likely to go for self-employment compared to people in the age group 18-34 and the odds ratio of 0.22 for age 35-64 indicates that people over 65 are 4.5 times more likely to go for self-employment than people in the age group 35-64. Highest degree achieved is not statistically significant at the 0.05 level based on the Wald test in the logistic regression analysis. In other words, highest degree achieved is not a determining factor in choosing self-employment. There are four categories of hours worked namely less than 20 hours, 21 – 40 hours, 41 to 55 hours and over 55 hours. Our reference group is over 55 hours. Even though hours worked is statistically significant at the 0.05 level, hours worked less than 20 hours is not statistically significant. This means that a person who works for less than 20 hours is as likely to go for self-employment as a person who works for more than 55 hours. This is consistent with the univariate analysis. Based on the odds ratio, an individual who works more than 55 hours per week almost 3 times more likely to be self-employed than an individual

Table 2. Attitudes toward tax evasion and self-employment by highest degree and hours worked per week

			Occupational Status		Total
			Self-Employed	Work for Someone Else	
Highest degree	Less Than High School & High School (68.1%)	Not wrong & a bit wrong	15.00%	85.00%	24.70%
		Wrong & seriously wrong	8.90%	91.10%	75.30%
		Total	10.00%	90.00%	100.00%
	Junior College (24.3%)	Not wrong & a bit wrong	11.80%	88.20%	12.40%
		Wrong & seriously wrong	12.20%	87.80%	87.60%
		Total	12.10%	87.90%	100.00%
	Graduate (7.2%)	Not wrong & a bit wrong	22.20%	77.80%	10.90%
		Wrong & seriously wrong	12.00%	88.00%	89.90%
		Total	13.00%	87.00%	100.00%
Hours worked	20 hrs or less (9.45%)	Not wrong & a bit wrong	33.30%	66.70%	12.20%
		Wrong & seriously wrong	18.50%	81.50%	87.80%
		Total	20.30%	79.70%	100.00%
	21 to 40 hrs (46.87%)	Not wrong & a bit wrong	13.00%	87.00%	18.80%
		Wrong & seriously wrong	6.70%	93.30%	81.20%
		Total	7.90%	92.10%	100.00%
	41 to 55 hrs (29.63%)	Not wrong & a bit wrong	11.40%	88.60%	19.00%
		Wrong & seriously wrong	10.10%	89.90%	81.00%
		Total	10.30%	89.70%	100.00%
	over 55 hrs (13.79%)	Not wrong & a bit wrong	31.60%	68.40%	17.60%
		Wrong & seriously wrong	15.70%	84.30%	82.10%
		Total	18.50%	81.50%	100.00%

who works 21 to 40 hours, and more than 2 times more likely to be self-employed than an individual who works for 41 to 55 hours.

We have categorized the attitude toward tax evasion into two groups. Our reference group is people with "wrong and seriously wrong" attitude toward tax evasion. The coefficient for the attitude of "not wrong and a bit wrong" is positive indicating that people with attitude of "not wrong and a bit wrong" are more likely to go self-employment. The odds ratio of 3.46 indicates that people with attitudes of "not wrong and a bit wrong" are 3.46 times more likely to be self-employed as compared to people with attitudes of "wrong and seriously wrong". Since this variable is statistically significant at the 0.05 we can conclude that there is a link between the attitude of "not wrong and a bit wrong" and choosing self-employment. This is consistent with hypothesis 1. We also include a variable of men with attitudes of "not wrong and a bit wrong" (an interaction variable male*"not wrong and a bit wrong"). This variable is not statistically significant at the 0.05 level signifying that attitudes influence on decision to go for self-employment is independent of the gender.

Table 3. Logistic regression analysis with self-employment (=1 and 0 otherwise) as a dependent variable

Variables	Estimate	Wald	Odds Ratio	Estimate	Wald	Odds Ratio
Constant	-0.30	**0.16**	0.74	-1.33	**0.75**	0.27
Male	0.55	4.55	1.73	0.66	4.90	1.94
Nor wrong and a a bit wrong	0.96	10.81	2.61	1.24	7.14	3.46
Reference Wrong and seriously wrong						
White	0.30	**0.79**	1.36	0.30	**0.77**	1.35
Age		29.48			28.62	
Age 18-34	-2.66	28.27	0.07	-2.63	27.14	0.07
Age 35-64	-1.58	12.59	0.21	-1.54	11.63	0.22
Reference Age over 65						
Education		4.40			4.28	
Less than high school & high school	-0.36	**0.75**	0.70	-0.33	**0.66**	0.72
Junior college	0.20	**0.23**	1.22	0.22	**0.27**	1.25
Reference Graduate						
Hours worked		12.35			12.67	
Hours worked less than 20	0.01	**0.00**	1.01	0.05	**0.01**	1.06
Hours worked 21 to 40	-0.96	8.22	0.38	-0.96	8.23	0.38
Hours worked 41 to 55	-0.76	4.92	0.47	-0.75	4.83	0.47
Reference Hours worked over 55						
Male * Not and a bit wrong				0.45	**0.59**	1.56
Number of observations		778			778	
Omnibus Chi-square test		63.44			64.01	

Income

We examine the factors that affect income. We have income data in ranges with the highest value of greater than \$110,000. We use mid-point of the data for analysis. However, highest income is right censored. So we cannot use mid-point of the highest range. So we use Tobit analysis with right censoring at \$110,000. Our independent variables are gender, race, age, education, whether self-employed, work hours, attitudes of "not wrong and a bit wrong", and self-employed*attitudes of "not wrong and a bit wrong". The Tobit analysis results are presented in Table 4.

We present four specifications of the Tobit analysis. All specifications have gender, race, education, whether self-employed, and work hours. Other three specifications include the attitudes of "not wrong and a bit wrong"; attitudes of "not wrong and a bit wrong" and attitudes of "not wrong and a bit wrong"*self-employed; and attitudes of "not wrong and a bit wrong"*self-employed. The independent variables of gender, race, age, education, whether self-employed, and work hours have identical signs in all specifications and are statistically significant at the 0.05 level. According to the Tobit analysis, men earn about \$10,500 more than women. Whites earn about \$3000 more than African Americans and others. People in the age group 35 – 64 earn about \$6000 more than people over 65. However, people in the age group 18-34 earn \$3500 less than people over 65. Incomes are positively influenced by education.

Table 4. Tobit regression model with income as a dependent variable

Variables	Estimate	t-Value	Estimate	t-Value	Estimate	t-Value	Estimate	t-Value
Intercept	56897.0	315.0	55883.0	361.3	55366.0	428.5	55457.0	377.1
Male	10595.0	108.3	10631.0	128.4	10607.0	154.6	10556.0	134.1
Reference Group: Female								
White	2831.0	18.7	2828.9	21.9	2875.0	26.8	2876.3	23.5
Reference Group: Other								
Age 18-34	-3549.8	55.0	-3385.3	62.11	-3425.2	74.6	-3532.3	66.7
Age 35-64	5968.8	54.0	5926.4	62.14	5893.6	74.4	5951.9	66.4
Reference Group: Over 65								
LT High & High School	-26087.0	227.3	-25977.0	267.1	-25952.0	321.1	-26029.0	280.7
Junior College	-16454.0	320.0	-16462.0	368.1	-16442.0	437.0	-16461.0	388.6
Reference Group: Graduate								
Employed	-11786.0	71.6	-12012.0	85.3	-12222.0	103.7	-12401.0	92.3
Reference Group: Self-Employed								
Work Hours 20 & less	-13679.0	964.0	-13766.0	1093.7	-13773.0	1291.3	-13395.0	1157.6
21-40 hours	-6042.5	70.2	-5980.3	81.7	-5994.9	98.5	-6035.5	86.7
41-55 hours	-254.7	4.6	-185.4	3.9	-222.2	5.57	-257.5	5.7
Reference Group: Over 55 Hours								
Wrong & seriously wrong			1293.0	9.9	1182.3	10.8		
Reference Group: Not Wrong & a Bit Wrong								
Not wrong, a bit wrong * self-employed					-826.5	36.4	- 2003.7	13.9
_Sigma	19427.0	36.4	19421.0	36.4	19421.0	36.4	19425.0	36.4
# of observations	690		690		690		690	
Log likelihood	-7628		-7628		-7628		-7628	
AIC	15281		15282		15284		15283	
Schwarz Criterion	15335		15341		15348		15342	

All t-values statistically significant at the 0.05 level.

People with less than high school, and high school earn about $26,000 less than graduates, and people with junior college earn $16,500 less than graduates. Incomes are positively related to hours worked. People who worked less than 20 hours, on an average, made about $13,800 less than people who worked over 55 hours. People who worked 21-40 hours made about $6000 less than people who worked over 55 hours. People who worked 41-55 hours made about $250 less than people worked over 55 hours. The self-employed made over $12000 more than people who worked for others. This affirms our hypothesis 2. Based on the Tobit regression analysis which includes a dummy for "wrong and seriously wrong" as an independent variable, the dummy variable is positive and statistically significant at the 0.05 level. This indicates that people with attitudes of "not wrong and a bit wrong" earn less income than people with attitudes of "wrong and seriously wrong" assuming everything else remaining equal. This affirms hypothesis 3. However, self-employed people with attitude of "not wrong and a bit wrong" toward tax evasion, make less than all other people.

DISCUSSION AND CONCLUSION

Multivariate analysis of self-employment (=1 otherwise 0) indicates that an individual with the attitudes of "not wrong and a bit wrong" is more likely to go for self-employment compared to an individual with the attitudes of "wrong and seriously wrong". A self-employed individual is likely to have a higher income than an individual who works for someone else. An individual with an attitude of "not wrong and a bit wrong" is likely to have a lower income than an individual with "wrong and seriously wrong" attitudes. A self-employed person with an attitude of "not wrong and a bit wrong" will also have a lower income than others assuming everything else remaining equal. So a person with an attitude of "not wrong and a bit wrong" will earn less whether self-employed or not and also a self-employed with "not wrong and a bit wrong" will have income less than others all else being identical.

Economic models are developed based on the assumption that people make choices rationally to maximize their payoffs. It is assumed that such models should not only explain how people should make choices but also what they will choose. However, Thaler (1980) argues that this may not be true and presents several situations where people make choices different from what is predicted by the economic theory. The situation discussed in this paper also falls in similar category.

Since higher taxes disincentivise risk-taking, policy makers argued that high tax rates are likely to impede entrepreneurship. For example, according to Bruce (2000), marginal and average tax rates on self-employment earnings are negatively related to the likelihood of self-employment. According to Gentry & Hubbard (2000) higher progressive tax system is negatively related to the likelihood of self-employment. However, most other empirical studies that examined personal income tax rates and entrepreneurial rates have found a positive relationship between these two rates. (Bruce & Mohsin, 2003). Moreover, studies that examined the likelihood of a person being an entrepreneur and tax rates have also found the positive impact of higher taxes on entrepreneurship (Long, 1982; Schuetze, 2000; Fan & White, 2003). According to Cullen & Gordon(2002), when tax rates are higher, deductions are higher should entrepreneurs need to write-off loses from self-employment against other incomes. However, others have attributed this divergence to the tax evasion opportunities self-employment provides (Georgellis & Wall, 2006). To sum up, according to this paper, a self-employed person earns more than a person who works for others. This is essential as self-employment income is uncertain and income from working for others is certain. If attitude toward tax evasion reflects likelihood of tax evasion, then an individual with attitude of less wrong toward tax evasion is likely to go for self-employment and this decision is regardless of the gender. In addition, a person who feels that tax evasion is less wrong and is self-employed is also likely to earn less than everyone else because tax savings from tax evasion makes up the difference in income. This provides a logical explanation for rise in self-employment with rising taxes.

REFERENCES

Adams, C. (1993). *For Good or Evil: The Impact of Taxes on the Course of Civilization*. London: Madison Books.

Allingham, M. G., & Sandmo, A. (1972). Income Tax evasion: A Theoretical Analysis. *Journal of Public Economics*, *1*(3-4), 323–338. doi:10.1016/0047-2727(72)90010-2

Alm, J. J., Martinez-Vazquez, & Torgler, B. (2010). Developing Alternative Frameworks for Explaining Tax Compliance. In J. Alm, J. Martinez-Vazquez, & B. Torgler (Eds.), Developing Alternative Frameworks for Explaining Tax Compliance (pp. 3-12). London: Routledge.

Alm, J., & Torgler, B. (2006). Culture differences and tax morale in the United States and in Europe. *Journal of Economic Psychology*, *27*(2), 224–246. doi:10.1016/j.joep.2005.09.002

Becker, G. (1968). Crime and Punishment: An Economic Approach. *Journal of Political Economy*, *76*(2), 169–217. doi:10.1086/259394

Birch, D. L. (1979). *The Job Generation Process* (Unpublished report). Washington, DC: MIT Program on Neighborhood and Regional Change for the Economic Development Administration, U.S. Department of Commerce.

Birch, D. L. (1981). Who Creates Jobs? *The Public Interest*, *65*(3), 3–14.

Birch, D. L. (1987). *Job Creation in America: How Our Smallest Companies Put the Most People to Work*. New York: Free Press.

Blanchflower, D. G. (2000). Self-employment in OECD Countries. *Labour Economics*, *7*(5), 471–505. doi:10.1016/S0927-5371(00)00011-7

Blum, W. J., & Kalven, H. Jr. (1953). *The Uneasy Case for Progressive Taxation*. Chicago: University of Chicago Press.

Boeri, T., & Garibaldi, P. (2002). *Shadow activity and unemployment in a depressed labour market*. CEPR Discussion paper, DP3433.

Boortz, N., & Linder, J. (2005). *The Fair Tax Book: Saying Goodbye to the Income Tax and the I.R.S.* New York: HarperCollins.

Bruce, D. (2000). Effects of the United States Tax System on Transitions into Self-Employment. *Labour Economics*, *7*(5), 545–574. doi:10.1016/S0927-5371(00)00013-0

Bruce, D., & Mohsin, M. (2003). *Tax Policy and Entrepreneurship: New Time Series Evidence*. Working Paper, University of Tennessee-Knoxville.

Cullen, J. B., & Gordon, R. H. (2002). *Taxes and Entrepreneurial Activity: Theory and Evidence for the U.S.* NBER Working Paper 9015.

Davis, J., Smith, T., & Mardsen, P. (2005). *General Social Survey, 1972–2004: Cumulative codebook*. Chicago, IL: National Opinion Research Centers.

Davis, S. J., Haltiwanger, J., & Schuh, S. (1996). Small Business and Job Creation: Dissecting the Myth and Reassessing the Facts. *Small Business Economics*, *8*(4), 297–315. doi:10.1007/BF00393278

Douhan, R. (2009). *Compulsory Education and Jack of all trades Entrepreneurs!* Working Paper Series 797. Research Institute of Industrial Economics, Stockholm, Sweden.

Edwards, C., & Mitchell, D. J. (2008). *Global Tax Revolution: The Rise of Tax Competition and the Battle to Defend It*. Washington, DC: Cato Institute.

Evans, D., & Jovanovic, B. (1989). An estimated model of entrepreneurial choice under liquidity constraints. *Journal of Political Economy*, *97*(4), 808–827. doi:10.1086/261629

Evans, D., & Leighton, L. (1989). Some empirical aspects of entrepreneurship. *The American Economic Review*, *79*, 519–535.

Fan, W., & White, M. J. (2003). Personal Bankruptcy and the Level of Entrepreneurial Activity. *The Journal of Law & Economics*, *46*(2), 543–567. doi:10.1086/382602

Feige, E. L. (1989). *The Underground Economies: Tax Evasion and Information Distortion*. Cambridge University Press. doi:10.1017/CBO9780511571749

Frey, B. S., & Pommerehne, W. W. (1982). Measuring the Hidden Economy: Though this be Madness, there is Method in it. In The Underground Economy in the United States and Abroad. D.C Heath and Co.

Gentry, W. M., & Hubbard, R. G. (2000). Tax Policy and Entrepreneurial Entry. *The American Economic Review*, *90*(2), 283–287. doi:10.1257/aer.90.2.283

Graetz, M., & Wilde, L. L. (1985). The Economics of Tax Compliance: Fact and Fantasy. *National Tax Journal*, *38*(3), 355–363.

Greenwood, S. (2007). *10 Excellent Reasons not to Hate Taxes*. New York: The New Press.

Gregory, M.A.G. (1998). Taxation: Catholic Social Thought and Classical Liberalism. *I J. Acct. Ethics & Pub. Pol'y*, 91-100.

Hall, R. E., & Rabushka, A. (1985). *The Flat Tax*. Stanford, CA: Hoover Institution Press.

Hultberg, N. (1996). *Why We Must Abolish the Income Tax and the IRS: A Special Report on the National Sales Tax*. Dallas, TX: AFR Publications.

Joulfaian, D., & Rider, M. (1998). Differential Taxation and Tax Evasion by Small Business. *National Tax Journal*, *51*(4), 675–687.

Kolm, A.S., & Birthe, L. (2003). *Does tax evasion affect unemployment and educational choice?* Economics Working Paper No: 22. Retrieved from papers.ssrn.com

Long, J. E. (1982). The Income Tax and Self-Employment. *National Tax Journal*, *35*(1), 31–42.

McGee, R. W. (2006). Three Views on the Ethics of Tax Evasion. *Journal of Business Ethics*, *67*(1), 15–35. doi:10.1007/s10551-006-9002-z

McGee, R. W. (Ed.). (2012). *The Ethics of Tax Evasion in Theory and Practice*. New York: Springer. doi:10.1007/978-1-4614-1287-8

Morales, A. (1998). Income Tax Compliance and Alternative Views of Ethics and Human Nature. *Journal of Accounting, Ethics &. Public Policy*, *1*(3), 380–399.

Neumark, D., Wall, B., & Zhang, J. (2011). Do small businesses create more jobs? New evidence for the united states from the national establishment time series. *The Review of Economics and Statistics*, *93*(1), 16–29. doi:10.1162/REST_a_00060

Pennock, R. T. (1998). Death and Taxes: On the Justice of Conscientious War Tax Resistance.*1 J. Acct. Ethics & Pub. Pol'y*, *58*, 58–76.

Pestieau, P., & Possen, U. M. (1991). Tax Evasion and Occupational Choice. *Journal of Public Economics*, *45*(1), 107–125. doi:10.1016/0047-2727(91)90050-C

Schlaes, A. (1999). *The Greedy Hand: How Taxes Drive Americans Crazy and What To Do about It*. New York: Random House.

Schuetze, H. J. (2000). Taxes, Economic Conditions and Recent Trends in Male Self-Employment: A Canada-U.S. Comparison. *Labour Economics*, *7*(5), 507–544. doi:10.1016/S0927-5371(00)00012-9

Slemrod, J. (2007). Cheating Ourselves: The Economics of Tax Evasion. *Journal of Economic Perspectives*, *21*(1), 25–48.

Slemrod, J., Blumenthal, M., & Christian, C. (2001). Taxpayer Response to an Increased Probability of Audit: Evidence from a Controlled Experiment in Minnesota. *Journal of Public Economics*, *79*(3), 455–483. doi:10.1016/S0047-2727(99)00107-3

Thaler, R. (1980). Toward a positive theory of consumer choice. *Journal of Economic Behavior & Organization*, *1*(1), 39–60. doi:10.1016/0167-2681(80)90051-7

Thorndike, J. J., & Ventry, D. J. Jr. (2002). *The Ongoing Debate on Tax Justice*. Washington, DC: The Urban Institute Press.

Torgler, B. (2002). Speaking to Theorists and Searching for Facts: Tax Morale and Tax Compliance in Experiments. *Journal of Economic Surveys*, *16*(5), 657–683. doi:10.1111/1467-6419.00185

Torgler, B. (2006). The Importance of Faith: Tax Morale and Religiosity. *Journal of Economic Behavior & Organization*, *61*(1), 81–109. doi:10.1016/j.jebo.2004.10.007

Torgler, B. (2008). What Do We Know about Tax Fraud? An Overview of Recent Developments. *Social Research*, *75*(4), 1239–1270.

U. S. Department of the Treasury. (2005b). *Understanding the Tax Gap. FS-2005-14*. Washington, DC: Author.

U.S. Department of the Treasury. (2005a). *Internal Revenue Service*. Tax Gap Facts and Figures.

U.S. General Accounting Office. (2012). *Tax Gap: Sources of Noncompliance and Strategies to Reduce It*. GAO-12-651T. Retrieved from http://gao.gov

Webber, C., & Wildavsky, A. (1986). *A History of Taxation and Expenditure in the Western World*. New York: Simon & Schuster.

Yannis, G. (2006). Entrepreneurship and the Policy Environment. *Federal Reserve Bank of St. Louis Review*.

Yitzhaki, S. (1974). A Note on Income Tax Evasion: A Theoretical Analysis. *Journal of Public Economics*, *3*(3), 201–202. doi:10.1016/0047-2727(74)90037-1

Chapter 4
Three Social Choice Rules:
An Experimental Approach

Andrei Marius Vlăducu
University of Bucharest, Romania

ABSTRACT

The authors analyze three social choice rules (plurality voting, approval voting and Borda count) from a behavioral economics perspective aiming three objectives: 1) if it is a viable solution to use these procedures during mass elections; 2) why individuals prefer a specific social choice rule and not another; 3) how status quo bias and framing effect influence the preference of individuals for a certain social choice rule. The research is conducted with 87 participants to a lab experiment and data suggest that for using approval voting and Borda count during mass elections is necessary to increase the people level of information about their benefits. When making a decision in a political or economic context seem that people tend to prefer simple plurality rule do to its availability and maybe because of its strong reliance with status quo bias.

INTRODUCTION

Individuals are often confronted with different choices, whether it is the choice between candidates at the next presidential elections, the choice of a future job or the university their children will attend. Each of us has a set of preferences regarding the alternatives we face. From this set, more often than not, we choose one alternative using various strategies to reach our desired goals. When our societies are confronted with situations where a decision involving interaction between multiple individuals is needed, (such as political elections, referendums) they use practical mechanisms to transform individual preferences into collective decisions. This type of mechanisms are generally known as social choice rules (Balinski, Michel; Laraki, Rida;, 2010). There is an entire list of social choice rules that are used or can be used, such as single non-transferable vote (used to choose the legislature in Japan), single transferable vote (known as Hare Rule or Cincinnati Rule), Borda count, Combs Rule, Copeland Rule, Condorcet winner, Simson-Kramer Rule, Kemeny-Young method, Kendall-Wei method, Jech method or majority voting (Levin, Jonathan; Nalebuff, Barry;, 1995). Some of them, like the majority vote, are

DOI: 10.4018/978-1-5225-1826-6.ch004

used more frequently than others, being known as usual procedures in human decision-making. How we build and apply these social choice rules can have a direct effect on individuals` behavior and the outcome we obtain. Duverger, 1963 [1951] argues that different voting rules produce different results in terms of the proportion in which votes are transformed into seats in the legislative. This phenomenon is most commonly known as *the mechanical effect of voting rules*. One direct implication of this effect is that voters who understand the mechanical implications of voting procedures could change their voting behavior, acting like strategic voters. Moreover, political agents can build their decisions – whether to enter the political competition or not – depending on how they anticipate the mechanical effect will influence voter's behavior.

Also, a particular social choice rule used in a specific context can produce political crisis and institutional blockages that could be avoided by using other rules that prove more efficient. In this sense, the history of US democracy provides a good example, known as the *Burr Dilemma*. During the first four US presidential elections (from 1788, 1792, 1796 and 1800) the official voting procedure used to elect the president was similar to approval voting[1]. During the 1800s presidential elections this procedure produced a draw between Thomas Jefferson and Aaron Burr. Under the US Constitution, in this case, the decision for electing the new president was transferred to the House of Representatives who needed 36 rounds to declare a president from one of the two candidates (who eventually turned out to be Thomas Jefferson). This situation led to an institutional deadlock threatening to escalate into a major political crisis and a possible civil war. Immediately after (in 1804), in order to avoid similar situations, approval voting was eliminated and replaced, under Amendment 12, with another voting procedure (majority voting) which granted each elector the right to choose one, and only one candidate from the list (Nagel, 2007, p. 43).

Nowadays we can select from many types of social choice rules when facing a decision. A good question is on what arguments we rely when we decide to use a specific social choice rule and not another? This question is important for at least two reasons. Firstly, it is possible that different social choice rules applied to the same decision making situation, could produce different outcomes. When speaking about political elections, there are consistent examples (different winners and ranking changes according to the procedure we use) who prove this finding (Brams, 1980), (Laslier & Van der Straten, 2008), (Balinski, Michel; Laraki, Rida;, 2010), (Vlăducu & Guțu, 2011, 2013), (Igersheim, Baujard, Gavrel, Laslier, & Lebon, 2015). Secondly, authors (Brams, 1980), (Felsenthal, Maoz, & Rapoport, 1993) consider that some of them are superior to others in terms of certain criteria. For example, if there are cyclical results, some voting procedures are better than others to surpass them. In this regard, approval voting is considered a procedure that gives voters the proper incentives to express their sincere preferences, eliminating strategic voting (Brams, Steven J; Fishburn, Peter C;, 2005), (Laslier & Van der Straten, 2008). Given these examples, the authors raise a number of questions in this chapter: how do we determine the social choice rule that best aggregates individual preferences into collective decisions? What are the reasons that lead individuals to prefer a social choice rule over another? Is the preference for a specific social choice rule influenced by the context in which decisions are made? If we prefer a social choice rule only by pure habit, degree of familiarity or because it simply represents the status quo, should we question the entire process of voting? Eventually, when referring to decision-making we need to eliminate various negative effects, such as strategic voting that are the result of some social choice rules.

There is consistent literature which uses an individualistic approach in analyzing social choice rules, primary dealing with their properties and axiomatic characteristics (May, 1952), (Fishburn, 1973, 1978), (Young, 1974) (Miroiu, 2004), (Xu, Yongsheng; Zhong, Zhen;, 2009). On the other hand, there are not so many research endeavors which examine how individuals understand voting procedures, the reasons individuals prefer some voting procedures over others or how factors such as context of choice and status quo bias influence individual preferences for a particular social choice rule. Starting from this discussion, in this chapter, the authors analyze three social choice rules (plurality voting, approval voting and Borda count) using the heuristics and biases approach from a behavioral economics perspective. In this regard, the authors formulated three research questions (I) analyzed by a laboratory experiment conducted with 87 participants: (I1) Considering three social choice rules (plurality voting, approval voting, Borda count) and a hypothetical decision making situation, which one is preferred by the participant to the experiment? (I2) Considering the decision of the participants to the experiment in (I1) how do they motivate their preference? (I3) How well do the participants to the experiment understand the social choice rules? And two hypothesis to be tested: (H1) the preferences of the participants to the experiment for one of the social choice rules is influenced by the context (political, social, and economic) in which the decision process take place. (H2) More powerful an individual`s preference for one of the three social choice rules is, the lower the status quo bias becomes.

In the first part of the chapter authors discuss the reasons which stand behind the decision to analyze the three social choice rules, their viability in real elections, framing effect and status quo bias. The second part consists of the experimental procedure and the results obtained and in the last section authors discuss the implications of the findings on social choice rules, the development of research in further directions and limits.

BIASES, HEURISTICS, AND SOCIAL CHOICE RULES

There are three main arguments on which the authors of this chapter based their decision to study these three social choice rules and not others. Firstly, approval voting and Borda count are considered to be the leading candidates in getting the official title of proper voting procedures that could be used in real elections (Alos-Ferrer, 2006). These are voting procedures that have been studied in detail by researchers of social choice theory, including the systematical assessment of their advantages and disadvantages, the way they operate in the real world elections and what kind of incentives they offer to political actors. Secondly, approval voting and Borda count began to gain popularity from being used in various situations of choice in the private or public sector. Thirdly, these social choice rules are simple enough that, when you test them in the lab there is no need to explain the process by which votes are counted, people naturally understand how it happens (Fishburn, 1978). Referring to social choice rules in general Balinski and Laraki (2010, p. 2) argue that they should meet the principal properties:

1. The social choice rules should be absolute in the sense that each person who chooses should use them to measure the merit of each competitor (alternative).
2. Social choice rules should be common in the sense that people who use them to choose should do so in a common language.

Given the experimental procedure that authors have constructed to analyze these social choice rules, it was a basic requirement to use intuitive and understandable voting procedures[2]. If there are some arguments for authors to choose to analyze approval voting and Borda count, regarding plurality voting, it is probably the most popular form of majority voting, it is a widely used voting procedure, particularly in political elections and generally in any situation in which individuals must come to an agreement in making a decision.

Studying social choice rules from a behavioral economics perspective is important because one of the objectives of this approach is to analyze the extent to which individuals are aware of the choices they make, given specific sets of institutions and a complex environment (Camerer & Loewenstein, 2004). Behavioral economics combines assumptions of cognitive psychology and microeconomics, trying to reunite them in order to provide a greater degree of predictability of human behavior and make public policies more realistic. The starting point of behavioral economics was a systematic critique of rational choice models, who produce wrong predictions whose consequences can be very costly at the social level (emergence of the 2008 economic crisis that few economists have anticipated) (Thaler, Misbehaving. The Making of Behavioral Economics, 2015). Even if individuals are seen as subjective utility maximizers, this perspective is not based on empirical evidence, but rather on axiomatic utility and subjective probability, without models to be tested in field trials (Selten, 2002). Recognition of other factors involved in influencing human behavior, other than prices, income, level of information etc., could be the first step to building more realistic policies that take into account of all these human limitations (Thaler & Sunstein, 2008). Firstly, Kahneman and Tversky, and then a number of other authors have systematically analyzed how individuals violate the assumption of rational choice theory (Tetlock & Mellers, 2002). There is a growing body of anomalies which proves that individuals tend to give more attention to reference points than to absolute levels of outcomes, losses outweigh gains or a systematic series of cognitive errors that contravene to the rational choice assumptions (Rabin, 1998). From this perspective, behavioral economics has two main research directions:

1. Research of individual judgments – the process by which individuals` estimates probabilities of reaching an output given some strategies, and
2. Research of decision making the process by which individuals tend to choose some alternatives, regarding their cognitive process (Camerer & Loewenstein, 2004, p. 9).

From this perspective, studying social choice rules is part of a broader field research of analyzing decision making process.

Another important aspect is the distinction between behavioral economics and experimental economics, two fields which are often erroneous seeing as they are so similar. If behavioral economics represents mostly the research field which allows research methods from psychology to be applied in economics, experimental economics assumes the application of experiments in economics. The main difference between those two is that behavioral economics proves to be eclectically in term of research methods in contrast to experimental economics which is defined in relation with experimental method (Loewenstein, 2007, pp. 110-111).

Framing effect and status-quo bias are two phenomena which are influencing human behavior, systematically studied by behavioral economists and other social scientist. For a better understanding of framing effect, suppose we are put in a situation in which we need to choose between two possible scenarios: An unusual plague resulting in the death of 600 people is about to start in the USA. Each of the two scenarios involves two types of solutions to counter this problem:

Scenario 1: If solution A is adopted, 200 people will be saved and if solution B is adopted, there is a probability of 1/3 that 600 people will be saved and a probability of 2/3 that no one will be saved. Which of these two strategies do you prefer?

Scenario 2: If solution C is adopted 400 people will die for certain and if solution D is adopted, there is a probability of 1/3 that no one will die and a probability of 2/3 that 600 people will die. Which of these two strategies do you prefer?

This situation is generally known as the *Asian disease problem*, being first used by Slovic and Liechtenstein (1983) as an example for better understanding the framing effect. Although the two scenarios are identical in terms of number of people dead/saved, individual preferences for one of the solutions differs according to the scenario used. In a research conducted with students, 72% choose solution A over B (scenario 1) and 78% choose solution D over C (scenario 2). Differences between preferences expressed by the participants to the experiment are determined by how the problems are expressed, either in terms of *being saved*, the reference point for the first scenario being *600 people will die*, either in terms of *will die for certain*, where the reference point for the second scenario being *no one will die* (Slovic & Lichtenstein, 1983, p. 601)[3]. The above example seems to illustrate the context dependence of preferences, although one fundamental assumption of rationality is that of invariance (Arrow, 1982)[4]. The alternative chosen depends exclusively on the set of alternatives within which the decision must be made, independently of how the alternatives are described.

Kahneman and Tversky (1979, 263) propose a new descriptive model of decision involving risk (prospect theory) by presenting another series of examples in which framing effect influence the process of decision making. The research conducted in behavioral economics emphasizes a list of biases and heuristics such as hindsight bias, curse of knowledge, law of small numbers, confirmation bias, anchoring effect or endowment effect who influence human decision making (Camerer & Loewenstein, 2004). The idea of framing effect generated reactions from economists considering that if this phenomenon will be examined, under different experimental conditions it will disappear. (Kunreuther & Slovic, 1978), (Grether & Plott, 1979), (Pommerehne, Schneider, & Zweifel, 1982), (Reilly, 1982) (Hamm, 1984) (Cubitt, Munro, & Starmer, 2004) conducted a series of experiments which attempted to test the existence of framing effect controlling different variables considered fundamental predictors for the appearance of this effect. The conclusion was that framing effect and reverse preferences was present in a significant degree in all the experimental models, influencing only the degree in which it manifested. Basically if you extrapolate this findings to social choice rules you could say that the way you define context of choice (political, economic, social) may influence the individual preferences for one of them. It is possible that political elections, where majority rule is the custom voting procedure, generate a stronger preference for these social choice rules compared with other decision making situations (for example, when you and your friends need to decide where to go on holiday this summer).

Another important aspect arising from behavioral economics which could influence the preference for one particular social choice rule is status-quo bias. Samuelson & Zeckhauser (1988) argues that the choices we make in real life are often accompanied by influential labels. For example, one of the labels that any alternative will inevitably carry with it is the status-quo, meaning that doing nothing or keeping a decision that is already working is always possible. Thus, faced with making a new decision, individuals choose to remain with the existing option which represents the status-quo. This bias is visible when we comply with existing policies, extension of an official mandate, buying the same products or the difficulties we face when we want to change our job. Regarding social choice rules, a pertinent question that authors ask in this chapter is whether the preference for a particular voting procedure is influenced by status-quo bias. An interesting example regarding the way status-quo bias works is in the analysis of organ donation rates (Johnson & Goldstein, Do Defaults Save Lives?, 2003). The authors wonder why the organ donation rates are so different between countries which, at first glance, appear similar (Austria and Germany, Belgium and Netherlands, Sweden and Denmark). Regarding the process of becoming an organ donor there are two possible situations:

1. Being an organ donor by default (implicit) and if you want to seize to be in this category you need to pass a bureaucratic process (opt-out system), or
2. Choosing to be an organ donor (opt-in system).

Opt-in and opt-out are the only two possible systems in which a person could trove in regard to organ donation consent. Theoretically the opt-out system is the better choice if we desire to increase the number of organ donors, because this king of status-quo influences individuals to remain faithful to it[5]. There is a series of explanations for this phenomenon: the possibility that individuals are likely to believe that status-quo is a recommendation issued by the government; any decision requires a certain degree of effort while accepting status-quo does not; a change in status-quo implies a phenomenon similar to prospect theory (losses outweigh gains) (Johnson & Goldstein, 2003, p. 1338). Another possible explanation is that the way status-quo is defined represents a powerful signal of an expert`s preferences (who are considered by ordinary people in a position that gives them legitimacy) to male informed policy recommendation. Status-quo bias tends to be a robust effect which is present in pension plans (Madrian & Shea, 2001), insurance decisions (Johnson, Hershey, Meszaros, & Kunreuther, 1993), end-of-life medical treatment (Kressel & Chapman, 2007), health care (Helpern, Ubel, & Asch, 2007) or car accidents (Thaler & Sunstein, 2008).

Framing effect and status-quo bias are two phenomena that can influence preferences of individuals for certain voting procedures, and their analysis is an important step in deciphering the relationship between behavioral economics and social choice rules.

METHOD, PROCEDURE, AND RESULTS

Methodologically, the analysis is circumscribed by the limits of the post-positivist approach of social sciences, which explains political phenomena by employing analytical methods that offer explanations for why the results of an action appear to be one and not another (Austen-Smith & Banks, 1998, p. 259). I have chosen the laboratory experiment as a research method for gathering and analyzing data. Some of the advantages of this method are its capacity to provide both quantitative and qualitative data and the fact that it can connect theoreticians and practitioners due to the fact that it allows researchers to observe a variety of features of the decisional process (Levitt & List, 2007, pp. 362-363). I have chosen hypothetical questions since this procedure allows the researcher to ask the participants a high number of questions. Psychological experiments such as this have two kind of underlying assumptions: a) that individuals usually know how to behave in such situations; b) that individuals have no reason to hide their true preferences (Thaler, 2015, p. 38).

Participants

The experiments have been conducted in May 2015 at the Faculty of Political Science of the National School of Political Studies and Public Administration Bucharest. 87 students (68% women, 32% men) have participated at the within-subjects design. Each participant received 20 lei for an experimental session of approximately one hour. The participants have been selected through the ORSEE program (Greiner, 2003) and prior to the experiments they have been informed about the three voting procedures and about the corresponding mechanisms through which individual preferences are turned into collective decisions.

Procedure

In order to respond to I1, I have analyzed the frequency of the responses given to Q1: "Imagine that you are a member in a group that has to choose among three alternatives, X, Y and Z. Within the group there are dissensions regarding the best option. You want to set up a rule according to which the decision should be taken. Taking into account the social choice rules presented above, which one of them is the most adequate in order to settle which one is the winning alternative? (You have 1 minute to answer)". All participants had to respond to this question. This question was addressed immediately after the organizers explained the three voting procedures. In order to respond to I2, I analyzed the answers given by the participants to Q2: "Taking into account the answer you have given to the previous question, please explain why you chose that particular social choice rule". In order to solve the operationalizing problems posed by open-ended questions, I have subsequently classified participants' answers in one of the following categories of arguments for a voting rule: the argument of simplicity and efficiency; the argument of sincerely revealing preferences; the argument of equity; the argument of consensus; the argument of the mechanical and psychological effects of a voting procedure; the argument of familiarity with a certain rule; other arguments. The taxonomy draws from the arguments put forward by (Fishburn P. C., 1978), (Alos-Ferrer, 2006), (Laslier, Jean-Francois; Sanver, Remzi M;, 2010) according to whom approval voting and the Borda count are the social choice rules easiest to comprehend by the participants.

The third research question (I3) has been answered by building a familiarity index for each of the three rules. The index comprises five criteria:

1. The correctness degree of each voting rule;
2. How intuitive the rule is perceived to be by the participants;
3. The degree of understanding of each respondent;
4. Perception of the degree of understanding of the other participants by each respondent; and
5. The degree of understanding regarding how individual preferences are aggregated into group decisions.

An index allowed me to incorporate the arguments from (Fishburn P. C., 1978), (Alos-Ferrer, 2006), (Laslier, Jean-Francois; Sanver, Remzi M;, 2010) regarding the simplicity of approval voting and Borda rule. My rationale has been that, if the participants understand those two rules, they should rank higher than they would have had they not been easily comprehended. Nonetheless, there are at least two potential criticisms that can be raised against a familiarity index:

1. It is impossible to determine how the participants interpret the five criteria employed by the index for judging the rules;
2. Although the rules are scored similarly by the participants, we cannot ascertain the intensity of their preferences[6].

These objections should be accounted for in any situation in which we ask an individual to rate a certain item (such as an object, a feature of an object, etc.). The participants' responses have been evaluated through a series of continuous variables, which entailed a grading system similar to the one used in the Romanian educational system (1 to 10[7]) for each of the five criteria and for each of the three voting rules. In order to obtain the familiarity index I aggregated all individual scores for each separate criterion, in order to obtain their mean.

In order to test H1I resorted to a within-subjects experimental design (more specifically, a pretest-posttest design). The graphical representation of the experiment looks like this:

Group A------------X----------0 Group A1R------------X-----------0

Group A------------X----------0 Group A2R------------X-----------0

Group A------------X----------0 Group A3R------------X-----------0

where:

X= subjecting a group to an experimental variable or a process whose effects are going to be measured
0 = observation or measurement through an instrument
X and 0 on the same row = applied to the same person
X and 0 on the same column = simultaneously occurring
Left-right axis = temporal dimension
R = random distribution.

The purpose of the experiment has been to test whether the context in which choices are taken influences participants' preference for a rule. Thus, the predictor variable CONTEXT refers to the way the context of choice has been defined (neutral, political, economic or social), and the outcome variable CHOICE measures whether the participant has maintained his preference for a rule in the both the neutral context and the specified contexts (political, economic, social contexts). Behavioral economics predicts that the predictor variable will influence the outcome variable, in that preference reversals will occur. In order to assess whether the prediction of behavioral economics holds, I compared the rules chosen by the participants in the neutral context (Q1) with those chosen in political, economic and social contexts. At this point it would be useful to provide an explanation regarding how I operationalized those contexts. By political contexts I mean a hypothetical situation in which participants have to choose the social choice rule that is going to be used in political electoral processes ("Suppose you are part of a group and you have to decide according to which rule the president of Romania will be chosen. There are disagreements within the group regarding the most appropriate candidate. Taking into account the fact that in the elections there will be three candidates, what social choice rule do you think that should be chosen by the group in order to nominate the winner?"). In what I call social contexts, the participants had to choose a rule that is going to be used for decision-making in social choices ("You and your friends try to decide where to spend New Year's Eve. There are three possible locations, all of which being endorsed by some of your friends. Which social choice rule would you use in order to choose a location?"). An economic context is a hypothetical situation in which the participants are asked to select the rule according to which economic decisions are taken ("You and your friends have gathered some money that you intend to invest. There are three potential investment opportunities. You and your friends disagree about which one of these would be the most advantageous. What social choice rule would you use in order to select one of the investment directions?"). A framing effect occurs whenever a participant opts for a different voting rule in the political, economic or social context from the one preferred in the neutral context.

In order to test H2 I carried out a within-subjects experiment, using a pretest-posttest design. The graphic representation looks like this:

Group A ------------- X ---------------- 0 Group A1R ------------- X---------------0

Group A ------------- X ---------------- 0 Group A2R ------------- X---------------0

Group A ------------- X ---------------- 0 Group A3R ------------- X---------------0

Through this experiment I wanted to observe whether designating a rule as the status quo has a disproportionate effect on the participants' choices. The predictor variable STATUS-QUO indicates the status quo. During the experiment, a rule could have been chosen in one of the following contexts:

1. The context in which there was no status quo, defined as the neutral context.
2. The context in which there existed a voting rule as the status quo.

The outcome variable REG_ALEASĂ (that is, chosen rule) is defined as the voting rule preferred by the participants in one of the above situations. Thus, the control group for H2 consisted of the choices being taken in the neutral context, whereas the experimental groups have been the following: a) the context in which approval voting was the status quo ("Suppose you are a student at a university which employs the approval rating for choosing the student representatives for the university council. According to this rule each student can approve any number of candidates. The winner is the most-approved candidate. Before the elections a referendum is organized in which you are asked what rule should be used starting with the next elections. Which rule would you choose?"); the context in which plurality rule was the status quo ("Suppose you are a student at a university which employs the plurality rule for choosing the student representatives for the university council. According to this rule each student can vote for a single candidate and the candidate who obtains 50% + 1 of the total number of votes is elected. Before the elections a referendum is organized in which you are asked what rule should be used starting with the next elections. Which rule would you choose?"); the context in which the Borda rule was the status quo ("Suppose you are a student at a university which employs the plurality rule for choosing the student representatives for the university council. According to this rule each student. Before the elections a referendum is organized in which you are asked what rule should be used starting with the next elections. Which rule would you choose?") In line with the predictions of behavioral economics, what I expected to happen was that the outcome variable would take different values as a result of the impact of the predictor variable, i.e. that most participants would opt for the X rule when X was the status quo, followed by the rule selected in the neutral context.

Results

The results of I1 are shown in Table 1.

The data shows that approval voting is the most preferred by the participants (43.7%), followed by Borda (34.5%) and plurality rule (21.8%). Taking into account the fact that the participants had been previously informed about the different ways the three rules aggregated individual preferences into collective decisions, one of the implications of the experiment is that approval voting and Borda constitute viable solutions for real-world elections. I also mention the fact that there were no cases of abstention at this stage. The results obtained in I2 show that the motivations put forward by the participants for their choices resonate with those mentioned by (Fishburn P. C., 1978), (Alos-Ferrer, 2006), (Laslier, Jean-Francois; Sanver, Remzi M;, 2010), overlaps occurring especially in regard to the efficiency and simplicity associated with Borda and approval voting. Nevertheless, there is no significant difference between the frequency of efficiency and simplicity arguments for approval voting and Borda in comparison with the frequency of the same arguments for plurality rule. Inter alia, one of the arguments for Borda and approval voting is that these rules allow the possibility of sincerely revealing one's preferences. Familiarity with plurality rule is a feature that is also shown by the data.

Participants' answers to I3 provided the value of the Familiarity Index for each of the three rules (along the five criteria of evaluation) are shown in Table 2.

The Familiarity index has the highest value for the plurality rule = 8.4276 (S.D. = 1.30), followed by approval voting = 8.4046 (S.D. = 1.25) and Borda = 7.8667 (S.D. = 1.42). However, if we look at the values taken by each criteria, we notice that the hierarchy changes. When it comes to people's perception on the correctness of each rule, Borda ranks first (8.72), followed by approval voting (7.90)

Table 1. Voting rule choose by the participants to the experiment in the neutral context

Approval Voting	Plurality Voting	Borda Count
38 [43.7%]	19 [21.8%]	30 [34.5%]

N = 87

Table 2. Familiarity index for each of the three social choice rules

Item	Approval Voting	Plurality Voting	Borda Count
Fairness	7.90	7.56	8.72
Intuitively	7.40	7.52	6.76
Personal understanding	9.22	9.46	8.10
Understanding by others	9.15	9.36	7.47
Reasoning	8.36	8.24	8.28
Familiarity Index	8.4046	8.4276	7.8667

and the plurality rule (7.56). The plurality rule is considered the most intuitive (7.52), closely followed by approval voting (7.40) and at a significant distance by Borda (6.76). On the personal understanding dimension plurality rule fares best once again (9.36); the plurality rule is followed by approval voting (9.22) and, at a significant distance once again, by Borda (8.10). When it comes to the perception of the degree of understanding of the other participants, the ranking looks as follows: plurality rule (9.36), approval voting (9.15) and Borda (7.47). In the case of the degree of understanding of how individual preferences are aggregated into group decisions, approval rating ranks first (8.36), followed by Borda (8.28) and plurality rule (8.24). When we transform the scores of each criterion in the Familiarity Index, we notice that there are small differences between approval rating and the plurality rule, whereas Borda lags behind.

The plurality rule is preferred by a plurality of participants in the political context. Approval voting rating ranks highest in the social context. In the economic context approval voting and the plurality rule share the first place in participants' preference orders. Only 34% of the participants have indicated that they prefer the same rule regardless of the context of choice. In order to assess whether there is a statistically significant difference between choices taken in each context, I have analyzed the data and obtained the results shown in Table 4.

The results prove the existence of the framing effect, in that the participants who chose a rule in the neutral context changed their preference order in the other contexts (7 out of 9 cases). In regard to the

Table 3. Social choice rule selected by the participants to the experiment depending on context

Social Choice Rule	Political Context	Economic Context	Social Context	Neutral Context
Approval Voting	N = 6 [20%]	N = 9 [34.6%]	N = 12 [38.7%]	N = 38 [43.7%]
Borda count	N = 8 [26.7%]	N = 8 [30.8%]	N = 9 [29.9%]	N = 30 [34.5%]
Plurality Voting	N = 16 [53.3%]	N = 9 [34.6%]	N = 10 [32.3%]	N = 19 [21.8%]
N	30	26	31	87

Table 4. Relation between the social choice rules selected in neutral context and in the experimental context

Situations	Social Choice Rule Selected in Q1/Social Choice Rule Selected in Q3	P Value
AV neutral context – AV political context	9 – 3	p > .05
AV neutral context – AV economic context	9 – 2	p > .05
AV neutral context – AV social context	9 – 6	p > .05
BC neutral context – BC political context	7 – 3	p > .05
BC neutral context – BC economic context	7 – 3	p > .05
BC neutral context – BC social context	6 - 3	p > .05
PV neutral context – PV political context	4 – 4	P < .05
PV neutral context – PV economic context	3 – 2	p > .05
PV neutral context – PV social context	3 – 3	p > .05

degree of confidence in the generalization of the findings to the whole population we notice that $p < .05$ for plurality rule when it is preferred in the political context.

H2 has been based on the assumption that if an individual prefers rule X in the neutral condition she should prefer it also when:

1. The rule represents an alternative to the status quo;
2. When the rule is the status quo. In regard to the percentage of participants who have maintained their preference order both in the neutral condition and under the conditions where the rule was the status quo the results are shown in Table 5.

More participants preferred Borda and approval voting where these rules have been the status quo in comparison with the neutral context. Table 6 sheds light on whether there have been instances of status quo bias.

Status quo bias has been statistically significant only for the Borda rule and for approval voting. When these rules have been the status quo, more participants preferred them in comparison to the situation where the participants faced the neutral condition.

Table 5. Relation in percent's between the situation when a social choice rule is choose in neutral context and the situation when it represents the status-quo

Social Choice Rule	Situation When the Social Choice Rule Represent the Status-Quo and It Is Selected	Situation When the Social Choice Rule Is in a Neutral Context and It Is Selected
Approval Voting	36.4%	43.7%
Borda Count	51.6%	36.4%
Plurality Voting	48.6%	27.3%

Table 6. Relation between the situation when a social choice rule is choose in neutral context and the situation when it represents the status-quo

Social Choice Rule	Situation When the Social Choice Rule Represent the Status-Quo and It Is Selected	Situation When the Social Choice Rule Is in a Neutral Context and It Is Selected	P Value
Approval Voting	7	10	P > .05
Borda count	16	10	P < .05
Plurality Voting	17	9	P > .05

CONCLUSION

The way individuals make decisions in complex situations represents a wide research domain which can be studied from different perspectives. Employing the instruments of behavioral economics in the study of voting rules represents a framework of analysis that adds an important piece to the puzzle of human decision-making. Taking into account the different effects produced by different voting rules, it is necessary to understand this phenomenon if we intend that individual and collective decisions prove to be optimal. To this end, we should examine both the mechanical and psychological effects produced by different voting rules. Last but not least, it is important to understand that even the context in which the voting rules work can influence the preference for one rule or another. In this chapter I discussed three voting procedures (plurality rule, approval voting and Borda), with the purpose of seeing whether using them in mass elections would be feasible. I have also emphasized the reasons why individuals preferred one procedure to the others and the way status quo bias and framing effects influence individual preferences. Taking into account the high number of participants (79%) who preferred in I1 to use approval voting and Borda, I consider that these two rules could be viable in mass elections. However, we should also factor in the level of information the participants possessed. All of them have been briefed regarding the way their preferences were aggregated into collective decisions by the two rules. Thus, one of the preconditions necessary for using these procedures in wider contexts is undertaking campaigns with the purpose of informing people of the way these rules work. An interesting result of I2 is that participants considered approval voting and Borda desirable in the neutral condition due to the fact that they allowed them to express their true preferences. Those participants who endorsed plurality rule have not put this argument forward. Taking into account the high number of participants (79%) who preferred in I1 to use approval voting and Borda, I consider that these two rules could be viable in mass elections. However, we should also factor in the high informational level of the participants. All of them have been briefed regarding the way their preferences were aggregated into collective decisions by the two rules. Thus, one of the preconditions necessary for using these procedures in wider contexts is undertaking some campaigns with the purpose of informing people of the way these rules work. An interesting result of I2 is that participants considered approval voting and Borda desirable in the neutral condition due to the fact that they allowed them to express their true preferences. Those participants who endorsed plurality rule have not put this argument forward. The possibility of revealing true preferences is an argument put forward by defendants of Borda and approval voting, which are mainly considered as embodying the property of strategy-profess. The results for I3 are not surprising, as most of the participants expressed familiarity towards the plurality rule. This is a well-known voting procedure, and participants have had firsthand experience with this rule. For instance, 93% of the participants responded affirmatively to the question of whether they voted in December 2014 (when the last elections for the Romanian Parliament had taken place). However, an interesting result is represented by the participants' perception of the fairness of the voting procedures, most of them believing that plurality rule is the least correct, followed by approval voting. The participants' perception is aligned with the main counterarguments put forward against plurality rule, that it disregards the profile of preference orderings and that it is susceptible to manipulation.

In regard to hypothesis H1, the preference invariance principle holds that most of the participants who preferred a certain rule in the neutral context should have maintained their preference order in the economic, political and social contexts. However, the preference invariance principle has been violated in 67% of the cases. Specifically, plurality rule is preferred in political contexts whereas the approval voting procedure in economic and social contexts. Furthermore, the data show that in 7 out of 9 cases the individuals who chose one voting rule in the neutral context had changed their option in economic, social and political contexts. This result can be explained by the framing effect. On the other hand, a statistically significant result has been obtained only for those participants who opted for plurality rule in the neutral, political and social contexts. Thus, the number of participants who preferred plurality rule in social and political contexts is statistically significant from the number of participants who chose plurality rule in the neutral context. A first implication of these results for behavioral economics is that framing effect occurs even when we deal with voting rules, in contradiction with the predictions of social choice theory. One way in which we can interpret the results is that plurality rule is preferred in political context because it is a more familiar rule in that domain, whereas it is not institutionalized in social and economic contexts.

Regarding H2, the results show that more people preferred Borda or the plurality rule when they had been the status quo than when there was no status quo. On the other hand, approval voting was preferred by 43.7% in the neutral context, and only 36.4% of the participants chose it when it had been the status quo. The most spectacular increase belonged to the plurality rule, preferred by 27.3% in the neutral condition and by 48.6% when it had been the status quo. Two conclusions can be drawn:

1. Approval voting is not susceptible to status quo bias and as such it would be easier to change it if it proved to be inefficient;
2. Plurality rule is the voting rule most affected by status quo bias. Taking into accoun the fact that many real-life choices are taken by plurality rule, this should be a worrisome result.

According to this interpretation, plurality rule seems to be preferred because it is so entrenched in day-to-day practice, not because of its intrinsic properties. This status quo bias towards the plurality rule could be a consequence of the power of habit, conformism, conservative behavior or ex post facto rationalization.

The limits of this research are those of any experimental method, such as internal and external validity problems. As social scientists, we can only build a series of filters that can improve upon the quality of the research and alleviate the problems arising from the experimental method itself. However, between internal and external validity there is a permanent tension. For instance, my research, being based on a lab experiment, fares better in regard to internal validity than in regard to the possibility of generalizing the results. Internal validity has been increased by informing the participants about the rules and about the decisions they had to take during the experiment, by carefully selecting the participants and by providing each participant with financial incentive. External validity had to suffer because all the participants had been students and because their number was relatively low for wide-scale generalization. Taking into account this limit, future research will have to expand the pool of participants so that they'll be both more numerous and more representative for the general population.

REFERENCES

Alos-Ferrer, C. (2006). A simple characterization of approval voting. *Social Choice and Welfare*, *27*(3), 621–625. doi:10.1007/s00355-006-0145-8

Arrow, K. J. (1982). Risk Perception In Psychology And Economics. *Economic Inquiry*, *20*(1), 1–9. doi:10.1111/j.1465-7295.1982.tb01138.x

Austen-Smith, D., & Banks, J. S. (1998). Social Choice Theory, Game Theory, and Positive Political Theory. *Annual Review of Political Science*, *1*(1), 259–287. doi:10.1146/annurev.polisci.1.1.259

Balinski, M., & Laraki, R. (2010). *Majority Judgement*. Cambridge, MA: MIT Press.

Baujard, A., Gavrel, F., Igersheim, H., Laslier, J.-F., & Lebon, I. (2015). *How voters use grade scales in evaluative voting*. Academic Press.

Baujard, A., Igersheim, H., Lebon, I., Gavrel, F., & Laslier, J.-F. (2014, June). Whos favored by evaluative voting? An experiment conducted during the 2012 French presidential election. *Journal of Electoral Studies*, *34*, 131–145. doi:10.1016/j.electstud.2013.11.003

Brams, S. J. (1980, September). Approval Voting in Multi Candidate Elections. *Policy Studies Journal: the Journal of the Policy Studies Organization*, *9*(1), 102–108. doi:10.1111/j.1541-0072.1980.tb00928.x

Brams, S. J., & Fishburn, P. C. (2005). Going from theory to practice: The mixed succes of approval voting. *Social Choice and Welfare*, *25*(2-3), 457–474. doi:10.1007/s00355-005-0013-y

Camerer, C. F., & Loewenstein, G. (2004). Behavioral Economics: Past, Present, Future. In C. F. Camerer, G. Loewenstein, & M. Rabin (Eds.), *Advances in Behavioral Economics* (pp. 1–52). Princeton, NJ: Princeton University Press.

Cubitt, R. P., Munro, A., & Starmer, C. (2004, July). Testing Explanations of Preference Reversal. *The Economic Journal*, *114*(497), 709–726. doi:10.1111/j.1468-0297.2004.00238.x

Duverger, M. (1963). *Political Parties: The Organization and Activity in the Modern State*. New York: Wiley. (Original work published 1951)

Felsenthal, D. S., Maoz, Z., & Rapoport, A. (1993, January). An Empirical Evaluation of Six Voting Procedure: Do They Really Make Any Difference? *British Journal of Political Science*, *23*(1), 1–27. doi:10.1017/S0007123400006542

Fishburn, P. (1973). *The Theory of Social Choice*. Princeton, NJ: Princeton University Press.

Fishburn, P. C. (1978). Axioms for Approval Voting: Direct Proof. *Journal of Economic Theory*, *19*(1), 180–185. doi:10.1016/0022-0531(78)90062-5

Greiner, B. (2003). *An Online Recruitment System for Economic Experiments*. Academic Press.

Grether, D. M., & Plott, C. R. (1979, September). Economic Theory of Choice and the Preference Reversal Phenomenon. *The American Economic Review*, *69*(4), 623–638.

Hamm, R. M. (1984). *The Conditions of Occurrence of the Preference Reversal Phenomenon*. Institute of Cognitive Science.

Helpern, S. D., Ubel, P. A., & Asch, D. A. (2007). Harnessing the Power of Default Options to Improve Health Care. *The New England Journal of Medicine*, *357*(13), 1340–1344. doi:10.1056/NEJMsb071595 PMID:17898105

Igersheim, H., Baujard, A., Gavrel, F., Laslier, J.-F., & Lebon, I. (2015). *Individual Behavior under Evaluative Voting: A Comparison between Laboratory and In Situ Experiments*. Academic Press.

Johnson, E. J., & Goldstein, D. (2003, November). Do Defaults Save Lives? *Science*, *302*(5649), 1338–1339. doi:10.1126/science.1091721 PMID:14631022

Johnson, E. J., Hershey, J., Meszaros, J., & Kunreuther, H. (1993). Making Decisions about Liability and Insurance. *Journal of Risk and Uncertainty*, *7*(1), 35–52. doi:10.1007/BF01065313

Kahneman, D., & Tversky, A. (1979, March). Prospect Theory: An Analysis of Decision under Risk. *Econometrica*, *47*(2), 263–292. doi:10.2307/1914185

Kressel, L. M., & Chapman, G. B. (2007). The Default Effect in End-of-Life Medical Treatment Preferences. *Medical Decision Making*, *27*(3), 299–310. doi:10.1177/0272989X07300608 PMID:17545499

Kunreuther, H., & Slovic, P. (1978). Economics, Psychology, and Protective Behavior. *The American Economic Review*, *68*(2), 64–69.

Laslier, J.-F., & Sanver, R. M. (2010). *Handbook on Approval Voting*. London: Springer. doi:10.1007/978-3-642-02839-7

Laslier, J. F., & Van der Straten, K. (2008). A live experiment on approval voting. *Experimental Economics*, *11*(1), 97–105. doi:10.1007/s10683-006-9149-6

Levin, J., & Nalebuff, B. (1995). An Introduction to Vote-Counting Schemes. *The Journal of Economic Perspectives*, *9*(1), 3–26. doi:10.1257/jep.9.1.3

Levitt, S. D., & List, J. A. (2007). What Do Laboratory Experiments Measuring Social Preferences Reveal about the Real World? *The Journal of Economic Perspectives*, *21*(2), 153–174. doi:10.1257/jep.21.2.153

Loewenstein, G. (2007). *Exotic Preferences. Behavioral Economics and Human Motivation*. Oxford, UK: Oxford University Press.

Madrian, B. C., & Shea, D. F. (2001). The Power of Suggestion: Inertia in 401(k) Participation and Savings Behavior. *The Quarterly Journal of Economics*, *116*(4), 1149–1187. doi:10.1162/003355301753265543

May, K. O. (1952, October). A Set of Independnet and Necessary and Sufficient Conditions for Simple Majority Decision. *Econometrica*, *20*(4), 680–684. doi:10.2307/1907651

Miroiu, A. (2004). Charachterizing Majority Rule: From profiles to societies. *Economics Letters*, *85*(3), 359–363. doi:10.1016/j.econlet.2004.05.003

Nagel, J. H. (2007, February). The Burr Dilemma in Approval Voting. *The Journal of Politics*, *69*(1), 43–58. doi:10.1111/j.1468-2508.2007.00493.x

Pommerehne, W. W., Schneider, F., & Zweifel, P. (1982, June). Economic Theory of Choice and the Preference Reversal Phenomenon: A Reexamination. *The American Economic Review*, *72*(3), 569–574.

Rabin, M. (1998, March). Psychology and Economics. *Journal of Economic Literature*, *36*, 11–46.

Reilly, R. J. (1982, June). Preference Reversal: Further Evidence and Some Suggested Modifications in ExperimentalDesign. *The American Economic Review*, *72*(3), 576–584.

Samuelson, W., & Zeckhauser, R. (1988). Status Qvo Bias in Decision Making. *Journal of Risk and Uncertainty*, *1*(1), 7–59. doi:10.1007/BF00055564

Selten, R. (2002). What Is Bounded Rationality? In *Bounded rationality, the adaptive toolbox* (pp. 13–36). Cambridge, MA: MIT Press.

Slovic, P., & Lichtenstein, S. (1983, Sep.). Preference Reversals: A Broader Perspective. *Preference Reversals: A Broader Perspective*, *73*(4), 596-605.

Tetlock, P. E., & Mellers, B. A. (2002, January). The Great Rationality Debate. *Psychological Science*, *13*(1), 94–99. doi:10.1111/1467-9280.00418

Thaler, R. H. (2015). *Misbehaving. The Making of Behavioral Economics*. New York: W.W. Norton & Company.

Thaler, R. H., & Sunstein, C. R. (2008). *Nudge. Improving Decisions About Health, Wealth, and Happieness*. New Haven, CT: Yale University Press.

Vlăducu, A., & Guțu, D. (2011, December). Un experiment asupra regulilor de vot. *Perspectives on Politics*, *4*(1), 99–111.

Vlăducu, A., & Guțu, D. (2013). Un experiment privind regulile de vot la alegerile locale din Chișinău – Republica Moldova. In A. Miroiu, & Ș. Cerchez (Eds.), *Competiția Politică în România* (pp. 190-224). Iași: Polirom.

Xu, Y., & Zhong, Z. (2009). Single profile of preferences with variable societies: A characterization of simple majority rule. *Economics Letters*, 1–3.

Young, H. P. (1974). An axiomatization of Bordas rule. *Journal of Economic Theory*, *9*(1), 43–52. doi:10.1016/0022-0531(74)90073-8

KEY TERMS AND DEFINITIONS

Approval Voting: A single-winner voting method used in elections. Each voter may *approve* (select) any number of alternatives from the set of alternatives. If there are *n* alternatives there will be 2^n possible outcomes for a voter`s ballot. It is also possible for the voter to select all of the alternatives or none of them. The winner is the most-approved (select) alternative.

Borda Count: A single-winner voting method used in elections. Each voter may rank alternatives, from the set of alternative, in order of his preference. Each alternative will receive a number of points according to her position in the hierarchy. Once all points have been counted the alternative with the most points is the winner.

Framing Effect: An effect from behavioral economics which stipulates that choices can be worded in a way that highlights the positive or negative aspects of the same decision, leading to changes in their relative attractiveness.

Heuristics and Biases Approach: A research program whose main goal is to understand the cognitive process that produce both valid and invalid judgments and to demonstrate errors of judgment, that is, systematic deviations from rationality.

Plurality Voting: A single-winner voting method used in elections. Each voter may select one, and only one, alternative from a set of alternative. The alternative who receive most votes is selected even if it not receive a plurality (50% + 1 of the votes cast).

Social Choice Rule: Practical mechanisms to transform individual preferences into collective decisions.

Status-Quo Bias: An effect from behavioral economics which stipulates that people prefer things to stay the same by doing nothing or by sticking with a decision made previously.

ENDNOTES

1 There are three elements who differentiate the two forms (old and new) of approval voting. The old form used during the first elections presented the following characteristics that the new form does not fulfill: a) an elector could not choose more than two alternatives from the list; b) for an alternative to win elections was needed to achieve a majority; c) the number of total voters was very small (69 in 1788, 138 in 1796 and 1800) (Nagel, 2007, p. 44).

2 This is the main reason why the authors decided to remove from the analysis more complex social choice rules such as single transferable voting or majority judgement.

3 If we look at solutions A and C we see that they are identical in terms of people who are saved and who will die. A solution (A) where 200 people will be saved for granted and 400 (out of 600) is identical with a solution (C) where 400 people will certainly die and 200 will be saved. The same logic applies for solutions B and D.

4 Arrow (1982, p. 7) argues that cognitive psychologists infirm this assumption, offering a full set of systematic examples.

5 People could avoid the decision being an organ donor because it can proove unpleasant and stressful to go through a complex bureaucratic process.

6 For instance, it is possible that a participant that rates approval voting's intuitiveness as a „7" does this on different grounds than another participant who rates the same rule and the same criterion in an identical way.

7 I used this system because the participants (who were students) were familiar with it.

Chapter 5
An Agent-Based Model to Forecast the Inflation Rate in the Eurozone:
Incorporating Microfoundations into Complex Behavioral Models

Juan Luis Santos
University of Alcala, Spain

Jagoda Anna Kaszowska
Cracow University of Economics, Poland

Tomás Mancha Navarro
University of Alcalá, Spain

ABSTRACT

The aim of the agent-based model presented in this chapter is to explain the determinants of inflation and to forecast the inflation rate in the Eurozone for the next five years. The behaviors of agents and their expectations are interrelated and explained by macroeconomic models applied to heterogeneous agents of three classes: individuals, companies and financial institutions. In addition, the behavior of public sector and central bank is also modeled with a single agent of each kind. Once the quantitative easing policy is implemented, the quantitative theory of money expects higher inflation rates in the long run. Inflation should remain low taking into account the Phillips-Curve. Last, according to the Aggregated Supply and Demand as well as to the Money Market equilibrium, the behaviors modeled allow forecasting low inflation. However, an external shock, as it would be an increase in the price of important commodities, can alter the inflation rate to a great extent.

DOI: 10.4018/978-1-5225-1826-6.ch005

INTRODUCTION

Agent-based models are increasingly applied to macroeconomic forecasting. However, they require high amounts of information of agents in terms of microdata and behavioral rules and they have only recently being used successfully thanks to several European Commission funded projects such as Eurace (Cincotti, Raberto & Teglio, 2012) and Mosips (Pablo-Martí et al., 2013; 2014). The aim of these initiatives is to improve the state of the art and they created massive agent-based models with millions of heterogeneous agents of different classes. The frameworks of these projects are the ones used as building blocks to develop the agent-based model presented in this chapter.

In the background section previous related research it is studied. The main flaw of past approaches is the lack of agents' variety with respect to classes (individuals, corporations, financial institutions, etc) and behavioral rules variety. Behavioral rules are a key point to the validity of an agent-based model and in Economics they tend to be selected from Microeconomic Theory. However, since 1970s Macroeconomic Theory incorporates microfoundations. These models have important drawbacks and should be replaced for agent-based models because their assumptions made them unable to predict disruptive changes in the economic growth such as the recent financial crisis (Colander et al., 2008) and also because the equational models have important flaws that can be solved with algorithmic models (Velupillai & Zambelli, 2015). However, they allow explaining macroeconomic variables such as Gross Domestic Product (GDP) growth. Therefore, they can be included in the set of behavioral rules of agents. In the chapter it is explained how it can be performed in an agent-based model aimed to forecast the inflation rate.

In the third section, the three macroeconomic theories that aim to explain inflation performance are explained. They are the quantitative theory of money, the Phillips curve and the aggregated supply and demand as well as to the money market equilibrium. In general, they forecast low inflation except in the case of the quantitative theory of money that allows forecasting a high inflation rate in the long run under some assumptions about the behavior of agents.

In the fourth section, the agent-based model is presented following Dahlem guidelines. It makes it possible to arrive to a set of scenarios that incorporate different assumptions to the model in order to assess how they would impact on the inflation rate in the Eurozone for the next five years.

The agent-based model is built in order to cope with the main objective of the chapter: to study how behavioral rules impact on the level of prices. The most important transactions in the economy are modeled and their results modify the subsequent states and behavior of agents in the economy. The central bank is explicitly modeled and its decisions are also taken into account. Imports and exports are also incorporated as they modify the performance of companies. In addition to the actual inflation rate simulated in every period in the baseline scenario that aims to replicate the actual economy, it is possible to introduce shocks in the model in order to measure how agents react to different scenarios. Three conditions are tested: inflationary tensions, deflationary tensions and an oil shock. The agent-based model developed allows the implementation of counterfactual analysis useful for monetary policy.

BACKGROUND

Complex agent-based macroeconomics is a research field recent that has benefited of the increasing availability of big amounts of available data, new systems that allow computing at a higher speed and the inadequacy of the previous paradigm, dynamic stochastic general equilibrium (DSGE) models. These

DSGE models are still used, but the number of researchers in the new approach is increasing thanks to the potential it has. However, texts such as 'Complex agent-based macroeconomics: a manifesto for a new paradigm' (Gatti, Gaffeo & Gallegati, 2010) are still recent. In this manifesto there is an explicit reference to macroeconomic variables such as inflation rate: "Levels and growth rates of aggregate output and employment, inflation [...] and all other typical macroeconomic occurrences and laws [...] are social phenomena that must be explained at a different level than microeconomic units". In addition, the authors claim monetary policy could be studied with more accuracy with agent-based models because the supervision of financial institutions is neglected in DSGE models, which assume efficient markets and perfect arbitrage.

Ashraf, Gershman, & Howitt (2013) use an agent-based model to show how inflation impact on the GDP growth by unsettling the mechanisms underlying transactions. In this model it is possible to measure the effect of a rise or a descent in inflation rate on the economic growth. This model shows the target of 2% of the majority of central banks in developed economies is too narrow because deviations of a ±1.5% do not have a clear effect on employment and GDP levels. This model minimizes the cost of high inflation rate and suggests the responsible organizations of monetary policy can relax their targets.

Another agent-based model (Salle, Senegas & Yildizoglu, 2013) intends to quantify the effect of stating an inflation target. The advantages of agent-based modeling on this regards are heterogeneity, bounded rationality and the capacity to learn from the past. Thus, if the monetary authority wants to achieve credibility, the inflation rate has to experience low volatility around the specified target. Agents can modify the expectations about inflation and the degree of confidence in the central bank target accomplishment. If the target it is not reached, an increasing portion of individuals and companies stop including the target inflation in their forecasting mechanism after several periods. In this way, it would be better a less explicit and more adaptable inflation rate target.

The study of business cycles is also one of the methodological approaches that can be improved with the use of agent-based model. For example, stabilization policies are usually studied with DSGE models, but agent-based models are increasingly used, as they offer more reliable results. For example, the last fiscal stabilization policies can be included in a model (Harting, 2015) that estimates its impact on companies' behavior allowing categorizing them by technological level. The impact on every agent is aggregated and this policy changes the aggregated output level in the long run. Other agent-based model that also explicitly focuses on the business cycle intends to measure the impact of consumers' confidence on economic activity (Závacká, 2015). The relations among heterogeneous consumers and producers who anticipate the level of growth of prices and GDP generates business cycle without complicated equational-based models that assume equilibrium takes place in every period.

Finally, there are three noteworthy recent examples of agent-based models aimed to study monetary policy. Giri, Riccetti, Russo and Gallegati (2016) research the effect of how interest rate changes produce bubble burst. Therefore, monetary policy decisions can be considered the starting point of the crisis events of 1929 and 2008. In addition, once the recession started, interest rate is also a key factor in the extension and magnitude of the crisis and zero interest rate can effectively prevent an additional slowdown. Secondly, Gualdi, Tarzia, Zamponi and Bouchaud, (2015) develop an agent-based model that has into account the potential non-linear effects of monetary policy. A small change may have little or no effect while an overreaction can produce economic instability. The conclusion of this model contrasts with the smooth effect usually detected with the alternative DSGE models. Lastly, Popoyan, Napoletano and Roventini (2016) study the interactions of macroprudential regulations with other monetary policies. In this agent-based model financial sector is correctly represented and allow the implementation of counterfactual analysis on Basel III new regulations.

The main drawbacks of previous agent-based approaches to the study of inflation are the excessive simplification of the economy and the exclusion in the analysis of current macroeconomic theories widespread in the economic agents. A truly meaningful agent-based approach may include public sector, a key agent that determines taxes, subsidies and represents between one third and a half of the GDP of advances economies. In addition, central bank is a reactive agent that modifies key variables such as the interest rate and the money supply. Moreover, external sector can be modeled as a whole and interact with companies, which export and import a high portion of their production. Changes in international prices such as the oil price have a significant impact on GDP growth and inflation and should be taken into account too. On the other hand, there are macroeconomic theories that explain inflation and previous macroeconomic agent-based models did not include them in the analysis. However, these approaches have microfoundations and have proven useful to forecast inflation. Thus, they can become part of the behavioral rules as agents have them into account when forecasting inflation.

MACROECONOMIC THEORIES TO EXPLAIN INFLATION

In the recent years the average inflation rate in the Euro Area decreased to a level close to zero, according to Harmonized Index of Consumer Prices (HICP). This rate is below the two percent goal of the ECB. Inflation is defined as the rate (%) at which the general price level of goods and services change, causing purchasing power to fall when it is positive. To explain inflation or the change of the price level in an economy, different theories exists, in this chapter we are going to elaborate and agent-based model that takes into account the main three of them applied for the Euro Area: Quantitative theory of the money, the Phillips curve, and aggregate supply and aggregate demand and the equilibrium in the money market. Based on the elaborations, a forecast of the future development of the inflation rate will be provided thanks to an agent-based model that includes the behaviors of the central banker, public sector, individuals, companies and financial institutions. These agents do not only have behavioral rules based on microeconomic theory findings, as it is usual, but they incorporate elements of the three macroeconomic theories most used to explain inflation rates.

Quantitative Theory of Money

The Quantitative Theory of the Money is based on the following Equation:

$$M * V = P * T \tag{1}$$

M represents the money supply, V the velocity of the money, P the price level, and T the volume of transactions in the economy. The money supply can be defined in different liquidity levels in economy. The most liquid form is M0 followed by M1, M2, and M3, each wider definition expand, or include, the definition of one level below. The money supply is managed by the central bank of the currency area, in the Eurozone by the ECB. After the financial crisis of 2007-2008, the ECB started an expansionary monetary policy as it can be seen on the quantitative easing program and the low interest rates monetary policy. Thanks to banking regulations, the ECB can control money supply. The main source of uncertainty emerges from the entities that are not directly by the regulations, the so called 'shadow bank system', which includes institutions which are not regulated, for instance asset managers. However, the lack of data makes it extremely difficult to investigate the influences of the 'shadow bank system' on inflation. Therefore, only the action of the ECB is observed, and thanks to the ECB, M increases. The growth rate of M3 and M1 has been above GDP in the Eurozone since the financial crisis but the inflation rate decreased.

The velocity of the money did not have a great variation in the last years. The left side of equation 1 increased in the post crises years, according to ECB policy aim and the actual data offered by the institution. The volume of transactions can be indicated by the GDP. The GDP has grown in the Eurozone since its existing, with the exception of crisis years 2008 and 2009, when there was relatively small a negative growth. Therefore, the first variable of the right side of equation 1 increases. M grew faster than T (GDP). With the assumption of a constant V, it can be followed, that inflation rate should be positive and in the long run at the level of:

$$\frac{1+\Delta M}{1+\Delta T\left(GDP\right)}-1=\Delta P\left(inflation\ rate\right) \quad (2)$$

The left side of equation 2 in the post crisis years was above the inflation rate. Therefore, inflation will rise in the Future according to the quantitative theory of money. This theory has wide evidence in countries of Europe and other advanced economies such as United States, were a recent research (Lanne, Luoto, & Nyberg, 2014) showed that it worked in the long run for the period 1947Q1-2013Q4, including the period of the Great Moderation.

The quantitative theory of money implies that the central bankers are aware of the potential increase of inflation and will implement corrective measures if the objective is exceeded. Agents such as public sector and companies only recently benefit from the quantitative easing policy in measurable ways, according to their size and indebtedness. The behavior of these agents it is modified. Namely, public sector can increase the expenditure level thanks to the reduction of debt service. In addition, big companies can increase their level of debt following the findings of Modigliani-Miller theorem under realistic assumptions (Joyce, Miles, Scott & Vayanos, 2012). The additional funding can be used to acquire other companies, to reduce the number of their shares in the stock market and to increase their investment only if the expected return on investment is high enough to compensate the uncertainty of a new recession. Consumers are affected by the alteration of the behavior of companies and public sector as they are public and private employees and they invest their money in government bonds and the stock market. In addition, individuals modify their expectations due to the overall effect of the monetary policy on GDP growth.

The Phillips Curve

The Phillips curve describes the relation between unemployment and inflation rate. In summary, it states that inflation reduces unemployment at least in the short run. Hence, when the ECB increase the money supply and supports inflation, unemployment will be reduced, and vice versa. The economy can buy employment decreasing the value of the currency (price level). This relation is called the sacrifice ratio, and is described as follows:

$$Sacrifice\ relation = \frac{points\ above\ 'natural'\ unemployment}{reduction\ of\ inflation\ rate} \tag{3}$$

The points above the 'natural' unemployment are the difference between the computed normal unemployment rate and the current unemployment rate. The so-called natural unemployment is a construct developed during 1970s. In that time it was necessary to adjust the macroeconomic models, because they didn't explain the situation in a sufficient correct way. This rate is explained, for instance, with the time that is needed to find a new job, or the required time to find a sufficient qualified occupation. The reduction of the inflation rate is the difference between the previous and the actual inflation rate. The sacrifice relation is the relation for this both variables and is different for every economy. However, in equation 3, when it is assumed that the sacrifice relation is constant, high unemployment could be compensated with a reduction of inflation, producing a low inflation rate.

Focusing on the development of the unemployment in the Eurozone and comparing the unemployment post and pre financial crisis, it can be seen, that unemployment is much higher post financial crisis. When it is assumed that the average long term unemployment is the natural unemployment, the Eurozone has unemployment above this natural unemployment. With a constant sacrifice relation, the inflation rate is lower than pre financial crisis and as long as unemployment is high, inflation rate will be low.

The Phillips curve shows that a reduction of the unemployment level will be interpreted as a signal of following inflation increase by the central bankers, which will modify their policy accordingly even if employment is not a target variable of ECB. In addition, changes in the unemployment rate modify the behavior of public sector via social expenses and other automatic stabilizers. Changes in monetary and fiscal policies modify subsequently the behavior of companies and individuals as their income level and expectations are modified.

One of the models that explain the inflation with the Phillips curve is Gordon's (1990) triangle model. Inflation in the following period depends on a constant μ, the current inflation π_t, the unemployment rate u_t and supply shock variables z_t. $\alpha^G(L)$ is the step-function restriction so the coefficients are equal within the groups of lags 1-4, 5-8, etc., and also that the coefficients sum to one because a unit root is imposed.

$$\pi_{t+1} = \mu + \alpha^G(L)\pi_t + \beta(L)u_t + \gamma(L)z_t \tag{4}$$

Aggregate Supply and Aggregate Demand and Equilibrium in the Money Market

The Aggregate Demand and Aggregate Supply describe the relation between the price level (P) and the output of an economy (GDP). The Money Market equilibrium describes the relationship between the Quantity of Money (M) and the interest rate (i). According to the Aggregate Supply and Aggregate Demand, price level rises according to for basic economic principles:

- Increase in the Money Supply,
- Decrease in the Aggregate Demand for Money,
- Decrease in the Aggregate Demand in goods and services, and

- Increase in the Aggregate Supply in goods and services.

Inflation can be driven from two sides: cost-push inflation and demand-pull inflation. On the one hand, the cost-push inflation takes place when the costs of production factors increase. In this way changes in the amount of raw materials such as oil, modify the equilibrium of supply and demand and affect the inflation through the agents of company class. In addition, in the last years we had many structural changes in Europe affecting labor factor in order to make it flexible the economy and boost the competitiveness, or in other words, reduce costs. When total income of the economy between the income distribution among capital income and income from work during the last 20 years is compared, it can be seen the change is in favor of capital income. Therefore, it can be followed, that the cost moderation supported the low inflation rates in the last years.

Capital effect can be seen from two perspectives, the asset in the statement of financial positions of the firms or as the financial perspective as equity and liability in of the statements of financial positions. Taking a look on the asset side, firms' balance sheets have a higher value than in the past and that means the costs for machinery are higher. This can be explained by inflation itself, because inflation drives prices of assets and machinery and by the new accounting methods. On the asset side, it is necessary to highlight that technologic development makes assets better and more efficient, therefore this yields in lower production costs. Analyzing equity and liability, that is, looking at the costs for an asset from the financial perspective, companies pay interests for its financing, interests for liabilities and costs of equity. Money supply expanded and costs of capital lowered. According to data for the last years, expansive monetary policy lowered costs of capital, and therefore, the costs of holding assets. Accordingly, raw materials and, in particular commodities, when increased their price affect positively to inflation and vice versa. However, it may depend more on supply and demand of the products defined by agents of the class companies.

According to commodities, the S&P GCSI Index makes it possible to conclude that after its crash they did not recover to the previous prices. In particular the oil price, recovered partially for a few years, but thanks to the increase of supply and the consumption reduction it decreased again. Therefore, raw materials, and particularly commodities and the oil, are cheaper post crisis and low inflation rates are supported as a result. To sum up, as described in this section, the indicators of cost-push inflation support most likely, with exception of the capital component, a low inflation rate as they modify the behavior of companies.

The demand-pull inflation occurs when aggregated demand increases. Aggregated demand is categorized by individuals, companies and public sector. According to individuals, thanks to high unemployment and the structural changes, aggregated demand decreased. What may increase aggregated demand is the low level of interest according to monetary policy on savings. For this class of agents, there is an incentive to spending instead of saving. Moreover, thanks to the low inflation rate, capital income (from equity and debt) should be lower post crisis. According to the public sector, when the data of pre and post crisis government spending is compared, government spending is on a lower level in most of the countries. Therefore, the demand of this agent supports a low level of inflation too. Finally, according to companies, when the public sector spends less and individuals spend less because of high unemployment, they should have less revenue and therefore also less expenses, in particular, in service-based industries, where costs could be reduced at a very fast rate. Even if the external sector demands more exports due to an increase in competitiveness, the behavior of agents of the class companies also contribute to arrive and maintain low inflation rate.

To conclude, with respect to the money market, as already outlined above developed as follows: the supply of the money increased, according to the expansionary monetary policy. This supports higher inflation rate and is desired to have an effect on the real economy. Interest rate decreased, if the demand for money is on a low level, this would support higher inflation rates additionally. The money market supports a higher inflation rate.

From this part of the analysis it is possible to consider that the aggregate supply and aggregate demand support mainly a low inflation rate and the money market supports a higher inflation rate. As it can be seen on the HICP, the inflation rate is close to zero in the recent years in the Eurozone. An increase of domestic demand could stimulate the economy in and increase inflation in the middle run. In the short term, a correct model would preliminary forecast a low inflation rate.

AN AGENT-BASED MODEL TO FORECAST THE INFLATION RATE

The agent-based model is constructed incorporating building-blocks of three finished public-funded projects. Eurace project (FP6 European Commission) incorporated parallel computing for macroeconomic policy design that included real economy, financial economy and the public sector (Deissenberg, Van der Hoog & Dawid, 2010; Cincotti, Raberto & Teglio, 2012). Mosips project (FP7 European Commission) focused on the real economy and public sector and expanded the behavioral rules of individuals and companies (Pablo-Martí et al., 2013; 2014). Finally, the project 'Analysis of systemic risk after the crisis emergence' (NCN Poland) focused on macroprudential policy and interbank markets (Kaszowska & Santos, 2014). It supplements the aspects not included in Eurace and Mosips projects related to interbank markets.

The next depiction of the model follows Dahlem guidelines for describing economic agent-based models (Wolf et al., 2011) that were developed after a high number of researchers agreed it was necessary a standard to describe complex agent-based models following an approach that allows the readers understand the main insight of the model focusing in the underlying concepts rather than in an enumeration of algorithms or equations.

Rationale

The object under consideration is the economy of a monetary union, in this case the Eurozone. They are considered goods and services markets, interbank markets and the government bonds primary market. The economy depicted is an open economy that transacts goods and services with the rest of the world modeled as a whole.

The intended usages of the model is forecasting of inflation and secondly, monetary policy analysis. The time period used is a quarter and agents explicitly forecast inflation for the next period taking into account their situation. It is possible to introduce different policies of the ECB and check their effectiveness. In addition ECB behaves reacting to changing conditions of the economy and especially the financial institutions performance.

The model predicts also the levels of unemployment, interest rate, GDP growth, public deficit and public debt, sector growth rate, non-performing loan rate of financial institutions, exports and imports. Nevertheless, these variables are not the focus of the model, the algorithms that affect them have structural validity but the process of calibration did not intend to and therefore their values in the model cannot be taken as actual forecasts.

Agents and Other Entities

There are three kinds of heterogeneous agents in the model: individuals, companies and financial institutions. In addition, there is a central bank, public administrations and external sector. The database is built from 2008Q1 in order to use the first periods of one quarter of duration to perform the calibration and validation according to the double mechanism described in Klügl (2008). First the model was tested for the internal structural validity, the relations between variables and agents. In a second stage, the behavioral validity is tested trough the results both at aggregate and agent level. This approach allows obtaining a model that is valid from a technical point of view and arrives in all the simulations to plausible results. In addition, the first periods are used for calibration and at the same time the behaviors of agents are checked in order to obtain a valid model.

Individuals have age expressed in years, which they increase by 0.25 each period. Individuals can be employed or not. If they are employed they have a company_id associated to them and a positive wage. If they are not employed they can have a positive subsidy received from the public administrations that represent retirement and disability subsidies and wages of public employees. Individuals can have positive amounts of deposits, loans and mortgages in a financial institution included in the model, denoted by bank_id. Individuals devote their income to taxes, savings and consumption in companies of different sectors that are included in the database. According to the paid prices they have their own perceived inflation in each period.

Companies produce goods or services each period and assign a price for them. Companies also have deposits and loans with a financial institution of the model, designated as bank_id. Their production is added to the stock, that it is updated after each period, decreasing with the amount that was sold. Companies need employees to produce, and they hire and fire them every period. They also have an owner who is an individual in the database, identified with an individual_id. He or she receives profits if the company is successful and incorporates them to their deposits. Companies can be in one of the different sectors. They face demand from consumers, public administrations, other companies and the rest of the world (exports). They need raw inputs for produce their goods and services from other companies in the data base (supply chain) and the rest of the world (imports). They pay profit taxes and the Value Added Tax (VAT) to the public administrations. They also compute their perceived inflation rate in each period according to the change in the prices of inputs.

The last class of agent, financial institutions, holds deposits, loans and mortgages of individuals and companies of the data base. They pay interest for deposits and receive income from loans and mortgages if companies and individuals can afford to pay them back. If agents with debts are bankrupted their liabilities are included. They also buy government bonds issued by public administrations and receive interest for it. They hold bank reserves in the ECB and participate in the interbank markets where they lend their excess of liquidity to other financial institutions with liquidity shortage.

There are three other entities: public administrations, central bank and the rest of the world:

- Public administrations collect taxes, purchase goods and services from companies, pay interest rate for the previously issued government bonds and give subsidies to individuals. During periods of low economic growth they tend to have deficit and they need to issue large amounts of public debt.

Figure 1. Agents and variables in the model
Source: Authors' elaboration.

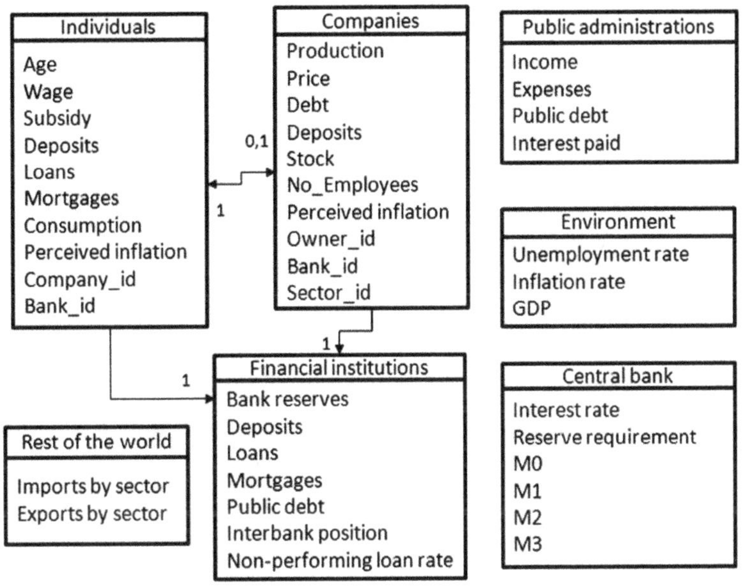

- The central bank fixes the interest rate and controls different definitions of money supply. They can offer or remove liquidity in the interbank market in order to manage inflation and guarantee the financial institutions are sufficiently stable.
- The rest of the world represents the rest of the economies. It only interchanges goods and services with companies and there are not financial relations.

Boundaries

There are several boundaries in the agent-based model described in this chapter. The majority of the models tend to hide them but it is highly advisable to state them in order to help identifying potential sources of inaccuracies and get rid of these boundaries in subsequent versions of the model or approaches by other researches. The first three ones are partially included in Pablo-Martí, Santos and Kaszowska (2015) that focuses on individuals. Most of the boundaries are solved in Mosips and Eurace projects, but in this case they would make the model too complex for the intended aims with no expected significant change. Others are highlighted in the section Further research directions and would need to be included in the system:

- The number of individuals and companies is fixed: there are not newborns, deceases, emigration, immigration and firm dynamics (bankruptcies, mergers and acquisitions, new firms). This boundary only has limited impact in the short term but it prevents using the model for long-term forecasting.
- Individuals decide about saving and consumption grouped in households but this class of agents is not included in the model to reduce the complexity. Households would require specific activities such as marriages and divorce, real estate investment and mobility to represent

- Individuals do not have gender, educational level, nationality, location and other characteristics that help to determine their labor status and financial position.
- Companies do not have product specialization, research and development activities and their financial statement and balance sheet is oversimplified.
- There is no stock market, cooperatives, and financial institutions are the only source of company funding excluding other mechanisms such as public loans, grants and business angels.
- Sectors are simplified into five: agriculture, manufactures, construction, business services and personal services.
- The real estate sector is not modeled and real estate bubbles and bursts are not included in the system. Thus, demand for the construction sector is smooth than in the actual economy.
- Companies only can hire and fire employees taking into account age and labor status. Companies and individuals have no location and this model cannot study different economic growth in European regions, which would lead to different inflation rates.
- When companies have difficulties to repay their loans, they reduce production but there are not bankruptcies and potential sector crises can be minimized.
- Financial institutions always decide to participate in interbank markets and concede loans and mortgages if companies and individuals are sufficiently solvent. This behavior does not have into account situations of systemic risk when banks prefer to leave the excess of liquidity in the central bank rather than lend it to other financial institutions. In those conditions, loans to individuals and companies are also significantly reduced as it happened during the some years after the recent financial crisis in Europe.
- Public administrations do not react to changes in the ruling parties and adapt their expense level to the political business cycle.
- All public administrations are aggregated into one agent and there are not different risk premiums for government bonds issued by countries incorporated in the monetary union.
- Central bank is independent and only cares about inflation rate and solvency of financial institutions under its supervision. In the case of ECB there are other objectives that are not strictly economic and are related to political concerns about Euro stability.
- The rest of the world acts in the baseline scenario as a steady object that only changes exports and imports in relation to changes in prices in the Eurozone, as a proxy of productivity. However, in the actual economy there are different countries that can adjust their local currency to be more competitive, they can experience diverse levels of growth and there are also trade agreements that might change imports and exports between commercial areas.

Relations

All the individuals of Eurozone are included in the system according to data from Eurostat. They have deposits in one and only one financial institution, where they also might have loans and mortgages. They can have a wage from one and only one company or a subsidy. In any case they pay income taxes. They decide which part of their net income it is spent and which part it is saved according to the life-cycle model of consumption and saving (Browning & Crossley, 2001) taking into account their net assets, their labor status and their age. By having deposits, individuals receive an interest rate from financial institutions (i) lower than the official one and they have an expectation about the inflation rate for next period (π_{t+1}^{agent}). The real return (r) as it appears in Fisher equation [5] can be different for every agent and it also conditions their decision about saving in addition to the standard life-cycle model.

$$i = r + \pi_{t+1}^{agent} \tag{5}$$

Companies are modeled according to information obtained from the database Amadeus that compiles information from public records. Companies need raw materials to produce and they are bought from other companies in the rest of the world (imports) and from other companies in the Eurozone according to the available data in the input-output matrix. In the case of positive profits they pay profit tax to public administrations and the owner of the company increases the deposits.

Financial institutions hold the deposits of individuals and companies paying an interest rate inferior to the one stated by the central bank and borrow money to these agents, asking for an interest rate superior to the official one. They need to deposit the statutory reserve requirement in the central bank and they buy the public debt issued by the public administrations. Finally, they participate in the interbank markets where the banks with liquidity surplus lend money to other with liquidity deficit, asking an interest rate slightly superior than the official one set by the central bank.

Figure 2. Agents and transactions in the model
Source: Authors' elaboration.

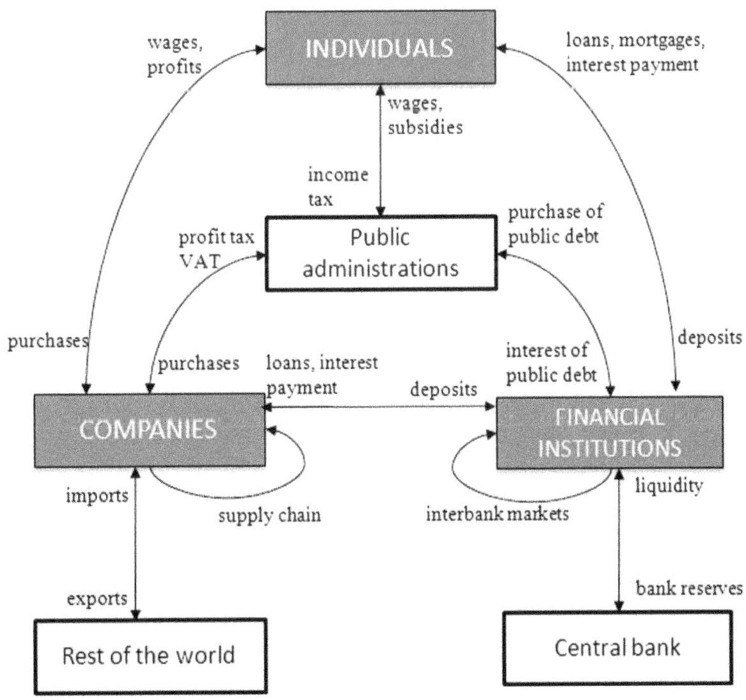

Activities

Individuals' consumption is done using fuzzy rationality. They consume a higher portion in companies with the lowest prices and those with a higher number of employees, as bigger companies have higher visibility and consumers only purchase in companies they have heard about before. Companies also decide their suppliers taking into account price and firm size. Bigger companies have access to more information as they have employees only devoted to select suppliers and they decide with a higher degree of rationality.

If individuals' income is below a threshold and their amount of deposits is zero they are not able to repay loans (short term) and mortgages (long-term). Financial institutions ask for different interest rate depending on the duration of the loan, as the interest rate in mortgages is lower because they have an asset in return. When a mortgage is not paid the bank cancels one half and the other half is included as a non-performing loan. This process represents an eviction. In the case of unpaid loans there are fully included as non-performing loan.

When company's stock is below a threshold they increase their number of employees and they decrease their staff when the stock of products is higher than another threshold. They prefer to hire and fire young employees but they also apply fuzzy rationality and sometimes choose a person near the retirement age.

Companies (c) update wages and public sector updates subsidies using the inflation on the last year (four periods). Companies decrease the amount spent in raw materials, wages and interest rate of the loans to deposits. They update their price in every period according to three determinants: previous experienced inflation (π_t^c), relative amount of stock and inflation expectation (π_{t+1}^c):

$$\Delta price_{c,t} = \pi_t^c \left(\frac{\alpha stock_c \,/\, production_c}{\sum stock_c \,/\, production_c} \right) \pi_{t+1}^c \tag{6}$$

In this way, the most successful companies tend to increase their prices more than the ones with a higher amount of stocks ($\alpha > 0$) but this change depends also on their costs and their expectations about inflation that can differ to a great extend.

Individuals and companies forecast inflation according to the three theories presented in the previous sections, assigning to them different weights θ:

$$\pi_{t+1}^{agent} = \theta_1 \left(\frac{1 + \Delta M_t}{1 + \Delta GDP_t} - 1 \right) + \theta_2 \left(\mu + \alpha^G (L) \pi_t + \beta(L) u_t + \gamma(L) z_t \right) + \theta_3 \left(\rho e_d \frac{\Delta GDP_t}{\Delta \sum stock_t} \right) \tag{7}$$

The coefficients θ are the percentage of likelihood they assign to each theory. They are between zero and one and sum the unit. The first one is related to the Quantitative Theory of Money (eq. 2), the second one to the Phillips curve (eq.4) and the third one to the Aggregated Supply and Aggregated Demand equilibrium and is equal to a constant multiplied by the price-demand elasticity and the relation between the variations of output and productive capacity.

During the calibration stage, every agent of the company and individual classes starts with the following coefficients θ, selected from uniform distributions:

$$Select\ randomly\ i, j, k = \{1,2,3\} \cdot \theta_i = u(0,1) \cdot \theta_j = u(0,1-\theta_i) \cdot \theta_k = u(0,1-\theta_i-\theta_j) \quad (8)$$

They compare their inflation expectation, the three ones obtained with $\theta_i = 1$ and the one they experience in the following period. They modify the weights increasing the one(s) that proved to be more accurate by max(1- θ_i, $0.01\theta_i$) and reducing the other(s) in order to maintain the sum of the three ones equal to the unit. This procedure is developed eight periods in order to keep enough amount of heterogeneity and assure a sufficient degree of rationality to the majority of agents. This procedure is also implemented in the agent-based model after the calibration has taken place. In Figure 3 it is possible to see the initial values, those after the calibration and the ones after twenty periods in the simulation.

The initial values of the three coefficients have an average near to one third. Their distributions are also very similar and they have a higher amount of lower values and the median locates near one fourth. In this way a positive portion of agents starts with one of the three weights close to one and if it was the optimal macroeconomic theory to forecast inflation in the agent-based model the weight would be one unit after the calibration.

After the calibration one third of agents assign a value equal to zero to inflation forecast based on Phillips curve, one fourth of agents assign a value below to 0.05 to inflation forecast based on Quantitative Theory of Money and only one twelfth do not rely on the Aggregated Supply and Demand equilibrium. In addition, less than 0.5% assign θ_1 or θ_2 a value higher than 0.95, while θ_3 is close to the unit for one out of six the agents. The average values are

$$\theta_1 = 0.23;\ \theta_2 = 0.2;\ \theta_3 = 0.67\ .$$

Once the simulation from 2011Q1 to 2015Q4 takes place, the likelihood assigned to each theory is slightly modified. The percentage of agents assigning a null or small weight to the first two macroeconomic theories increases to 30% and 40% respectively. It is worthy to note that the third theory decrease its mode to the range from 0.9 to 0.95. This can indicate the other two theories might have some advantages for a number of companies and individuals when they are have a low but positive weight. After the simulation the averages values are

$$\theta_1 = 0.18;\ \theta_2 = 0.16;\ \theta_3 = 0.76\,.$$

Finally, inflation rate in the environment object of the database is updated as:

$$\pi_t = \sum \Delta price_{c,t}\left(production_{c,t} - \Delta stock_{c,t}\right) \quad (9)$$

In this way, every company decision of updating prices is weighted for its demand in the current period, expressed as the difference between the amount produced and the change in stock. In the case a company has no demand all the production would be stockpiled and its contribution to the inflation rate calculation of that period would be null.

Figure 3. Calibration and simulation of weights of macroeconomic theories for inflation expectations
Source: Authors' elaboration.

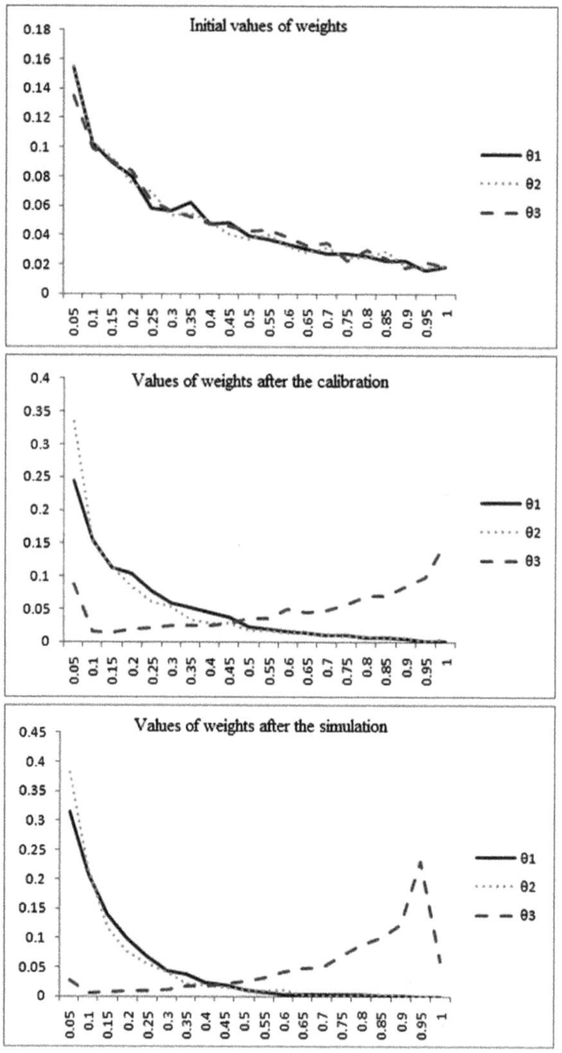

SOLUTIONS AND RECOMMENDATIONS

The agent-based model presented in the last section allows forecasting not only inflation and the average inflation expectation for the next quarter. In the baseline scenario the actual data for all the variables and calibrated coefficients is included in the model in order to simulate the inflation rate for the period 2008Q1 to 2021Q4. Next, there are introduced three scenarios: Oil shock were the price of this commodity would increase to 150$ in the period 2016Q1 to 2021Q4. Second, inflationary tensions are incorporated in the model with an increase in public expenditure of 5% and increase in exports of 5% for the period 2016Q1 to 2021Q4. Last, deflationary tensions with an equivalent decrease in public expenditure and exports in these five years.

The main difficulty of the model with respect to previous inflation performance took place during 2009 and 2010. During this period the austerity of public administrations reduced significantly aggregated demand. In the agent-based model fiscal policy variations do not take place as they are the result of political decisions rather than the application of optimal behavioral rules of the government. After 2011 the model fits better the inflation rate of the Eurozone and it forecast a low inflation rate for the period 2016 to 2021. In the future, *ceteris paribus*, the model forecast an inflation increase until 2018Q1, when the inflation rate would be 2.68%. From that point it would slightly decrease and would stay near the 2% target of the ECB. As it can also be seen in figure 4, market-based expectations in 2012 estimated a constant inflation near the target, but in the beginning of 2015 the low price of oil and the uncertainty about economic growth anticipated several years of inflation rate below 1%.

An oil shock, as defined by Hamilton (2003) is the nonlinear relation between oil price and macroeconomic performance. When the oil price change suddenly GDP growth and other macroeconomic variables such as inflation and unemployment rate vary in the following periods and their changes can exceed the one in oil price that set off the dynamics. In addition, oil shocks tend to be higher when oil price increase. In the simulated scenario the price of oil barrel increase to 150$ in 2016Q1 and continues with that price during the remaining periods of the simulation. Inflation rate increases up to 3.3% in 2017Q2, and has a slightly higher rate than the baseline scenario for the rest of the simulation. Nevertheless, the forecasted automatic adjustment in the monetary policy implemented by the ECB allows arriving to a value close to the target of 2% inflation rate.

Figure 4. Inflation forecast of the agent-based model from 2008 to 2021
Source: European Central Bank and authors' elaboration.
Note: Market-based inflation expectations refer to zero-coupon swaps of 1 to 10 years.

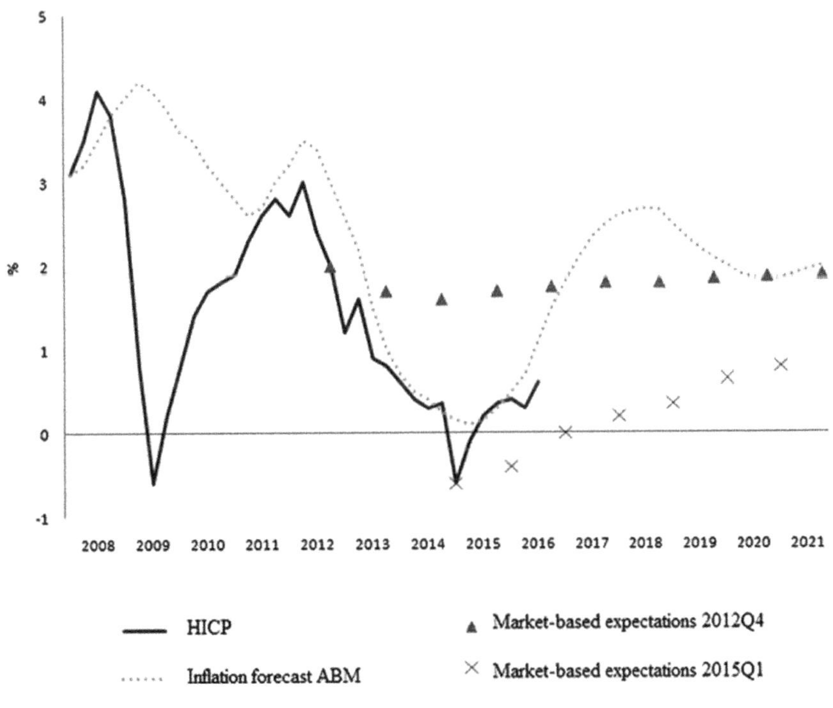

Figure 5. Inflation forecasts of the agent-based model from 2016 to 2021
Source: Authors' elaboration.

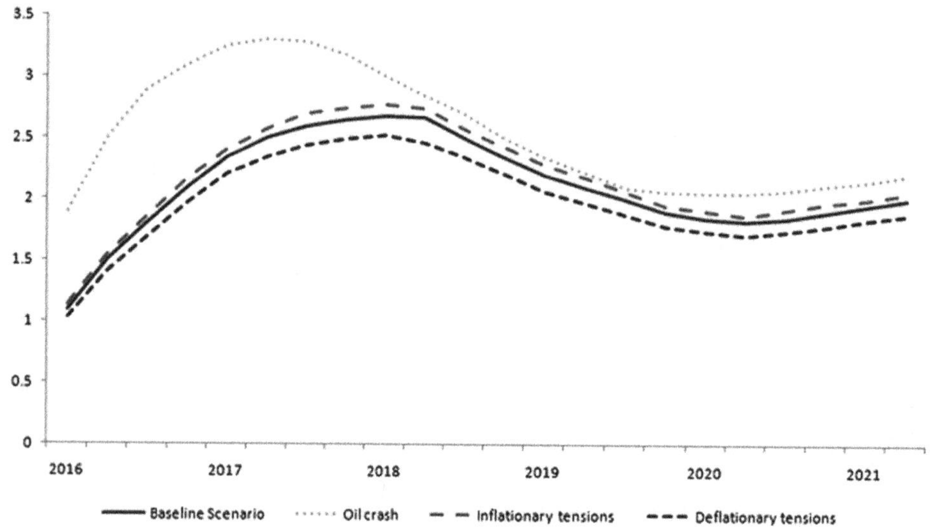

Finally, deflationary and inflationary tensions initiated with 5% variation in public expenditure and exports have little impact on inflation in the agent-based model. On the one hand, currently companies have capacity surplus and an increase in demand will not necessarily generate higher inflation rate. On the other hand, an additional decrease in demand would trigger additional expansionary monetary policy from the ECB and the negative effect would be partially corrected.

FUTURE RESEARCH DIRECTIONS

The implemented agent-based model intends to forecast inflation rate in the Eurozone and compute market-based expectation. Although it is a promising research field, most of previous attempts did not use real data. In this case the model uses actual data for individuals, companies and financial institutions of the Eurozone but still there are some assumptions that should be enhanced in order to improve the accuracy. Once this objective is achieved, the period of the simulation can be decreased to one month instead of one quarter and the model can introduce seasonality in the inflation rate.

In addition, it would be desirable if a future version of the model can generate macroeconomic variations such as oil shocks and other inflationary and deflationary tensions. In order to implement this feature it would be necessary to include regional financial markets and to model the interrelations among agents located in different countries of the Eurozone. Companies, individuals, financial institutions and the public sector in several countries face uncertainties and problems that other areas currently do not have. The classification of agents in countries would make the behavioral rules more complex but the model would be able to forecast not only the average inflation rate in the Eurozone but the one in each country.

The results of the model would improve if interbank markets are modeled in order to allow systemic risk. This would increase the difficulty of ECB supervision but the effects on inflation in the short and long run could be significant. In addition, this improvement would benefit of the modeling of real estate market in order to link construction activities with credit market of households in a realistic way.

Finally, this agent-based model shows it is possible and convenient to include standard macroeconomic models in the behavioral rules of agents when their use is extended and the only alternatives would be the estimation with time series or the assumption of the same value of the variable as in the previous period.

CONCLUSION

Previous attempts to forecast inflation with agent-based models are recent and they did not include macroeconomic theories with microfoundations in agents' behavioral rules. This can improve predictions and make models more realistic in terms of decision-making processes and agents' learning.

A meaningful agent-based model to study inflation has to model individuals, companies, financial institutions, public sector and the central bank in order to simulate both the real and financial economy and their interrelations. The central bank has to implement the monetary policy adjusting its action to changes in inflation but also taking into account economic growth and potential problems in financial institutions. Public administrations have a key and sometimes neglected impact in the real economy, purchasing goods and services, collecting taxes and providing subsidies. In addition, they fund public deficit issuing government bonds, which are one importance part of financial transactions. Finally, the incorporation of the rest of the world in the model is highly advisable, not only for the importance of imports and exports of services and manufactures goods, but especially because imports of commodities in advanced economies has a great impact in the macroeconomic performance.

The developed model allows agents to have into account the forecasts with the Quantitative Theory of Money, the Phillips curve and the Aggregated Supply and Aggregated Demand equilibrium. During the period 2008 to 2015 the latest one is the most useful for the majority of agents but the three are incorporated to the forecast of inflation in a significant portion of agents.

Currently, the Eurozone has low inflation and in the simulations the inflation rate will remain low, increasing until 2018 and exceeding the target of 2%. The simulation is performed with no unforeseen change in issues such as public expenditure, financial stability, foreign trade and price of commodities. The model was able to replicate the inflation rate in the Eurozone for the period 2011 to 2015. However, contractive fiscal policies in the previous years were not taken into account and the inflation rate forecasted was higher than the actual one. Nevertheless, this is not a drawback of the model and can be seen as a counterfactual analysis studying the case of the macroeconomic performance without discretionary actions of European governments during the period immediately after the recent financial crisis.

REFERENCES

Ashraf, Q., Gershman, B., & Howitt, P. (2013). How Inflation Affects Macroeconomic Performance: An Agent-Based Computational Investigation. *Macroeconomic Dynamics*, 1-24.

Browning, M., & Crossley, T. F. (2001). The life-cycle model of consumption and saving. *The Journal of Economic Perspectives*, *15*(3), 3–22. doi:10.1257/jep.15.3.3

Cincotti, S., Raberto, M., & Teglio, A. (2012). The Eurace macroeconomic model and simulator. In Agent-based Dynamics, Norms, and Corporate Governance. In *Proceedings of the 16th World Congress of the International Economic Association*. Palgrave.

Colander, D., Howitt, P., Kirman, A., Leijonhufvud, A., & Mehrling, P. (2008). Beyond DSGE models: Toward an empirically based macroeconomics. *The American Economic Review*, *98*(2), 236–240. doi:10.1257/aer.98.2.236

Deissenberg, C., Van der Hoog, S., & Dawid, H. (2010). EURACE: A massively parallel agent-based model of the European economy. *Applied Mathematics and Computation*, *204*(2), 541–552. doi:10.1016/j.amc.2008.05.116

Gatti, D. D., Gaffeo, E., & Gallegati, M. (2010). Complex agent-based macroeconomics: A manifesto for a new paradigm. *Journal of Economic Interaction and Coordination*, *5*(2), 111–135. doi:10.1007/s11403-010-0064-8

Giri, F., Riccetti, L., Russo, A., & Gallegati, M. (2016). *Monetary Policy and Large Crises in a Financial Accelerator Agent-Based Model.* MPRA Paper No. 70371.

Gordon, R. J. (1990). U.S. Inflation, Labor's Share, and the Natural Rate of Unemployment. In *Economics of Wage Determination*. Springer-Verlag. doi:10.1007/978-3-642-84134-7_1

Gualdi, S., Tarzia, M., Zamponi, F., & Bouchaud, J. P. (2015). *Monetary Policy and Dark Corners in a stylized Agent-Based Model.* arXiv e-prints.

Hamilton, J. D. (2003). What is an oil shock? *Journal of Econometrics*, *113*(2), 363–398. doi:10.1016/S0304-4076(02)00207-5

Harting, P. (2015). *Stabilization policies and long term growth: Policy implications from an agent-based macroeconomic model.* Technical Report 6. Bielefeld Working Papers in Economics and Management.

Joyce, M., Miles, D., Scott, A., & Vayanos, D. (2012). Quantitative Easing and unconvencional monetary policy – an introduction. *The Economic Journal*, *122*(564), 271–288. doi:10.1111/j.1468-0297.2012.02551.x

Kaszowska, J., & Santos, J. L. (2014). The Role of Risk Perception in the Systemic Risk Generation and Amplification: Agent-Based Approach. *ACRN Journal of Finance and Risk Perspectives*, *3*(4), 146–170.

Klügl, F. (2008). A validation methodology for agent-based simulations. In *Proceedings of the 2008 ACM symposium on Applied computing* (pp. 39-43). ACM. doi:10.1145/1363686.1363696

Lanne, M., Luoto, J., & Nyberg, H. (2014). *Is the Quantity Theory of Money Useful in Forecasting US Inflation?* Working Paper No. 2014-26. School of Economics and Management, University of Aarhus.

Pablo-Martí, F., García-Tabuenca, A., Gallo, M. T., Santos, J. L., del Val, M. T., & Mancha, T. (2013). MOSIPS Agent-based model for predicting and simulating the impact of public policies on SMEs. In *Proceedings of the European Conference on Complex Systems 2012* (pp. 399-413). Springer International Publishing. doi:10.1007/978-3-319-00395-5_50

Pablo-Marti, F., Garcia-Tabuenca, A., Santos, J. L., Gallo, M. T., del Val, M. T., & Mancha, T. (2014). Macroeconomic Forecasting with Agent-Based Models: Prediction and Simulation of the Impact of Public Policies on SMEs. In Advances in Computational Social Science (pp. 139-155). Springer Japan.

Pablo-Martí, F., Santos, J. L., & Kaszowska, J. (2015). An agent-based model of population dynamics for the European regions. Emergence. *Complexity and Organization*, *17*(2), C1.

Popoyan, L., Napoletano, M., & Roventini, A. (2016). *Taming Macroeconomic Instability: Monetary and Macro Prudential Policy Interactions in an Agent-Based Model.* Working Paper 6/2015. ISI Growth.

Salle, I., Senegas, M. A., & Yildizoglu, M. (2013). *How transparent about its inflation target should a Central Bank be? An Agent-Based Model Assessment.* Working paper No. 2013-24. Groupe de Recherche en Economie Théorique et Appliquée.

Velupillai, K. V., & Zambelli, S. (2015). Simulation, computation and dynamics in economics. *Journal of Economic Methodology*, *22*(1), 1–27. doi:10.1080/1350178X.2015.1004933

Wolf, S., Bouchaud, J. P., Cecconi, F., Cincotti, S., Dawid, D., Gintis, H., . . . Paroussos, L. (2011) Describing economic agent-based models, Dahlem ABM documentation guidelines. In *Proceedings of the 100th Dahlem conference on new approaches in economics after the financial crisis.*

Závacká, J. (2015) Monetary policy during the business cycle. In *Proc. 11th International Conference on Strategic Management and its Support by Information Systems 2015*, (pp. 329–338).

KEY TERMS AND DEFINITIONS

Agent-Based Model: Model that is built using a bottom-up approach. The modeler starts defining the behavioral rules of heterogeneous agents that represent a population and their interactions make it possible to study and forecast a set of aggregate variables for the complete population.

Deflation: Reduction of the level of prices of the majority of goods and services in an economy during a period of time. The most volatile products such as fresh food and energy are excluded in the calculation in order to get to deflation only if most of the products in the consumer basket are decreasing their prices.

European Central Bank: The central bank of the countries of the European Union which have adopted the euro as their currency. Its central mission is to maintain the stability of prices in a level close and inferior to two percent in order to contribute to economic growth and keeping the purchasing power of the euro.

Inflation: Extensive growth in prices over time that reduces the purchasing power of money. It is the general case for most of the economies and central banks aim to reach a small and positive inflation. Negative inflation is named deflation while high positive values are named hyperinflation.

Macroeconomic Foundations: Behavior of individual agents such as consumers and firms is related not only to the standard microeconomic theory but also to the new macroeconomic developments since 1970s.

Monetary Policy: Part of the economic policy focused on price stability. It is usually performed by the Central Bank and it follows the strategy of monetary aggregates control or the strategy of inflation rate direct supervision.

Money Supply: Total amount of money in a economy during a period of time. Money can have different definitions from only currency to currency and bank money such as deposits and other financial liabilities.

Oil Shock: Effect on oil price of a significant and unforeseen change in oil production. It can be the effect of a war, economic blockade and disruptive technological change.

Phillips Curve: Empirical model that describe the inverse correlation between the inflation rate and the unemployment rate. Milton Friedman stated that it is only applicable in the short term.

Chapter 6
An Examination of Selfish and Selfless Motives:
A Review of the Social Psychological and Behavioral Economics Literature

Gabriela Carrasco
University of North Alabama, USA

Eric Kinnamon
Alabama A&M University, USA

ABSTRACT

Current behavioral economics/game theory and social psychology literature have been captivated by the idea of altruism and egoism. In large part, these two disciplines have tried to determine the foundation of selfish and selfless behavior, without much result. The current chapter examines the root issues associated with this inquiry and argues for a shift in attention towards factors associated with cooperation. As such, empirical research from both disciplines is presented to show the advancements in relation to identification of these factors. Additionally, the authors offer a possible solution to the fractured literature in the form Weber, Kopelman, and Messick's (2004) dual process model in an effort to merge findings from both disciplines in an attempt progress this line of research.

INTRODUCTION

The topic of selfish and selfless behavior has captured the interest of philosophers, academics, researchers, and practitioners across a variety of disciplines, including biology, mathematics, sociology, psychology, economics, and political science. As a species, we have pondered the antecedents to, benefits of, and meaning behind selfish and selfless thoughts and behaviors. This duality is exemplified by Ayn Rand "greed is good" vs Louis Blanc "to each according to his needs". Why have so many dedicated so much time to these two motives? Perhaps it is because as humans we have encountered both motives in our own lives and have found them appealing and valuable. Additionally, it is common for humans

DOI: 10.4018/978-1-5225-1826-6.ch006

to seek information out about a situation in order to understand and predict behavior and outcomes. As such, we are frequently evaluating our own and other people's intentions. Thus our ability to recall past experiences and form predictions of human behavior allows us to also postulate about the benefits and risks inherent in both strategies.

The original intent of this chapter was to provide a review of the literature in selfish and selfless motives and behavior. However, there is a great deal of information from a variety of disciplines that at times seems to contradict itself. In part, this is due to the use of multiple terms for the same process or variable. Thus, the authors of this chapter will first provide a list of terms and their definitions that will be used throughout. These terms and definitions are important as they may help clarify some of the inconsistent results in the cross-discipline literature.

Following the definitions, this chapter will examine selfish and selfless motives and behavior by reviewing the social psychological and behavioral economics literature. In particular, the chapter will examine factors that influence selfish (i.e., non-cooperative) vs. selfless (i.e., cooperative) behavior in both disciplines. The authors will then discuss how the selfish/selfless literature in both disciplines can be synthesized by a dual process model. Finally, the authors will briefly discuss how the literature in this area may benefit business management, politics, and social issues.

BACKGROUND

In order for selfish or selfless behavior to occur there must be at least two individuals, the target of the behavior and the executor of the behavior. Additionally, selfish or selfless behavior can only occur within the exchange of a resource (e.g., time, money).

Social Dilemmas

According to Van Lange, Balliet, Parks, and Van Vugt (2014) a social dilemma is a situation whereby non-cooperation, or a selfish action, is beneficial for the individual in the short-term; however, non-cooperation by the group will be detrimental for the group members in the long run. The dilemma occurs when an individual is forced to choose between their own well-being now (i.e., selfish behavior) or work with the group in a long-term (i.e., selfless) investment of the resource. Similarly, Dawes and Messick (2000) goes further by suggesting that the dilemma occurs when "reasonable and rational" decisions at the individual level lead to less benefits, thus coaxing the individual to act "unreasonably and irrationally" (p. 111). Social dilemmas have been a pervasive issue addressed in religion, philosophy, natural and social sciences, politics and business.

Mixed Motives

Social dilemmas present a problem because of mixed motives. Mixed motives are dueling or inconsistent motives that have the potential to influence an individual in seemingly unpredictable ways. In the case of social dilemmas, an individual must choose between actions based on pure self-interest or actions with the group in mind. According to Van Lange et al.(2014) mixed motives are based off of three main arguments: individuals are driven to do well for oneself, the outcome of a situation is, in part, based on others' actions, and non-cooperative behavior on an individual's part opens up the door for possible retaliation from others (p. 13). Thus, an individual's actions in a mixed-motive situation take into account the potential outcomes, the individual, the group, and the exchange between the individual and group.

MAIN FOCUS OF CHAPTER

Issues, Controversies, Problems

A great deal of literature and research has gone into understanding how individuals will behave in these situation. Of particular interest is whether individuals will behave altruistically or egoistically. Unfortunately, the literature does not provide a clear answer on the basis of altruistic or egoistic behavior. The authors of the current chapter suggest that a major issue preventing clarity in the literature is ambiguous terminology. As such, this chapter will first identify and define some of the more commonly used terms in the literature.

Definitions

1. **Prosocial Behavior:** According to Dovidio et al.(2006), prosocial behavior includes a broad range of actions that benefit other individuals outside of the agent, or executor. According to Dovidio et al.(2006) there are various types of prosocial behavior including helping, altruism, and cooperation.
2. **Helping:** Dovidio et al.(2006) define helping as "an action that has the consequence of providing some benefit to or improving the well-being of another person" (p. 22). It is important to note that the intent of the executor is not a significant factor in the definition but that there is a difference in power between the two parties involved, such that the target and executor in a helping relationship are "not equal partners" as the executor has a resource the target needs (p. 27).
3. **Altruism:** The distinguishing trait between helping and altruism is the intent behind the prosocial behavior. While altruism is still decidedly prosocial behavior it is based on the ultimate well-being of another person, outside of the executor (Batson, 1991; Dovidio et al.,2006). As such, Dovidio et al. (2006) defines altruism as a helpful act that, "is carried out in the absence of obvious and tangible rewards for the helper" (p. 26).
4. **Cooperation and Non-Cooperation:** Dovidio et al. (2006) suggest cooperation is based on group members participating in various forms to achieve the group's common goal. Thus, cooperation is an exchange between group members for the benefit of the overall group. Non-cooperation, then, is when an individual, or group of individuals, choose to not participate in the group exchange. This lack of cooperation impacts the group and promotes self-interest.
5. **Egoism:** According to Dovidio, Piliavin, Schoeder, and Penner (2006) egoism occurs when an individual in focused on his/her own welfare. Dovidio et al.'s definition is broad and intent based. Being egoistical, therefore, does not preclude an individual behaving positively towards another person. In fact, there is an long-running and ongoing debate on whether egoism is at the base of prosocial behavior (Batson, Ahmad, and Stocks, 2011; Dovidio et al., 2006).

While social psychological literature focuses on terms such as altruism and egoism, prosocial and self-interest, and selfish and selfless, the behavioral economics literature relies on terms such as cooperation and non-cooperation. Although these labels are often used interchangeably we suggest that these terms imply different phenomenon and should be used according to the appropriate context.

The terms altruism/egoism and selfish/selfless all imply intent and allow for a subjective evaluations of the agent as either good or evil. Additionally, by using these judgment-based terms, we are in effect implying that one behavior is preferred over another.

In a similar vein, the use of self-interest/prosocial behavior also is prone to subjective evaluations; however, the intent of the action appears to be clearer in these terms such that we are focused on the self or the group. The self-interest and prosocial terms are similar to the cooperative and non-cooperative terms used in the behavioral economics literature

The behavioral economic literature's use of cooperative and non-cooperative behavior focuses on the outcome. While this type of research does commonly vary factors in the research design, the dependent variable is consistently behavior. Consequently, the behavioral economics literature allows us a largely unbiased view of the factors that influence cooperation versus non-cooperation. As such, we will use the terms cooperative/non-cooperative for the remainder of the chapter.

The remainder of the chapter is an attempt to identify the major factors in both behavioral economics and social psychology that impact cooperative behavior. Each of these disciplines has strengths and weaknesses in this literature. For example, the behavioral economics literature presents an opportunity to examine decisions in a variety of scenarios. These scenarios help explain what structural and situational factors influence cooperation. Unfortunately, traditional game theory has focused on rational choice and expected utility models that have not addressed varying motives behind decisions. The social psychological literature attempts to addresses factors such as motives, values, identity, and the impact of group forces on the individual. Unfortunately, the social psychological literature has not adopted a unifying model or strategy for examining decision making in different scenarios.

Thus, the authors begin by examining factors associated cooperation in behavioral economics and game theory then follow up with an examination of factors related to social psychology and cooperation.

Behavioral Economics/Game Theory: Factors Influencing Cooperation

Both behavioral economics and game theory are in the business of examining decision making. However, while behavioral economics integrates the fields of economics and psychology, game theory involves the use of models, or strategic games (Osborne, 2004). These strategic games allow us to examine individual and group preferences, choices, and, ultimately, behaviors in a variety of interactive situations. Strategic games consist of one or more players, or decision makers, who are given a set of actions they can take in the game. Each player is also assumed to have a set of preferences, or ideal outcomes with respect to how other players and he/she will respond in the game. Thus, once a player understand the rules and potential outcomes of a strategic game, his/her future actions are to some extent based on the expectations formed of the other players.

Parks (2015) identifies the two modern approaches to cooperation in social dilemmas as the "economic" approach and the "sociability" approach. According to the author, the economic approach, "assumes that humans are inclined against cooperation" while the sociability approach, "assumes that humans are inclined towards cooperation" (p. 527). The behavioral economics and game theory literature provides mixed findings on whether humans are inherently cooperative or non-cooperative. Instead, the behavioral economics and game theory research provides us with rich literature addressing the factors that increase and diminish cooperation. While the literature in this area provides a variety of factors, we have narrowed down the focus to two major areas of interest: game structure and individual differences.

Cooperative Games: Game Structure

It is important to note that cooperative and non-cooperative behavior can be influenced by the type of strategic game he/she is playing. Although there are a variety of strategic games (see Osborne, 2004), Parks (2015) distinguishes between three social dilemma games of particular importance: the Prisoner's Dilemma Game, the public goods game, and the common pool game.

In all three instances the player must choose between maximizing their own utility (i.e., proself behavior) and cooperating with the group to maximize the group's outcome (i.e., prosocial acts). An individual's preferred set of actions, or game strategy, varies for each game as each game reflects a different set of possible payoffs. These payoffs are based not only on the individual's action but also the action of the other players in the game. Thus, each individual player has an opportunity to affect each other's payoffs through his/her actions.

Prisoner's Dilemma

In the Prisoner's Dilemma Game, each player can either cooperate with the other player or make a selfish decision and save himself/herself. Because the player's outcome is in part dependent on the choice made by the other player, each player optimal choice should be to forego the cooperative route and be selfish.

Public Goods Game

In a public goods game, players contribute a certain amount of money to a group fund. Any money not allocated to the group remains as a payoff for the individual. However, group members can receive a bonus if the group fund meets a threshold. Thus, it benefits the players in the group to cooperate by allocating funds to the group.

The Common Pool Dilemma

The common pool dilemma is similar to the public good game in that individuals will benefit when the group works together. In this scenario group members can harvest from a group resource but must manage their size of their harvest so as to not overuse and deplete the resource. Group members can harvest large quantities thus gaining more resources than other group members; however, depletion of the resource ends the game and prevents further harvesting. It is in the group members' best interest to cooperate by maintaining the resources adequately replenished while simultaneously harvesting from the pool.

The manner in which these games are structured and framed reward (or punish) certain strategies. Thus, cooperation or non-cooperation is, in part, based on the structure of the game employed.

Game Information

According to Parks (2015), "in the typical social dilemma, information is sparse". However, information can be manipulated in experiments. Moreover, the amount and type of information provided to participants has been shown to influence cooperation or non-cooperation.

For example, players will modify their behavior depending on the amount of information regarding the resource pool in a public goods game. In fact, proselfs are more likely to maintain consistently high consumption of the group resource regardless of whether the group resource was being depleted (Brucks and Van Lange, 2007). This is untrue for prosocials which attempt to protect the group resource unless prosocial learn that other members are not cooperating, in which case prosocials abandon their cooperative behavior.

Information can also take the form of other player's previous behavior. Boone, De Brabander and Witteloostuijn (1999) found that players, who were originally proself in a one-shot Prisoner Dilemma game increased their level of cooperation when the game extended into rounds. These authors surmise that players understood the benefits of cooperating in these repeated games.

On a similar note, Ockenfels and Werner (2013) asked players in a dictator game to estimate the amount typically transferred to recipients by other dictators and the amount expected by recipients using scales with varying midpoints (i.e., low midpoints vs. high midpoints) before sending their recipient any funds. The results from this study indicated that dictators who viewed a scale with a higher midpoint and who guessed the average amount expected by the recipient sent on more money, on average, to their recipient. This suggests that the manner in which the information is framed will affect the degree an individual cooperates.

Individual Factors

In addition to game structure factors, the literature also identifies certain factors related to the individual that influence cooperation. Individual factors include, among other things, values and personality traits. Both values and personality traits are considered to be stable phenomenon that influence behaviors. Values are beliefs that individuals have regarding the worthiness of a particular object, person, or idea. Personality traits are aspects of an individual's unique characteristics that remain fairly stable through time and situations. While some will argue that individual differences are important in the decision making research, the literature has provided conflicting results. Research in this area has examined whether different personal value systems and personality traits will sway an individual to cooperate or not cooperate.

Social Value Orientation (SVO)

SVO can be defined as an individual's tendency in evaluating his/her own self-interest and the interest of other people (Balliet, Parks, and Joireman, 2009). SVO is thought to be a relatively stable value that dictates to what degree individuals are proself or prosocial (Bogaert, Boone, and Declerck, 2008; Haesevoets, Folmer, and Van Hiel, 2015). However, the relationship between SVO and cooperation is dependent on the game structure and situational factors.

For example, Haesevoets, Folmer, and Van Hiel (2015) examined whether scores on social value orientation, social dominance orientation and right-wing authoritarianism would predict behavior across games. The authors found only weak to moderate relationships between behaviors across games based on these beliefs. The authors conclude that behavior in one game is insufficient to predict behavior in another game. Similarly, Balliet, Parks, and Joireman's (2009) meta-analysis on social value orientation in social dilemmas found only weak to moderately strong relationship between social value orientation and cooperation in social dilemmas. This relationship was moderated by the game structure (i.e., public good dilemma vs. resource dilemma) and whether the participants were paid or not paid based on their decisions.

Personality Traits

Boone, De Brabander and Witteloostuijn (1999) examined how four personality traits (i.e., locus of control, self-monitoring, sensation seeking, and Type A behavior) influenced cooperative/non-cooperative behavior in five different Prisoner Dilemma scenarios. Two of the scenarios were one-shot situations, where participants either did not receive information regarding the other player's past behavior (i.e., game #1) or did receive information regarding the other player's past behavior (i.e., game #2). The remaining three scenarios included multiple rounds where players made simultaneous choices. In game #3, players knew there was a total of 12 rounds to play, in game #4, players were unaware of the number of rounds to be played, and in game #5, players were notified that 12 rounds would be played but the payoff matrix was modified to reinforce cooperation.

Boone et al, (1999) found that individuals high in internal locus of control were more likely to cooperate than individuals high in external locus of control, high in self-monitoring, and high in sensation seeking were more likely to cooperate consistently than individuals who scored low on these traits. While not statistically significant, the authors also found that individuals low in Type A behaviors were more likely to cooperate in these scenarios than individuals high in Type A behaviors.

Other research on traditional personality traits such as the components of the Big Five personality traits (i.e., Openness, Conscientiousness, Agreeableness, Extraversion, and Neuroticism) are less straightforward.

For example, Hirsch and Peterson (2008) found that certain aspects of Agreeableness and Extraversion have an impact on cooperative/non-cooperative behavior. In their study, Hirsch and Peterson used a repeated Prisoner's Dilemma scenario, where players participated in 10 trials with the same partner. In this study, players who scored high on the withdrawal aspect of Neuroticism or scored high on the enthusiasm aspect of Extraversion were more likely to cooperate with the other player. The authors suggest that the Neuroticism-withdrawal and Extraversion-enthusiasm components trigger punishment and reward systems, respectively, and thus influence cooperation.

Koole, Jager, van den Berg, Vlek, and Hofstee (2001) found main effects of Agreeableness and Extraversion on cooperative behavior. Moreover, these researchers also found that the structure of the game impacted cooperation/non-cooperation in conjunction with these measured personality traits.

Koole et al, (2001) examined cooperation in a public goods game between players and simulated others. In addition to measuring Agreeableness and Extraversion, the researchers also manipulated the feedback players received regarding the use of resources such that some participants were told that the resources were being used reasonably (i.e., sustained) or overused (i.e., rapid depletion).

Interestingly, Koole et al. (2001) found a quadratic trend that reflected an increase of resource use in the first trials followed by a decreases of resource use in the future trials. In line with the idea that personality traits can influence cooperation/non-cooperation, Koole et al.(2001) also found that individuals high in Extraversion were less likely to cooperate than individuals low in Extraversion. As expected, individuals high in Agreeableness were more likely to cooperate than individuals low in Agreeableness.

In fact, both the main effect of Extraversion and main effect of Agreeableness on cooperation were further explained by three-way interactions between Personality (i.e., Extraversion or Agreeableness), resource use feedback, and the quadratic trend. In fact, these researchers found that players with high Extravert scores in the sustained-use condition consumed more of the resource than players with low Extravert scores in the same condition. Likewise, players who scored high on Agreeableness were more likely to cooperate, or consume less of the resource, than players who scored low on Agreeableness in the sustained-use condition.

Additionally, players with high Extravert scores in the rapid-depletion condition used the resource consistently throughout the rounds while players with low Extravert scores first increased then decreased their consumption of the resource. Players in the rapid-depletion condition who scored high on Agreeableness were more likely to maintain a consistently low consumption rate of the resource when compared to players who scored low on agreeableness in the same condition.

Both personality traits and value systems are considered to be static qualities that should, in theory, lead to consistent behavioral outcomes across situations. The inconsistent results in the literature does not generally take into consideration the possibility that these personality traits and values are dynamic and inclined to change. In their proposal for synthesizing economics and personality research, Borghans, Duckworth, Heckman, and ter Weel (2008) argue that personality traits do change in time.

Another possibility, as evident by the Koole et al. (2001) research is that the mixed findings on the impact of personality traits on cooperation/non-cooperation may be further clarified by examining the interaction between personality, or individual traits, and the situation.

Whereas behavioral economics has examined the structural and individual factors that influence cooperation and non-cooperation, very little has been done to examine the impact the group's influence on the individual has on the process. This is where social psychology can provide some insight into cooperative versus non-cooperative behavior in groups.

Social Psychology: Factors Influencing Cooperation

Psychology is the scientific study of human behavior both internal (e.g., emotions, thoughts, beliefs) and external (e.g., overt behavior). Psychology, in general, focuses on the individual. Social psychology, a subfield in psychology, is interested in examining the exchange between the individual and the group. In particular, social psychology proposes that other people, real or imagined, will have an impact on individual's emotions, thoughts, and behaviors. Similarly, social cognitive psychology examines how cognitive processes, such as information storage, retrieval, and recall, will be influenced by other people.

It is easy to imagine how another individual may force or manipulate an individual into modifying their behavior; however, social psychology and social cognitive psychology explain more than these obvious examples of social forces on individual reactions. In fact, both social psychology and social cognitive psychology suggest that individuals modify their behavior on their own, without direct influence from other people, when other people are around or even suspected to be around. Consequently, even the mere idea of another person is sufficient to have an impact on an individual.

Why do we grant such power to other individuals?

A major tenet in both social and social cognitive psychology is that we are not single agents living in a vacuum. Our internal behavior, decisions, and overt behavior are, in part, based on the environment. Although not traditionally viewed as such, other humans are elements of the environment and thus have the potential to impact human behavior.

Group Factors

Social Motivation

As such, we are motived to seek out other individuals and form groups, participate in interpersonal activities, and maintain in good standing with society. This is the premise behind social motivation (Forgas, Williams, and Laham's, 2005). Consequently, humans are thought to hold other individuals, and the group, in high regard because of our innate need to affiliate with other individuals.

Baumeister and Leary (1995) theorize that individuals have a need to belong which is characterized by the need:

1. Frequent interactions with others, and that
2. These interactions elicit a sense of attachment which can be represented by a need to continue the relationship, emotionally involvement, and perceived stability (p. 500).

These authors clearly identify this as a need, not a drive, and suggest that this need must be met in order to attain psychological and physical well-being. The need to belong theory is well regarded and accepted in social psychology. The subsequent theoretical and empirical work that stems from this theory suggest that it benefits us to behave positively towards the group as our membership can be revoked.

Interdependence

The need to belong strongly suggests that affiliating ourselves with others is adaptive. We function easier in a group and benefit psychologically and physically from the interactions. Thus, interdependence occurs when individuals in the group are impacted, physically and psychologically, by the other group members' behaviors. As such, group members come to realize that behaving positively towards the group will, in the long run, benefit them as well. Van Lange et al.(2014) point out that an individual realizes that his/her outcomes are, in part, based on the group's behavior. Consequently, interdependence is functional in so much as our own survival and maximum potential are impacted by the group and its other members. Thus, the individual's efforts should be focused on benefit the group, as well as maximizing their own individual outcome.

Interestingly enough, a set of people in a group begin to function as an entity with the overall group's well-being in mind. As such, rules and norms are developed and enforced in an effort to maintain the group working effectively. Norms, then, are behavioral guidelines established by the group for the benefit of the group and its members. Norms can take the form of scripts and schemas. Scripts are a delineated outline of expected behaviors that an individual adheres to when in a particular social situation, such as the set of behaviors a person performs when eating out or entering an elevator. Social schemas are a set of predetermined and generally agreed upon traits and expected behaviors associated to a categorical stimulus, such as an accountant, athlete, or academic. We use schemas to predict the utility of and behavior from the individual. Norms provide us information regarding procedures, allow us more predictive power in our social interactions, and can provide a sense of security from ambiguous stimuli, forces, or processes.

For the most part, norms are considered beneficial for the group, in that they maintain order, and for the individual, in that they provide clarity. It is important to remember, however, that norms are a means of enforcing group behavior from an individual. It is equally important to remember that groups are dynamic entities and, as such, are bound to change. Consequently, the norms formed in these groups are also bound to change.

The authors of the current chapter suggest that cooperative and non-cooperative behavior can be considered a norm.

Norm of Reciprocity

Once such norm is the norm of reciprocity, which states that individuals are prone to reciprocate others' behaviors. According to Gouldner (1960) the norm of reciprocity is based off of two principles: (a) individuals will help individuals that have helped them in the past and (b) individuals will not harm individuals that have helped them in the past (p. 171).

In respect to group behavior, then, individuals are expected to reciprocate cooperative and non-cooperative behavior exhibited by other group members.

There is research to support the idea that individuals attempt to modify behavior of others when they deviate from the script. Gintis, Bowles, Boyd, and Fehr (2003) call this strong reciprocity. According to the authors, strong reciprocity is a schema that promotes personal cooperation with others and the punishment of those who are non-cooperators. Fehr and Fischbaher (2004) and Fehr and Rockenbach (2004) review literature suggesting that strong reciprocity is evident at the neural level such that the brain responds to cooperators and punishment of defectors in a positive manner and inequitable outcomes in a negative manner. These reviews points to the enforcement of cooperative norms in human behavior.

Individual Factors

Goals

Human behavior is thought to be driven by goals. Goals are a desired outcome or objective that can manifest either consciously or automatically but will, inevitably, influence an individual's behavior. We are thought to have a hierarchy of goals that are activated at different times and in different situations. Ultimate goals are the end goal while instrumental goals are benchmarks used to reach the ultimate goal.

There is a potential for these goals to contradict or overpower each other. Huang and Bargh (2014) propose the idea that that goals themselves are "selfish" in that activation of a goal motivates the individual to complete the goal without much thought to other factors. In fact, Noval (2016) found that by reducing an individual's focus on the desired outcome, she was able to also decrease unethical behavior.

Goal activation and completion are dependent on the individual and the situation. For example, Batson (1991) claims that, "both egoistic and altruistic motives may evoke a variety of behaviors or no behavior at all. A motive is a force. Whether this force leads to action depends on the behavioral options available in the situation, as well as on the strength of both the motive and of congruent and conflicting motivational forces present at the time" (p. 9).

In respect to cooperative and non-cooperative behavior, we suggest that identifying the active goal will help determine the course of action an individual may take. However, the context in which the individual finds himself/herself will determine which goal is activated.

Contextual Factors

For the purposes of this chapter, context is more than the situation. The context of a situation is the phenomenon that is developed from the exchange between the individual, the group, and the environment. The context is not merely the situation but rather the interpretation of the situation by an individual.

The self is a term used in psychology to understand the individual, his motives, and his actions. It represents the malleable knowledge an individual has about himself. The agent self is a component of the overall self that acts as the executor of the individual's will. Thus, the concept of the self is important to our current conversation as it the self is the starting point of an individual's identity. Additionally, the individual's active self-dictates which goals are activated.

For example, Frimer, Shaefer, and Oakes (2014) manipulated whether individuals saw themselves as an agent ("self as executor") or an actor ("watched self"). Frimer et al, found that individuals modified their goals based on whether they were in an actor mode or an agent mode, with actors agreeing with more prosocial motives and agents agreeing with self-interest motives.

The importance of the context on cooperative/non-cooperative behavior is becoming evident in the literature (Fortat, Denant-Boemong, and Funaki, 2012, Henrich, Boyd, Bowles, Camerer, Fehr, Gintis, and McElreath, 2001; La Barbera, Ferrara, and Boza, 2014). Lozada, D'Adamo, and Fuentes (2011) argue that altruism is not only intrinsically rewarding but also based on the social context. The authors point out the importance of the individual and the collective group in influencing cooperation within an organization. Similarly, Dovidio et al. (2006) point out that prosocial behavior is defined by society, thus a "given behavior is not inherently or universally prosocial (or antisocial for that matter)" (p. 21). A behavior is deemed prosocial or antisocial by society, which is susceptible to change. Thus, any behavior can be regarded as positive or negative. It is important to note this as it speaks to the dependence of prosocial, or cooperative/non-cooperative, behavior on the context.

We suggest that the context is the crucial component in understanding cooperative and non-cooperative behavior. Importantly, a context can be learned, primed, or at least manipulated in settings. As such, organization behavior can be modified according to the context presented to the individuals.

We briefly identify three major factors we believe have an impact on cooperative/non-cooperative behavior in a group or an organization. These factors are: group identity (i.e., in-group/out-group), trust, and procedural justice. At the core, these three factors reflect the importance of the context, or the individual's perception of the group, its function, and its reliability.

In-Group and Out-Group Identity

In-group/out-group bias are two theories that often get grouped together; however, it is important to note that they are two distinctive theories. These two theories are closely related and are two sides of the same coin. In-group bias, also called in-group-out-group bias, in-group bias, intergroup bias, or in-group favoritism bias is a theory that purposes individuals favor or more highly regard the individual's in-group positively. Out-group bias is also known as out-group homogeneity effect or out-group homogeneity bias. Out-group bias purposes that individuals in the out-group will more likely to be categorized and stereotypes/overgeneralizations will be attributed to them.

Individual group membership is a fluid item, hierarchical, has varied strength, and is a perception of the individual. The individual does not have to be 'part' of the team, but they perceive themselves to be part of the team (e.g. sports fans that consider themselves or identify with a certain team or club).

Some identities are relatively fixed such as an individual's race, age, or gender where other can change with time or situational context. While going to school an individual will identify with individuals in the school, but more closely related to those in their own class. After graduation and many years have passed the 'all alumni' identity will get stronger for that institution and 'class of 2010' identity will fade. What is important about in-group bias is the positive aspects individuals give to the members of their in-group and similarly out-group derogation of the out-group being a threat to the in-group. Literally, in-group members are better, nicer, more trust worthy, and individuals are more likely to share resources with then those in the in-group then those in the out-group. Social identity theory posit that a portion of the individual's self-concept (and thus self-esteem) is derived from their group memberships. So the individual is not being magnanimous when they perceive their in-group to be more trustworthy, they are part of the trust worthy group and are themselves more trustworthy. When the group does well, they are part of the good. Realistic conflict theory (also known as realistic group conflict theory) is a theory that posit that the intergroup conflict that arises between the in-group and out-group are a result of conflicting goals or finite resources (i.e. limited resources or fixed pie scenario). This theory would suggest you would see less cooperation and more competition with individuals in the out-group versus those in the in-group.

On the flip side of the coin regarding out-group bias, the in-group is heterogeneous, the out-group is homogeneous. We are unique but they are alike. This thought pattern can lead to stereotypes and ethnocentrism which can modify the cooperative behavior with out-group individuals.

Optimal Distinctiveness Theory

At the very least, what we can take away from this is the importance the group has on the individual. In some cases, the group conformity does overwhelm the individual but the individual can also go against the group. It should be noted, however, that the individual and the group work in unison. In the optimal distinctiveness theory, Marilyn Brewer (1991) suggests that individuals attempt to find a balance between the group identity and the individual identity such that individuals are motivated to seek the optimal balance of the two extremes of in-group distinctiveness and in-group assimilation in order to maintain group membership. In a nutshell, individuals all want to be special, but individuals don't want to be different from the group. Optimal distinctiveness theory is especially interesting, an individual will only be as different as the group allows so they can remain a part of the group. So non-conformist will adhere to their non-conformist peers' conformity. So those social 'rebels' that dress in goth, dye their hair weird colors, or have unusual hairstyles, will conform to their in-groups standards. Thus they won't dress in a traditional prom dress out of fear of being expelled/teased/rejected by their peers for not being a non-conformist.

Trust

From an interpersonal perspective, trust is the ability to depend or rely on another individual. Trust in an individual is based on the principle of reciprocity such that your behavior will be reciprocated in kind and you will not subject to unnecessary harm. In essence, an individual makes themselves susceptible to others' actions but anticipates equal treatment. Trust can take many forms, according to Dunning and Fetchenhauer (1991) trust can manifest in the beliefs we have of others or actions towards others.

Interestingly enough, the literature makes a strong general assumption that humans should not be trusted. This assumption crosses sociological, psychological and economic literature. In fact, Dunning and Fetchenhauer (1991), and others, go so far as to argue that trusting other individuals is irrational.

Nevertheless, trust is a crucial component examined in the behavioral economics and social psychological theories and research. While trusting may be considered irrational, it occurs quite frequently in the literature. The literature is riddled with examples of trust being a core issue in group decisions. For example, Yamagashi and Cook (1993) examined the effects of trust, group dynamics (i.e., group-generalized structure vs. network-generalized structure), and dissemination of group member actions on average contribution in multiple trials. These authors found that an individual's general level of trust, which was measured prior to participating in the study, was related to the average amount contributed such that those high in trust contributed significantly more than those low in trust.

Yamagashi and Cook also found a trust X structure interaction such that individuals with higher trust in the network-generalized exchange structure contributed on average more than individuals low on trust in the same structure and more than both trust types in the group-exchange structure. This interaction is important, in light of the main effect of trust the authors also found, because this speaks to the importance of context. According to the authors, the group-exchange structure is susceptible to free loading and thus even individuals high in trust will be weary to trust others in this situation. Thus, Yamagashi and Cook state that "the relationship between trust and generalized exchange varies depending on the structure of the generalized exchange situation.

Procedural Justice

Procedural justice looks to the fairness in group processes and social interactions. If a group executes suitable procedural justice, then members in the group are treated fairly and equitably. Thus, procedural justice ties into both in-group and out-group identity and trust.

Additionally, seeking equity through procedural justice may be a motive unto itself.

Batson (1991) argues that some motives may be neither egoistic nor altruistic and uses the advancement of justice as an example, which he calls "upholding a principle of justice" (p. 9). Batson, Ahmad, and Stocks call this "principlism" or "upholding a moral principle" (p. 106).

In either case, focusing on a principle such as procedural justice has the benefit of creating group cohesion (i.e., in-group bias), setting a goal for the group, and reinforcing trust with the group members.

One common thread amongst in-group/out-group, trust, and procedural justice is that these reflect the interaction between the group and the individual.

The individual seeks information from the group in order to determine whether they are vulnerable or protected, whether the group has a reasonable sense of justice, and whether they will be treated equitably.

SOLUTIONS AND RECOMMENDATIONS

Dual Process Models

Thus far the behavioral economic and social psychological approaches, while similar, have remained fairly distinct from each other in this chapter. Luckily, Weber, Kopelman, and Messick (2004) address how these two fields can be integrated through the lens of a dual process model in their seminal review of decision making in social dilemmas. This dual process model outlines how individuals can process information and select appropriate situational rules using either shallow processing based on heuristics or a more complex and adaptive approach.

According to Weber et al. (2004), the individual assesses the situation, or context, before choosing a set of rules to follow. In assessing the situation, the individual takes into consideration situation cues and personal identity. This information allows the individual to determine which rules are appropriate the individual in a particular situation. The shallow process is analogous to quick decisions based on automatic processing and behavior whereas the more complex processing requires more conscious thought. According to the authors, we move from the shallow processing, which requires less energy and less deliberation to a more conscious and considered processing, when

1. Two or more conflicting values are made salient,
2. An individual is confused about the norms or rules required in a particular situation, or
3. The situation itself is "vague, ambiguous, or unpleasant" (p. 286).

Weber et al.(2004) suggest that individual differences such as social motives, personality, and personal history and situational factors such as task structure, decision structure, and perceptual factors will are important factors in assessing the situation. As been noted earlier in the chapter, behavioral economics and game theory have taken exceptional steps in addressing similar situational and individual factors that influence decision making. Add to that information acquired by social psychology regarding social influences in cooperation and this model has the potential to have strong predictive power in the realm of cooperative behavior.

FUTURE RESEARCH DIRECTIONS

Both behavioral economics and social psychology have amassed a treasure trove of empirical literature that helps to explain cooperative behavior in individuals and groups. With the introduction and integration of dual process models in the literature it is highly likely that a clearer picture of the factors influencing cooperation will develop. The impact of the current and future research in this area has the potential to influence business management, political, social, and educational realms.

According to Parks (2015) the literature on cooperation in social dilemmas may help dissuade the "lone wolf" phenomenon, whereby individuals refute the potential effectiveness and efficiency associated with groups. That is not say that individual work may in some instances be more productive than group work; however, humans have traditionally not functioned well in solitude. In fact, humans are considered both social and cultural animals that prosper in groups. As such, it would benefit us all to understand when cooperation would benefit the individual and the group. Additionally, we should examine how factors related to the individual, the group, and the context impact cooperation.

For example, we find more direct and effective methods of reducing depletion of resources (e.g., community office supplies, travel funds, energy consumption) in the workplace by understanding how individuals perceive these resources. Additionally, we may find ways motivate potential voters to participate in local and federal elections by understanding the impact of social value orientations on social issues. Similarly, by understanding how social value orientations and personality influence community action for individuals from different cultures and socioeconomic statuses.

CONCLUSION

On a final note, although the literature continues to debate whether humans are inherently selfish or selfless, we might be better served to synthesize the theories and literature in both behavioral economics/game theory and social psychology. Both disciplines have focused on different perspectives based on their unique strengths and weaknesses. While consolidating the literature may initially prove difficult, the benefits would certainly outweigh the costs. Additionally, the literature in both domains may progress to future questions, such

1. To what degree can cooperative behavior be learned and fostered, and
2. What the long term effects of cooperative behavior are for the individual and the group.

REFERENCES

Balliet, D., Parks, C., & Joreman, J. (2009). Social value orientation and cooperation in social dilemmas: A meta-analysis. *Group Processes & Intergroup Relations*, *12*(4), 533–547. doi:10.1177/1368430209105040

Baston, C. D. (1991). *The altruism question: Towards a social-psychological answer*. Hillsdale, NJ: Lawrence Erlbaum Associates.

Baston, C. D., Ahmad, N., & Stocks, E. L. (2011). Four forms of prosocial motivation: Egoism, altruism, collectivism, and principlism. In D. Dunning (Ed.), *Social motivation*. New York, NY: Psychology Press.

Baumeister, R. F., & Leary, M. R. R. (1995). The need to belong: Desire for interpersonal attachments as a fundamental human motivation. *Psychological Bulletin*, *117*(3), 497–529. doi:10.1037/0033-2909.117.3.497 PMID:7777651

Bogaert, S., Boone, C., & Declerck, C. (2008). Social value orientation and cooperation in social dilemmas: A review and conceptual model. *The British Journal of Social Psychology*, *47*(3), 453–480. doi:10.1348/014466607X244970 PMID:17915044

Boone, C., De Brabander, B., & van Witteloostuijn, A. (1999). The impact of personality on behavior in five Prisoners Dilemma games. *Journal of Economic Psychology*, *20*(3), 343–377. doi:10.1016/S0167-4870(99)00012-4

Borghans, L., Duckworth, A. L., Heckman, J. J., & ter Weel, B. (2008). The economics and psychology of personality traits. *The Journal of Human Resources*, *43*(4), 972–1059. doi:10.3368/jhr.43.4.972

Brucks, W. M., & Van Lange, P. A. M. (2007). When prosocials act like proselfs in a commons dilemma. *Personality and Social Psychology Bulletin*, *33*(5), 750–758. doi:10.1177/0146167206298569 PMID:17440204

Dawes, R. M., & Messick, D. M. (2000). Social Dilemmas. *International Journal of Psychology*, *35*(2), 111–116. doi:10.1080/002075900399402

Dovidio, J. F., Piliavin, J. A., Schoeder, D. A., & Penner, L. A. (2006). *The social psychology of prosocial behavior*. New York, NY: Taylor and Francis Group.

Dunning, D., & Fetchenhauer, D. (1991). Understanding the psychology of trust. In D. Dunning (Ed.), *Social motivation* (pp. 103–126). New York, NY: Psychology Press.

Fehr, E., & Fischbacher, U. (2004). Social norms and human cooperation. *Trends in Cognitive Sciences*, *8*(4), 187–190. doi:10.1016/j.tics.2004.02.007 PMID:15050515

Fehr, E., & Rockenbach, B. (2004). Human altruism: Economic, neural, and evolutionary perspectives. *Current Opinion in Neurobiology*, *14*(6), 784–790. doi:10.1016/j.conb.2004.10.007 PMID:15582384

Forgas, J. P., Williams, K. D., & Laham, S. M. (2005). *Social motivation: Conscious and unconscious processes*. New York, NY: Cambridge University Press.

Fortat, V., Denant-Boemont, L., & Funaki, Y. (2012). *Coordination and cooperation in an assurance game: A cross-cultural experiment.* Unpublished manuscript, Economics Department, University of Rennes, Rennes, France.

Frimer, J. A., Schaefer, N. K., & Oakes, H. (2014). Moral actor, selfish agent. *Journal of Personality and Social Psychology*, *106*(5), 790–802. doi:10.1037/a0036040 PMID:24749822

Gintis, H., Bowles, S., Boyd, R., & Fehr, E. (2003). Explaining altruistic behavior in humans. *Evolution and Human Behavior*, *24*(3), 153–172. doi:10.1016/S1090-5138(02)00157-5

Gouldner, A. W. (1960). The norm of reciprocity: A preliminary statement. *American Sociological Review*, *25*(2), 161–178. doi:10.2307/2092623

Haeseveoets, T., Folmer, C. R., & Van Hiel, A. (2015). Cooperation in mixed-motive games: The role of individual differences in selfish and social orientation. *European Journal of Personality*, *29*(4), 445–458. doi:10.1002/per.1992

Henrich, J., Boyd, R., Bowles, S., Camerer, C., Fehr, E., Gintis, H., & McElreath, R. (2001). In Search of Homo Economicus: Behavioral Experiments in 15 Small-Scale Societies. The American Economic Review, (2), 73.

Hirsch, J. B., & Peterson, J. B. (2009). Extraversion, neuroticism, and the prisoners dilemma. *Personality and Individual Differences*, *46*(2), 254–256. doi:10.1016/j.paid.2008.10.006

Huang, J. Y., & Bargh, J. A. (n.d.). The Selfish Goal: Autonomously operating motivational structures as the proximate cause of human judgment and behavior. *Behavioral and Brain Sciences*, *37*(2), 121–135. PMID:24775120

Koole, S. L., Jager, W., van den Berg, A. E., Vlek, C. A. J., & Hofstee, W. K. B. (2001). On the Social Nature of Personality: Effects of Extraversion, Agreeableness, and Feedback about Collective Resource Use on Cooperation in a Resource Dilemma. *Personality and Social Psychology Bulletin*, *27*(3), 289–301. doi:10.1177/0146167201273003

La Barbera, F., Cariota Ferrara, P., & Boza, M. (2014). Where are we coming from versus who we will become: The effect of priming different contents of European identity on cooperation. *International Journal of Psychology*, *49*(6), 480–487. doi:10.1002/ijop.12073 PMID:25355671

Lozada, M., D'Adamo, P., & Fuentes, M. A. (2011). Beneficial effects of human altruism. *Journal of Theoretical Biology*, *28912-16*. doi:10.1016/j.jtbi.2011.08.016 PMID:21872608

Noval, L. J. (2016). On the misguided pursuit of happiness and ethical decision making: The roles of focalism and the impact bias in unethical and selfish behavior. *Organizational Behavior and Human Decision Processes*, 1331–16. doi:10.1016/j.obhdp.2015.12.004

Ockenfels, A., & Werner, P. (2014). Scale manipulation in dictator games. *Journal of Economic Behavior & Organization*, *97*, 138–142. doi:10.1016/j.jebo.2013.11.002

Osborne, M. J. (2004). *An introduction to game theory*. New York, NY: Oxford University Press.

Parks, C. D. (2015). Determinants of cooperation in social dilemmas. In D. A. Schoeder & W. G. Graziano (Eds.), *The Oxford handbook of prosocial behavior (pp. 524 – 547)*. New York, NY: Oxford University Press.

Van Lange, P. A. M., Balliet, D., Parks, C. D., & Van Vugt, M. (2014). *Social dilemmas: The psychology of human cooperation*. New York, NY: Oxford University Press.

Weber, J. M., Kopelman, S., & Messick, D. M. (2004). A conceptual review of decision making in social dilemmas: Applying a logic of appropriateness. *Personality and Social Psychology Review*, *8*(3), 281–307. doi:10.1207/s15327957pspr0803_4 PMID:15454350

Yamagishi, T., & Cook, K. S. (1993). Generalized Exchange and Social Dilemmas. *Social Psychology Quarterly*, *56*(4), 235. doi:10.2307/2786661

Chapter 7
Consumer–Retail Structure Interrelations as Seen in the Young Consumers' Photographs of Retail Environments

Pirjo Laaksonen
University of Vaasa, Finland

Ari Huuhka
University of Vaasa, Finland

Martti Laaksonen
University of Vaasa, Finland

ABSTRACT

This chapter seeks to understand the multidimensionality of urban consumption and the nature and the levels of consumer – retail structure interrelations. A holistic conceptual framework of urban consumption is proposed. It views the needs, wants, and desires as the motivating forces for consumer behavior, and conceptualizes the dimensions of consumption space and the forms that consumption takes within these dimensions (the platforms of consumption). Qualitative data (respondent-generated photographs and written explanations) is used to exemplify the forms of consumption within the proposed platforms.

INTRODUCTION

Urban consumption contexts, city centers and down town shopping areas are multidimensional spaces where consumer behavior can take diverse forms depending on the nature of the consumer – retail structure interrelations. From the economic point of view urban consumption contexts are, at the aggregate level, dynamic interchanges between supply and demand. On the supply side, retail structure (e.g., location, number and variety of stores) and on the demand side, market characteristics (e.g., market size, income) affect the nature of consumption. If this view is adopted, quantitative indicators

DOI: 10.4018/978-1-5225-1826-6.ch007

like households' monetary spending for commodity consumption in a given geographic area could tell about the nature of consumption.

However, many aspects of urban consumption cannot be apprehended only with quantitative terms. When shopping consumers not only use their monetary and time related recourses but also their cognitive and emotional resources. Besides, consumption does not necessary have to involve the use of money to acquire material possessions. Consumption context itself can be the primary object of consumption, an experienced space where the experiencing takes place beyond shopping and the commodity world. Such aspects of urban consumption, at the level of lifestyles, individual's experiences, concern more qualities than quantities. They arise from the interplay between consumer intrinsic motivations and extrinsic retail structural and environmental factors. The intrinsic and extrinsic factors enable and impede consumer behavior, the behavioral patterns, activities and experiences that take place in urban consumption context.

The postmodern view of consumption questions and contradicts many assumptions in modern marketing and economic theories concerning for instance the nature of consumer market, consumer's role in the market, and the rationality of consumers' decision-making. Furthermore, fulfillment of needs or wants are not regarded the primary drivers for consumption. Instead, an emphasis is placed on the qualities in consumption, consumers' passions and desires, subjective and holistic experiences, and on the use of products, brands and symbols for identity construction. Processes such as globalization retailing and fragmentation of consumer demand have on their part created and facilitated market conditions for such aspects of consumer behavior to come into view (e.g., Smart & Smart, 2003). The omnipresence of global fast fashion chains for instance allows consumers across cultures to be engaged with similar lifestyles, visual and symbolic consumption and forms of self-expression. Consumers have access to global brands and store formats. They can have relationships with brands, stores, and commercial places.

Urban consumption contexts, not anymore just shopping malls, shopping centers or other managed and branded retail establishments, but increasingly also public commercial parts of city centers are purposely developed or regenerated as places to be consumed and experienced and where the boundaries between public and private consumption spaces are blurred (e.g., Hernandez & Jones, 2005). Often shopping experiences, entertainment and leisure are emphasized. Despite this tendency, it is misleading to view urban consumption contexts, city centers in particular, merely as places where the consumption is driven by consumers' desires or their hedonic motivations. They are also places for more ordinary forms of consumption, the routine type of purchasing and buying activities that are linked to person's daily lives.

The purpose of this chapter is to explore and conceptualize the consumer – retail structure interrelations. The multidimensionality of urban consumption spaces and the seemingly diverging views on the motivations and drivers of consumptions calls for a holistic and integrative conceptualization of the character of urban consumption. The chapter has two objectives. The primary objective is to conceptually model the dimensions of consumption space and the forms that consumption takes within these dimensions (the platforms of consumption). The secondary objective is to empirically exemplify the forms of consumption within the proposed platforms. Qualitative visual research approach is adopted for the empirical analysis. The data (the respondent-generated photographs and written explanations) was collected among Finnish university students (61 respondents). The consumption context is Finnish retail structure, a modern retail setting that is dominated by large retail groups and their relatively uniform chains. The empirical aim is to inquire, first, how young consumers (as a homogeneous consumer group in Finland) are related to at different levels to the prevailing retail structure, and second, what the visual and textual material tells about their behavioral patterns with regard to these levels.

The chapter is structured into six sections. This introductory section is followed by the conceptual framework section. It begins with discussion about the motivations and drivers for consumer behavior. Then the assumptions concerning the dimensions of consumption space and the platforms of consumption are put forward. The empirical research section describes the research setting, summarizes key findings and discusses about limitations. It is followed by conclusions section and finally by discussion section.

CONCEPTUAL FRAMEWORK

Motivations and Drivers of Consumption

People have many roles as consumers. The motivations and drivers for their behavior vary individually and by circumstances. Also consumers' resources, not only available monetary and time related, but also emotional and cognitive resources affect behavior. Thus, consumption involves trade-offs and compromises between accessible choices. Consumer might be in one occasion a busy fill-in shopper and in another occasion a variety seeker or a leisure shopper who merely enjoys shopping for pleasure with friends. The first premise of the conceptual framework is that behavioral patterns, activities, and experiences in the urban consumption context arise from three kinds of driving forces: needs, wants and desires of consumers. These drivers can be viewed as three distinct approaches to understand the motivations and goals in consumers' behavior. Besides, each set of drivers can be linked to characteristic consumer behavior features and corresponding retail structural and environmental preconditions (Table 1).

The Maslowian approach, the basic hierarchical structuring of human needs, has in contemporary research been amended and expanded (Kenrick et al., 2010). However, traditionally, due to its universal nature and its implicit assumptions of the links between the different levels of needs and the corresponding product benefits sought by consumers, it has influenced marketers' view of consumers as need-fulfilling individuals (Solomon, 2002: 108-109). The immediate physiological need for nourishment for

Table 1. Consumer behavior features and corresponding retail structural preconditions

	Consumer Behavior Features	Retail Structural Preconditions
Needs-driven	Routine purchasing behavior: • Obtain commodities to fulfill needs • Use and allocation of monetary resources • Reactive behavior	Adequate supply and quantity: • Existence and number of stores (mainly offline stores) • Access and location of stores • Cross-category assortment in the store
Wants-driven	Selective buying behavior: • Select and make choices among alternatives • Use of money and time, cognitive energy • Active, often reactive behavior	Diversity and quality: • Variety of stores (both offline and online stores) • Within-category assortment in the store • Brands • Product attributes and qualities
Desires-driven	Shopping and lifestyle related behavior: • Use of money, often mostly time, cognitive and emotional recourses • Holistic experiences • Social relations • Recreation, leisure and entertainment • Active non-reactive behavior	Retail environment and consumption space: • Variety and quality • Atmospherics and aesthetics • Retail formats • Branded places • Multichannel retail environment

instance could be considered as the driver for fill-in grocery shopping. Similarly, the need for esteem could motivate person to acquire luxury items. Even partly correct, it would be all too one-dimensional to understand consumer behavior only from a person's need-fulfillment point of view. In the conceptual framework needs-driven consumption is acknowledged at the level of routine purchasing behavior related to the obtaining of goods and basic commodities. At this level consumers mainly use and allocate their monetary resources. The existence of sufficient number of stores, their locations, access to them, and the basic supply of products in the stores in terms of cross-category assortments would be the necessary minimum retail structure requirements for the needs-driven consumption.

Motivations to buy and do shopping arise also from consumers' diverse wants. That is especially the case when consumers are involved in selective buying behavior. A person wants to acquire a particular product with certain attributes or qualities or a particular brand. Even if the processes of searching, comparing and evaluating alternatives and deciding do not lead to the actual acquisition of the product, the selective behavior use consumers' time and cognitive resources. The process and the complexity of decision-making vary depending on for instance whether consumer is in the process of acquiring high-involvement or low-involvement products. Often wants-driven consumer is considered to be more rational decision-maker than a needs-driven consumer. This is not always the case since consumers' wants are not always rational and cannot be understood with absolute terms. Thus, as pointed out by O'Shaughnessy (1987, p. 82), the rationality should be understood as matter of degree ranging from the highly rational to the irrational, noting also that the rationality of decisions does not necessarily lead to correct choices. On the supply side the enabling preconditions for selective buying behavior concern primarily the issues of diversity and quality such as the variety of stores available to consumers (both offline and online), the range of brands carried in the stores and the depth of assortment in these stores. Retailers can control retail settings in order to facilitate consumers' choices and reactive behavior (Esbjerg & Bech-Larsen, 2009; Inman, Winer & Ferraro, 2009).

In the conceptual framework the desires-driven consumption is recognized at the level of consumers' shopping and lifestyle related behavior. Such behavior has also many recreational, social and hedonic aspects and motives. The increasing role of consumers' desires and passions as the motivating forces for shopping and the experiencing of the retail environment has been pointed out by many authors (Holbrook & Hirschman, 1982; Jackson & Thrift, 1996; Pine & Gilmore, 1999; Belk, Ger & Askegaard, 2003; Kozinets, 2008). Recreational shopping may concern more about leisure and social relations, subjective time than obtaining goods (e.g., Bellenger & Korgaonkar, 1980; Shields, 1992; Brusdal & Lavik, 2008). Besides, consumers might seek enjoyment, entertainment and holistic experiences with hedonic motivations. From the viewpoint of post-modern consumption consumers are not the end users of the value chain but active co-producers of the customer value (e.g., Firat & Dholakia, 2006, p. 138). Desires-driven consumption extends beyond the commodity world. Thus qualities of the retail environment, atmospherics and aesthetics and a consumer's subjectively experienced dimensions of consumption space are important facilitators for consumers' desires-driven behavior.

Dimensions of Consumption Space

The second premise of the conceptual framework is that consumption contexts are multidimensional spaces. Thus, not only spatial and physical structuring but also functional, social, and mental aspects of consumption context are acknowledged. The five types of experiences (sense, feel, think, act, and relate) proposed by Schmitt's (1999) are the foundation of dimensions of consumption space (Figure 1). The four dimensions are perceived place (sensing and thinking), used space (doing), lived space (social relations and interactions), and experienced space (emotional experiences). The dimensions are overlapping: they extend beyond each other. Thus, consumers' holistic experiencing of the consumption context can deal with all the dimensions, but the experiencing can also be limited to only one or few dimensions.

An individual gets information of the environment, its spatial structure and organization through sensory experiences (e.g., Golledge & Stimson, 1990). The perceived place refers to sensing and thinking, the person's perceptions and understanding of the spatial and physical structuring of the consumption space. Physical landmarks (e.g., buildings, parks, stores) and paths (e.g., streets, pedestrian areas) help the individual to orientate and navigate in the environment (e.g., Israel, 2003). Besides, built environments are also used spaces, the behavioral settings for activities, events and everyday occasions. The experiencing of built environment can involve doing something or just being in the environment. The functions for which the spaces are used by people may not be the same for which the space is originally designated (e.g., Woolley et al., 1999; Woolley & Johns, 2001). The lived space concerns social-identity experiences. These range from being together or in solitude, doing something with other, to see other people and to be seen by others (e.g., Brusdal & Lavik, 2008). Consumption spaces are also social contexts, socially constructed settings for social relations and interaction (e.g., Golledge & Stimson, 1990; Knox, 2005). Consumption spaces are also experienced spaces, where an individual's emotions and moods can arise from the interaction of the mind and the environment, as in the perceptual or the aesthetic experiencing of the physical place (sensing and thinking) (e.g., Tuan, 1974; Burns, 2000; Isaacs, 2000).

Figure 1. Dimensions of consumption space

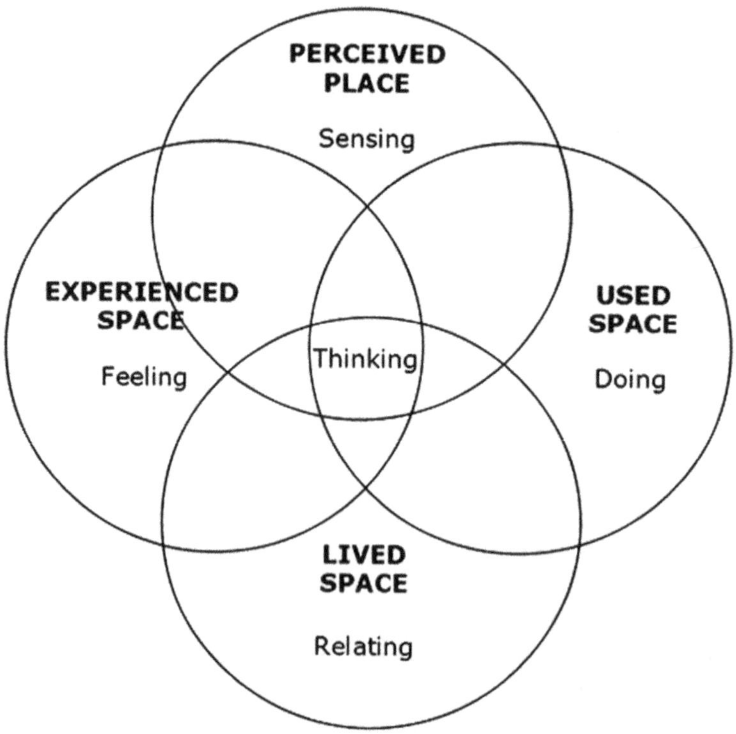

Platforms of Consumption

The third premise of the conceptual framework is that the overlapping dimensions of consumption space are viewed as platforms of consumption (Figure 2). The platforms are:

1. Routine purchasing behavior,
2. Selective buying behavior,
3. Shopping and lifestyle related behavior, and
4. Immersion and experiences beyond shopping and the commodity world.

The framework recognizes consumers' active role in transforming the behavioral setting of a consumption space into a stage for social interaction, symbolic consumption, and holistic experiences (e.g., Pine & Gilmore, 1999). Consumers have different roles depending on the platforms. The roles vary from passive to active and from reactive audience to active actors. Furthermore, the concept of mental state is introduced. It refers to consumers' mental and subjective world that can expand beyond the world of shopping and experiences.

The first platform is the setting for routine purchasing behavior. The consumer is primarily concerned about "Can I buy the goods I need in this place?". In the second platform consumer behavior is primarily selective and reactive. Consumers are buying and doing shopping and involved in activities. However, though more active than needs-driven shoppers, consumers are reactive audience (e.g., Baron et al., 2001). They are mainly concerned about "What can I buy and do in the place?" or "What do I select". The third platform gives consumers' an access to the world of social interaction, symbolic consumption, and holistic experiencing. Here consumer behavior is typically recreational shopping behavior and experiencing. Shopping can be essential part of their lifestyles. Consumers' role is more active: they can be viewed as the actors in the stage (e.g., Pine & Gilmore, 1999). They are concerned about "How the place serves me?", "For what I can use the place?", or "With whom can I share and experience the place". In the fourth platform consumption departs from the realm of commodity consumption. The fourth platform offers a consumer the access to the mental and subjective world (mental state). Besides, this is the platform for immersion (e.g., Pine & Gilmore, 1999), and for the experiences that exists beyond the shopping and commodity world. In immersion the consumption context is an authentic and inseparable part of person's life and identity. Through every day practices, habits and activities, a person can have an access to desired lifestyles. Due to the linkages between consumption and a person's habitual behavior, consumption begins to partly take forms are similar to those in the first platform.

EMPIRICAL RESEARCH

The empirical objective is to exemplify the diverse forms of consumption within the four platforms. Qualitative research approach was adopted in order to explore the qualitative dimensions proposed by the conceptual framework. It was assumed that visual material, photographs of stores taken by consumers themselves could uncover the diversity concerning consumers' attachment to the prevailing supply structure. The integrated framework for visual social research put forward by Pauwels (2010) provided guidelines for the planning and implementing of this visual research project. The respondent generated photographs were selected as the origin of the visual data (Pauwels, 2010). Moreover, the important

Figure 2. Platforms of consumption

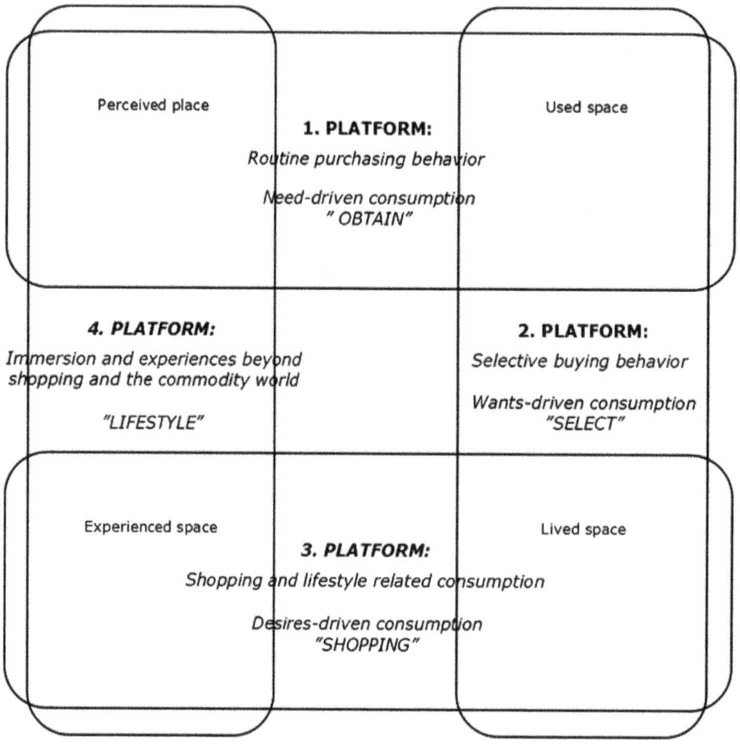

image-external context was taken into account by supplementing the visual data with respondents' written explanations (Pauwels, 2010).

Homogenous Finnish consumer group, a sample of university students was chosen. Besides, practical reasons like convenience sampling and the easy access to visual material through the course assignment favored the decision. The data was collected as an assignment in retail marketing course offered at the bachelor level. The participants were second year students. The data contains the respondent-generated photos and written explanations submitted by 61 students (43 women and 18 men). The task given to participants was short and straightforward (Appendix). They were asked to take four photos of retail environments: the first, where the person goes just to obtain something, the second, where the person goes to when she wants to compare and select, the third, where the person enjoys and wants to shop, and the fourth, that is or would be part of the person's lifestyle. They were also asked to write why they had made the selection.

The photos were in general snapshot type digital images taken mostly with mobile phone cameras. They were different from the stylish and glossy generic images used for instance in advertisements. The environments depicted in the photos clearly belonged to the living sphere close to the respondents. Two thirds of the photos depicted store interiors. The assignment contained no advice to take certain stores or environments or photos of certain format. Although it was expected that the photos would depict physical retail environments and be taken by the respondents themselves, some images were taken from the web especially when they were selected to represent desired lifestyle, or when the on-line environment (a print screen copy of the website) was the person's favorite place to shop.

Privacy and ethical issues were brought up in the written explanations: taking photos places where photographing is forbidden, or copyright of photo if downloaded from the web. Many photos of empty looking store interiors imply that respondents may have avoided to show people. Such factors might have influenced some respondents to take photos of stores that were conveniently accessible to them. However, some respondents wrote also than it had not been easy to choose a suitable environment to be depicted in the environment.

The empirical analysis was guided by two key questions: first, what is young consumers' attachment to the different levels (platforms) in the prevailing retail structure, and second, what the visual and textual material tells about their behavioral patterns with regard to these levels. The data analysis was conducted across the four retail environments. The respondents are treated as homogeneous consumer group.

FINDINGS

Stores by Platforms

The stores mentioned and depicted in photos were classified into 20 categories representing different retail sectors (Table 2). Food and daily goods stores as well as kiosks and fast food restaurants were most often the store for need-driven behavior. Interestingly same grocery chains were also mentioned as places for compare and choose. Food courts and eco-stores selling local produce and ecological food products were mentioned in relation to lifestyle related consumption.

Hennes & Mauritz and Zara were female respondents' favorite places to do shopping for clothes. Only few respondents mentioned those typical fast fashion stores as representing their lifestyles. Instead, smaller boutiques and design-oriented clothing stores as well concept stores were mentioned as lifestyle related retail environment.

Specialty stores were mentioned across all types of retail environments. For instance, book stores could be environments where something needed was get. Besides, they could represent places where the respondents enjoyed spending free time and doing shopping or their favorite places representing their lifestyles. Some of the retail environments were typically places meant especially for female customers. Well-being stores and beauty stores selling cosmetics were mentioned as favorite places for selective behavior, shopping and lifestyle related consumption. Also shops selling health and dietary supplements were mentioned.

In lifestyle related consumption wider range of different stores were mentioned. The specialty stores were for instance stores selling more expensive design products, store closely related to respondent's hobbies (e.g. pet shops, video rentals, record shops, travel agencies etc.). High number of sport stores was mentioned both by women and men.

Respondents' Explanations by Photos

Among the reasons mentioned were preferences for particular environments, evaluative judgments, emotional expressions (e.g. I love fashion and shopping; I don't like shopping) and references to future aspirations (e.g. lifestyle is accessible in the future). Also consumer resources, in particularly the scarcity of money (e.g. limited student budget) and time (be in a hurry) were mentioned. The explanations were predominantly positive. The assignment might have leaded the respondents to think something

Table 2. Stores depicted (classified by retail sectors and by platforms)

	Obtain	Select	Shopping	Lifestyle
Food and daily goods stores	37	16		
Food specialty stores		2		
Food courts and eco-stores				4
Kiosks and fast food restaurants	8			1
Cafés				2
Liquor stores		6		1
Clothing stores		1	29	6
Boutiques & specialty clothing stores				7
Specialty stores	4	5	6	13
Well-being & beauty stores		5	3	6
Sport stores		1		12
Pharmacies	6			
Opticians & eyewear stores	3	1		
On-line stores		5	3	1
Home electronics stores		5		
Furniture stores		2		
Interior decoration stores			5	5
Department store		3	4	1
Shopping centers			6	
Other	3	9	5	2
Total	61	61	61	61

that the person "wants to do". An unexpected finding was that social aspects of shopping, friends were not explicitly mentioned in the explanations. In the light of data young consumers' shopping seems to be relatively solitary, self-contained, activity. However, the positive social aspects came out implicitly in the respondents' remarks about their hobbies. The negative social aspects like crowded stores came out explicitly in some explanations.

The imperative to get a certain product was seen in the explanations of the first photo. All explanations were relatively similar. Typically, the respondents referred to the availability of basic necessities in the store, to the good location of the store (close proximity), and to the possibilities to do quick shopping (convenience). Besides, typical stores, soft discounters and hypermarkets, are selected because of their functional reasons.

Example: This store (a soft discounter) is small and the selection is narrow but I can buy all my basic food and household products. Usually I go to this store when I have only a few products to buy or when the other stores are not open. ... This is not an attractive or cozy environment, and I stay there only few minutes: I buy the products and I go away. Service station forecourt stores and kiosks are similar stores but they have higher prices.

The explanations of the second photo a referred to broad assortments, the pleasantness of the indoor environment, practical product displays that facilitate selection, the possibility to make price and quality comparisons, and the presence of store personnel to help the customer in selecting the product.

Example: I took this photo because I go to Citymarket (a hypermarket) mostly when I buy food. Citymarket has a good selection and thus usually I can choose the cheapest alternative. I usually buy daily food items. This store has also a good selection of cosmetics, so I can at the same time compare the prices of make-up products.

The explanations of the third photo touched on product assortments and the existence of the right kind of products and brands that the person felt like her own. The products typically were clothing but also products related to person's hobbies. Not anymore only the names of the retail chains but also the names of the brands began to appear in the explanations. Also retail environmental factors such as the appealing store atmosphere, the feeling evoked by the store, the attractiveness of product displays were mentioned. Also attributes like reasonable prices or good quality were mentioned.

Example: I chose this shop Sokos Emotion (a beauty store) because I love beauty care products and fragrances. I am interested in them and ready to use time and money to buy them. Usually I find information about the new products beforehand and then go this shop to see them. The store is peaceful (the customers are adults, no children running around). The sales persons are immaculate and the service is professional and friendly. I become glad when I buy the products I love in a nice environment.

Example: Hennes&Mauritz (a clothing store). There are plenty of different clothes and accessories, different styles and now also shoes. The clothes are cheap but also good quality and fashionable. Therefore I can spend lots of time to do shopping. However, I don't enjoy being there on Saturdays or when crowded, because the store is full of people and the products are messily on display. But on other times the store is clean, with plenty of light, and it's cozy. This is the store where I can drop in even when I don't need any particular product. This is the store where I can leave and be satisfied even though I hadn't found I had been looking for.

The explanations of the fourth photo concerned the quality and luxury products and the aesthetic qualities of the retail environments. Also hobbies were often mentioned. The explanations began to be related to values and to issues that were important to the respondents (e.g. ethical issues, origin of the products). Respondents' relationship with stores and brands differed from those of the third photo. Now stores could be "trusted friends" and brands "represent my personality".

Example: (a pet shop). This is the retail environment that is part of my lifestyle. We have always had pets at home and I love animals. I like to go pet shops to buy new toys and snacks to my pets. I also like to go these shops just to see new items even when I don't have any intention to buy.

Example: In my mind Stockmann (a department store) represents quality, trust and better service. Stockmann has always been part of my and my family's lifestyle. My family has always patronized Stockmann and maybe also for that reason I have a strong emotional bond with Stockmann. Stockmann is for me like a trusted friend that makes me feel myself important and respected.

The wording of the assignment allowed the respondents to think about not only their present lifestyles as a student but also their desired lifestyles. Although desired and valued, some forms of consumption, were not yet concretely accessible or possible to the respondents due to for instance limited monetary recourses. It was also found that some behavioral patterns, as proposed by the conceptual framework, are closely related to consumers' habitual behavior.

Example: (a food court). I would like to use more organic products when cooking and to select local products more often; and if possible to buy my food directly from the producer without any extra middlemen.

Example: (an interior decoration store). I like very much design, furniture, decorating and beautiful items. Because design is relatively expensive I don't yet have afford it, but I wish that in the future design would be part of my lifestyle.

Example: I chose R-Kioski (a kiosk), I patronize it surprisingly often. I can quickly get coffee and other small purchases and, above all, in Helsinki I load my travel card in R-Kioski. They are located in good places and they are easy and quick to deal with. I have busy and speedy lifestyle and I seldom have patience to queue in the normal store just for the sake of chewing cum. Besides, the coffee costs one euro. That's good for my wallet.

Limitations

The task given to the students resulted rich data containing respondent-generated photos and written explanations. It was supposed that the photos and related explanations could be used to exemplify the diverse forms of consumption that take place in the different platforms. Besides, it was assumed that by allowing the respondents to express themselves both with photos and written explanations, this method would bring forth associations and preferences that could not be caught solely with written data. However, the research setting and the data have several inherent limitations that are worth taking into account. The first limitation is the small size of the convenience sample. Although it can be considered as fairly sufficient in explorative and qualitative studies it does not allow wider generalizations. The second limitation concerns the wording of the assignment. It might have guided the respondents to seek explanations that are all too self-evident or unsurprising for instance. A more indirect inquiry might have been better in this sense. The task guided the person to explain (by taking the photo and by writing) her relationship with the retail environment. However, in actual consumption situations a great deal of consumer behavior is unconscious. Consumers are not automatically aware of the motivating forces of their behavior or the rationales of their choices (e.g. Etzioni, 2011). The third limitation, an issue worth noticing is that the characteristic behavior proposed to take place in the fourth platform could not be fully explored with this data. The task worked sufficiently well at the level consumer lifestyles but could not fully touch the issues of immersion and the consumer identities.

CONCLUSION

The chapter has seek to explore and understand the varied and multidimensional nature of urban consumption, in particularly the consumer – retail structure interrelations. The theoretical challenge was to provide a holistic and integrative conceptualization of the character of urban consumption. The conceptual framework was based on three premises: first, consumer behavior is driven by consumers' needs, wants and desires, second, consumption contexts are multidimensional spaces, and third, the overlapping dimensions of consumption space form distinct platforms of consumption. The four platforms are routine purchasing behavior, selective buying behavior, shopping and lifestyle related behavior, and immersion and experiences beyond shopping and the commodity world.

The empirical challenge was to exemplify, with the help of visual research methods, the forms that consumption takes in within the platforms. The data showed that certain retail environments are linked to several platforms. This supports the conceptual framework's assumption of the interrelatedness of the platforms. For instance, a hypermarket was mentioned as place for routine purchasing behavior and for selective behavior. Besides same store could be used differently by a same person depending on what motivated the behavior.

Also a pattern of increased diversity regarding the selected retail environments and reasons given was noted. There was least diversity at level of routine purchasing behavior. The more the consumption moves from the level of selective buying behavior to the realm of shopping and lifestyle related consumption, the more diverse the retail environments and the reasons given were. At the level of shopping and lifestyle related behavior the consumers' attachment to the retail structure was seen not only their preferences to particular stores, products and brands but also to their hobbies, lifestyles and personal identities. The arguments began to be related to the values that were important to them. Thus it seems that certain retail environments are able to activate certain type of values. This finding is in line with the views presented by Holbrook (1999).

DISCUSSION

The focus of this chapter has been on the various forms that consumption can take in urban consumption settings as a result of consumer – retail structure interrelations. The concept of platform of consumption was proposed to represent these forms of consumption within urban setting. Urban consumption is a highly context dependent phenomenon. It concerns choices and daily life behavior that have been addressed within behavioral economics. These behaviors include for instance preferential choices to visit particular stores, buy particular products and brands. This chapter has sought to understand urban consumption holistically. The multidisciplinary approach to consumer – retail structure interrelations has made possible to take into account routine, selective, and life style related behavior as well as consumer behavior related to a consumer's experiences beyond shopping and the commodity world. Also future research on urban consumption would benefit from integrating premises from behavioral economics, marketing and economic geography. Besides, future research should sensitively acknowledge the many ongoing trends that are expected to affect the supply and demand, in particular the retail structural preconditions that impede and enable different forms of consumption in urban contexts.

The digital disruption, the merging physical and digital forms of commerce has brought about and many fundamental changes in supply (retail structural changes), in demand (consumer behavior). In demand side, digitalization is resulting retail format variation, including off-line and on-line hybrids (e.g., Betancourt, 2016; Hortacsu & Syverson, 2015). Digitalization is also shaping demand side, consumer behavior, by giving consumers multiple-touch points to interact with products, brands, store, and increasing importantly with other consumers (e.g., The Boston Consulting Group, 2014). Future research on the consumer-retail structure interrelatedness should examine how the digital dimension of place and the many different ways it is related to consumers' consumption practices (e.g., Pink, 2012). There are many alternatives to approaches and methods to study consumer behavior in online contexts. However, as shown by Agosto (2002), future research on online consumer behavior (e.g., preferential choices and search behavior) will benefit from the application of the fundamental ideas, tools and models put forward within behavioral economics (see e.g., Kahneman & Tversky, 1984; Rieskamp et al., 2006; Camerer & Loewenstein, 2004).

In supply side, retail structural changes are brought about by investments to large scale retail formats, in particular shopping centers (e.g., Cushman & Wakefield, 2016). Urban shopping centers are becoming multipurpose and multifunctional establishments are planned to be places where different forms of consumption, in particularly recreational and experiential are combined. Thus shopping centers increasingly are having characteristics of hybrid consumption systems (e.g., Bryman, 2004). The conceptual framework put forward in this chapter helps to understand holistically the motivations that drive consumers to patronize such environments. However, due to the increased complexity of such environment, there is need for studies that examine how consumer behavior within such hybrid consumption environments are related to different types of values (e.g., economic, social or hedonic) triggered by particular aspects of the consumption setting and situations. Besides, there is need for studies that focus on the urban macro-environment and acknowledge the increasing important role of the general urban atmospheric factors (e.g., Löfgren, 2014) in urban development and place branding projects.

There are also interesting future research opportunities to examine how particular micro consumption environments act as social consumption setting. Recent studies by Mendelson & Papacharissi (2011) and by Pyyry (2016) show how visual research methods can provide interesting insights into the nature of immersion and social interactions in young consumers' lifes. There is need for research on consumers' choices, in particular how consumers form preferences for their favorite "third places" (e.g., Oldenburg & Brissett, 1982; Belk, 2013) that they habitually want to patronize. Besides future research would benefit from the application behavioral economics approach (e.g., Kahneman et al., 2004: White & Dolan, 2009) to analyze consumers' daily life activities as well as consumer psychological issues such as well-being.

Finally, opportunities for future research on urban consumption arise from the ongoing changes concerning how future markets will be structured. Recent research (e.g. Capgemini, 2015) illustrates and discusses how mainly due to consumer behavior related drivers, in the future the consumer value is increasingly created in value networks centered on customer rather than in traditional supplier-retailer-consumer value chains. Future multidisciplinary research on urban consumption should acknowledge these emerging market realities. A challenging question for future research is, how new market and value constellations (or assemblages, see e.g. Arsel, 2016) create economic, social or hedonic value to urban consumers.

REFERENCES

Agosto, D. E. (2002). Bounded rationality and satisficing in young peoples web-based decision making. *Journal of the American Society for Information Science and Technology*, *53*(1), 16–27. doi:10.1002/asi.10024

Arsel, Z. (2016). Assembling markets and value. In R. Canniford & D. Bajde (Eds.), *Assembling consumption. Researching actors, networks and markets* (pp. 32–41). London, UK: Routledge.

Baron, S., Harris, K., & Harris, R. (2001). Retail theater. The intended effect of the performance. *Journal of Service Research*, *4*(2), 102–117. doi:10.1177/109467050142003

Belk, R. W. (2013). Extended self in a digital world. *The Journal of Consumer Research*, *40*(3), 477–500. doi:10.1086/671052

Belk, R. W., Ger, G., & Askegaard, S. (2003). The fire of desire: A multisited inquiry into consumer passion. *The Journal of Consumer Research*, *30*(3), 326–351. doi:10.1086/378613

Bellenger, D. N., & Korgaonkar, P. K. (1980). Profiling the recreational shopper. *Journal of Retailing*, *56*(3), 77–92.

Betancourt, R. R. (2016). Distribution services, technological change and the evolution of retailing and distribution in the twenty-first century. In E. Basker (Ed.), *Handbook on the economics of retailing and distribution* (pp. 73–94). Cheltenham, UK: Edward Elgar. doi:10.4337/9781783477388.00012

Brusdal, R., & Lavik, R. (2008). Just shopping? A closer look at youth and shopping in Norway. *Young. Nordic Journal of Youth Research*, *16*(4), 393–408. doi:10.1177/110330880801600403

Bryman, A. (2004). *The Disneyization of society*. London, UK: Sage Publications Ltd.

Burns, A. (2000). Emotion and urban experience: Implications for design. *Design Issues*, *16*(3), 67–79. doi:10.1162/07479360052053333

Camerer, C. F., & Loewenstein, G. (2004). Behavioral economics: Past, present, future. In C. F. Camerer, G. Loewenstein, & M. Rabin (Eds.), *Advances in Behavioral Economics* (pp. 3–51). Princeton, NJ: Princeton University Press.

Capgemini. (2015). *Rethinking the value chain. New realities in collaborative business*. Retrieved from: https://www.capgemini.com/

Cushman & Wakefield. (2016). *European shopping centre development report*. Available: http://www.cushmanwakefield.com/en/research-and-insight/2016/european-shopping-centre-development-report-april-2016/

Esbjerg, L., & Bech-Larsen, T. (2009). The brand architecture of grocery retailers: Setting material and symbolic boundaries for consumer choice. *Journal of Retailing and Consumer Services*, *16*(5), 414–423. doi:10.1016/j.jretconser.2009.06.002

Etzioni, A. (2011). Behavioral economics: Towards a new paradigm. *The American Behavioral Scientist*, *55*(8), 1099–1119. doi:10.1177/0002764211412355

Firat, A. F., & Dholakia, N. (2006). Theoretical and philosophical implications of postmodern debates: Some challenges to modern marketing. *Marketing Theory*, *6*(2), 123–162. doi:10.1177/1470593106063981

Golledge, R. G., & Stimson, R. J. (1990). *Analytical behavioral geography*. London, UK: Routledge.

Hernandez, T., & Jones, K. (2005). Downtown in transition. Emerging business improvement are strategies. *International Journal of Retail & Distribution Management*, *33*(11), 789–805. doi:10.1108/09590550510629392

Holbrook, M. B. (1999). Introduction to consumer value. In M. B. Holbrook (Ed.), *Consumer value. A framework for analysis and research* (pp. 1–28). London, UK: Routledge. doi:10.4324/9780203010679.ch0

Holbrook, M. B., & Hirschman, E. C. (1982). The experiential aspects of consumption: Consumer fantasies, feelings, and fun. *The Journal of Consumer Research*, *9*(2), 132–140. doi:10.1086/208906

Hortacsu, A., & Syverson, C. (2015). The ongoing evolution of US retail: A format tug-of-war. *The Journal of Economic Perspectives*, *29*(4), 89–112. doi:10.1257/jep.29.4.89

Inman, J. J., Winer, R. S., & Ferraro, R. (2009). The interplay among category characteristics, customer characteristics, and customer activities on in-store decision making. *Journal of Marketing*, *73*(5), 19–29. doi:10.1509/jmkg.73.5.19

Isaacs, R. (2000). The urban picturesque: An aesthetic experience of urban pedestrian places. *Journal of Urban Design*, *5*(2), 145–180. doi:10.1080/713683961

Israel, T. (2003). *Some place like home. Using design psychology to create ideal places*. Chichester, UK: John Wiley & Sons.

Jackson, P., & Thrift, N. (1996). Geographies of consumption. In D. Miller (Ed.), *Acknowledging consumption. A review of new studies* (pp. 204–237). London, UK: Routledge.

Kahneman, D., Krueger, A. B., Schkade, D. A., Schwarz, N., & Stone, A. A. (2004). A survey method for characterizing daily life experience: The day reconstruction method. *Science*, *304*(5702), 1776–1780. doi:10.1126/science.1103572 PMID:15576620

Kahneman, D., & Tversky, A. (1984). Choices, values, and frames. *The American Psychologist*, *39*(4), 341–350. doi:10.1037/0003-066X.39.4.341

Kenrick, D. T., Griskevicius, V., Neuberg, S. L., & Schaller, M. (2010). Renovating the pyramid of needs: Contemporary extensions built upon ancient foundations. *Perspectives on Psychological Science*, *5*(3), 292–314. doi:10.1177/1745691610369469

Knox, P. L. (2005). Creating ordinary places: Slow cities in a fast world. *Journal of Urban Design*, *10*(1), 1–11. doi:10.1080/13574800500062221

Kozinets, R. V. (2008). Brands in space: New thinking about experiential retail. In T. M. Lowrey (Ed.), *Brick & mortar shopping in the 21st century* (pp. 3–15). Mahwah, NJ: Lawrence Erlbaum.

Löfgren, O. (2014). Urban atmospheres as brandscapes and lived experiences. *Place Branding and Public Diplomacy*, *10*(4), 255–266. doi:10.1057/pb.2014.26

Mendelson, A. L., & Papacharissi, Z. (2011). Look at us. Collective narcissism in college student facebook photo galleries. In Z. Papacharissi (Ed.), *A networked self. Identity, community, and culture on social network sites* (pp. 252–273). New York, NY: Routledge.

O'Shaughnessy, J. (1987). *Why people buy*. New York, NY: Oxford University Press.

Oldenburg, R., & Brissett, D. (1982). The third place. *Qualitative Sociology*, *5*(4), 265–284. doi:10.1007/BF00986754

Pauwels, L. (2010). Visual sociology reframed: An analytical synthesis and discussion of visual methods in social and cultural research. *Sociological Methods & Research*, *38*(4), 545–581. doi:10.1177/0049124110366233

Pine, B. J., & Gilmore, J. H. (1999). *The experience economy: Work is theatre & every business a stage*. Boston, MA: Harvard Business School Press.

Pink, S. (2012). *Situating everyday life*. London, UK: Sage Publications Ltd.

Pyyry, N. (2016). Participation by being: Teenage girls hanging out at the shopping mall as ´dwelling with´. *Emotion, Space and Society*, *18*, 9–16. doi:10.1016/j.emospa.2016.01.006

Rieskamp, J., Busemeyer, J. R., & Mellers, B. A. (2006). Extending the bounds of rationality: Evidence and theories of preferential choice. *Journal of Economic Literature*, *44*(3), 631–661. doi:10.1257/jel.44.3.631

Schmitt, B. (1999). Experiential marketing. *Journal of Marketing Management*, *15*(1-3), 53–67. doi:10.1362/026725799784870496

Shields, R. (1992). Spaces for the subject of consumption. In R. Shields (Ed.), *Lifestyle shopping. The subject of consumption* (pp. 1–20). London, UK: Routledge.

Smart, A., & Smart, J. (2003). Urbanization and the global perspective. *Annual Review of Anthropology*, *1*(32), 263–285. doi:10.1146/annurev.anthro.32.061002.093445

Solomon, M. R. (2002). *Consumer behavior: Buying, having, and being*. Upper Saddle River, NJ: Prentice-Hall.

The Boston Consulting Group. (2014). *The digital future. A game plan for consumer packaged goods*. Available: https://www.bcgperspectives.com/

Tuan, Y.-F. (2003). *Space and Place. The perspective of experience*. Minneapolis, MN: University of Minnesota Press.

White, M. P., & Dolan, P. (2009). Accounting for the richness of daily activities. *Psychological Science*, *20*(8), 1000–1008. doi:10.1111/j.1467-9280.2009.02392.x PMID:19549079

Woolley, H., Dunn, J., Spencer, C., Short, T., & Rowley, G. (1999). Children describe their experiences of the city centre: A qualitative study of the fears and concerns which may limit their full participation. *Landscape Research*, *24*(3), 287–301. doi:10.1080/01426399908706564

Woolley, H., & Johns, R. (2001). Skateboarding: The city as a playground. *Journal of Urban Studies*, *6*(2), 211–230. doi:10.1080/13574800120057845

KEY TERMS AND DEFINITIONS

Desires-Driven Consumption: Typically shopping and lifestyle related behavior, that can include holistic experiencing of the environment as well as social and recreational aspects of consumption. It can also extend beyond shopping and the commodity world.

Dimension of Consumption Space: Conceptualized in this study as perceived place (sensing and thinking), used space (doing), lived space (social relations and interactions), and experienced space (emotional experiences).

Needs-Driven Consumption: Typically routine and reactive purchasing behavior like grocery shopping to obtain commodities to fulfill basic needs.

Platform of Consumption: Theoretical abstraction, a concept that refers to dimension of consumption space within which consumption takes distinct forms.

Respondent Generated Photographs: Visual research method used in this study. Photos that were taken by the respondents themselves and complemented with their written explanations to take into account the image-external context.

Urban Consumption Context: Multidimensional consumption spaces especially within city centers and down town shopping areas.

Wants-Driven Consumption: Typically active and selective buying behavior to make choices among alternatives. It can include reactive behavior.

APPENDIX: THE TASK GIVEN TO THE RESPONDENTS AS COURSE ASSIGNMENT

Take four different photos:

1. Photo: retail environment, where I go just to obtain what I need.
2. Photo: retail environment, where I go when I want to compare and select.
3. Photo: retail environment, where I enjoy and want to do shopping.
4. Photo: retail environment, that is or could be part of my lifestyle.

Write an explanation, in which you tell about each photo why you took or selected just that one.

Chapter 8
Relational Dynamics:
The Flood Solution - Sustainable Energy and Rural Tourism

David Stefan Bathory
Bathory International, USA

ABSTRACT

The effects of global warming are becoming apparent through- out the world. Europe has begun to experience more severe winters and increased rain (Steffen, 2011). Massive flooding in South Eastern Europe has devastated communities and repeatedly strains the economy of these regions resulting in mass trauma to the residents of multiple countries (Sito-Sucic & Djurica, 2014). Intergenerational effects of trauma (Bathory & Celik, 2014; Kaitz, Levy, Ebstein, Faraone, & Mankuta, 2009) have been noted to be an increasing world-wide concern. These traumatic effects are not only psychologically based but result in structural and functional changes within the brain and body (D. Bathory, 2012; D. S. Bathory, 2013a, 2013b; van der Kolk, Roth, Pelcovitz, Sunday, & Spinazzola, 2005). This chapter explores the application of decision making and Relational Dynamics to mass victims of floods by creating healing sites of sustainable energy and rural tourism to assist mass victims of natural disaster flooding.

OVERVIEW

Psychological trauma occurs without regard to age, race, gender, ethnicity socio-economic status, or setting. From common place events such as car accidents and natural disasters such as floods, life threatening events are rampant throughout the world (De Zulueta, 2007). Massive floods and other natural disasters are on the rise due to global warming and the devastation, both to people and property are becoming more substantial. Seventy-two people died in Hurricane Sandy in the United States in October of 2012 (Sharp, 2012) and there was an estimated $70 billion in damage as compared to Hurricane Katrina that resulted in over $100 billion in damages and 1,836 deaths in 2005 (Stone, 2012). In 2014, South Eastern Europe and the Balkans were devastated with the worst floods in over 120 years. Over 1 million people were affected when three months of normal rainfall fell in a matter of hours, 62 people died in these flood waters (Sito-Sucic & Djurica, 2014) and there was an estimated €1.55 billion worth of damage.

DOI: 10.4018/978-1-5225-1826-6.ch008

The end result, is that floods kill, they leave behind economic fallout that takes years to replace and repair, from debris removal, to reconstruction of homes, buildings, and infrastructure, and rebuilding families lives that have been washed away.

Relational Dynamics is a non-linear theory of how we interact with others and things. At the base of Relational Dynamics, is the ability to move non-cooperative relationships into those of cooperation. In the case of floods and disasters, Relational Dynamics provides a means for people to heal from the devastation and loss and form positive interactions with weather and water again. Relational Dynamics was generated from theories within mathematics (chaos (Gleick, 1987) and game theories (Nash, 1950)) and psychology (personality, social, cultural, neurobiological and trauma) (Freud, 1905 (1962)) (Jung, 1916 (reprinted 2002)) (Maslow, 1943) (Erkison, 1963) (Frankel, 1963). Within Behavioral Economics, Relational Dynamics provides a means of exploring both the aspects of personal and monetary losses and ways to repair and rebuild from disasters, as well as understand basic interactions and cooperation.

Economics has relied on three principles related to behavior rationality, willpower and selfishness. These principles have guided economics into a static corner of attempting to predict outcomes in the all too human world of diversity. In 1955, Herbert Simon proposed unlimited information processing capabilities and called it "bounded rationality" and applied this concept to decision making (Simon, 1955; Simon, 1959). Kahneman et al. has explored the human factor or departures from rational choice within judgements, beliefs and decision making (Kahneman & Tversky, 1974; Kahneman & Tversky, 1979; Kahneman, Slovic, & Tversky, 1982; Kahneman, 2003).

Kahneman said, Economists often critize psychological research for its propensity to generate lists of errors and biases, and for its failure to offer a coherent alternative to the rational-agent model. This complaint is only partly justified. Psychological theories of intuitive thinking cannot match the elegance and precision of formal normative models of beliefs and choice, but this is just another way of saying that rational models are just psychologically unrealistic. Furthermore, the alternative to simple and precise models is not chaos. Psychology offers integrated concepts and mid level generalizations, which gain credibility from their ability to explain ostensibly different phenomena in diverse domains. (Kahneman, 2003, p.1449)

Psychological theory and these behavioral economic models still do not provide a way in which human behavior that is seldom purely rational, can be explained. Models do not have to be linear in mathematics, economics or psychology, yet the majority are linearly based. Relying on cause and effect, sequential logic, and supply and demand does not provide an accurate description of the interaction of humans with each other, or with objects. Relational Dynamics provides a novel approach to understanding the interplay of the drives for dominance and acceptance in understanding the process that occurs when two or more players attempt to interact. Within in this dynamic, there is the ability to form cooperative interactions from what was once non-cooperative, as well as destroy cooperation, or create chaos and misunderstanding. Relational Dynamics is useful for managers and others within the field of behavioral economics to understand how to create cooperation with individuals or groups (Bathory D., 2015a), assist with helping to heal painful experiences such as psychological trauma from disasters (Bathory D. S., 2013; Bathory D. S., 2013a) and understand human interactions with objects (as it can be applied to advertising and marketing, human resources, employment, and customer dispute/satisfaction). It has been applied in Art in finding ways for artist to convey important messages through their work in sculptures such as monuments. (Bathory & Lajbenšperger, 2014; Bathory D. S., 2013). Relational Dynamics has been applied to education in creating models for entrepreneurship in helping to define what factors are found in success (Bathory D. S., 2012). It has been applied in models for healthcare delivery and systems in finding ways for providers to work more effectively with their treatment populations (Bathory D., 2015; Bathory D., 2014). Relational Dynamics has been applied to decision making and architectural design to assist with creating cooperative processes in restoration and building (Bathory D. S., In press; Bathory D. S., 2016a), as well as healing structures that interact with people (Bathory & Lajbenšperger, 2014; Bathory D. S., 2013). Within decision making, Relational Dynamics helps to understand the difference between rational and non-rational thought processes and the theory has been applied to trauma, resiliency (Bathory D., 2012a) and personality theory within psychology. (Bathory D., 2014; Bathory D., 2015a; Bathory & Celik, 2014; Bathory D. S., 1993; Bathory D. S., 2014b; Lasser & Bathory, 1997) Lastly, in an effort to show the importance of cooperation as a superior strategy over competition, Relational Dynamics has been applied to Evolutionary Biology in a proof for evolution (Bathory D. S., 2015). An interdisciplinary overview of Relational Dynamics is provided in Cross Disciplinary Perspectives with Relational Dynamics (Bathory D. S., 2016).

CULTURE AND RESILIENCY

The role or influence of culture on people's response to trauma has been addressed through Sotero's (2006) Model of Historical Trauma and other studies. A related concept and application of trauma work is research completed in Serbia, Bosnia and the Balkan Region on national identity, after the dissolution of Yugoslavia, (Biro, Mihić, Milan, & Logar, 2002; Đorđevic, 2003; Puhalo, 2003; Đorđević, 2007). The Western Concept of a National Identity is tied to sharing a common space, political and governing structure and recognized citizenship. The Non-Western view of National Identity involved a "subjective feeling related to genetic lineage and common ancestors." ((Đorđević, 2007, p.387). The Non-Western National Identity is that of of what Jung (Jung, 1916 (reprinted 2002)) called the collective unconsicous (shared history, myths, and archetypes). Đorđević (2007) completed a factor analysis of National Identity within Serbia comparing data from both 2003 and 2006 and determined there is an embedded factor of identity by this collective unconsious that exists outside of a country's borders. (Đorđevic, 2003; Đorđević, 2007) This embedded identity is what we refer to as a Psyche. It ties the history, traditions and share culture into an identity that can exist outside of traditional Western views of a National Identity and is resilient over time.

Viktor Frankel's interpretation of surivival in concentration camps describes attributes to those factors identified as essential to resiliency (Frankel, 1963). Serbians were found to have the following commonalities by Zunjić (1999): a traditional Greek-European way of thinking, being critical and self-reflective, and socio-cultural ties to their history, arts and religion ethnicity and mental belonging as part of their psyche. In 2006, the views of relationships among ethnic groups were studied on a continuum of flexiability. Flexibility is defined as the "degree to which they tolerate change among national identity." (Đorđević, 2007), p.385

Refugee studies conducted with a population exposed to the Marmara Earthquake in which 17,000 people were killed and 44,000 injuried (Aker, Onen, & Karakilic, 2007) points to cultural differences affecting the treatment of people exposed to disasters and trauma and decribes both the influence of Turkish and Muslim values related to the expression of symptoms and recovery. Aker (2007) sites other studies conducted by Sabucuoglu who investigated Bulgarian refugees and Yurbay who treated Albanian

Muslim children who were refugees from Kosovo and also found the importance of including cultural values in their treatment as well as a high resiliency within these populations.

In Sotero's Conceptual Model of Historical Trauma, a dominant culture oppresses a population or social group and creates an effect that increases exponentially- affecting the oppressed group's physical health, sociocultural, political, and economic status (Sotero, 2006). Cultural resiliency and other protective factors can influence the effects, as can mitigating or aggravating factors in later generations, as was found in the Native Hawaiian population (Ka'opua, Braun, Browne, Mokuau, & Park, 2011). Combining this research with that of other studies on resiliency in children, refugees and adults (Luther, Cicchetti, & Becker, 2000; Hoge & Pollack, 2007; Almedon, 2008; Atkinson, Martin, & Rankin, 2009) suggests some common factors in building resiliency. These factors are: problem solving (or using abstraction), collectivism (or a sense of group obligation over that of an individual), flexibility (an easy going personality), responsibility (with an internal locus of control), self-esteem, and communication.

Resiliency has been defined as an ability to respond positively to adverse events (Rutter, Tuma, & Lann, 1988) as a multidimensional process of adaptation (Almedon, 2008) and as an adaption despite adversity (Luther, Cicchetti, & Becker, 2000; Atkinson, Martin, & Rankin, 2009) The use of abstract thought was noted in children (Atkinson, Martin, & Rankin, 2009) to be a potential aggravating or mitigating factor dependent upon their family's communication and dynamics.

Bathory (2012a) completed an analysis of cultural values and dynamics comparing the Hawaiians Islands and the Balkan Region. In this study the following significant historical events and values were examined: exposure to trauma, and core values and beliefs: conquests, occupations and settlers, governing philosophies, healthcare and education, devastating illnesses, public healthcare/education, business and commerce, arts and culture, self-expression in sports, arts and creativity, emotions, trust, honor and value of others, home and sharing of knowledge, and communication. Information from these core values was then applied in rating the degree of influence a value had within the culture (high, moderate, or low) to better understand resiliency. Both the Hawaiians and the people of the Balkan Region were found to score high on cultural resiliency factors and have maintained their identities through their belief systems, values and the arts. Romanians share similar cultural characteristics and values as other people of the Balkan Region with the exception of self-esteem. Romanians tend to see themselves and their country as less powerful and less able than their Balkan allies.

Resiliency is influenced by culture and genetics, socioeconomic factors, as well as individual differences such as exposure to mutliple traumas and the response by others to these events. When an individual faces a life threatening event within a culture where they have no cohorts, their individual differences (genetics and life experiences) can have a greater impact than under other circumstances. In cultures where trauma is experience in mass (such as in wars or disasters) the underlying cultural values and collective dynamics have great influence on the expression of trauma. Cultural expression of these massive traumatic events is expressed on a continuim from emotionally overwhelmed or to supressed emotions, as if nothing unusual has occurred (De Zulueta, 2007). In the Balkans, where wars occurred over ten years ago, the experience of death, bombings, and interruption of life is a shared experience and expressed as life goes on- we will rebuild and survive. (Bathory D. S., 2013; Bathory D., 2012a; Bathory D. S., 2013a). With massive flooding, as experienced in 2010, 2011, 2012 and 2014 in Southeastern Europe and the Balkan Region, this same expectation, to rebuild and continue, is domainant.

In a meta-analysis of studies completed on resiliency it was concluded that to study resiliency requires a conglomeration of different fields within psychology, biology, anthropology, and economics (Almedon, 2008). In this analysis, clinical and community psychology (pathology), developmental psychology (studies of risk and resiliency in children), social work (studies of abuse), positive psychology (resiliency after trauma), theory and treatment by existentialism are interfaced with biology, anthropology, and economics. While Sotero's Model includes issues such as aggravating factors of war, devastating illness, systematic efforts of dismantling of the cultural, and economic and educational oppression and their role in enhancing resiliency, additional information is needed to explain cultural dynamics and resiliency. (Bathory D. S., 1993; Lasser & Bathory, 1997; Sotero, 2006)

Cultural growth can be partially explained within a traditional stage theory but is more accurately described using a model that allows for both progressions by steps, and reworking steps under new schemata with the ability to jump or skip between issues utilizing a reciprocal causal framework. Reciprocal causality is defined as "the result of events influencing themselves or mutually influencing each other. That is, they are interactive such that causes simultaneously can be effects for the same effects for which they are causes and vice versa." (Lasser & Bathory, 1997, p.149).

RELATIONSHIPS

In order to discuss Relational Dynamics it is necessary to first explore the premise of a basis for a working relationship. Figure 1 shows the difference between working relationships and non-working relationships and helps to define an operational definition of Relationship. Along the left side are a list of connections that parallel how invested we are in making this a working relationship. There is a continuum of involvement that spans from intense investment (love and hate) to where I am so disinterested that I don't even bother to look for commonalities. Relational Dynamics began with the idea of how relationships move from being non-cooperative, or indifferent to cooperative or working. Relationships can be either working or indifferent, where I am invested in a working relationship, or I really don't care about the other person in an indifferent one.

In working relationships, we wish for the other to understand us, even if it is a remote wish. Our relationship may be argumentative, but our desire is still to be understood, or to find a means to cooperate.

Figure 1.

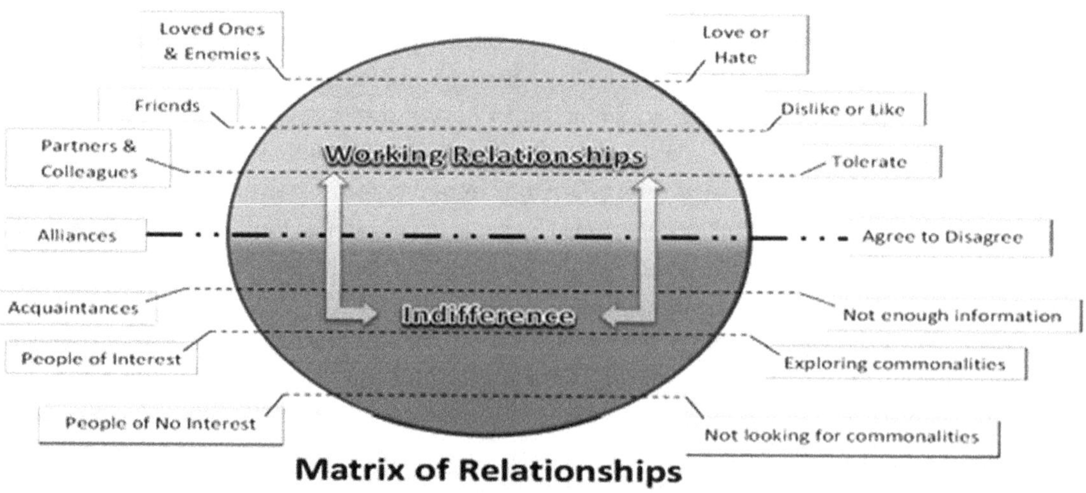

The exception to this is found when we pretend to have a working relationship, but there is no interest or desire to cooperate (often encountered in diplomatic forums), or where competition is valued over cooperation (such as academic settings and corporate environments, where cheating is used to gain advantage over others). In businesses where cooperation is valued over competition, the outcomes are often greater than what would have been developed or created independently. On the right side of Figure 1, are the corresponding feelings associated with the type of relationship. In Relationships where we have indifference, we care less and less about if the other person understands us. Just as in working relationships, we care more and more about if someone we are invested in, understands. Cooperation requires understanding, while competition to survive requires no understanding. If I ultimately kill everyone else off and am the last survivor, I may have won the competition, but in the end exterminated myself and my species. One needs only to look at corporate politics and the success and failure of businesses to see the destructiveness of competition among its employees and between companies. When we work together towards any goal, our probability of success increases, just as our probability of failure increases as we compete more and more. Figure 1 (Bathory D. S., 2013a) provides a comparison of working versus non-working relationships and their paired psychological state.

RELATIONAL DYNAMICS

Relational Dynamics was developed from a combination of psychodynamic, psychosocial, psychoneurological, non-linear mathematics and game theory in an attempt to understand the complexity of social interactions changing from non-cooperative to cooperative. It can also be applied to areas such as cultural development, art, architecture, behavioral economics, evolutionary biology, psychopathology, and psychological trauma. There are two main drives within relationships, acceptance and dominance. Dominance it the need to subjugate others and follows a continuum from force, control, influence and altruism. Force and control are selfishly motivated, that is the object is to gain more for the self than for others, while influence and altruism are more cooperatively motivated. True cooperation goes beyond the needs of the self and looks towards the needs of others and an overall benefit to a group or species. Acceptance is the need to join with others by similarities, congruence, or acknowledgement. Within this drive we are motivated individually, or driven by the opinions of others. The greater movement toward cooperative thoughts and behavior, the less invested a person is on the impact their actions have directly on them. In Acceptance we are most self-involved when we worry about punishment and least self-involved when we are concerned about our reputation, on individual and then group bases. Punishment is based in a 100% risk, I get caught or I do not get caught and so the attraction to win at all odds is high. Reputation is much more complex, it is how others will perceive our competence, our success and whether they will risk investing in us. Reputation can be based upon what is real (our accomplishments), what is fantasy (what is believed by others), and what is our potential (what we may be able to do based upon our luck and talents) or a combination of the three. In Relational Dynamics these two drives affect what strategies we chose to use to try to communicate with others and get our needs met. Our communications are based from a psycho-social strategy (or a particular way in which we view the world). The psychosocial strategies of Relational Dynamics are: Trust, Will, Purpose, Competence, Proof, Passion, Share, and Conjoint Wisdom.

Trust

Based upon Erikson's (1963) concept of trust when he examined both individuals and society, the basis of interaction begins with the ability to form relationships. A child forms trust when adult caregivers respond to their signals of distress. Interactions based in a trust strategy involve ideas such as, will someone come and save us, lead us, or give us correct information? If I cannot trust you, or have faith in you, I will reject you as a person of worth. I may still interact with you but my expectations, within our relationship, are few. You will, or will not provide me with something. I will not depend upon you, if I have no faith in you.

Will

Autonomy is seen as part of the separation of an individual from others. In terms of developmental psychology Freud, (1905) described this process of identification with the same sex parent and subsequent rejection as part of developing an independent self. Freud defined these as part of the Oedipal and Electra Complexes. As an infant develops object permanence around 18 months of age, and things are now separate from the child because they can appear and disappear, there is a development of an independent being. Within a relationship, if I am insecure about my own abilities, or insecure about you, I may choose to use a strategy of Will. I do the task myself, with the belief that I minimize harm to myself. The irony of this strategy is that I actually maximize my vulnerability by being alone. If I fail it is because of me alone; I am in isolation. When groups are insecure about their own abilities they tend to isolate and refuse interaction and input from others. As they become more secure or sure of their own abilities they too, look to others as a more welcome resource.

Purpose

Meaning or purpose, has been described as paramount in survival of individuals (Frankel, 1963). Viktor Frankel was a physician who was held in a concentration camp during World War II and noted that those who survived in the camp were the people who could find meaning in their life. Those individuals in the camps who could not find meaning, became ill, or died at the hand of others. Having a purpose, or meaning within our lives moves us toward working with others. If I wish to accomplish something, but do not have all the information or skills I need to obtain it, I begin to see the value of working with others to gain these key resources. In order to work with this strategy, I must have a sense of who I am. I must be defined sufficiently to complete a simple self-inventory. In this self-inventory, I assess do I have this information or skill, or not? If I cannot do this assessment, I am left with confusion. I have no sense of my own talents, no internal storage banks upon which I can rely for resources. Within a culture, this definition of purpose is also defining in essence who we are and how we define ourselves as members of a group. In determining meaning or purpose the group is questioning; Who are we? Why are we here? What do we hope to accomplish?

Competence

Erikson (1963) describes striving to demonstrate one's abilities and competency as Industry. Industry is doing, but it is first an internal analysis of whether I have the skills and abilities to accomplish some task. If I am interacting with another, I need to know not only if have a skill or ability on file, but a further assessment of how good am I at this particular task. This allows me the ability to strategize how much of my competence I will offer or share with another. If my assessment says I am unable to do certain things or do not have these skills, I find I am inferior and I am unable to complete whatever is required. I have omitted, or am void of these abilities. When a cultural or assimilates, they often lose their competency. The more powerful group does not value the same principles and values as the other culture and either punishes, or targets areas the minority group has held in esteem. (Sotero, 2006) When an individual evaluates their competency they complete an internal self-assessment and if faced with a lack of skills can either find a means of gaining these aptitudes, or they can attempt to overlook, or omit these absent abilities.

Proof

Proof, or evidence of what we are able to do is our way of showing our competence. Freud (1905) and Erikson (1963) both looked at the ability to demonstrate or prove oneself as evidence of maturity into adulthood. Within a relationship we demonstrate our competency and thereby establish the proof of our abilities, we lay our cards on the table, here is what I can do and here is what I cannot. If we cannot prove our abilities or do not have these abilities, we can lie. Lying is an act of commission, we intentional portray something as it is not. Proof is based in evidence, it is what you have done or can do.

Passion

Erikson, Frankel, and Freud all address passion within the developmental context of individuals (Freud, 1905 (1962); Erkison, 1963; Frankel, 1963). Expressing passion in relationships, or in work, is seen not only as proof of what we value, but as where we dedicate our energies or libido. Frankel cites passion and meaning as what made it possible for him and others to survive the brutality of a concentration camp. Passion is a powerful, but risky strategy, in that it delves highly into our emotions. Within passionate relationships, emotions divide respondents into two categories: those who can identify or understand our standpoint, and those who reject us. Passion tied with logical evidence often sways others into changing their beliefs. The difficulty lies in assessing whether the logical evidence is true, because we can be persuaded to change our beliefs based on lies. If someone cannot be persuaded to the same viewpoint, they become disinterested or indifferent to the cause. This strategy is very successfully used in political campaigns where the candidates and their supporters are often very passionate, and when paired with facts often bring those who were once opposed to become supporters. It also reflects the indifference politicians encounter when they are unsuccessful in engaging support.

Share

Sharing is the ability to be open and transparent. Sharing is reciprocal. It is impossible to share with someone if they are unable to be open in return, for then what is given becomes expertise, evidence or proof. Sharing encourages the other to cooperate. In looking at later stages of development both Erikson (1963) and Frankel (1963) explore the need for individuals to share their knowledge and abilities. Frankel identified this as so core to the human psyche that without this ability we perish under stressful conditions. Sharing implies a level of integrity, within a group where there is no fear of someone finding something that is less than perfect. Sharing allows for change and growth. If your information is better than mine in a sharing environment I assimilate your data, or ideas. Sharing tends to expand information beyond what each party beings to the table. The old adage, the sum is greater than its parts, is a good analogy for sharing and what develops because of reliance upon its use. If I cannot openly share, but I am attempting to look like I am being transparent, I must deceive you. I can use a variety of tactics to create deception, from omitting information, knowingly provide false information, or allow for partial or full misrepresentation.

Altruistic Wisdom

Erikson (1963) discussed wisdom for the individuals as reviewing their life accomplishments or failures with accuracy, as his last stage of development. Maslow (1943) points to a higher level of consciousness where individuals are able to transcend their own needs and welfare for the greater good of others. Few people are noted to reach these last stages of Erikson and Maslow, but this is not so within Relational Dynamics. When a parent chooses to have their child vaccinated against small pox, a disease that is not currently a threat or present within the world's population, they are acting out of altruistic wisdom. Despite the risk that may be involved to their individual child do to reactions to vaccines, this parent is looking out for the good of all people. Reactions to vaccines can result in compromised immune systems that challenge a child's ability to survive, allergies that cause systemic breakdowns and permanent dysfunction of organs, or ultimately death. If I am unable to act altruistically but am trying to portray my actions as such, I am being selfish, or have my own best interests at heart, rather than what is best for the whole. Acts of martyrs are often viewed as being altruistic, but it depends upon the internal motivation for the act being completed rather than the act itself. If as a parent, I comply with getting a vaccine simply out of my ignorance of the potential harm to my child, I am not acting out of altruistic wisdom. If I am an assassin and believe I am taking the life of another as a means of helping the world to become a better place, my act may be based in altruistic wisdom. The morality of my action, needs to be weighed outside of my internal motivation. This is how as a social system we condone wars, the act of killing the soldiers from the other side is viewed as saving us. The larger social system of the world then judges our acts to determine if they were for the good of all, for the good of a few, or merely selfish acts.

Within Darwin's evolutionary content of survival of the fitness (Darwin, 1859 (reprinted 1982)), altruism makes no sense. To value one's own ability to genetically survive less than the species is an act of altruism. Darwinian Theory cannot account for this kind of behavior, yet it is present in both humans and animals. Dawkin's (1989) further explored this concept in the Selfish Gene, where the predominant motive was to perpetuate an individual's genes into the next generation was challenged by Nowak (2011) in his work on the cooperative gene. The cooperative gene is in contrast to selfishness, in that it looks to continue the species or like genetics over the individual. It can be argued that common acts such as fighting for the civil liberties of people in other nations (or who are genetically unrelated) are acts beyond cooperation, they are in the best interest of the species.

Figure 2 contains a diagram of Relational Dynamics, it shows how the Drives of Acceptance (containing punishment and reputation) and Domination (encompassing force, control, influence and altruism) interface with history and the Psychosocial Strategies (represented by numbers) and the three types of History that interface within a relationship with one or more individuals, or between an individual and an object(s).

The psychosocial strategies of Relational Dynamics are not fixed and we adapt how we attempt to get our needs met by altering our strategies based upon our personal, collective and collaborative histories. In other words, in most interactions, we strive for cooperative understanding with who or whatever we are interacting. Dependent upon where the initiator of an interaction begins and the dynamic with the other person (the respondent) the two will volley back and forth until they can either find a common ground (a matched strategy) or they will remain in conflict. This dance between the two (or more) is the dynamic within the relationship. Just as the drives of Acceptance and Dominance function to meet our individual needs, the strategies we choose reflect components of our personality but fluctuate in our desire to reach a cooperative understanding. The exception to this is demonstrated with Personality Disorders, here, a psychological pattern of attempting to interact with others in relationships is stagnant due to an inability to alter psychosocial strategies, or is missing motivational needs around the drives of Acceptance and Dominance (Bathory D., 2015a) . The other exception is when one or more parties has the intention of not cooperating. This is demonstrated in strategies such as defectors, who believe that they will win by out maneuvering their opponents. The irony, is that they may win in the moment, becoming dominant over the other(s), but if the interactions continue over time, they lose. The cost to defecting is losing Acceptance of the others in the relationship and usually results in a breakdown of all gains in cooperation. Species and people who cooperate have superior outcomes over the long run (Nash, 1950; Axelrod, 2006; Nowak, 2011). When the two (or more people) are able to match, they hit an equilibrium point where everything resets back to new relational beginning. The difference between the first interaction, the second and subsequent interactions, is history.

See Figure 2 for how the histories are intertwined with the other concepts of Relational Dynamics. Our personal history, is what we have experienced, retained and created within fantasy, or delusion, as our past. In essence, it is what we claim as our experience. Delusion and fantasy are incorporated into

Figure 2.

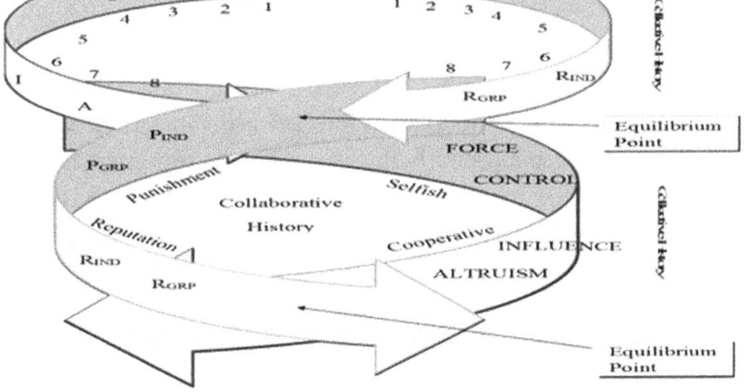

this history, because our experiences do not need to be real in order to be categorized and sequenced into our memory. Our memory is a combination of reality and fiction and our personal history is created from these stored memories. The collective history is based from Carl Jung's concept of the collective unconscious. Here a historical sequence of data is stored from our genetic ancestry and culture. It is partially responsible for why we have like preferences for things like styles of music, spices and foods with others who share our heritage. It also accounts for stored memories of significant trauma that is encoded into our genetic sequence, so that we do learn from our ancestors. I may have never encountered a large cat, like a mountain lion or tiger, but if we go back far enough in my ancestry, one (or more) of my ancestors has, and I carry both the fear of these potential predators and an innate knowledge of how to fight them. If I travel to a country of ancestral origin, I will encounter customs, language, food and pieces of the culture that I may have never been exposed to previously, yet I may feel a natural connect and comfort with them. This is evidence of Jung's concept of a collective unconscious and gives us a collective history. There is also evidence of a collective unconscious found in universal symbols, archetypal messages within art and monuments (Bathory & Lajbenšperger, 2014) and findings that support retention of traumatic memories in future generations (Bathory & Celik, 2014). The collaborative history is what happens between one or more individuals, or objects within an encounter. When we interact with another or interface with an object, we begin to create our collaborative history. We store information of each and every interaction we have with another. With each interaction our collaborative history builds and it can also include a realm of fantasy or delusion that is shared between us. Our personal and collective histories influence our collaborative history in what and how each of us chooses to disclose, suppress, or alter within an exchange. As humans, we retain the ability to consciously omit information from others and ourselves that not all animals possess this ability to deceive. Within our histories, we can erase or replace events consciously and unconsciously.

Neurobiology and Trauma

In 1914, Walter Cannon's ground breaking research determined the neurobiological pathways related to stress and their neurochemical basis (Cannon, 1914). Janet (1925) eloquently described the psychological complex of trauma, displayed by countless victims he treated from abuse victims and battle fatigue that were brought for treatment in the asylum where he cared for patients after World War I. He noted that dissociation was a key factor in their presentation, in addition to these individuals having temporarily lost their ability to function in their daily lives with the onset of the traumatic event. Of the populations treated within psychiatry facilities during this time period, few were considered to fully recover; trauma victims were the exception. Pavlov (1927) furthered neuroscience and learning theory, when he was able to define conditioning and reflexes. Here neuropsychology was able to begin to understand how to influence behavior through the paradigm of stimulus and response. Maier and Seligman's (1976) experiments with dogs and shock, lead to the theory of learned helplessness that has been applied to both depression and post-traumatic stress disorder. In learned helplessness the victim gives up after fruitless attempts to change its situation and loses hope for any outside intervention. Van der Kolk's (1987) work on psychological trauma combined knowledge in the field of trauma for over 100 years and created a model for explaining the neurobiological foundations and effects of trauma on the human brain and body. He was able to pair the neuroscience with the psychological expression of trauma and demonstrate how it is stored and retrieved within the body differently than other experiences. Bathory explored the psychological, neuro-biological and developmental consequences of trauma in children who were exposed to the murder of a parent (Bathory D. S., 1993), and proposed a novel theory that incorporated neurobiological trauma studies through history as well as developmental models that were being explored by Sroufe and Rutter (1984) and Rutter and Lann in (1988). In treating hundreds of children, adults and families exposed to life threatening events and designing clinical programs for their treatment (Bathory D. S., 1993; Lasser & Bathory, 1997) noted that individual and group treatment for psychological trauma could never reach the countless number of people who were exposed to events so severe that it alters their lives both psychologically and neurologically. This hypothesis has led to Relational Dynamics being applied to other venues outside of psychology such as Behavioral Economics and Architectural Design in order to discover ways to create mass interventions.

Since this time, work in psychological trauma has focused on refining theory and a more detailed understanding of the neurochemical changes related largely to pharmaceutical interventions. Research, in this area, has focused on the role of norepinephrine (NE) and primarily disregarded the influence of dopamine (DA) (van der Kolk, Roth, Pelcovitz, Sunday, & Spinazzola, 2005). Van der Kolk (1987) pioneered much of the more recent research in trauma theory beginning in the 1980's and there have been too numerous studies undertaken to begin to cite within the context of this paper the volumes of work completed in this area Perry explored the biological changes within the brains of children exposed to trauma and noted there were physical changes in structure and neurotransmitter function (Perry, 1993). The role of catecholamines (β adrenergic) and glucocorticoids within the hippocampal/pituitary axis (HPA) have been noted to atrophy in studies associated with stress and depression (McEwen, 2000; Mtra & Sapolsky, 2008). Subsequent studies have demonstrated organic brain alterations due to stress are centered in these same neural structures (Arnsten, 2009) (Jackowski, de Araujo, de Lacerda, & Mari, 2009; Nitschke, et al., 2009; Shackman, McManamin, Maxwell, Greischar, & Davidson, 2009).

When mammals are exposure to trauma (defined as life threatening events), neurotransmitters, and pathways within the brain that are involved in the natural response to stress can result in permanent biological or organic alterations. There a three major neurotransmitters involved in the response to trauma: norepinephrine (NE), dopamine (DA) and serotonin (5HT). These neurochemicals interact with each other in a symbiotic feedback system, balancing the necessary physical and emotional response to life threatening situations. When people are exposed to severe trauma an overload of NE creates an imbalance within the other systems and a rebound effect that can take months or years to return to stasis. In the case of repeated trauma, the body's response can result in a permanent depletion of receptors sites for one or more of these neurotransmitters, a release of larger amounts of neurotransmitters to create an excitatory or inhibitory response within efferent and afferent neurons as well as within the response of neural brain pathways. (Cannon, 1914; Pavlov, 1927; Maier & Seligman, 1976; Loewy, 1986; Bathory D. S., 1993; McCleery & Harvey, 2004; van der Kolk, Roth, Pelcovitz, Sunday, & Spinazzola, 2005; Ford, Phillips, & Williams, 2009; Jackowski, de Araujo, de Lacerda, & Mari, 2009) The amygdala is associated with transferring emotional responses to the prefrontal cortex that is a factor in affect regulation, interpretation of emotion and the processing of complex information (McEwen, 2000; Mtra & Sapolsky, 2008; Nitschke, et al., 2009). Cortisol which drives the HPA axis and SAM can result in changes due to allostatic load effecting memory (McEwen, 2000). The prefrontal area is not normally engaged in the immediate response to traumatic events but is highly involved later in adults as they process the experience. (Peres, Nasello, & Moores, 2008; Shackman, McManamin, Maxwell, Greischar, & Davidson, 2009; Arnsten, 2009). Figure 3 describes the interaction within these neurotransmitters and major pathways and regions of the brain related to trauma.

Figure 3.

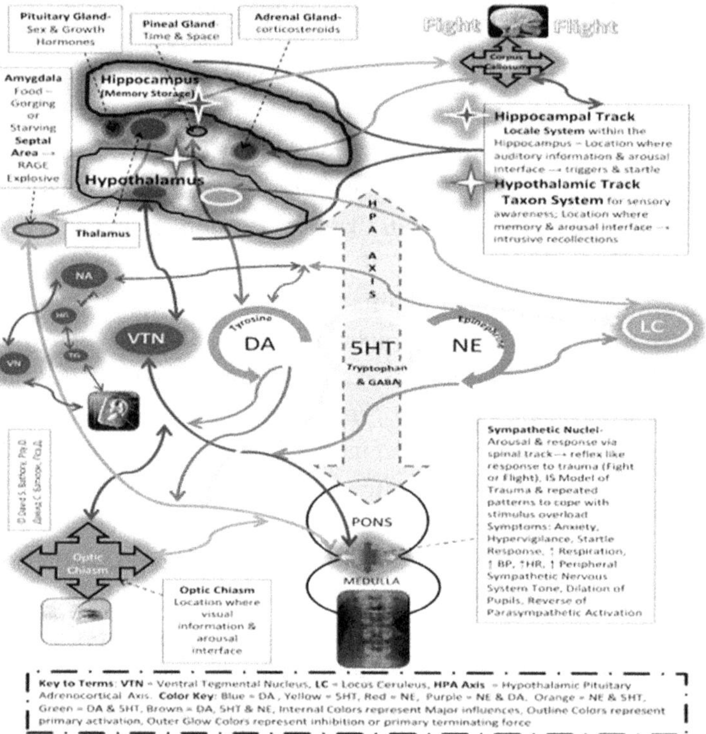

Relational Dynamics and Trauma

Trauma effects many of our interactions with the world by altering our storage and recall of senses and memory. The age at which a trauma occurs also encodes information differently. When interacting with others who have experienced trauma, the relationship needs to acknowledge these effects in order to gain the ability for movement. Traumatic experience is fixated, like that found in Personality Disorders (Bathory D., 2015a) Psychological Trauma in its most severe pathological expression results in Post-Traumatic Stress Disorder (PTSD). Here an individual is subjected to random relieving of their past trauma in the form of flashbacks, intrusive memories of the trauma and hypervigilance in an attempt to avoid re-triggering these experiences via sensory memory. Not all people who experience similar psychological trauma manifest the same symptoms. Some victims are able to overcome life threatening events with what appears to be little change while others are devastated. PTSD appears to mimic a brain injury in how it alters specific systems and functions of the brain. The mid-brain (hippocampus and hypothalamus) is particularly targeted by trauma. Encoding life threatening trauma is akin to laying the pavement for a 20 lane highway through the brain. The neural tracks that are formed are flooded by activation of Norepinephrine and stimulation of nerve thresholds. As these pathways are reinforced, messages fly through these centers to trigger instance responses. The role of Dopamine is to counter act the effects of Norepinephrine, but when excess Dopamine is available in the brain, it results in the ability to create flashbacks (a sensory replaying of events as if they are occurring again). Serotonin provides the ability for the body to begin to create a narrative of the event, moving it from sensory and reactive memory to higher brain processing centers within the cortex. Unfortunately, when there is no longer a true threat the response that is triggered is not always beneficial. If we were able to simply obliterate these trauma formed pathways, we would risk the survival of the individual, because they would then be unable to respond by a fight, flight (Cannon, 1914), or freeze pattern that is an essential response to threats. Adults recover from PTSD at a higher rate than children due to their ability to form new associations in their cortex that override more basic brain functions. Figure 4 (Bathory D. S., 2013) provides a breakdown of symptoms and their role in memory, cognition, affect, and physical expression associated with NE, 5HT and DA in response to stress or trauma.

Within Relational Dynamics dependent upon the age and development of the individual different fixations within the psychosocial strategies emerge. For example, a person exposed to trauma as an infant, will most likely have a fixation on trusting others or resort to the use of Will as their preferred strategy. As one matures, and develops psychosocially, the number of psychosocial strategies that are available for use increases. Adults who experience trauma have the greatest number of alternative strategies to cope with the onslaught of traumatic sequelae and neurobiological changes. Figure 5 provides the psychological effects of trauma by age and the preferred psychosocial strategies of Relational Dynamics when trauma occurs at the corresponding age group.

Application-Rural Tourism and Sustainable Energy

If a shallow canal were dug from a higher altitude that sloped continually downward, and this was lined with suspended solar panels that had limited movement: the runoff from rain and melting snow could be harnessed for power. These panels would be under the water's surface, by approximately .25 meter, and the canal would be a no more than a meter in total depth. By having the panels able to oscillate and be attached to a bar that passes through their center, the motion of the water passing over would create hydroelectric power. The fitting for the bars needs to limit the ability of movement, yet still create enough motion to make power. The bars would attach to a small turbines and run to a larger generator. See Figure 6.

Figure 4.

Figure 5.

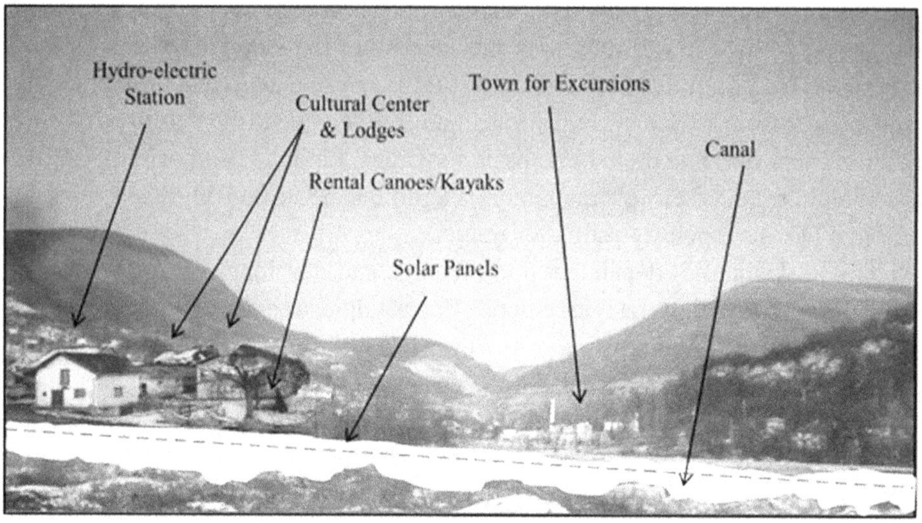

Figure 6.

	Dopamine (DA) Memory & Arousal	Serotonin (5HT) Affect & Memory	Norepinephrine (NE) Arousal & Affect
Memory	Sensory Motor memory Sensory Account of event Proprioception (Location in Space) Locomotion (movement) Sequencing (in time)	Affective Memory Feelings associated with events or triggers Sequencing of events allowing a narrative account of the trauma	Arousal Memory Immediate proprioception Immediate locomotion
Cognition	Dissociation Attention Hypervigilance Intrusive recollections Flashbacks Recurring Nightmares	Preoccupations & intrusive thoughts Processing of feelings (guilt, self-reflection, responsibility) Cognitive increases or decreases, or slowing of thoughts Narrative account of event & feelings	Distortion of time Fight or Flight Cortical inhibition or flooding thoughts Hypervigilance Dissociation Attention Use of Taxon System Bypass of normal Sensory Motor Information & retrieval
Affect	Irritability Rage & explosive outbursts	Labile moods Profound emotions Emotions associated with event	Loss of interests, pleasures or obsession Anxiety Rage & explosive outbursts
Physical	Psychomotor retardation Appetite Disturbances Sleep deregulation & nightmares Hormone & Endocrine deregulation Long term hypervigilance	Appetite disturbances Insomnia (due to intrusive thoughts) Hormone & Endocrine deregulation Changes in eye contact, energy level	Immediate fight or flight response (↑ HR, ↑ BP, ↑ Respirations, anxiety, startle response, ↑ peripheral & sympathetic tone response (shutdown of nonessential functions), dilation of pupils, eventual resetting of CNS

When the water flows over the panels and generates power, it also creates waves or a phenomenon similar to white water river rapids. These white water rapids can be used in tourism for canoeing, kayaking, and inner tubing in the spring, summer, and fall months. During the winter, when the water freezes, the panels can be moved into a stationary position and create a surface for ice skating, tobogganing/sledding. Water can flow over the panels creating an uneven surface and moving surface. The natural slope of the surface becomes flat when the panels are stationary and during freezing temperatures. While stationary, the solar panels would still function as they are placed beneath a thin layer of fresh water ice. This change in the position of the panels permits solar power to be harnessed over all four seasons (the exception would be when it becomes too cloudy, debris covers the surface of the water or overcast and sun light is very limited).

If these channels or canals begin in mountainous regions, the runoff that may cause flooding can be diverted from existing rivers when snow melts or from heavy rains. Larger reservoirs can be created to hold water supplies in some areas and control the release of water, block debris, and reduce sediment to keep the water clear via gates.

Along the routes, a cultural center and lodge, recreational rentals for equipment, outdoor camping, and restaurants can be provided for tourist and visitors. A hiking trail can be created alongside the canal that passes through each site where a hydro-electric generator is located. Local crafts and traditions can be featured at events and festivals to promote tourism and the retention of ancestral customs and heritage such as music, art, theater, and dance. If small towns or cities are nearby, electric buses or trains could transport people for excursions to local attractions (museums, castles, churches/temples, universities, etc.). Area residents can be trained and hired to monitor the hydroelectric generator, solar panels, be water, and hiking guides, teach sports, maintain rental equipment as well as fill positions in hospitality.

This type of project is usually best implemented in phases. Phase I would begin with a smaller example of the overall project, in order to demonstrate its' sustainability and profit. In Phase II a larger area (or number of channels and trails) could be created and in Phase III these pathways connected to form a web of interconnecting waterways and power for the entire region or country. Electric power could be sold to neighboring areas, as well as fresh water (if there is a surplus). Figure 7 describes what a Phase I portion may look like when completed.

Neurobiological and Psychological Rationale for This Project

Global warming and its subsequent climatic changes have been predicted to continue, as a result of these effects, Europe appears to be entering a time period when winter temperatures will be lower and there is increased precipitation. As a result of these changes in climate there has been increased flooding in spring due to melting snow from higher elevations, and from larger amounts of rainfall. Many people are displaced from their homes either temporarily or sometimes permanently due to these flooding disasters. In some communities the devastation has been so severe, entire towns, communities or countries have been effected (Steffen, 2011; Sharp, 2012; Sito-Sucic & Djurica, 2014). Natural disasters have both psychological and neurological residual effects to people. Most people do not exhibit psychological symptoms so severe that they warrant mental health diagnoses and treatment: they are able to continue functioning in their daily lives and have relationships with others. To assist these individuals with the impact of a disaster or multiple disasters, there are interventions that can be made to communities and nations (Almedon, 2008; Bathory D. S., 2013). In this instance, creating sites where water power is harnessed and utilized for electricity (heat, air conditioning, and general power needs) assists the

Figure 7.

Factor		Age 0 to 5	Age 6 to 12	Age 13 to 18	Age 18 Plus
Psychological Presentation	Self	Helpless, Passive, Defenseless, Unable to take action or alter Trauma, Magical Powers	Helpless but not passive observer, survivor guilt, expressed as Identification with the aggressor. Belief of no control over destiny	Personal ownership of actions, loss of a sense of being vulnerable, sensitive, feelings of guilt, a belief that there will be no future, live for the moment	Ownership of actions, able to take action and see their role or actions in the event. Survivor guilt or identification with the aggressor, future exists but there is a lack of commitment to it.
	Symptoms	Nightmares, Flashbacks with sensory focus, withdrawn, subdued, aloof, re-enactment of central action of trauma. Aggression and activity, look like Attention Deficit Hyperactivity	Cognitive constriction, decline or improved school performance, either aggressive or avoidant, re-dramatizations of trauma. Poor social skills, nightmare and flashbacks with the ability to sequence events, looks like ADHD or Bipolar Disorder	Antisocial identity formation and poor work values versus premature adulthood, guarded, ability for abstract though allows for sequencing paired with responsibility, fear of stigma and labelling, looks like ADHD or Bipolar Disorder	Life is futile, inability to commit in relationship or work, can be paired with antisocial or borderline personality disorder, episodes of major depression and often looks like Bipolar Disorder
	Responses	Regression, denial in fantasy, action and affect, wish fulfilment, dissociation, sublimation and accommodation	Denial by cognitive style of forgetting, repression, inability for spontaneous though, primativation, somatization, dissociation, sublimation and accommodation.	Turning against self to distract from anxiety and painful memories/feelings, guilt, dissociation, somatization, primativation, repression, regression, sublimation, and accommodation	Repression, dissociation, denial, somatization, repression, sublimation and accommodation.
Psychosocial Strategy Preferences with stress		Trust, Will	Trust, Will, Purpose, Competence	Trust, Will, Purpose, Competence, Proof, Passion	Trust, Will, Purpose, Competence, Proof, Passion Share, Altruism

economy, redefines what was once harmful to be helpful, and provides a sustainable green power source (independent of oil and natural gas).

In the circumstance of repeated severe flooding or devastation by flooding, the ability to control and interact with water in a positive manner may assist with healing. For adults, controlling the flooding can be accomplished by employment involved in the project (e.g. monitoring and maintaining the hydro-electric plant, teaching canoeing and kayaking). Traumatized adults have full access to all the psychosocial strategies in helping them to address their trauma from the flooding. If they are fixated in a particular area, it is most likely due to having experienced a similar trauma in their earlier life, a co-morbid personality disorder, or complex trauma. Complex trauma is repeated exposure to psychological traumatic events. Adolescents may be involved in rebuilding and maintaining the natural life and trails around the canal, as they need to reform a safe relationship with water and nature. As they are able to utilize multiple psycho-social strategies, they can choose from any of the following to address their traumatic experience; Trust, Will, Purpose, Competence, Proof, or Passion. Adolescents who are able to see their impact in readjusting from a traumatic experience are less likely to feel that they are helpless victims. This is important, because developmentally, they are at a point in time where feeling empowered determines their ability to be functional and resilient adults. Becoming knowledgeable environmental activists in caring for the land and water also assists adolescents with their healing process. Preschoolers often focus on the most salient feature of a trauma, in the case of a flood it may be the rising water, and the fear found in what adults see as a potential life threatening event. A contained pool or smaller area that is staffed by school age children, who can teach water safety, canoeing and kayaking skills, creates a venue of mastery for the school age children and a natural environment of healing for preschoolers. This focuses on strategies, for the preschoolers, related to their Trust and Will and for the school age children addresses Trust, Will, Purpose, and Competence. Both of these roles will assist the school age children and the preschoolers in building their resiliency to trauma. Senior citizens may provide a multitude of support in teaching and guidance roles, as they are the holders of cultural values and are invested in the betterment of their children and ancestors. As seniors do not encode trauma differently than mature adults, their choice of psychosocial strategies encompasses all eight positions. To generate successful recovery from trauma, interventions must provide appropriate cultural, age and developmentally alternatives. Interventions designed for adults are not successful with younger children and adolescents.

In marketing tourism, or any product or service, the underlying principles of culture and trauma theory as applied to the target audience must be considered. It is paramount to include the target audience's age, sex, and other background information such as socioeconomic status, and education. While it is advantageous to be aware of the culture and populations being worked with by understanding their cultural dynamics but to also essential realize the potential permanent or long term harm that can occur when this type of information is misused. For example, breaking trust with a person, population, or nation, where there has already been experience with dominance and force often leads to never being able to reconcile the betrayal. It is necessary to match a group or culture's cultural dynamics, in order to be able to begin a meaningful relationship. Once this interpersonal dynamics is reached, the process of moving forward or coming to a mutual agreement is possible (even when the mutual agreement is to disagree).

In cases of natural disasters and wars unaddressed trauma effects not only the people who are directly exposed, but can involve their unborn children and others exposed to the occurrence by the media, creating even larger exposed populations (Kaitz, Levy, Ebstein, Faraone, & Mankuta, 2009; Bathory & Celik, 2014). This can result in hypervigilance, detachment, more incidents of physical and substance abuser, addictions, as well as an increase in the number of personality disorders (e.g. borderline, antisocial, avoidant personality disorders) for their children. Often increases in anxiety related illnesses, such as gastrointestinal disorders, migraine/cluster headaches, decreases in immunity and a variety of other medical conditions and symptoms can arise. It behooves a public health conscious region or country to find ways to help their residents heal from traumatic events rather than wait for the ensuing manifestations of mental illness and disease.

DISCUSSION AND CONCLUSION

The application described in this chapter focuses on rural tourism and sustainable green energy as a means of healing mass trauma, but also will improve living conditions and the economics for a region or country. In providing mass interventions to populations exposed to trauma and who are not in need of traditional mental health treatment, Relational Dynamics paired with our current understanding of trauma theory, allows people to heal before becoming potentially more harmed, or disabled. The outcome of providing interventions to the currently exposed generation impacts the next generation both psychologically and neuro-biologically. If interventions are made in a thoughtful manner they can provide economic and psychologically benefits for the current generation and generations to come. Relational Dynamics began from the roots of exploring the basics of understanding relationships and grew into how to assist large groups of people affected by life threatening events that better their lives and the lives others. Relational Dynamics has been applied in the areas of Architecture, Behavioral Economics, Education, Evolutionary Biology, Healthcare, and Psychology.

In creating future applications for Relational Dynamics, John Nash's (1950) non-cooperative game theory can be looked to for guidance. He describes the concept of looking for the best solution for all as being advantageous over that of one. Nash's theory has been applied to a variety of disciplines since its conception with the same outcome: When resources are pulled together towards a best (or common) solution – all may win or benefit rather than there be a "loser". Nash stated, "There are situations in politics in which, effectively a group of interests involved in a non-cooperative game without being aware of it, the non-awareness helping to make the situation truly non-cooperative," (Nash, 1950)(p23). [1]

In this quote, Nash was insightful as to the potential applications of his work in game theory and its ability to be utilized in other fields. A combination of the ability to work towards the common welfare within the context of what is morally best, we have described, as con-joint wisdom. Most world diplomacy and business still relies on strong arm tactics and dominance, either by physical, psychological, or economic actions. Influence in business and diplomacy is largely more manipulative than truly a con-joint process; as Nash stated; an underlying agenda makes negotiations that are perceived to be collaborative as actually being intended to create the opposite result. When leaders are able to work con-jointly worlds can change by peaceful means because they are able to look for the "best" solution for all involved rather than themselves. In business, con-joint relationships focus on the welfare of all. Often public health campaigns are an example of a con-joint process, such as the tobacco industry's efforts to decrease smoking and providing people with current information on the risks of smoking that is supported by both governments and the industry.

In earlier marketing strategies the tobacco corporations were focused on profit, gaining a larger market, and controlling all research and information regarding smoking. By these private corporations providing the funding for the majority of research completed on the effects of smoking, they controlled consumer information. It required government interventions to open this stronghold and in some countries smoking advertisements were banned or scrutinized heavily to ensure their target audience were not minors. Rather than these corporations responding by continued lawsuits, they were able to not only comply to the laws, but to take a higher ethical or developmental stance and see the benefit of a greater good (public health). These companies now fund most of the anti-smoking programs and campaigns throughout the world. Despite the dissemination of excellent information and state of the art interventions, they have not lost their market of smokers; this points to the ability for business to function with a greater social consciousness.

In looking at diplomatic relationships, intimate and marketing there is a progression of lessening dominance and oppression that mirrors the dynamics from positions of force, control, and influence to con-joint or cooperative. In business ventures, the majority of the world powers still rely on tactics of force (takeovers), control (market restrictions), or as with influence - are barely able to consider the other's point of view (mergers and elimination of the competition). These tactics are not only antiquated but are ineffectual in most situations; in a global world there is business and the ability for profit for everyone if it is undertaken in a cooperative manner. Since Relational Dynamics can be used to determine the best strategies to apply when trying to create responses of force, control, influence or altruism in others, it is also subject to being misused by people whose intent is to deceive or manipulate. In reality this is no different than the abuse of any psychological theory that provides understanding of the human psyche, but because of Relational Dynamics ability to be applied to so many different fields the risk of its misapplication grows exponentially. It is this author's intent that this theory not aide or encourage the negative manipulation and destruction of others.

The applications of Relational Dynamics are only as limited as topics that include human relationships; but as with any knowledge and understanding of people's vulnerabilities and strengths, it is meant to be used within the premise of Hippocrates Oath "to do no harm first" (Hippocrates, 2009). The challenge remains for the populous of the world to take information we learn about how humans function and use this knowledge for the betterment of all, rather than mere individual profit or control over others.

REFERENCES

Aker, A. T., Onen, P., & Karakilic, H. (2007). Psychological Trauma: Research and Practice in Turkey. *International Journal of Mental Health*, *36*(3), 38–57. doi:10.2753/IMH0020-7411360306

Almedon, A. (2008). Resilience Research and Policy, Practice Discourse in Health, Social, Behavioral and Environmental Sciences Over the Past Ten Years. *African Health Sciences*, 5–13.

Arnsten, A. (2009). Stress Signaling Pathways that Impair Prefrontal Cortex Structure and Function. *National Review of Neuroscience*, 410-422.

Atkinson, P., Martin, C., & Rankin, J. (2009). Resilience revisited. *Journal of Psychiatric and Mental Health Nursing*, *16*(2), 137–145. doi:10.1111/j.1365-2850.2008.01341.x PMID:19281544

Axelrod, R. (2006). *The Evolution of Cooperation*. Basic Books.

Bathory, D. (2012). The Preservation of a Cultural Psyche: A Comparison of the Hawaiian Islands and the Balkan Peninsula.*Hawaii University International Conference of Arts and Humanities* (pp. 1-21).

Bathory, D. (2014). Healing Worldwide Wounds- Applied Trauma Theory and Relational Dynamics. *International Journal of Applied Behavioral Economics*, *3*(2), 1–14. doi:10.4018/ijabe.2014040101

Bathory, D. (2015a). Behavioral Health and Relational Dynamics. *International Journal of Applied Behavioral Economics*, *4*(2), 36–52. doi:10.4018/ijabe.2015040103

Bathory, D. (2015b). Personality, Relationships, and Decision Making with Relational Dynamics. *International Journal of Applied Beahvioral Economics*, 52-74.

Bathory, D., & Celik, F. (2014). Intergenerational Trauma & Relational Dynamics. In *Proceedings of the 5th Global Conference on Trauma*. Prague: Interdisciplinary Net.

Bathory, D., & Lajbenšperger, N. (2014). The Collective Mind in Design and Relational Dynamics. *Зборник Матице Српске за Ликовне Уметхости*, 209-223.

Bathory, D. S. (1993, July). *Psychological, Neurobiological and Developmental Consequences of Trauma in Children* (Unpublished Doctoral Dissertation). Forest Institute of Professional Psychology, Honolulu, HI.

Bathory, D. S. (2012). Entrepreneurial Characteristics and Relational Dynamics. In *Proceedings of CReBUS 9th International Conference on Higher Education and Entrepreneurship*. Bucharest, Romania: EU & CReBUS.

Bathory, D. S. (2013a). Applied Psychological Trauma Theory and its Reflection in Architecture: Wounds and Memorials. In A. Кадујевић (Ed.), Простори Памћења Spaces of Memory Volume 1 Architecture (pp. 375-394). Belgrade, Serbia: Faculty of Philosophy University of Belgrade & Museum of Applied Art.

Bathory, D. S. (2013b). Economics and Practical Applications for Applied Trauma Theory: Sustainable Engery and Rural Tourism. *International Journal of Applied Behavioral Economics*, *2*(2), 41–55. doi:10.4018/ijabe.2013040103

Bathory, D. S. (2014). The Mugs of Reflection & Relational Dynamics. *5th Global Conference on Trauma*. Prague, Czech Republic: Interdisciplinary Net.

Bathory, D. S. (2015). The Proof for Evolution and Coming Out of Prison with Relational Dynamics. *International Journal of Applied Behavioral Economics*, *4*(1), 58–69. doi:10.4018/ijabe.2015010104

Bathory, D. S. (2016a). *Interdisciplinary Perspectives with Relational Dynamics*. IGI Global. Retrieved from http://www.igi-global.com

Bathory, D. S. (2016b, May 20). Design and Decision Making. In *Design and Decision Making*. Belgrade, Serbia: University of Belgrade.

Bathory, D. S. (in press). Stress Decision Making and Relational Dynamics. *International Journal of Applied Behavioral Economics*.

Biro, M., Mihić, V., Milan, P., & Logar, S. (2002). Did Socio-Political Changes in Serbia Changed the Level of Authoritariansm and Ethnocentrism of Citizens? *Psihologija*, 37-47.

Cannon, W. B. (1914). The Emergency Function of the Adrenal Medullla in Pain and the Major Emotions. *The American Journal of Physiology*, 356–372.

Darwin, C. (1859). *The Origin of the Species*. London: Penguin Books. (reprinted 1982)

Dawkins, R. (1989). *The Selfish Gene*. Oxford Press.

De Zulueta, C. (2007). Mass Violence and Mental Health: Attachment and Trauma. *International Review of Psychiatry (Abingdon, England)*, *19*(3), 221–233. doi:10.1080/09540260701349464 PMID:17566900

Đorđevic, J. (2003). Jedan Pokušaj Klasifikacije Teorijskih Rasmatranja Nacionalnog Identiteta. *Psihologija*, 125-140.

Đorđević, J. (2007). Primordialistic Concept of National Identity in Serbia. *Psihologija*, 385-397.

Erkison, E. (1963). *Childhood and Society*. New York: Norton.

Ford, C., Phillips, D., & Williams, J. (2009). The Time Course of Dopamine Transmission in the Ventral Tegmental Area. *The Journal of Neuroscience*, 133344–133352. PMID:19846722

Frankel, V. (1963). *Man's Search for Meaning*. New York: Pocket Books.

Freud, S. (1962). Three Essays on the Theory of Sexuality. Basic Books.

Gleick, J. (1987). *Chaos: Making a New Science*. Penguin Books.

Hippocrates, . (2009). *The Corpus*. New York: Basic Books.

Hoge, E. A., & Pollack, M. (2007). Resilience: Research Evidence and Conceptual Considerations for Post-traumtic Stress Disorder. *Depression and Anxiety*, *24*(2), 139–152. doi:10.1002/da.20175 PMID:16892420

Jackowski, A., de Araujo, C., de Lacerda, A., & Mari, J. (2009). Neurostructural imaging findings in chidlren with post-traumatic stress disorder: Brief Review. *Psychiatry and Clinical Neurosciences*, *63*(1), 1–8. doi:10.1111/j.1440-1819.2008.01906.x PMID:19154207

Janet, P. (1925). *Psychological Healing: A historical and clinical study*. New York: MacMillan.

Jung, C. (1916). *Psychology of the Unconscious*. Dover-Mineola, NY: Yard and Company. (reprinted 2002)

Kahneman, D. (2003). Theories of Decision Making in Economics. *The American Economic Review*, 1449–1475. doi:10.1257/000282803322655392

Kahneman, D., Slovic, P., & Tversky, A. (1982). *Judgement under Uncertainty: Heuristics and Biases*. Cambridge, UK: Cambridge University. doi:10.1017/CBO9780511809477

Kahneman, D., & Tversky, A. (1974). Judgement under uncertainty: Heuristics and Biases. *Science*, 1124–1131.

Kahneman, D., & Tversky, A. (1979). Prospect Theory: An anlaysis of Decision under risk. *Econometrica*, *47*(2), 263–291. doi:10.2307/1914185

Kaitz, M., Levy, M., Ebstein, R., Faraone, S., & Mankuta, D. (2009). The Intergenerational Effects of Traums from Terror: A Real Possiblity. *Infant Mental Health Journal*, *30*(2), 158–179. doi:10.1002/imhj.20209

Kaopua, L., Braun, K., Browne, C., Mokuau, N., & Park, C. (2011). Why Are Native Hawaiians Under-represented in Hawai(i)s Older Adult Population? Exploring Social and Behavioral Factor of Longevity. *Journal of Aging Research*, *2011*, 1–8. doi:10.4061/2011/701232 PMID:21966592

Lasser, K. J., & Bathory, D. S. (1997). Reciprocal Causality and Childhood Trauma: An Application of Chaos Theory. In *The Psychological Meaning of Chaos* (pp. 147–176). Washington, DC: American Psychological Association. doi:10.1037/10240-006

Loewy, A. (1986). *Central Regulation of Autonomic Functions*. New York: Oxford University Press.

Luther, S., Cicchetti, D., & Becker, B. (2000). The Construct of Resilience: A Critical Evaluation and Guidelines for Future Work. *Child Devleopment*, 543-562.

Maier, S., & Seligman, M. (1976). Learned Helplessness: Theory and Evidence. *Journal of Experimental Psychology. General*, *105*(1), 3–46. doi:10.1037/0096-3445.105.1.3

Maslow, A. (1943). A Theory of Human Motivation. *Psychological Review*, *50*(4), 370–396. doi:10.1037/h0054346

McCleery, J., & Harvey, A. (2004). Integration of Psychological and Biological Approaches to Trauma Memory: Implications for Pharmacological Prevention of PTSD. *Journal of Traumatic Stress*, *17*(6), 485–496. doi:10.1007/s10960-004-5797-5 PMID:15730067

McEwen, B. (2000). Allostasis and Allostatic Load: Implications for Neuropsychopharmacology. *Neuropsychopharmacology*, *22*(2), 108–124. doi:10.1016/S0893-133X(99)00129-3 PMID:10649824

Mtra, R., & Sapolsky, R. (2008). Acute corticosterone treatment is sufficent to induce anxiety and amygdloid dendritic hypertrophy.*Proceedings of the National Academy of Science*, 5573-8.

Nash, J. (1950). *Non-cooperative Games* (Unpublished Doctoral Dissertation). Princeton University, Princeton, NJ.

Nitschke, J., Sarinopoulous, I., Oathes, D., Johnstone, T., Whalen, P., Davidson, R., & Kalin, N. (2009). Anticipatory Activationn in the Amydala and Anterior Cingilate in Generalized Anxiety Disorder and Prediction of Treatment Response. *The American Journal of Psychiatry*, 1–10. PMID:19122007

Nowak, M. (2011). *Super Cooperators: Altruism, Evolution, and Why We Need Each Other to Survive*. Free Press.

Pavlov, I. (1927). *Conditioned reflexes: An investigation of the Physiological Activity of the Cerebral Cortex*. New York: Dover.

Peres, F. M., Nasello, A., & Moores, K. (2008). Traumatic memories: bridging the gap between functional neuroimgaging and psychotherapy. *Australian and New Zealand Journal of Psychiatry*, 478-488.

Perry, B. (1993). Neuro-development and the Neurophysiology of Trauma I: Conceptual Consideration for Clinical Work with Maltreated Children. *The Advisor*, 14-18.

Puhalo, S. (2003). Etnička distanca građana Repubike Srpske i Feeracije BiH prema narodima bivše. *Psihologija*, 141-156.

Rutter, M., Tuma, A., & Lann, I. (1988). *Assessment and Diagnosis in Child Psychopathology*. Guilford Press.

Shackman, A., McManamin, B., Maxwell, J., Greischar, L., & Davidson, R. (2009). Right Dorsolateral Prefrontal Cortical Activity and Behavioral Inhibition. *Psychological Science*, *20*(12), 1500–1506. doi:10.1111/j.1467-9280.2009.02476.x PMID:19906125

Sharp, T. (2012, November 27). *livescience*. Retrieved from www.livescience.com

Simon, H. (1955). A Behavioral Model of Rational Choice. *The Quarterly Journal of Economics*, *69*(1), 99–118. doi:10.2307/1884852

Simon, H. (1959). Theories of Decision Making in Economics and Behavioral Science. *The American Economic Review*, 253–283.

Sito-Sucic, D., & Djurica, M. (2014, May 19). *Floods affect over 1 million in Balkans, destruction terrifying*. Retrieved from Reuters: www.moblie.reuters.com

Sotero, M. (2006). A Conceptual Modela of Hisotrical Trauma: Implications for Public Health Practice and Research. *Journal of Health Disparities Research and Practice*, 93-108.

Sroufe, L., & Rutter, M. (1984). The Domain of Psychopathology. *Child Development*, *55*(1), 17–29. doi:10.2307/1129832 PMID:6705619

Steffen, A. (2011). *World Changing: A User's Guide for the 21st Century*. New York: Abrams.

Stone, C. (2012, November 2). *US News and World Report*. Retrieved from www.usnews.com

van der Kolk, B. (1987). *Psychological Trauma*. Washington, DC: American Psychiatric Press.

van der Kolk, B., Roth, S., Pelcovitz, D., Sunday, S., & Spinazzola, J. (2005). Disorders of Extreme Stress: The Empirical Foundation of a Complex Adaption to Trauma. *Journal of Traumatic Stress*, *18*(5), 389–399. doi:10.1002/jts.20047 PMID:16281237

Zunjić, S. (1999). An Introduction to the Study of Serbian Philosophy. *Gledšita*, 5-77.

ENDNOTE

1 Quote and citation with permission of The Princeton Archives, Princeton University, Princeton, NJ, USA.

Chapter 9
Engineers' Perceptions of Contract Types' Performances for Highway Construction Projects

Fani Antoniou
Aristotle University of Thessaloniki, Greece

Georgios N. Aretoulis
Aristotle University of Thessaloniki, Greece

Dimitrios K. Konstantinidis
Alexander Technological Educational Institute, Greece

Glykeria P. Kalfakakou
Aristotle University of Thessaloniki, Greece

ABSTRACT

Research focuses on the perceptions of engineers towards highway projects contract types' (CTs) performance and their respective selection criteria (SC). A questionnaire survey evaluated the CTs against the selected criteria. The SPSS database's sample consisted of 91 engineers from Greece and abroad. Factor analysis identified groups of selection criteria representing the performance of each CT and reflecting the engineers' perceptions. Patterns of changes in engineers' assessment of the contract types' performance were noted and justified. Apart from the total sample, analysis considered participants' subgroups, such as Greek and foreign engineers, and experienced engineers in the private and public sector. Nationality and experience of participants influence the factors' content. Moreover, a number of criteria tend to cluster together irrespective of CT and engineers' profile. These pairs of criteria include all uncertainties' criteria, Scope and Process Uncertainty, Contractual Difficulties and Claims, and finally Value for Money and Criticality of Schedule.

DOI: 10.4018/978-1-5225-1826-6.ch009

INTRODUCTION

The construction industry is mostly concerned with one – of – a – kind projects. This, naturally, creates difficulties for effective management control (Aretoulis et al., 2006). Construction projects shape the built environment in which people live and work (Rose & Manley, 2011). According to Baccarini (1996) the construction process may be considered the most complex undertaking in any industry. Indeed, construction is a product-oriented activity that has many dimensions. One of these dimensions is the business side of construction. The business aspects of construction require the establishment of contractual relationships with a wide range of parties. The central role played by contracts is reflected by the fact that construction firms are referred to as "contractors" (Halpin & Senior, 2011).

Since the late 1980's early 1990's the importance of choosing the most appropriate CT has been evident in the construction industry (Veld & Peeters, 1989; Ward & Chapman, 1995). It is a fact that the construction professional must not only be able, technically, to build the building, but must be able to get it built amid all sorts of adverse forces that have a power today that they have never had before. In some cases, the power is legislated and in some cases it is not, but in all cases it is capable of slowing or halting the project (Lancaster, 2001).

Highway construction projects are multidisciplinary projects. The project stakeholders are people with very different background and objectives. Ojo et al. (2011), highlighted the complexity of construction projects because they bring together professionals within the building industry to form an organizational team to acquire the building.

The procurement process of any major infrastructure project includes the design phase, tender phase and construction phase. In the design phase the Owner determines the need for the realization of the project, carries out a feasibility study and completes the required designs either through an internal design team or through outsourcing. In the tender phase the project budget and tender documents are prepared by the Owner based on the definitive design and a construction tender procedure is carried out according to the relevant legislation and the chosen Project Procurement System (PPS). Finally, during the construction phase the project is constructed according to the contractual documents and supervision is achieved on behalf of the Owner in-house or by outsourcing to a Construction Manager (CM). The major participants in the above procedure are the Owner, also known as the Client, the Design Consultant, Contractor and Construction Manager (CM). The PPS chosen defines the number and types of contracts drawn up between the major participants. The number and type of contractual relationships between the major participants are crucial in terms of time, cost and quality achievement of the resulting project.

Badenfelt (2011) suggested that: "Tensions are frequent and serious in interorganizational projects in which the contracting parties share uncertainty about many important changes that occur after the contract is signed and production begins". Therefore, it was anticipated that a whole body of law has grown up around the many facets of contractual relationships. Because these issues remain constant for most construction situations, contract language in the construction industry has been normalized over many years and a variety of standard contract forms have developed (Halpin & Senior, 2011).

Selection of the most suitable CT may partly define project's success. Research has focused on available CTs and their characteristics, SC to consider during the process of identifying the best performing CT, and even multicriteria decision making applications to facilitate the selection process. SC along with their weights define the dominant CT. Other SC have equal significance and other are assigned lower weights during the decision making process. This fact leads to the creation of latent groups of SC based on the assessment and evaluation of the criteria's significance. Therefore, this paper examines the perception of engineers regarding the performance of CTs against selection criteria. Research, tries to identify these groups of criteria. In this context, a factor analysis takes place based on the total sample, then focuses on the Greek and foreign participants, and finally considers the most experienced engineers in public and private construction sector. Clusters of criteria are created against each contract type. The research highlights the factor content in each case and provides a rational interpretation of the outcome based on the engineers' profile.

In the following sections a literature review is carried out regarding CTs and SC, then methodology and findings are presented and discussed. Finally, conclusions and future work are highlighted.

LITERATURE REVIEW

Contract Types and Selection Criteria

A project is a temporary and unique endeavour undertaken to deliver a result (Vidal et al., 2011). Liu et al. (2012) suggested that in a project, work is typically divided into work packages which are contracted to different contractors. However, the number of contractors and the contract type are parameters which influence the project complexity (Bosch-Rekveldt et al., 2011). Focusing on the contractor selection, Ng and Skitmore (2001) presented an empirical study aimed at ranking prequalification criteria for contractors on the basis of perceived total cost–benefit to stakeholders.

Incorporation of incentives in various contract types is widely considered in current highway projects realization. In this context, Tang et al. (2008) focused on the incentives which have been increasingly applied to align the objectives of participants in the delivery of construction projects.

Cost overruns in transportation infrastructure projects is a frequent phenomenon creating tensions and claims among the contracting parties. Flyvbjerg et al. (2002) cited in Doloi (2011) indicated that in the United States, a comparative study conducted on actual and estimated costs showed that the costs in transportation infrastructure projects were significantly underestimated.

Goodrum et al. (2009) developed a decision - making system for accelerating the process of roadway construction by providing the necessary time to develop the design and contract agreements to accommodate and facilitate types of accelerated construction methods.

Irfan et al. (2011) considered fixed-duration and fixed-deadline contracts. Their research presents mathematical relationships between highway project duration and the magnitude of the planned cost, project type and contract type. Lai and Lam (2010) researched the importance of perceived performance criteria and identified timely completion of the project as the most important performance criterion, followed by profit, environmental protection and quality.

Construction projects are extremely complex endeavors. According to Mayer and Argyres (2004) and Wang et al. (2008) cited in Bröchner and Badenfelt (2011) one strategy for reducing complexity of contracting is to rely on standard forms of contracts.

Meng and Gallagher (2012) suggested that application of incentives aligns the objectives of different project parties and focuses efforts to important performance improvement. The contractor in an incentive project needs to make both internal and external efforts.

Chan et al. (2011) focused their research on target cost contracts (TCC) or guaranteed maximum price (GMP) contracts. They provided empirical evidence concerning identification, ranking and comparison of the key risk factors encountered with these forms of procurement.

Principal component factor analysis was used by Cheung et al. (2009) in order to classify identified aggressive–cooperative drivers of construction contracting.

Anastasopoulos et al. (2010), using data on maintenance contracts from around the world, developed models that compare several contracting methods.

The literature review showed that for public works contract types, there are numerous reports relating to

1. The evaluation of their performance in terms of the final cost, duration and quality of resulting project (Boukendour & Bah, 2001; Howard et. al., 1997; ITA, 1996; Paul & Gutierrez, 2005; Turner & Simister, 2001),
2. Proposals for new contracting methodologies (Wilmot & Cheng, 2003).
3. Proposals for new or combinations of award criteria (Lambropoulos, 2007; Padhi & Mohapatra, 2009; Ungern-Sternberg, 1994) or even modifications of the lowest bid criteria (Wang et.al., 2006)
4. The evaluation of contractor performance under contracts containing incentives for early completion, lower cost and better performance (Author et al., 2012; Arditi, 1997; Bower et. al., 2002; Jaraiedi et. al., 1995; Tang et. al., 2008) and e) proposals of methods for calculating incentives (Al-Subhi Al-Harbi, 1998; Arditi & Yasamis 1998; Berends, 2000; Jafaari, 1996; Shr & Chen, 2003; 2004).

Following the international literature and current practice in Greece, it was concluded that the CTs to be investigated are shown in Table 1 and Table 2.

The choice of evaluation criteria was based on the results of an extensive literature review into the most commonly considered evaluation criteria. Table 3 depicts the chosen selection criteria to be included in this research, as they were the most frequently proposed in the quoted research papers. The selection criteria that were included in the survey against which each CT was rated on a Likert scale from 1 to 5, are shown in Table 4 along with an explanation of each rating scale.

Table 1. Contract types

Contract Type	Short Description
Cost plus fixed fee (CPFF)	The client reimburses the contractor for all audited costs & pays a fixed amount for the contractor's services.
Cost plus percentage fee (CPPF)	The client reimburses the contractor for all audited costs & pays an additional percentage fee.
Cost plus incentive fee (CPIF)	All justified costs are paid but the final fee depends on the actual costs as compared to target cost, delivery and/or performance achievements.
Incentive/ Disincentive for time reduction (ID/T)	The contractor is paid in addition to the agreed payment method a bonus (incentive fee) if the project is completed earlier and pays a penalty (disincentive fee) if it is completed after.
Fixed price incentive (FPI)	The contractor is paid his actual costs in addition to an agreed upon fee while he guarantees that the total cost to the owner will not exceed maximum amount.
Lump sum / fixed price (LSFP)	The client pays a fixed price to the contractor irrespective of the actual cost.
Unit price method (UPM)	The contractor commits to fixed prices for pre-specified units of material or work required for the project. Payment is the sum-product of the unit prices and the actual units used.

Antoniou et al. 2012.

Table 2. Literature review on CTs

No.	Author	Year	CPFF	CPPF	CPIF	ID/T	FPI	LSFP	UPM
1	Herten and Peeters	1986			√	√	√		
2	Veld and Peeters	1989	√	√	√	√	√	√	√
3	Ward and Chapman	1994	√		√			√	
4	Herbsman et. al.	1995				√			
5	Jaraied et. al.	1995				√			
6	Ward and Chapman	1995	√	√	√		√		
7	ITA working group	1996	√			√		√	√
8	Jaafari	1996			√	√			
9	Arditi et. al.	1997				√			
10	Howard et. al.	1997	√		√	√			
11	Al-Harbi	1998	√		√		√		
12	Arditi and Yasamis	1998			√	√			
13	Herbsman and Glagola	1998				√			
14	Berends	2000	√		√		√	√	
15	Boukendour and Bah	2001	√				√		
16	Turner and Simister	2001	√	√				√	√
17	Broome and Perry	2002		√	√			√	
18	Bower et. al.	2002			√	√			
19	Bubshait	2003			√	√	√		
20	Piarc	2003		√	√				√
21	Shr and Chen	2003				√			
22	Shr and Chen	2004				√			
23	Missbauer and Hauber	2005							√
24	Olsen and Osmundsen	2005			√		√		
25	Paul and Gutierrez	2005	√	√				√	√
26	Boukendour	2007	√	√			√	√	√
27	Gruneberg et. al.	2007							
28	Lambropoulos	2007							√
29	Tang et al.	2008			√	√			
30	Padhi et. al.	2009							
31	Bröchner and Badenfelt	2011	√	√	√		√		
32	Chan et. al.	2011b					√		
33	Chan et. al.	2011a					√	√	
34	ITA working group 3	2011							√
35	Rose and Manley	2011			√	√			
36	Meng and Gallagher	2012	√	√	√	√	√	√	

Antoniou et al. 2013.

Table 3. Selection criteria as found in the literature

Selection Criteria (Freq)	Source
Cost Uncertainty (7)	Veld and Peters 1989, Ward and Chapman 1994, ITA 1996, Berends 2000, Boukendour and Bah 2001, Bower et. al. 2002, Carty 1995
Uncertainty of Scope (5)	Veld and Peters 1989, Ward and Chapman 1994, ITA 1996, Boukendour and Bah 2001, Turner and Simister 2001, Carty 1995
Process Uncertainty (2)	Veld and Peters 1989, ITA 1996, Turner and Simister 2001
Value for Money (2)	Ward and Chapman 1994, ITA 1996
Criticality of Schedule (4)	Veld and Peters 1989, Jaraiedi et.al. 1995, Herbsman and Glagola 1998, Bower et. al. 2002
Performance Criticality (5)	Veld and Peters 1989, Ward and Chapman 1994, Jaraiedi et.al. 1995, Berends 2000, Bower et. al. 2002
Availability of extra resources (4)	Veld and Peters 1989, ITA 1996, Berends 2000, Turner and Simister 2001
Contractual Difficulties (3)	ITA 1996, Berends 2000, Turner and Simister 2001
Claims (3)	Jaraiedi et.al. 1995, Herbsman and Glagola 1998, Berends 2000

Antoniou et al. 2012.

Table 4. Explanation of rating scale for each selection criteria used in survey

Criteria	Each CT Was Rated as 5 (in a Scale of 1 to 5) for Optimum Performance When
Cost Uncertainty	It is difficult to estimate the final construction cost and the client wishes to avoid the risk of cost escalation
Uncertainty of Scope	The technical characteristics of the project are not specifically defined
Process Uncertainty	Construction methodologies are unknown at start or are expected to be complex
Value for Money	It provides the most efficient method for obtaining value for money
Criticality of Schedule	The duration of the contract is critical
Performance Criticality	It provides incentive for excellent quality and avoids cutting corners
Availability of extra resources	It requires adequate staff in numbers and experience to supervise and/or manage the contract
Contractual Difficulties	It is simple to implement and does not require specialised calculations
Claims	It reduces the number of claims expected

Antoniou et al. 2012.

RESEARCH METHODOLOGY AND FINDINGS

The aim of the current research was firstly to identify the factors in the case of each CT per sample and try to explain the factors' content. Then the research identified and compared variations in the factors' content across same contract types but different participants' samples. The research methodology is depicted in Figure 1.

Figure 1. Research methodology

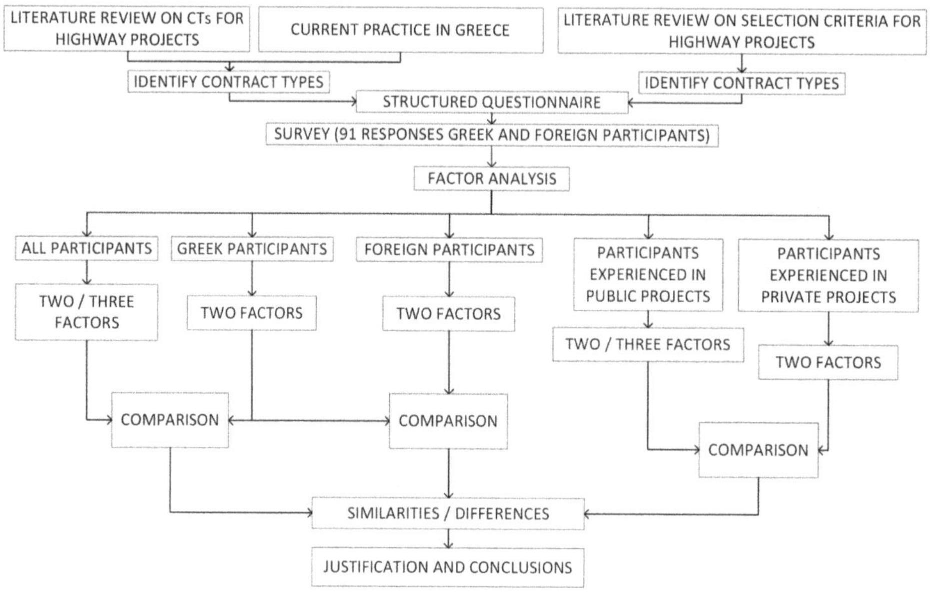

Definition of Factor Analysis

Factor analysis identifies unobserved variables (factors) that explain patterns of correlations within a set of observed variables. It is often used to identify a small number of factors that explain most of the variance embedded in a larger number of variables. It can also be used to generate hypotheses regarding the composition of factors (Hinton et al., 2004; Field, 2009; Mooi & Sarstedt, 2011). In other words, factor analysis is concerned with whether the covariances or correlations between a set of observed variables can be explained in terms of a smaller number of unobservable constructs known either as latent variables or common factors (Landau & Everitt, 2004). The approach employed in this paper is the Exploratory Factor Analysis (EFA).

According to Field (2009), factor analysis identifies common factors among a group of variables. This methodology reduces the dimensions of the problem and creates new variables, called "factors", thus explaining correlations that exist in data. The interesting thing in this type of analysis is that it tries to further explain data structure despite the volatility (variation). The process thus, determines occurring unobserved variables (factors), and explains relationships between groups of the observed variables.

According Pramangioulis (2008), "the steps of factorial analysis include the following:

1. **Investigation of Correlations' Existence:** The simple correlation coefficient calculates the correlation between two variables while ignoring the rest. The usefulness of factor analysis focuses on its ability to calculate the correlation, after subtracting the effect of other variables. In order to use factor analysis, partial correlation coefficients should be small (Pramangioulis, 2008). A measure to compare the relative magnitude of the correlation coefficients of the partial correlation coefficients is the Kaiser-Meyer-Olkin (KMO) statistical measure calculated as follows:

$$KMO = \frac{\sum_j r_{ij}^2}{\sum_j r_{ij}^2 + \sum_j a_{ij}^2} \tag{1}$$

where r_{ij} and a_{ij} are the sample correlation coefficients and partial correlation respectively. If the value of KMO is great, then the data is suitable (> 0.5) for factor analysis (Pramangioulis 2008).

2. **Export of Factors:** According to the SPSS User's Guide (2004), methods that can be used by SPSS for extracting the factors include:
   a. Analysis of the main components (Principal Components Analysis).
   b. Unweighted least squares method (Unweighted Least-Squares Method).
   c. Method of generalized least squares (Generalized Least-Squares Method).
   d. Maximum likelihood method (Maximum-Likelihood Method).
3. **Rotation of the Factors:** Then are the so-called "rotation factors" to make factors more interpretable. Rotation maximizes the value of the loading of each variable in one of the exported factors, while minimizing the loading on all of the other factors. This process clarifies which variables correspond to which factors (Field, 2009).
4. **Assessment of the Performance of Factors for Further Statistical Use:** These factors are expressed as a linear combination of the original variables, where each factor can be written as:

$$\begin{aligned} F_1 &= \alpha_{11} \cdot X_1 + \alpha_{12} \cdot X_2 + \ldots + \alpha_{1m} \cdot X_m \\ F_2 &= \alpha_{21} \cdot X_1 + \alpha_{22} \cdot X_2 + \ldots + \alpha_{2m} \cdot X_m \\ &\ldots \\ F_k &= \alpha_{k1} \cdot X_1 + \alpha_{k2} \cdot X_2 + \ldots + \alpha_{km} \cdot X_m \end{aligned} \tag{2}$$

The coefficients a_{ij} are the variables' X_{ij} score on F_i factor and should not be confused with the loadings. When the model has been estimated by the method of principal components, the factors are accurate, can be calculated without error, something that does not exist when the maximum likelihood method is used. Note that the new variables have mean 0 and are uncorrelated since the model is rectangular (Pramangioulis, 2008).

Questionnaire Survey and Description of Pool of Respondents

The main questionnaire survey was conducted during the last two years, 2010 - 2012. The survey collected 91 answers from engineers with various roles and involvement in project realization, such as designers, constructors, contractors, public authorities, funding managing authorities and academians, from Greece and abroad. The first part of the questionnaire, was devoted to the participants, who responded to a number of personal questions regarding their professional background that included: nationality, gender, current professional status, years of experience in design, construction, supervision and project management, years of experience in public and private sector, years of experience with various CTs.

The questionnaire presented and explained the various CTs along with their performance criteria and the range of grading the various CTs.

Questionnaires were completed through interviews and emails. The survey participants were highly experienced engineers, involved in the procurement of extensive highway construction projects. Furthermore, participants should represent all the types of stakeholders involved in the project realization. Greek participants were selected based on the degree of involvement in highway project contracting. The greatest highway project in Greece, during the last years was "Egnatia" and most of the participants were actively involved. Foreign participants were chosen according to their experience with the research topic, through a relevant conference workshop. From the total of 91 responses, Greek participants were 65 and foreign participants were 26. Foreign participants' nationalities are presented in the following table. From the total of 26 Foreign participants only 2 of them have worked both in Greece and abroad.

Regarding current occupational status, 14 are in highway design, 26 in Construction Supervision, 31 respondents are currently employed in project management or what is known in Greece as the Superior Authority and finally 20 respondents are in construction. Participants with public sector experience represent the 78% of the sample, while participants with some private sector experience represent 70% of the pool of respondents. Finally, 75 male and 16 female participants took part in the survey. As far as the quality of the sample is concerned, the result of the Cronbach's Alpha computation (= 0,919) reveals that the measure has high internal consistency.

SPSS Database Architecture and Content

The SPSS Database includes 91 cases (engineers), both Greek and Foreign participants. The variables include data concerning the profile of the survey participants, namely: origin, current occupational status, years of experience in project design, project supervision and project management, years of experience in public and private sector, years of experience with each contract type and project procurement method. All data were properly codified and transformed into categorical type. In order to record the evaluation of each contract type against each criterion, a composite variable was proposed, which reflects the way each CT performs against each criterion "Contract Type per Criterion". In this case the total variables are 84. There is one variable for each contract type against each criterion (63 variables). The other 21 variables included demographics and experience per certain projects, contract types and procurement systems, which were not used in factor analysis. Factor analysis considered the following samples and number of factors:

- **Whole Sample:** 2 and 3 factors,
- **Greek and Foreign Participants:** 2 factors, and
- **Experienced Engineers in Public and Private Projects:** 2 factors.

Table 5. Nationality of foreign participants

Italy	Australia	Usa	Belgium	Uk	Hungary	Romania	Spain	New Zealand	Austria	France	Malaysia	Japan	Ireland
1	1	4	1	7	2	1	1	1	1	1	1	2	2

In each case the results were presented, compared and discussed. Initially, the SPSS database which consisted by 91 respondents was divided into two distinct databases of Greek and foreign participants. Then, the database was rearranged to focus on engineers with a significant (over 10 years) experience in public and private projects. The number of CTs and SC was 7 and 9 respectively. The analysis was run 7 times, (one time per each of the seven Contract Types). Two and three factors were selected to be created. Analysis assumed that the created factors did not correlate with each other, thus the varimax rotation was selected and the chosen method for extraction was principal component analysis. All results had very high determinant scores and adequate KMO scores. The factor analysis' results will be presented in the following paragraphs along with the KMOs scores.

Three-Factor Analysis: All Participants

In this case for each contract type there exist three factors and each one of them includes a number of criteria. Table 6 presents the results for each CT, for the whole sample.

Table 6 shows that in most cases certain criteria tend to group together under certain contract types. In most cases "Uncertainty of Scope" groups with "Process Uncertainty" which is something to be expected. Both criteria are also associated with the initiation of the project. When the project scope is uncertain, the processes of the project are not defined in detail, as well. The relationship among these criteria could be characterized as cause and effect. When such a relationship exists among a number of criteria, participants tend to group them together. In this case, it is not only the similarities that group criteria together, but also a causal relationship. In addition, in most factors "Contractual Difficulties" group together with "Claims", which is also expected. Claims are caused by events which are not covered in the original contract. Furthermore, claims could be considered as a sub-product of the contractual difficulties or even a possible outcome. It could be also considered as a cause and effect relationship. Similarly, "Value for Money" tends to group with "Criticality of Schedule". These results appear to be quite logical and remain almost constant across the various contract types. Time and cost, in construction projects, usually go hand in hand. In the mind of engineers, the concepts of time, cost and quality are united. For the contractor, an increase in the project schedule causes an increase in the project cost. Considering the project owner, each highway project that delays, causes money or loss of income for the public. It is true that when the project schedule deviates, then associated costs occur. Furthermore, "Performance Criticality" accompanies "Availability of Extra Resources" and groups with "Process Uncertainty".

One of the goals is to explain how and why the factors form in regard with the contract type under consideration. More precisely focusing on each CT, it can be suggested that:

- **Unit Price Method (UPM):** The first factor appears to collect all uncertainties Table 6. Factor two, refers to financial and contractual matters, and factor three deals with quality, time and resources. This type of contract is considered useful when it is difficult to precisely define the quantities (uncertainty of scope and cost) prior to tendering (Carty, 1995; Permanent International Association of Road Congresses' (PIARC), 2003; Turner & Sinister, 2001). This explains why factor (1) attracts all the uncertainties. In addition, factor (1) includes criteria usually associated with the project initiation while factors (2) and (3) with project execution and performance. Moreover, factor (1) includes a number of concerns and considerations to be dealt by the contractor. Factor (2) mostly concerns both parties, namely the project owner and the contractor. In the

Table 6. Results of factor analysis: 91 participants (factors: three)

CTs/KMO	Factors – Sample of 91 Respondents		
	1	2	3
UPM / 0,66	Uncertainty of scope	Contractual difficulties	Performance criticality
	Process uncertainty	Value for money	Criticality of schedule
	Cost uncertainty	Claims	Availability of extra resources
ID/T / 0,69	Value for money	Availability of extra resources	Criticality of schedule
	Cost uncertainty	Claims	
	Process uncertainty	Contractual difficulties	
	Performance criticality		
	Uncertainty of scope		
FPI / 0,6	Performance criticality	Value for money	Claims
	Process uncertainty	Cost uncertainty	Contractual difficulties
		Uncertainty of scope	Criticality of schedule
			Availability of extra resources
LSFP / 0,49	Uncertainty of scope	Criticality of schedule	Contractual difficulties
	Process uncertainty	Value for money	Cost uncertainty
	Performance criticality	Claims	
	Availability of extra resources		
CPIF / 0,51	Claims	Uncertainty of scope	Performance criticality
	Contractual difficulties	Process uncertainty	Criticality of schedule
	Cost uncertainty	Availability of extra resources	Value for money
CPPF / 0,57	Contractual difficulties	Value for money	Performance criticality
	Process uncertainty	Cost uncertainty	Availability of extra resources
	Claims	Criticality of schedule	
	Uncertainty of scope		
CPFF / 0,58	Performance criticality	Value for money	Contractual difficulties
	Availability of extra resources	Cost uncertainty	Claims
	Uncertainty of scope	Criticality of schedule	
	Process uncertainty		

case of factor (3), another point of view could be that "Availability of Extra Resources" associates with "Schedule" and "Quality". This could be characterized as a causal relationship.

- **Incentive/Disincentive for Time Reduction (ID/T):** The core and critical parameter in this type of contract is project duration. Table 6, shows that "Criticality of Schedule" is indeed identified as a special parameter, as it represents a single factor (3) by itself. In comparison to the UPM CT it can be observed that the criteria describing pre-tendering uncertainties remain together and are joined by performance criteria (Value for money and Performance Criticality). The remaining factor collects the criteria relating to contractual execution (Availability of Extra Resources, Claims and Contractual Difficulties).

- **Fixed Price Incentive (FPI):** "Claims" and "Contractual Difficulties" again appear to team together. Factor (2) focuses on cost and scope criteria. Indeed one of the most sensitive aspects and vulnerabilities that threaten this type of CT are related to project scope according to international literature (Chan et al., 2011). The third factor includes two main sub-groups that usually cluster together, which are namely:
  - Claims and Contractual Difficulties,
  - Criticality of Schedule and Availability of Extra Resources.
- **Lump Sum/Fixed Price (LSFP):** According to literature this type of CT is usually associated with significant contractual disputes and the cost risk always falls on the contractor. This is clearly highlighted in the 3rd factor (Contractual Difficulties and Cost Uncertainties). In addition, factor (2) refers mainly to cost and schedule concerns. In the 1st factor, "Uncertainty of Scope" and "Process Uncertainty" are associated with quality and the need for extra resources to ensure that quality cuts are not attempted by the contractor in order to increase the profit margin.
- **Cost Plus Incentive Fee (CPIF):** Alike UPM, ID/T, FPI, CPPF, CPFF, "Claims" and "Contractual Difficulties" team again, since any change in the project scope causes contract / incentives renegotiation if the initial tender cost estimate is not accurate. Within the second factor "Uncertainty of Scope" clusters together with "Process Uncertainty" similarly with the case of UPM, ID/T, LSFP, CPIF, CPPF and CPFF. These two types of uncertainties may require additional personnel and experience ("Availability of Extra Resources"). Factor (3) includes the three criteria relating to the project performance (time, cost and quality).
- **Cost Plus Percentage Fee (CPPF):** The first factor is the most heavily loaded with criteria. Once again "Contractual Difficulties" and "Claims" go hand in hand. The latter are followed by "Process Uncertainty" and "Uncertainty of Scope". Indeed this contract is useful in the case that the project scope is not clearly defined from the beginning. The second factor considers time and cost issues while the third factor deals with quality and resources.
- **Cost Plus Fixed Fee (CPFF):** In this case factor (3), which is clearly occupied by the team of "Contractual Difficulties" and "Claims", deals with contract negotiation. The second factor is identical with the second factor of the CPPF contract type, concerning mainly cost and time. "Process" and "Scope" uncertainties are once more clustered together.

In almost all CTs "Uncertainty of Scope" and "Process Uncertainty" cluster together. In 4 out of 7 cases (CTs), "Performance Criticality" and "Availability of Extra Resources" team together. Furthermore, "Contractual Difficulties" and "Claims" are joined together in 6 out of 7 cases.

Three - Factor Analysis: Participants with Public Service Experience Over 10 Years

It is possible that each sub-group of respondents may have a different perspective regarding the performance of each CT against the selected criteria. The research moves on to focus on the most experienced engineers. Thus, the analysis was carried out on the ratings provided by those participants with greater than 10 years' experience in public sector. These results are shown in Table 7 and it can be seen that the resulting factor groups were almost identical with the corresponding ones from the whole sample, except for the CPPF and the CPFF contract types. CPPF, while allowed according to Greek law, is only employed in practice for small scale projects while the CPFF is not employed for Greek public work projects and this could partly explain the outcome.

Table 7. Results of factor analysis: public service experience over 10 years (factors: three)

CTs/KMO	Factors – Sample of 52 Respondents with Public Service Experience over 10 Years		
	1	2	3
UPM / 0,61	Uncertainty of scope	Contractual difficulties	Performance criticality
	Process uncertainty	Claims	Value for money
	Cost uncertainty		Availability of extra resources
	Criticality of schedule		
ID/T / 0,55	Value for money	Availability of extra resources	Criticality of schedule
	Cost uncertainty	Claims	
	Process uncertainty	Contractual difficulties	
	Performance criticality		
	Uncertainty of scope		
FPI / 0,65	Performance criticality	Value for money	Claims
	Process uncertainty	Cost uncertainty	Contractual difficulties
		Uncertainty of scope	Availability of extra resources
		Criticality of schedule	
LSFP / 0,38	Uncertainty of scope	Criticality of schedule	Contractual difficulties
	Process uncertainty	Value for money	Cost uncertainty
	Availability of extra resources	Claims	Performance criticality
CPIF / 0,47	Claims	Uncertainty of scope	Performance criticality
	Contractual difficulties	Process uncertainty	Criticality of schedule
	Availability of extra resources	Cost uncertainty	Value for money
CPPF / 0,53	Cost uncertainty	Uncertainty of scope	Claims
	Availability of extra resources	Process uncertainty	Contractual difficulties
	Value for money		Criticality of schedule
	Performance criticality		
CPFF / 0,52	Performance criticality	Cost uncertainty	Value for money
	Uncertainty of scope	Contractual difficulties	Criticality of schedule
	Process uncertainty	Availability of extra resources	Claims

Table 10 shows that comparing CTs with similar philosophy, the following could be concluded:

- The CPFF, CPPF and CPIF contract types have identical factors' content,
- LSFP and UPM contract types have a lot of similarities in their factors' content,
- FPI and CPIF also have a lot in common and only "Contractual Difficulties" are different among these contract types.

Table 11 presents the results of factor analysis regarding Greek engineers.
Table 12 presents the results of factor analysis regarding foreign engineers.

Table 8. Results of factor analysis: public service experience over 10 years (factors: two)

CTs/KMO Types/ KMOS	Factors – Sample of 52 Respondents with Public Service Experience over 10 Years	
	1	2
CPFF / 0,52	Uncertainty of scope	Contractual difficulties
	Value for money	Availability of extra resources
	Cost uncertainty	Criticality of schedule
	Performance criticality	
	Process uncertainty	
	Claims	
CPPF / 0,52	Cost uncertainty	Process uncertainty
	Value for money	Uncertainty of scope
	Availability of extra resources	Contractual difficulties
	Performance criticality	Criticality of schedule
	Claims	
CPIF / 0,47	Claims	Value for money
	Cost uncertainty	Performance criticality
	Uncertainty of scope	Availability of extra resources
	Process uncertainty	
	Contractual difficulties	
	Criticality of schedule	
IDT / 0,55	Uncertainty of scope	Contractual difficulties
	Performance criticality	Criticality of schedule
	Cost uncertainty	Claims
	Process uncertainty	Availability of extra resources
	Value for money	
FPI / 0,65	Claims	Uncertainty of scope
	Availability of extra resources	Value for money
	Performance criticality	Cost uncertainty
	Process uncertainty	Criticality of schedule
	Contractual difficulties	
LSFP / 0,38	Uncertainty of scope	Cost uncertainty
	Performance criticality	Value for money
	Availability of extra resources	Claims
	Process uncertainty	Criticality of schedule
		Contractual difficulties
UPM / 0,66	Process uncertainty	Value for money
	Uncertainty of scope	Performance criticality
	Cost uncertainty	Availability of extra resources
	Claims	Contractual difficulties
	Criticality of schedule	

Table 9. Results of factor analysis: private service experience over 10 years (factors: two)

CTs/KMO	Factors – Sample of Respondents with Private Service Experience over 10 Years	
	1	2
CPFF / 0,48	Performance criticality	Value for money
	Claims	Cost uncertainty
	Process uncertainty	Criticality of schedule
	Uncertainty of scope	
	Contractual difficulties	
	Availability of extra resources	
CPPF / 0,64	Uncertainty of scope	Value for money
	Process uncertainty	Cost uncertainty
	Contractual difficulties	Criticality of schedule
	Performance criticality	
	Claims	
	Availability of extra resources	
CPIF/ 0,51	Uncertainty of scope	Value for money
	Process uncertainty	Cost uncertainty
	Criticality of schedule	Contractual difficulties
	Performance criticality	Availability of extra resources
	Claims	
IDT / 0,45	Performance criticality	Criticality of schedule
	Uncertainty of scope	Claims
	Process uncertainty	Availability of extra resources
	Value for money	Contractual difficulties
	Cost uncertainty	
FPI / O,54	Process uncertainty	Value for money
	Performance criticality	Criticality of schedule
	Uncertainty of scope	Cost uncertainty
	Contractual difficulties	Availability of extra resources
		Claims
LSFP / O,57	Process uncertainty	Value for money
	Uncertainty of scope	Criticality of schedule
	Performance criticality	Cost uncertainty
	Availability of extra resources	Claims
		Contractual difficulties
UPM / 0,57	Uncertainty of scope	Criticality of schedule
	Cost uncertainty	Claims
	Process uncertainty	Contractual difficulties
	Value for money	Availability of extra resources
	Performance criticality	

Table 10. Results of factor analysis: 91 participants (factors: two)

CTs/KMO Types	Factors – Whole Sample	
	1	2
CPFF / 0,58	Uncertainty of scope	Value for money
	Performance criticality	Cost uncertainty
	Process uncertainty	Criticality of schedule
	Availability of extra resources	
	Claims	
	Contractual difficulties	
CPPF / 0,57	Uncertainty of scope	Value for money
	Process uncertainty	Cost uncertainty
	Claims	Criticality of schedule
	Performance criticality	
	Contractual difficulties	
	Availability of extra resources	
CPIF / 0,51	Uncertainty of scope	Value for money
	Performance criticality	Cost uncertainty
	Process uncertainty	Criticality of schedule
	Availability of extra resources	
	Claims	
	Contractual difficulties	
ID/T / 0,69	Performance criticality	Criticality of schedule
	Cost uncertainty	Availability of extra resources
	Uncertainty of scope	Claims
	Value for money	Contractual difficulties
	Process uncertainty	
FPI / 0,6	Cost uncertainty	Process uncertainty
	Criticality of schedule	Performance criticality
	Value for money	Uncertainty of scope
	Contractual difficulties	Claims
		Availability of extra resources
LSFP / 0,49	Value for money	Uncertainty of scope
	Claims	Performance criticality
	Cost uncertainty	Process uncertainty
	Criticality of schedule	Availability of extra resources
	Contractual difficulties	
UPM / 0,66	Uncertainty of scope	Contractual difficulties
	Process uncertainty	Value for money
	Cost uncertainty	Criticality of schedule
		Claims
		Performance criticality
		Availability of extra resources

Table 11. Results of factor analysis: Greek engineers (factors: two)

CTs/KMO	Factors of Greek Participants' Sample	
	1	2
CPFF / 0,54	Performance criticality	Cost uncertainty
	Uncertainty of scope	Value for money
	Availability of extra resources	Criticality of schedule
	Process uncertainty	Contractual difficulties
		Claims
CPPF / 0,52	Process uncertainty	Value for money
	Uncertainty of scope	Cost uncertainty
	Claims	Performance criticality
	Criticality of schedule	
	Availability of extra resources	
	Contractual difficulties	
CPIF / 0,51	Claims	Uncertainty of scope
	Cost uncertainty	Process uncertainty
	Contractual difficulties	Availability of extra resources
	Value for money	Performance criticality
	Criticality of schedule	
ID/T / 0,68	Cost uncertainty	Criticality of schedule
	Value for money	Availability of extra resources
	Performance criticality	Claims
	Uncertainty of scope	Contractual difficulties
	Process uncertainty	
FPI / 0,58	Uncertainty of scope	Performance criticality
	Cost uncertainty	Process uncertainty
	Criticality of schedule	Claims
	Value for money	
	Availability of extra resources	
	Contractual difficulties	
LSFP / 0,42	Claims	Uncertainty of scope
	Value for money	Performance criticality
	Cost uncertainty	Availability of extra resources
	Contractual difficulties	Process uncertainty
	Criticality of schedule	
UPM / 0,65	Process uncertainty	Value for money
	Uncertainty of scope	Contractual difficulties
	Cost uncertainty	Claims
	Criticality of schedule	Availability of extra resources
	Performance criticality	

Table 12. Results of factor analysis: foreign participants' (factors: two)

CTs/KMO	Factors - Foreign Participants	
	1	2
CPFF / 0,49	Scope uncertainty	Value for money
	Claims	Criticality of schedule
	Process uncertainty	Cost uncertainty
	Performance criticality	Availability of extra resources
	Contractual difficulties	
CPIF / 0,37	Scope uncertainty	Criticality of schedule
	Process uncertainty	Performance criticality
	Claims	Cost uncertainty
	Availability of extra resources	Contractual difficulties
		Value for money
CPPF / 0,57	Scope uncertainty	Value for money
	Process uncertainty	Cost uncertainty
	Contractual difficulties	Criticality of schedule
	Claims	
	Performance criticality	
	Availability of extra resources	
FPI / 0,25	Process uncertainty	Cost uncertainty
	Scope uncertainty	Value for money
	Performance criticality	Criticality of schedule
	Availability of extra resources	Contractual difficulties
		Claims
ID/T / 0,58	Performance criticality	Contractual difficulties
	Process uncertainty	Availability of extra resources
	Cost uncertainty	Criticality of schedule
	Scope uncertainty	
	Claims	
	Value for money	
LSFP / 0,37	Criticality of schedule	Scope uncertainty
	Cost uncertainty	Process uncertainty
	Value for money	Performance criticality
	Claims	Availability of extra resources
	Contractual difficulties	
UPM / 0,47	Process uncertainty	Criticality of schedule
	Cost uncertainty	Availability of extra resources
	Scope uncertainty	Performance criticality
	Value for money	Claims
	Contractual difficulties	

COMPARISON OF FACTOR ANALYSIS RESULTS

Comparison among Whole Sample and Greek Engineers

The Contract Types used in Greek Public's Works Projects are UPM, LSFP and CPPF. The results per CT will be compared among all and Greek Engineers. In each case, the first part of the Table 13 represents the results of factor analysis in the case of Greek participants and the second table part represents responses from all participants.

In the case of CPFF CT the difference is that the Greek respondents group the performance criteria along with two of the contractual execution criteria (Contractual difficulties and Claims).

In CPPF contracts the majority of criteria are assigned to the same factors. The differences focus on "Performance Criticality" and "Criticality of Schedule", which both have exchanged places among the two factors. Greek participants consider necessary for the 2nd factor to include the "Quality" parameter, while all respondents associate "Scheduling" concerns with the cost issues.

In the CPIF type of contract, the contractor has a motive to work more efficiently for himself and for the owner, too. There exist two main core factors. These are: Factor (1) "Value for Money", "Cost Uncertainty" and "Criticality of Schedule", Factor (2) "Uncertainty of Scope", "Performance Criticality", "Process Uncertainty" and "Availability of Extra Resources" while "Claims" and "Contractual Difficulties" move across the factors.

The core concept of the CT ID/T is time. As a consequence "Criticality of Schedule" is the main criterion encapsulating this idea. Thus, the concept of the particular CT is mostly straightforward and the participants logically share the same view. Considering the ID/T CT, it is interesting to note that the factor content is completely identical.

In the case of FPI, the 91 participants' proposed factors seem more anticipated. Factor (1) refers to cost, schedule and contract issues, whereas factor (2) associates process, scope uncertainty, quality with "Availability of Extra Resources" and "Claims".

LSFP is one of the most common in Greece. The interesting thing is that factors are completely identical. This means that both groups generally agree. Factor (1) deals with money, time and contract issues. Factor (2) deals with quality, project uncertainties and extra resources.

UPM is also a CT usually used in Greece. "Criticality of Schedule" and "Performance Criticality" in the Greek engineers sample are moved in factor 1. In other words "Scheduling" and "Quality" are the two criteria moving across factors. In the case of the whole sample and exactly like the case of the three factors (Table 6), "Uncertainties" are joined together and constitute a single factor. This outcome is expected due to the UPM CT.

Comparison among Public and Private Sector Experienced Participants (Two Factors)

The comparison of the results in these two cases reveal that the LSFP and ID/T contracts have exactly the same criteria content. The other contract types have differences in their factors' content.

Table 13. Comparison of Greek and 91 participants (factors: two)

CPFF	Performance criticality	Cost uncertainty
	Uncertainty of scope	Value for money
	Availability of extra resources	Criticality of schedule
	Process uncertainty	Contractual difficulties
		Claims
CPFF	Uncertainty of scope	Value for money
	Performance criticality	Cost uncertainty
	Process uncertainty	Criticality of schedule
	Availability of extra resources	
	Claims	
	Contractual difficulties	
CPPF	Process uncertainty	Value for money
	Uncertainty of scope	Cost uncertainty
	Claims	Performance criticality
	Criticality of schedule	
	Availability of extra resources	
	Contractual difficulties	
CPPF	Uncertainty of scope	Value for money
	Process uncertainty	Cost uncertainty
	Claims	Criticality of schedule
	Performance criticality	
	Contractual difficulties	
CPIF	Claims	Uncertainty of scope
	Cost uncertainty	Process uncertainty
	Contractual difficulties	Availability of extra resources
	Value for money	Performance criticality
	Criticality of schedule	
CPIF	Uncertainty of scope	Value for money
	Performance criticality	Cost uncertainty
	Process uncertainty	Criticality of schedule
	Availability of extra resources	
	Claims	
	Contractual difficulties	
ID/T	Cost uncertainty	Criticality of schedule
	Value for money	Availability of extra resources
	Performance criticality	Claims
	Uncertainty of scope	Contractual difficulties
	Process uncertainty	

continued on next page

Table 13. Continued

ID/T	Performance criticality	Criticality of schedule
	Cost uncertainty	Availability of extra resources
	Uncertainty of scope	Claims
	Value for money	Contractual difficulties
	Process uncertainty	
FPI	Uncertainty of scope	Performance criticality
	Cost uncertainty	Process uncertainty
	Criticality of schedule	Claims
	Value for money	
	Availability of extra resources	
	Contractual difficulties	
FPI	Cost uncertainty	Process uncertainty
	Criticality of schedule	Performance criticality
	Value for money	Uncertainty of scope
	Contractual difficulties	Claims
LSFP	Claims	Uncertainty of scope
	Value for money	Performance criticality
	Cost uncertainty	Availability of extra resources
	Contractual difficulties	Process uncertainty
	Criticality of schedule	
LSFP	Value for money	Uncertainty of scope
	Claims	Performance criticality
	Cost uncertainty	Process uncertainty
	Criticality of schedule	Availability of extra resources
	Contractual difficulties	
UPM	Process uncertainty	Value for money
	Uncertainty of scope	Contractual difficulties
	Cost uncertainty	Claims
	Criticality of schedule	Availability of extra resources
	Performance criticality	
UPM	Uncertainty of scope	Contractual difficulties
	Process uncertainty	Value for money
	Cost uncertainty	Criticality of schedule
		Claims
		Performance criticality
		Availability of extra resources

Comparison among Greek and Foreign Participants (Two Factors)

Similarly, the LSFP contract has exactly the same criteria content. All the other CTs have smaller or more extensive differences. One interesting phenomenon is that "Claims" and "Contractual Difficulties" most of the times tend to cluster together in the case of Greek participants.

CONCLUSION AND FUTURE RESEARCH DIRECTIONS

The paper identified the perceptions of engineers regarding the performance of CTs against selected criteria for highway construction projects. This is achieved by examining the results of factor analysis based on the scores obtained by each CT against each SC. Furthermore, research investigated the way SC tend to cluster together and therefore are considered by the engineers, as a unit. The research then examines the mechanisms that create these clusters' contents. Moreover, the paper provides a comparison among different samples of participants. In this context, the paper considers the CT and participants' profile and rationalizes the findings.

The findings suggest that clustering approaches of criteria could be divided into three distinct cases. Firstly, criteria cluster under the influence of the examined CT, secondly criteria which cluster due to the profile of the participant and finally the criteria that cluster irrespective of the participant's profile or the CT. It is true that the philosophy behind the function of each CT influences the way the criteria shape each factor.

Through the factor analysis it becomes obvious that different CTs are associated with different criteria factors. This is mainly caused by the special characteristics of each CT, which are reflected through the criteria factors. These factors that originate from the participants' judgment, communicate, in an indirect manner, the participants' perception of performance of each CT.

Another interesting finding includes the variations in the factors' content regarding the sample of participants. In some cases the whole sample compared to the Greek participants produced factors with limited but interesting variations. This fact along with the results of the foreign participants suggests that the nationality of participants is associated with the assessment of performance of each CT against each SC. Especially in the case of the 91 Participants the analysis' results of the 3 factors are in complete accordance with the international literature. The respondents' experience in years, type of projects, role-involvement, legislation, nature of project, professional "culture" and procurement method influence the participants' answers. In the comparison among engineers experienced in public and private sector the LSFP and ID/T contracts present identical factors among these two samples. Similarly, Greek and Foreign participants provide the same factors in the case of the LSFP contract.

The research approach shows that it is very difficult to assign a unique semantic label to each group of criteria. At the same time, there are a number of criteria that tend to cluster together irrespective of CT and participants' profiles. These pairs of criteria include:

- Uncertainties criteria: Cost, Scope and Process Uncertainty,
- Scope and Process Uncertainty,
- Contractual Difficulties and Claims,
- Value for Money and Criticality of Schedule, and
- Performance Criticality and Availability of Extra Resources.

Examining the factor creation, one parameter that could not be predicted is the apprehension of the criteria. The respondents' common interpretation of the definition of the survey criteria is critical to their evaluation of each CT. Respondents assess the criteria not necessarily as standalone but as groups or supplements to each other. In the case where participants don't have adequate experience with certain types of contracts then the grouping of criteria could be based on conceptual proximity. A number of secondary considerations explaining the grouping of criteria into factors could include:

- Conceptual or semantic similarity,
- Engineers' point of view,
- Criteria associated with a certain project stage,
- Type of criteria relationship:
    - Supplementing one another,
    - Cause and Effect,
    - Antagonistic .
- Standard Concepts (Cost/ Time/ Quality), and
- Criteria describing performance.

To facilitate the final conclusions, Tables 6 to 13 were combined and were reformed using the code names of the selection criteria (SC1-SC9) according to Table 14 into Tables 15 and 16.

This two combined tables highlight a tendency for no identical grouping of SC when selecting CT nor by respondents group and neither per CT. The only exception is the CT BP / X, which shows the same grouping for three factors and two factors per group, except for the survey participants from abroad.

The overall conclusion is that in all the cases the grouping of SC change per CT according to the group in question. Therefore, all have a different perception of the relations between the SC and hence the independence of the SC is confirmed. This element is important for the application of Multi Attribute Utility Theory. Then the averages will be considered along different groups per CT and SC to determine to what extent the research variables are correlated to the expert profiles.

This paper identified the perceptions of engineers regarding the performance of CTs against SC, and highlighted the way these perceptions change relatively to the profile of the decision maker. Understanding

Table 14. Codification of selection criteria

Selection Criteria	Codification
Cost Uncertainty	SC1
Uncertainty of Scope	SC2
Process Uncertainty	SC3
Value for Money	SC4
Criticality of Schedule	SC5
Performance Criticality	SC6
Availability of extra resources	SC7
Contractual Difficulties	SC8
Claims	SC9

Table 15. Comparison of 3-factors' analyses

CT/KMO	**All Respondents**			**CT/KMO**	**Experience in Public Projects > 10 Years**		
	1	**2**	**3**		**1**	**2**	**3**
CPFF / 0,58	SC2	SC1	SC8	CPFF / 0,52	SC2	SC1	SC4
	SC3	SC4	SC9		SC3	SC7	SC5
	SC6	SC5			SC6	SC8	SC9
	SC7						
CPPF / 0,57	SC2	SC1	SC6	CPPF / 0,53	SC1	SC2	SC5
	SC8	SC4	SC7		SC4	SC3	SC8
	SC9	SC5			SC6		SC9
	KE3				SC7		
CPIF / 0,51	SC1	SC2	SC4	CPIF / 0,47	SC7	SC1	SC4
	SC8	SC7	SC5		SC8	SC2	SC5
	SC9	KE3	SC6		SC9	SC3	SC6
ID/T/ 0,69	SC1	SC7	SC5	ID/T/ 0,55	SC1	SC7	SC5
	SC2	SC8			SC2	SC8	
	SC3	SC9			SC3	SC9	
	SC4				SC4		
	KE6				SC6		
FPI / 0,6	KE3	SC1	SC5	FPI / 0,65	SC3	SC1	SC7
	SC6	SC2	SC7		SC6	SC2	SC8
		SC4	SC8			SC4	SC9
			SC9			SC5	
LSFP / 0,49	SC2	SC4	SC1	LSFP / 0,38	SC2	SC4	SC1
	SC6	SC5	SC8		SC3	SC5	SC6
	SC7	SC9			SC7	SC9	SC8
	KE3						
UPM / 0,66	SC1	SC4	SC5	UPM / 0,61	SC1	SC8	SC4
	SC2	SC8	SC6		SC2	SC9	SC6
	KE3	SC9	SC7		SC3		SC7
					SC5		

Table 16. Comparison of 2 – factors' analyses

All Participants			Greek Participants			Participants from Abroad			Experience in Public Projects >10			Experience in Private Projects >10		
CT/ KMO	1	2	CT/ KMO	1	2	CT/ KMO	1	2	CT/ KMO	1	2	CT/ KMO	1	2
CPFF	SC2	SC1	CPFF	SC2	SC1	CPFF	SC2	SC1	CPFF	SC1	SC5	CPFF	SC2	SC1
0,58	SC3	SC4	0,54	SC3	SC4	0,49	SC3	SC4	0,52	SC2	SC7	0,48	SC3	SC4
	SC6	SC5		SC6	SC5		SC6	SC5		SC3	SC8		SC6	SC5
	SC7			SC7	SC8		SC8	SC7		SC4			SC7	
	SC8				SC9		SC9			SC6			SC8	
	SC9									SC9			SC9	
CPPF	SC2	SC1	CPPF	SC2	SC1	CPIF /	SC2	SC1	CPPF	SC1	SC2	CPPF	SC2	SC1
0,57	SC3	SC4	0,52	SC3	SC4	0,37	SC3	SC4	0,52	SC4	SC3	0,64	SC3	SC4
	SC6	SC5		SC5	SC6		SC7	SC5		SC6	SC5		SC6	SC5
	SC7			SC7			SC9	SC6		SC7	SC8		SC7	
	SC8			SC8				SC8		SC9			SC8	
	SC9			SC9									SC9	
CPIF /	SC2	SC1	CPIF /	SC1	SC2	CPPF	SC2	SC1	CPIF /	SC2	SC4	CPIF/	SC2	SC1
0,51	SC3	SC4	0,51	SC4	SC3	0,57	SC3	SC4	0,47	SC1	SC6	0,51	SC3	SC4
	SC6	SC5		SC5	SC6		SC6	SC5		SC3	SC7		SC5	SC7
	SC7			SC8	SC7		SC7			SC5			SC6	SC8
	SC8			SC9			SC8			SC8			SC9	
	SC9						SC9			SC9				
ID/T/	SC1	SC5	ID/T/	SC1	SC5	ID/T/	SC1	SC5	ID/T/	SC1	SC7	BP/X/	SC1	SC5
0,69	SC2	SC7	0,68	SC2	SC7	0,58	SC2	SC7	0,55	SC2	SC5	0,45	SC2	SC7
	SC3	SC8		SC3	SC8		SC3	SC8		SC3	SC8		SC3	SC8
	SC4	SC9		SC4	SC9		SC4			SC4	SC9		SC4	SC9
	SC6			SC6			SC6			SC6			SC6	
							SC9							
FPI /	SC1	SC2	FPI /	SC1	SC3	FPI /	SC2	SC1	FPI /	SC3	SC1	FPI /	SC2	SC1
0,6	SC4	SC3	0,58	SC2	SC6	0,25	SC3	SC4	0,65	SC6	SC2	O,54	SC3	SC4
	SC5	SC6		SC4	SC9		SC6	SC5		SC7	SC4		SC6	SC5
	SC8	SC7		SC5			SC7	SC8		SC8	SC5		SC8	SC7
		SC9		SC7				SC9		SC9				SC9
				SC8										
LSFP /	SC1	SC2	LSFP /	SC1	SC2	LSFP /	SC1	SC2	LSFP /	SC2	SC1	LSFP /	SC2	SC1
0,49	SC4	SC3	0,42	SC4	SC3	0,37	SC4	SC3	0,38	SC3	SC4	O,57	SC3	SC4
	SC5	SC6		SC5	SC6		SC5	SC6		SC6	SC5		SC6	SC5
	SC8	SC7		SC8	SC7		SC8	SC7		SC7	SC8		SC7	SC8
	SC9			SC9			SC9				SC9			SC9

continued on next page

Table 13. Continued

All Participants			**Greek Participants**			**Participants from Abroad**			**Experience in Public Projects >10**			**Experience in Private Projects >10**		
CT/ KMO	**1**	**2**	**CT/ KMO**	**1**	**2**	**CT/ KMO**	**1**	**2**	**CT/ KMO**	**1**	**2**	**CT/ KMO**	**1**	**2**
UPM / 0,66	SC1	SC4	UPM / 0,65	SC1	SC4	UPM / 0,47	SC1	SC5	UPM / 0,66	SC1	SC4	UPM / 0,57	SC1	SC5
	SC2	SC5		SC2	SC7		SC2	SC6		SC2	SC6		SC2	SC7
	SC3	SC6		SC3	SC8		SC3	SC7		SC3	SC7		SC3	SC8
		SC7		SC5	SC9		SC4	SC9		SC5	SC8		SC4	SC9
		SC8		SC6			SC8			SC9			SC6	
		SC9												

of the various viewpoints could facilitate contract negotiations among the project stakeholders. As part of the future work factor scores could be examined in order to provide more detailed conclusions and factor analysis could be conducted on selected samples associated with the experience of participants with each CT. Finally, a further research approach will consider the application of game theory concepts.

ACKNOWLEDGMENT

Financial support of this research work by the Research Committee of Alexander Technological Educational Institute of Thessaloniki is gratefully acknowledged.

REFERENCES

Al-Subhi Al-Harbi, K. M. (1998). Sharing fractions in cost-plus incentive-fee contracts. *International Journal of Project Management*, *16*(2), 73–80. doi:10.1016/S0263-7863(97)00013-6

Anastasopoulos, P., Anastasopoulos, Ch., McCullouch, B. G., Gkritza, K., Mannering, F. L., & Sinha, K. C. (2010). Cost savings analysis of performance-based contracts for highway maintenance operations. *Journal of Infrastructure Systems*, *16*(4), 251–263. doi:10.1061/(ASCE)IS.1943-555X.0000012

Antoniou, F., Aretoulis, G. N., Konstantinidis, D., & Kalfakakou, G. P. (2012). Selection criteria used for the choice of contract type for major highway construction projects. *Procedia - Social and Behavioral Sciences Journal*, *48*, 3508–3517.

Antoniou, F., Aretoulis, G. N., Konstantinidis, D., & Kalfakakou, G. P. (2013). Engineers perception and assessment of contract types for highway construction projects. *International Journal of Applied Behavioral Economics*, *2*(4), 1–24. doi:10.4018/ijabe.2013100101

Arditi, D., Khisty, J., & Yasamis, F. (1997). Incentive/disincentive provisions in highway contracts. *Journal of Construction Engineering and Management*, *123*(3), 302–307. doi:10.1061/(ASCE)0733-9364(1997)123:3(302)

Arditi, D., & Yasamis, F. (1998). Incentive/Disincentive contracts: Perceptions of owners & contractors. *Journal of Construction Engineering and Management*, *124*(5), 361–373. doi:10.1061/(ASCE)0733-9364(1998)124:5(361)

Aretoulis, G. N., Angelides, D. C., Kalfakakou, G. P., Fotiadis, G. S., & Anastasiadis, K. I. (2006). A prototype system for the prediction of final cost in construction projects. *International Journal of Operational Research, Special Issue*, *6*(3), 423–432.

Baccarini, D. (1996). The concept of project complexity a review. *International Journal of Project Management*, *14*(4), 201–204. doi:10.1016/0263-7863(95)00093-3

Badenfelt, U. (2011). Fixing the contract after the contract is fixed: A study of incomplete contracts in IT and construction projects. *International Journal of Project Management*, *29*(5), 568–576. doi:10.1016/j.ijproman.2010.04.003

Berends, T. C. (2000). Cost plus incentive fee contracting - experiences & structuring. *International Journal of Project Management*, *18*(3), 165–171. doi:10.1016/S0263-7863(99)00076-9

Bosch-Rekveldt, M., Jongkind, Y., Mooia, H., Bakker, H., & Verbraeck, A. (2011). Grasping project complexity in large engineering projects: The TOE (Technical, Organizational and Environmental) framework. *International Journal of Project Management*, *29*(6), 728–739. doi:10.1016/j.ijproman.2010.07.008

Boukendour, S. (2007). Preventing post-contractual opportunism by an option to switch from one contract to another. *Construction Management and Economics*, *25*(7), 723–727. doi:10.1080/01446190701392994

Boukendour, S., & Bah, R. (2001). The guaranteed maximum price contract as call option. *Construction Management and Economics*, *19*(6), 563–567. doi:10.1080/01446190110049848

Bower, D., Ashby, G., Gerald, K., & Smyk, W. (2002). Incentive Mechanisms for Project Success. *Journal of Management Engineering*, *18*(1), 37–43. doi:10.1061/(ASCE)0742-597X(2002)18:1(37)

Bröchner, J., & Badenfelt, U. (2011). Changes and change management in construction and IT projects. *Journal of Automation in Construction*, *20*(7), 767–775. doi:10.1016/j.autcon.2011.01.001

Broome, J., & Perry, J. (2002). How practitioners set share fractions in target cost contracts. *International Journal of Project Management*, *20*(1), 59–66. doi:10.1016/S0263-7863(00)00035-1

Bubshait, A. A. (2003). Incentive/disincentive contracts and its effects on industrial projects. *International Journal of Project Management*, *21*(1), 63–70. doi:10.1016/S0263-7863(01)00078-3

Carty, G. J. (1995). Construction. *Journal of Construction Engineering and Management*, *121*(3), 319–328. doi:10.1061/(ASCE)0733-9364(1995)121:3(319)

Chan, D. W., Chan, A. P., Lam, P. T., & Wong, J. M. (2011a). An empirical survey of the motives and benefits of adopting guaranteed maximum price and target cost contracts in construction. *International Journal of Project Management*, *29*(5), 577–590. doi:10.1016/j.ijproman.2010.04.002

Chan, D. W. M., Chan, A. P. C., Lam, P. T. I., Yeung, J. F. Y., & Chan, J. H. L. (2011b). Risk ranking and analysis in target cost contracts: Empirical evidence from the construction industry. *International Journal of Project Management*, *29*(6), 751–763. doi:10.1016/j.ijproman.2010.08.003

Cheung, S. O., Yiu, T. W., & Chiu, O. K. (2009). The aggressive–cooperative drivers of construction contracting. *International Journal of Project Management*, *27*(7), 727–735. doi:10.1016/j.ijproman.2008.09.001

Doloi, H. K. (2011). Understanding stakeholders perspective of cost estimation in project management. *International Journal of Project Management*, *29*(5), 622–636. doi:10.1016/j.ijproman.2010.06.001

Field, A. (2009). *Discovering Statistics using SPSS* (3rd ed.). SAGE Publications Inc.

Flyvbjerg, B., Holm, M. S., & Buhl, S. (2002). Underestimating costs in public works Projects. Error or lie? *Journal of the American Planning Association*, *68*(3), 279–295. doi:10.1080/01944360208976273

Goodrum, P. M., Wan, Y., & Fenouil, P. C. (2009). A decision-making system for accelerating roadway construction. *Journal of Engineering. Construction and Architectural Management*, *16*(2), 116–135. doi:10.1108/09699980910938000

Gruneberg, S., Hughes, W., & Ancell, D. (2007). Risk under performance-based contracting in the UK construction sector. *Construction Management and Economics*, *25*(7), 691–699. doi:10.1080/01446190601164097

Halpin, D. W., & Senior, B. A. (2011). *Construction Management* (4th ed.). John Wiley & Sons, Inc.

Herbsman, Z. J., & Glagola, C. R. (1998). Lane rental - innovative way to reduce road construction time. *Journal of Construction Engineering and Management*, *124*(5), 411–417. doi:10.1061/(ASCE)0733-9364(1998)124:5(411)

Herbsman, Z. J., Tong Chen, W., & Epstein, W. C. (1995). Time is money: Innovative contracting methods in highway construction. *Journal of Construction Engineering and Management*, *121*(3), 273–281. doi:10.1061/(ASCE)0733-9364(1995)121:3(273)

Herten, H. J., & Peeters, W. A. R. (1986). Incentive contracting as a project management tool. *International Journal of Project Management*, *4*(1), 34–39. doi:10.1016/0263-7863(86)90060-8

Hinton, P. R., Brownlow, C., McMurray, I., & Cozens, B. (2004). *SPSS Explained*. New York: Routledge, Taylor and Francis Group.

Howard, W. E., Bell, L. C., & McCormick, R. E. (1997). Economic principles of contractor compensation. *Journal of Management Engineering*, *13*(5), 81–89. doi:10.1061/(ASCE)0742-597X(1997)13:5(81)

Irfan, M., Khurshid, M. B., Anastasopoulos, P., Labi, S., & Moavenzadeh, F. (2011). Planning-stage estimation of highway project duration on the basis of anticipated project cost, project type, and contract type. *International Journal of Project Management*, *29*(1), 78–92. doi:10.1016/j.ijproman.2010.01.001

ITA Working Group. (1996). ITA position paper on types of contract. *Tunneling & Underground Space Technology*, *11*(4), 411-429.

ITA Working Group 3. (2011) *Contractual Practices*. International Tunneling and Underground Space Association. Retrieved from http://www.ita-aites.org/fileadmin/filemounts/general/pdf/ItaAssociation/ProductAndPublication/WorkingGroupsPublication/WG3/ITA_Report_N6_WG3_P.pdf

Jaafari, A. (1996). Twinning time & cost in incentive-based contracts. *Journal of Management Engineering*, *12*(4), 62–72. doi:10.1061/(ASCE)0742-597X(1996)12:4(62)

Jaraiedi, M., Plummer, R. W., & Aber, M. S. (1995). Incentive/disincentive guidelines for highway construction contracts. *Journal of Construction Engineering and Management*, *121*(1), 112–120. doi:10.1061/(ASCE)0733-9364(1995)121:1(112)

Lai, I. K. W., & Lam, F. K. S. (2010). Perception of various performance criteria by stakeholders in the construction sector in Hong Kong. *Construction Management and Economics*, *28*(4), 377–391. doi:10.1080/01446190903521515

Lambropoulos, S. (2007). The use of time & cost utility for construction contract award under European Union Legislation. *Building and Environment*, *42*(1), 452–463. doi:10.1016/j.buildenv.2005.08.002

Lancaster, P. J., Plotkin, E. S., Lerner, J. N., & Morris, M. D. (2001). *Construction in Cities Social, Environmental, Political, and Economic Concerns*. New York: CRC Press LLC.

Landau, S., & Everitt, B. S. (2004). *A Handbook of Statistical Analyses using SPSS*. Chapman & Hall/CRC Press LLC.

Liu, L., Wang, X., & Sheng, Z. (2012). Achieving ambidexterity in large, complex engineering projects: A case study of the Sutong Bridge project. *Journal of Construction Management and Economics*, *30*(5), 399–409. doi:10.1080/01446193.2012.679948

Mayer, K. J., & Argyres, N. S. (2004). Learning to contract: Evidence from the personal computer industry. *Organization Science*, *15*(4), 394–410. doi:10.1287/orsc.1040.0074

Meng, X., & Gallagher, B. (2012). The impact of incentive mechanisms on project performance. *International Journal of Project Management*, *30*(3), 352–362. doi:10.1016/j.ijproman.2011.08.006

Missbauer, H., & Hauber, W. (2006). Bid calculation for construction projects: Regulations and incentive effects of unit price contracts. *European Journal of Operational Research*, *171*(3), 1005–1019. doi:10.1016/j.ejor.2005.01.014

Mooi, E., & Sarstedt, M. (2011). *A Concise Guide to Market Research. The Process, Data, and Methods Using IBM SPSS Statistics*. Berlin: Springer-Verlag.

Ng, S. T., & Skitmore, R. M. (2001). Contractor Selection Criteria: A Cost–Benefit Analysis. *IEEE Transactions on Engineering Management*, *48*(1), 96–106. doi:10.1109/17.913169

Ojo, S. O., Aina, O., & Adeyemi, A. Y. (2011). A comparative analysis of the performance of traditional contracting and design-build procurements on client objectives in Nigeria. *Journal of Civil Engineering and Management*, *17*(2), 227–233. doi:10.3846/13923730.2011.574449

Olsen, T. E., & Osmundsen, P. (2005). Sharing of endogenous risk in construction. *Journal of Economic Behavior & Organization*, *58*(4), 511–526. doi:10.1016/j.jebo.2003.09.019

Padhi, S. S., & Mohapatra, P. K. J. (2009). Centralized bid evaluation for awarding of construction projects – A case of India government. *International Journal of Project Management*, *28*(3), 275–284. doi:10.1016/j.ijproman.2009.06.001

Paul, A., & Gutierrez, G. (2005). Simple probability models for project contracting. *European Journal of Operational Research*, *165*(2), 329–338. doi:10.1016/j.ejor.2004.04.005

Permanent International Association of Road Congresses' (PIARC). (2003). *Procurement of works, goods and services by road administrations.* PIARC Technical Committee, C15 Report.

Pramangioulis, P. (2008). *Guide to data analysis using SPSS.* Athens: Athens University of Economics and Business. Department of Statistics.

Rose, T., & Manley, K. (2011). Motivation toward financial incentive goals on construction projects. *Journal of Business Research*, *64*(7), 765–773. doi:10.1016/j.jbusres.2010.07.003

Shr, J. F., & Chen, W. T. (2003). A method to determine minimum contract bids for incentive highway projects. *International Journal of Project Management*, *21*(8), 593–599. doi:10.1016/S0263-7863(02)00056-X

Shr, J. F., & Chen, W. T. (2004). Setting Maximum Incentive for Incentive/Disincentive contracts for Highway Projects. *Journal of Construction Engineering and Management*, *130*(1), 84–93. doi:10.1061/(ASCE)0733-9364(2004)130:1(84)

Tang, W., Qiang, M., Duffield, C. F., Young, D. M., & Lu, Y. (2008). Incentives in the Chinese Construction Industry. *Journal of Construction Engineering and Management*, *134*(7), 457–467. doi:10.1061/(ASCE)0733-9364(2008)134:7(457)

Turner, J. R., & Simister, S. J. (2001). Project contract management and a theory of organization. *International Journal of Project Management*, *19*(8), 457–464. doi:10.1016/S0263-7863(01)00051-5

Ungern-Sternberg, T. (1994). Quality incentives in auctions for construction contracts. *International Journal of Industrial Organization*, *12*(1), 89–104. doi:10.1016/0167-7187(94)90029-9

Veld, J., & Peeters, W. A. (1989). Keeping large projects under control: The importance of contract type selection. *International Journal of Project Management*, *7*(3), 155–162. doi:10.1016/0263-7863(89)90034-3

Vidal, L.-A., Marle, F., & Bocquet, J.-C. (2011). Measuring project complexity using the Analytic Hierarchy Process. *International Journal of Project Management*, *29*(6), 718–727. doi:10.1016/j.ijproman.2010.07.005

Wang, E. T. G., Ju, P.-H., Jiang, J. J., & Klein, G. (2008). The effects of change control and management review on software flexibility and project performance. *Information & Management*, *45*(7), 438–443. doi:10.1016/j.im.2008.05.003

Wang, W. C., Wang, H. H., Lai, Y. T., & Li, J. C. C. (2006). Unit-price-based model for evaluating competitive bids. *International Journal of Project Management*, *24*(2), 15–166. doi:10.1016/j.ijproman.2005.06.002

Ward, S., & Chapman, C. (1994). Choosing contractor payment terms. *International Journal of Project Management*, *12*(4), 216–221. doi:10.1016/0263-7863(94)90045-0

Ward, S. C., & Chapman, C. B. (1995). Evaluating fixed price incentive contracts. *Omega*, *23*(1), 49–62. doi:10.1016/0305-0483(94)00047-E

Wilmot, C. G., & Cheng, G. (2003). Estimating Future Highway Construction Costs. *Journal of Construction Engineering and Management*, *129*(3), 272–279. doi:10.1061/(ASCE)0733-9364(2003)129:3(272)

KEY TERMS AND DEFINITIONS

Contract Types: Documents describing in legal terms the project stakeholders' obligations and rights.
Engineer: The person responsible for the realization of a project.
Highway Construction Projects: Main infrastructure projects, leading to development.
Perception: The belief or the point of view of a person.
Selection Criteria: A number of parameters to be considered during the decision making process.

Chapter 10

An Integrative Approach to Study on Consumer Behavior towards Plug-In Hybrid Electric Vehicles Revolution:

Consumer Behavior towards Plug-In Hybrid Electric Vehicles

Nadia Adnan
Universiti Teknologi PETRONAS, Malaysia

Imran Rahman
Universiti Teknologi PETRONAS, Malaysia

Shahrina Md Nordin
Universiti Teknologi PETRONAS, Malaysia

Pandian Vasant
Universiti Teknologi PETRONAS, Malaysia

Muhammad Amir Noor
London Metropolitan University, UK

ABSTRACT

Transport electrification has experienced major deviations for the last few decades. Current investigation towards the implication of green technologies to decrease pollution and increase diffusion of renewable energy in the transportation sector are achieving more attention. The significance of plug-in hybrid electric vehicles (PHEVs) play a key role towards the policy option to reduce the environmental concern. There are major uncertainties in the diffusion of PHEVs timing of market distribution among consumers. However, there has been a considerable effort made towards the benefit of PHEVs demand. Yet, the debates on consumer behavioral economics towards the adoption of electric vehicles are less recognized. Researchers highlight the significance of PHEVs from a combined perspective considering PHEVs which allows bi-directional flow of electricity. However, it mainly focuses on interface among technology adoption and consumer behavior includes many other aspects such as individual adoption behavior, vehicles performance, environmental concern and power system demand.

DOI: 10.4018/978-1-5225-1826-6.ch010

INTRODUCTION

Modern studies on green technologies for transportation sector are attaining attraction among the research communities from diverse parts. In this wake, Plug-in hybrid electric vehicles (PHEVs) have a bright future because of their battery system and charging facilities from the traditional power system. Numerous investigators have demonstrated that a great amount of decreases in greenhouse gas emissions and the growing reliance on oil could be accomplished by the transport electrification (Caramanis & Foster, 2009). Although road transportation is not considered as the leading source of greenhouse-gas emissions, but it contributes the major part of the emission. Transportation in recent days are the major unsustainable source of energies, depend on the liquid fossil fuels. Research suggest that the transportation sector at present consume over 55% of oil and emit around 25% of CO2 in total (Howey, 2012). With the introduction of Electric vehicles technology marked a considerable amount of carbon-free transportation in current market trend. By keeping a close consideration of the research on electric vehicle technology, where the main idea was to in cooperated electrically charged battery supported vehicles i.e. PHEVs came into the current market trend. We scale out our domain to study their potential introduction from an integrated perspective. Furthermore, we extend our domain to observe its interactions between technology and economic behavior and its market diffusion influence. Several studies and analysis are extended by taking major confirmations and verifications from Western Europe and North America and Asia in general. On the contrary, the analysis of energy implications is also being kept in close consideration throughout the world. However, Figure 1 displays the energy implication around the world.

The current marketing trend suggests that the transport sector is accountable for over 27% of total energy utilization. In the wake of future growth, it is expected to increase by 50% possibly by 2035 (Tran, Banister, Bishop, & McCulloch, 2012). Keeping in mind overall 94% dependency on oil fuel, passenger vehicle considered to be another source of CO2 emissions weigh up to 6.3 Gt or over 24% in general of

Figure 1. Energy implication around the world
Source: Ellabban, Abu-Rub, & Blaabjerg, 2014.

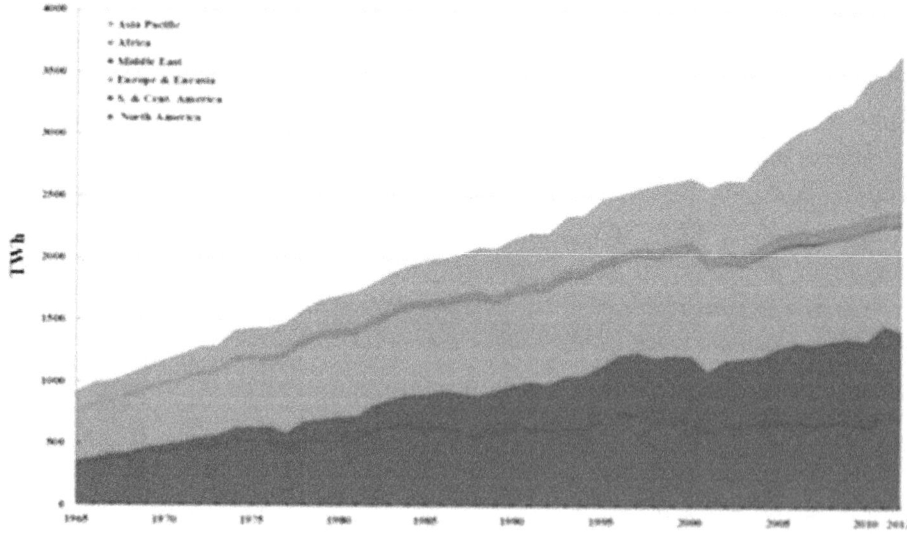

the total, on the other hand electricity generation (40%), industrial usage (16%), building usage (12%), agricultural sector and other usage (8%) (Tran et al., 2012). Figure 2 shows the statistics.

In a border sense, reduction of CO_2 emission encounters a couple of major key issues which address overall changing trend in the volume of travel as well as the total fuel efficiency towards the actual mode of travel (Tong, Jaramillo, & Azevedo, 2015). Since early 90's till last quarter of 2004, traveling through Light-Duty Vehicles (LDVs), including public transportation namely passenger cars, buses, and sports cars, at major countries increased by 15% (Tong et al., 2015). Research suggests that the increment goes from 13,000 to 15,000 km per person annually specially in Organization for Economic Co-operation and Development (OECD) countries. Heavy Duty Vehicles (tonne-km per capita) increased to 36% along with the global air travel increment of 90% since 90's (Howey, 2012). Rapid growth in transportation led to air travel, road freight, and Low-voltage differential signaling LDVs. However, second major impact that influences the trend of CO_2 emission is considered as high oil consumption or economic downturns. Based on recent findings one can hardly predict about these recent trends would hardly reverse in future. Under the supposition of the current trend, we observe that the lower average rates of vehicle purchasing within emerging economies along with rapid increment in gross domestic product (GDP) rates, increased the overall vehicle travel. Figure 3 shows the alternatives LDVs scales.

The study suggests that the passenger vehicles contribute a total of 60–70% of CO2 emissions, as compared to other vehicles. Suitable enforcement of energy policies should be implemented to cope with the passenger vehicle fleet. Another study points a major change in emission, where they highlight the adoption of PHEVs by the year 2050 which will predictably minimize CO2 emissions by 70–85%

Figure 2. Greenhouse gas emissions by sector
Source: Khondaker et al., 2016.

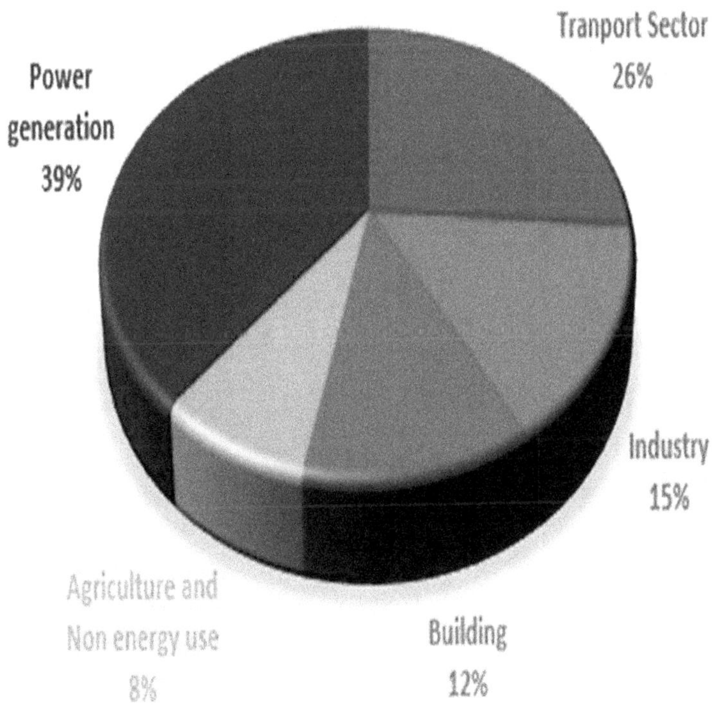

Figure 3. Alternatives LDVs scales
Source: Dulac, 2012.

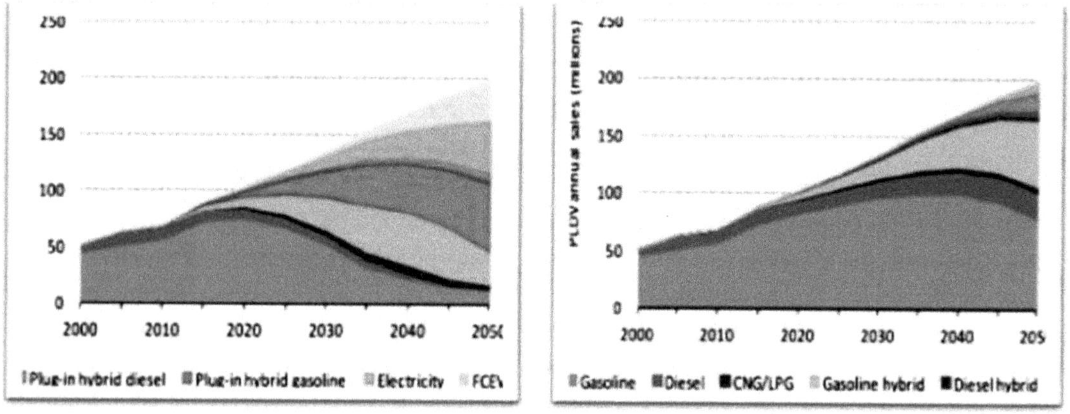

**For a more accurate representation of this figure, please see the electronic version.*

in total. Although the main benefits of CO2 will always proportionally rely on low-carbon electricity, considering that PHEVs will have a significant role in overall domestic and power sectors are covered below. Figure 4 shows vehicles mileage supplied by different vehicles technologies including PHEVs.

In future, transportation sector will be depending much on the development of this new era of electric vehicles. Indeed, the adoption of electric vehicles (EVs) has brought significant market success over the past decade. Vehicles are classified into three groups: internal combustion engine vehicles (ICEV), hybrid electric vehicles (HEV) and all- electric vehicles (AEV) (Tie & Tan, 2013). Plug-in hybrid electric vehicles (PHEVs) which are very recently introduced promise to boost up the overall fuel efficiency by holding a higher capacity battery system which can be directly charged from conventional power grid system, that helps the vehicles to operate continuously in "all-electric-range" (AER). All-Electric

Figure 4. Vehicles mileage supplied by different vehicles technologies
Source: Seixas et al., 2015.

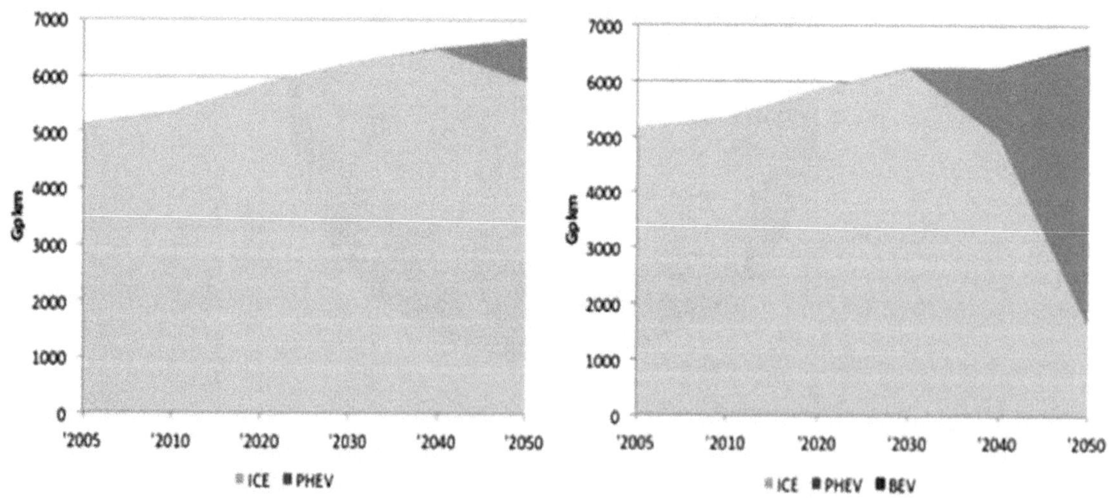

Vehicles or AEVs is a kind of transport which use electric power as only sources to run the system. Plug-in hybrid electric vehicles with a connection to the smart grid can own all of these strategies. Hence, the widely extended adoption of PHEVs might play a significant role in the alternative energy integration into traditional power systems (Lund & Kempton, 2008). On the other hand, if we look at the global policy scenario considering by the year 2035, pushed a total of 16% of new car trades to be PHEVs. Significantly, the demand for transport electricity will increase to over 125 million tons of oil equivalent with 90% for PHEVs. Oil-sourced road transport accumulates more than 80% of total oil consumed and could be a major source of oil savings. As predicted w.r.t current marketing trend by the end of 2035, LDVs will accumulate a total of 75-80% of oil savings, reducing around 400 Mt of CO_2 (Tran *et al.*, 2012). These are the consideration that set up a trend of potentially empowering the LDVs to overcome the CO_2 emission and reserve fuel consumption. With the impact of high volume of PHEVs in transportation trend, oil consumption still marks a significant rate of CO_2 emission of up to 77%. The consumption of biofuels along with fuel injection system could participate actively in the forthcoming mode of transportation. The rise of PHEVs in the current market, as well as developed marketing trend, could possibly get hit with alternate fuel technologies (Millo, Rolando, Fuso, & Mallamo, 2014). Current stats suggests that industrial research and development are marking their ways with an innovative approach and efficient engineering towards the efficiency of advanced fuel as well as biofuel engines. In comparison to that, acquisition of PHEVs might not mark an advancement because of the adoptive trend of existing technologies. A precise research suggests that modern ICE vehicles could possibly get 15–30% overall efficiency gains in upcoming years. Considering the current marketing trend, PHEVs (Rahman *et al.*, 2016) will have to compete for a significant market of advanced and biofuel with a trendy portrayal of zero CO_2 emission and to decarbonize transportation in general with consideration of market uncertainties. A thorough research indicates efficient energy saving potential whereas the technological and behavioral economic dynamics of diffusion of PHEVs has not been covered.

There is a need of efficient consumer adoption towards PHEVs technologies in order to solve highly diverse problems like energy management, cost reduction, efficient charging station etc. with different objectives and system constraints (Rahman *et al.*, 2015). Moreover, adoption of PHEVs also gives behavior economics benefits to the nation which is related to the effects of psychological, social, cognitive, and emotional factors on the economic decisions of individuals and the consequences for market prices, returns, and the resource allocation (Jain & Ahuja, 2013).One of the main targets is to facilitate the proper interaction between the consumers economic behavior towards the adoption of PHEVs.

CONTRIBUTION OF THIS CHAPTER

The purpose of this chapter is to contribute towards the research study of the diffusion of plug-in hybrid vehicles among consumer specifically to find out the impact trend of learning on consumer's decision towards hybrid technology adoption. Our main research evaluates major interactions between technology and behavior with respect to the magnitude of scales, containing systematic influences between bulk power system demand and PHEVs (Becker, Sidhu, & Tenderich, 2009). Along with local connections between provided charging arrangement and scenarios of driving, singular adaptive behavior with the policy as well as forecasting consequences plays a huge role towards the adoption of PHEVs. Our finding in this chapter covers two major aspects: the diffusion of the hybrid vehicle and technological diffusion. This research includes the factors of PHEVs adoption by taking the account of important features and ambiguity about quality and learning for this sustainable technology. Furthermore, it also covered a major portion of technological diffusion by considering the case of ambiguity and diverse quality. Innovative designs and models of hybrids from multiple makers add up diverse qualities in marketing trends. With this attractive approach and variance, consumers getting different nuances of PHEVs in terms of quality and type of vehicles, keeping this fact in consideration we can easily measure the effect of different quality and their consumer adoption.

BACKGROUND

The vehicular network recently accounts for around 25% of CO_2 emissions and over 55% of oil consumption around the world. Carbon dioxide is the primary greenhouse gas emitted through human actions like combustion of fossil fuels (coal, natural gas, and oil) for energy and transportation. Several researchers have proved that a great amount of reductions in greenhouse gas emissions and the increasing dependence on oil could be accomplished by electrification of transport sector (Holtz-Eakin & Selden, 1995). The EV was invented in 1834. During the last decade of the 19th century, a number of companies produced EVs in America, Britain, and France. In London, there were Electric Cab Company's taxis (Ellabban *et al.*, 2014). However, due to the limitations associated with the batteries and the rapid advancement of ICE vehicles, EVs have almost vanished from the scene since 1930 (Klass, 2016). Nevertheless, in the early 1970s, some countries, compelled by the energy crisis, started the rekindling of interests in EVs. In 1976, the U.S. launched the Electric and Hybrid Vehicle Research, Development and Demonstration Act, Public Law 94-413 (Yuan & Miyazaki, 2013). In the beginning of the 21st century, California had a mandate on the use of zero emission vehicles (Hu, Sun, Li, & Pan, 2014). Today, EVs are mainly used for small vehicles and short distance applications due to the limitation of batteries. In London, due to a new mandate of using zero emission vehicles in the down town, around 900 small EVs recently have been used (Hori, 2012). With the aid of intelligent transportation systems, EVs can be used as a car sharing system, when the user will travel for longer distances, the user can change to another fully charged EV at the midway service station.

Electric Vehicle Technology

As the Conventional vehicles (CVs) runs on internal combustion engines (ICEs), which consume petroleum fuel, that burns and emits a significantly larger quantity of greenhouse gasses. Whereas Advanced Fuel Vehicles (AFVs) designed to operate on dual fuel consumption namely petroleum and diesel also include EVs, bio-fuel vehicles, fuel cell vehicles, compressed natural gas (CNG) vehicles etc. Electrical vehicles (EVs) are specifically designed with either fractional or entire thrust propulsion source supplied from electricity. Along with its numerous ranges and the combination of HEV with ICE and electrical motor shares a larger portion of fuel economy as compared to similar sized vehicle. Some companies offered HEVs including the Toyota Prius, Ford Escape Hybrid, and Honda Civic Hybrid. The Plug-in Hybrid Electric Vehicle (PHEV) has a smaller internal combustion engine in comparison to the HEV, the introduction of a larger battery able to run the vehicle to cover an estimated mileage of 20 to 60 miles (Hori, 2012). Furthermore, with the help of an external electrical source PHEVs battery get recharged by just plugging in. Being flexibly adjusted with a rechargeable battery as an alternate fuel efficient system, PHEVs also adhere another flexibility of conventional fuels such as petroleum, biofuels etc. for a longer journey. For instance, if we look around in the present market PHEVs are associated with renowned brands such as Chevrolet Volt and Toyota Prius Plug-in Hybrid (Rahman et al., 2015a; Rahman, Vasant, Singh, & Abdullah-Al-Wadud, 2014). The main approach of any PHEVs is to acquire power through a rechargeable electric battery and support of up to 100 miles run on a fully charged battery. The core representation of PHEVs is to serve a purpose of 'carbon free' transportation. Whereas, renewable energy plays a vital role to generate electricity for charging. For instance, Nissan leaf, Mitsubishi i-MiEV, and Tesla Roadster acquired technology for its PHEVs (Graham-Rowe et al., 2012). However, categories of EVs present in Figure 5 shows three different variants each with a unique range of electrically driven mechanism depending on the strength and capacity of the battery.

COMPARATIVE STUDIES ON DIFFERENT TYPES OF ELECTRIC VEHICLES

The proper choice of purchasing a vehicle is not an easy task. There are different sort of choices which varies person to person. Consideration of buying an HEV or PHEV increases another factor into an already tough decision. The consumers need to distinguish among deferent types of electric vehicles before taking the decision to buy one of those. Different types of electric vehicles are described below.

Conventional Hybrids

Some of the conventional Hybrids such as Prius from Toyota merge both the gasoline type of engine with a motor (electric). Conventional hybrid vehicles have a battery and an electric motor. These types of vehicles cannot simply plugged-in into the grid and easily recharged. Moreover, the batteries of these

Figure 5. Different type of electric vehicles

	Conventional	Hybrid-Electric	Plug-in Hybrid Electric	Battery Electric
	CV	HEV	PHEV	BEV
Power Convertor	Engine	Engine & Motor	Engine & Motor	Motor
Battery Pack	-	Small	Medium	Large
Gasoline 	✓	✓	✓	
Electricity 			✓	✓

hybrids are only charged by the energy that captured during the time of braking which is also known as 'regenerative braking'. The conversion of kinetic energy into the electrical energy occur during this type of braking (Yilmaz & Krein, 2013). Whereas, this energy is usually wasted in the traditional vehicles. The electric motor normally works with the traditional gasoline-powered engine in order to decrease the use of gasoline or even permit the gasoline engine to turn off in total depending on the type of hybrid. The introduction of hybrid fuel-saving mechanisms can radically boost up the fuel economy. For instance, the model named '2014 Honda Accord hybrid' reaches a joint 47 miles per gallon (mpg) compared to a joint 30 mpg for the non-hybrid type at 12,000 miles a year and $4/gallon gasoline, that means saving more than $575 per year.

Plug-in Hybrid Electric Vehicles (PHEVs)

Plug-in Hybrid Electric Vehicles (PHEVs) are same as that of traditional hybrids with both IC engine and electric motor but PHEV batteries can be recharged by plugging into a charging outlet (Graham-Rowe *et al.,* 2012). Now the question arises about the validity of introducing PHEV in the place of a conventional hybrid. The answer is quite simple: unlike other conventional hybrids, Plug-in Hybrids can substitute electricity from the traditional grid for the gasoline. For example, the model '2014 Ford Fusion Energy' can travel around 21 miles by the use of electricity, and the model '2014 Chevy Volt' can travel about 28 miles before the gasoline motor kicks in (Al-Alawi & Bradley, 2013). Though the stats doesn't appears to be long ways, various folks normally drive their cars less than stated distance every day. Recent survey by UCS stated that about 54% of the car driver reported driving less than forty miles per day. Furthermore, use of electrical energy instead of gasoline is far inexpensive and cleaner for most of the people. The average price to drive hundred miles by the use of electricity costs only $3.45 compared to $13.52 for driving hundred miles on gasoline (Borba, Szklo, & Schaeffer, 2012).

Battery Electric Vehicles (BEVs)

Battery Electric Vehicles run exclusively on electricity via on-board batteries that are charged by plugging into an outlet or charging station. The Nissan LEAF, Fiat 500e, and Tesla Model S fall into this category, though there are many other BEVs in the market. These vehicles have no gasoline engine, longer electric driving ranges compared to PHEVs, and never produce tailpipe emissions (though there are emissions associated with these charging vehicles, which UCS has previously examined).The BEVs on the market today generally go around 60 to 80 miles per charge, though a Tesla can travel over 200 miles on a single charge. A recent UCS survey found that a BEV range of 60 miles would fit the weekday driving needs of 69 percent of U.S. drivers. As battery technology continues to improve, BEV ranges will extend even further, offering an even larger number of drivers the option of driving exclusively on electricity.

Fuel Cell Electric Vehicles (FCEVs)

Fuel Cell Electric Vehicles (FCEV) use an electric-only motor like a BEV but storing this energy is quite difficult because of the requirement of a big tank. Instead of recharging a battery, FCEVs store hydrogen gas in a tank. The fuel cell in FCEVs combines hydrogen with oxygen from the air to produce electricity. The electricity from the fuel cell then powers an electric motor, which powers the vehicle just like a BEV. And like BEVs, there is no smog-forming or climate-changing pollution from FCEVs tailpipe – the only byproduct is water. Unlike BEVs or PHEVs, however, there is no need to plug-in FCEVs, since their fuel cells are recharged by refilling with hydrogen, which can take as little as 5 minutes at a filling station. But just as producing electricity to charge a plug-in hybrid vehicle creates emissions, producing hydrogen also generates emissions. Hydrogen made today from natural gas produces about the same total emissions per mile as charging a plug-in vehicle with electricity generated from natural gas. But when made from renewable sources like biomass or solar power, hydrogen can be nearly emission free. Moreover, hydrogen fueling infrastructure, like public electric vehicle charging stations, is still ramping up and mostly available in California, USA. With increased state and federal policies aimed at helping get more of these vehicles on the road, FCEVs can become a large part of our future transportation systems. Although out of all these electric vehicles PHEVs considered as finest technology till date. Why PHEVs remain the finest technology among electric vehicle we can see it in characteristics of different electric vehicles given below.

CHARACTERISTICS OF BEVs, HEVs, PHEVs, and FCVs

The characteristics of different electric vehicles are shown in Table 1.

Table 1. Characteristics of BEVs, HEVs, PHEVs, and FCVs

Types of EVs	Battery EVs	Hybrid EVs	Plug-in Hybrid EVs	Fuel Cell EVs
Propulsion	Electric motor drives	• Electric motor drives • Internal combustion engines	• Electric motor drives • Internal combustion engines	Electric motor drives
Energy system	• Battery • Ultracapacitor	• Battery • Ultracapacitor • ICE generating unit	• Battery • Ultracapacitor • ICE generating unit • Charging port	• Fuel cells • Need battery/ Ultracapacitor to enhance power density for starting
Energy source and infrastructure	Electric grid charging facilities	Gasoline stations	Electric grid charging facilities	• Hydrogen • >Hydrogen production and existing infrastructure
Characteristics	• Zero emission • High energy efficiency • >Independence on crude oils • Relatively short range • High initial cost • Commercially accessible	• Very low emission • Higher fuel economy as compared to traditional vehicle • Longer driving range • Higher cost as compared ICE vehicles	• Very low emission • Higher fuel economy as compared to HEV • Longer driving range than HEV	• Ultra low emission • High energy efficiency • Satisfied driving range • High cost • Under development
Major issues	• Battery size and battery management • charging facilities • Higher cost	• Proper control, optimization and management • Battery sizing	• Engine use • required for accelerations and speeds • Grid connectivity	• Fuel cell cost, cycle life, reliability • Hydrogen infrastructure

Source: Contestabile *et al.*, 2011.

DESCRIPTION OF PHEVS TECHNOLOGY

The PHEVs vehicle run by the electricity supplied through the grid (unconventional) and stored in an on-board battery as well as refined liquid fuel in an internal combustion engine. The PHEVs are different from hybrid vehicles available in the present market (such as the Toyota Prius). The PHEVs completely empowered by a battery for a limited distance and can be recharged from provided electrical grid for further locomotion. Apart from this fixed distance, all-electric range vehicle works as an off-grid (or conventional) hybrid, with the fuel economy benefits resulting depend on the battery and electric motor to minimize efficiency losses in general. Whereas, PHEVs get more power and energy from the battery in comparison to conventional hybrids .The main reason is that they depend completely or entirely on the electricity that stored in a battery for propulsion. The main hindrance towards the commercialization of the PHEVs is battery efficiency and economical behavior among the consumers (Khondaker et al., 2016). Since a decade, battery KVA and energy per unit volume has shown gradual improvement in terms of unit cost. While the cost of battery packs for vehicles remain unchanged and required larger in size, while on-road usage performance and safety remain unconfirmed. Lithium-ion is commonly used in batteries of the PHEVs, which provides extended power and energy per unit volume as compared to nickel metal hydride or any other type of batteries (Kalghatgi, 2014). PHEV models that are being developed currently are supported by lithium-ion batteries. Lithium-ion battery is usually used in personal electronics gadgets experience barriers to its use in vehicles. Additionally, apprehensions for safety, durability and performance attaining these set objectives at the reasonable cost is the main challenge (Jain & Ahuja, 2013). Several experts of batteries efficiency rely on production at a large scale which will help them to minimize a cost of the battery, however, the picture is not clear that the cost will permit to PHEVs stand across conventional vehicles anytime soon. A brief summary related to the significance of PHEVs is described in below.

BENEFIT OF PLUG-IN HYBRID ELECTRIC VEHICLE ADOPTION

The PHEVs depend on batteries having large storage to stand for any financial or environmental profits comparative to old hybrids as well as ICE vehicles, the features and design concerns related to batteries of PHEV play a significant role in the possible acceptance of PHEVs. Consumer approvals and adaptation will be associated with the battery cost, operating cost, power and performance, battery cycle and calendar life and safety along with other extended features. Summaries of the recent market of battery technology for PHEV applications for the future objectives (Graham-Rowe *et al.*, 2012; Rahman *et al.*, 2014; Rahman *et al.*, 2016). Hybrid Electric vehicles can leave the impression to the level of consumer's adoption. In the upcoming section, we explain the main features of PHEVs adoption. Whereas, Figure 6 illustrates the vehicle electrification comparison.

Figure 6. Vehicle electrification comparison
Source: Becker et al., 2009.

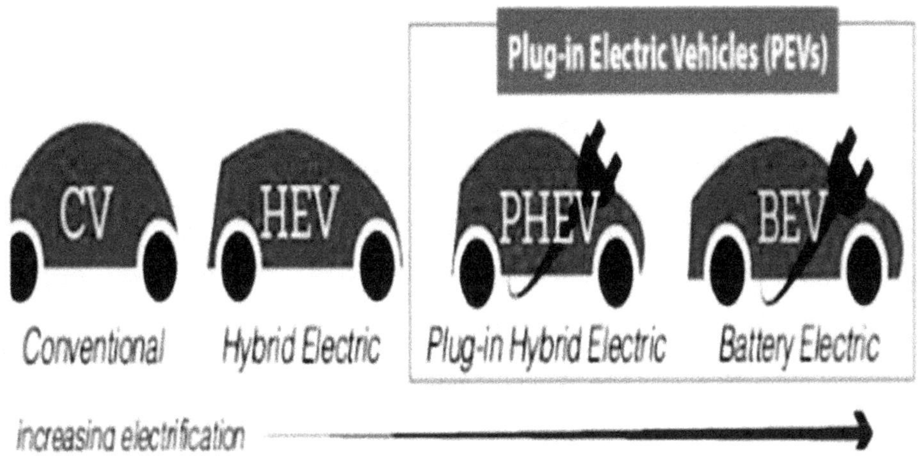

KEY FACTORS OF CONSUMER INCENTIVES TOWARD PHEVS ADOPTION

Consumer Preferences Perspective

In the line of this study, we found out that the conventional consumers are ready to adopt PHEVs at the same cost or equivalent to that of gasoline vehicles only if it values reduces up to an average of $10,000 to $20,000 in general (Howey, 2012). In comparison, consumers are ready to purchase PHEVs if they have multiple ranges of vehicles available (Becker et al., 2009; I. Rahman, P. M. Vasant, B. S. M. Singh, & M. Abdullah-Al-Wadud, 2015b). At mainstream level, consumers show their interest towards the adoption of PHEVs.

- **Willingness to Pay:** Willingness to pay high fuel prices and environmental benefits are the key factors that are being observed by the consumers while preferring PHEVs as an alternate energy source. An industrial survey conducted to observe the major factors across different vehicle market trends in the various region (United States, European Union, Asia, Japan & China) that could favorably influence PHEVs adaptation(Johansson & Mattsson, 2012). Although the environment and fuel savings marked the highest rank, on the other hand government incentives to lower the ownership cost prove to be an important factor effect. Extended research suggested that shortage of access point for charging, high pricing were the major deterrents in the direction of adoption. Charging convenience kept in consideration in almost every survey conducted, where consumers showed an agreement to acquire convenient charging and more than 50% consumers agree to pay up to $500 to $1,000 with reduce charging duration from eight to four hours daily. However empirically there were often discrepancy in collaborating between consumer's statements and actual willingness of payments. The EU (European Union) recent analysis suggested that about 16 percent of the consumers were first movers and are most likely to purchase or lease a PHEVs, whereas over 50% eager to ponder over in future. Moreover, thirty-one percent would not preferably accept PHEVs technology. It shows that over half of the surveyed consumers could hardly incentivize to adopt PHEVs. By probing further as shown in almost half or around 43% consumers actually interested to pay the cost of premium and shows that more than 55% expected to pay less than €15,000 as per statistics. However, government incentives, which directly imply the PHEVs would need to overcome the price competition with Internal Combustion Engine (ICE) cars to make a positive mark which can possibly trigger adoption.

- **Informing Consumers:** Informing consumers is the high cost of PHEVs premium payment and the overall absence of inclination to spend a premium for savings of fuel and eco-friendly advantages. In this point most of the consumers are unaware of the cost management of PHEVs and the benefit of fuel efficiency with respect to CO_2 emissions. Although consumers consider efficiency of fuel as the topmost benchmarks while making a purchase with accumulated discount of around 18 to 30%. Therefore it is also beneficial for future cost cutting standards that decreases the fuel prices where payback periods reduced up to 2-3 years. This suggests some major market flaws exists in consumer decision-making w.r.t fuel pricing. While in the USA, study suggests that the customers usually kept a justification of simply initial 3 years savings of fuel that demonstrate the real economic significance of a fourteen-year PHEV life by around 60 percent. The main reason for the failure of market is the absence of duration as well as aimed consumer info about traditional vehicle's emission of CO_2, mileage of traveling and cost effectiveness. Consecutively, while initial purchase, vehicle attributes namely performance, thrust, engine size, and brand image are considered as the higher priority than that of vehicle emissions and fuel consumption. However, in Malaysia overall information about CO_2 emissions becomes mandatory on every car brand advertised. It used to be restricted only for the car showroom, although late decision-making process already made an immense impact on buyers to look for the key attribute of CO_2 emission while purchasing. Within Malaysia, nearly 80% of car buyers hardly look at the vehicle's CO_2 emission rating before purchase.
- **Social Norms:** Customer understanding and absence of provided information about PHEVs cost-benefit along with the present market place architecture, where high-emission type vehicles are linked with socio-economic rank, are a vital obstruction for the adoption of PHEVs. Customer survey suggested that a solid bridge between buying behavior, societal surroundings, possession, identity, and rank are all associated directly. Social norms highly influence purchase decision making, where buyers look for financial savings along with improved fuel economy to pursue a higher-specification cars. This current market reflection in reviews shows that customers are not keen to negotiate the performance of vehicle as well as elegance. With the clear understanding and proper information, we are now beginning to acquire healthy purchasing motivations from the early adoption of hybrid technology, which can educate us towards the direction of PHEVs adoption. Scientific study reveals that there exists still a vast range of elements encouraging hybrid type adoption of innovative technology. Strong influential factors that made the impact on vehicle purchasing decisions are financial stability, eco-friendly ethics, policy-associated advantages, lifestyle, and status. Over a period of time Hybrid technology made a symbolic image portrayed by driving a hybrid shows a strong adoption factor and become an ideology that hybrid-car ownership reflects a particular community's status and norms. Extended research is required to decouple consumer behavior from the social norms of identity and status encircled ICE-vehicle ownership

to incentivize PHEVs adoption. The slowest of all available methods is Level-1 charging. In the United States, Level-1 charging uses a standard 120V/15A single-phase outlet which is grounded, such as NEMA 5-15R. The connection may use a standard J1772 connector into the electric vehicle ac port. No additional infrastructure is required for home or business sites. At night, low off-peak rates for charging are likely to be available. The total cost of a residential Level-1 charging infrastructure has been estimated around \$500 - \$880 (De Sousa, Silvestre, & Bouchez, 2010; Morrow, Karner, & Francfort, 2008).

Behavioral Economics Perspective

Behavioral economics explores why consumer makes irrational decisions, and why and how their behavior does not follow the predictions of economic models. Biggest economic obstacle towards the adoption of the PHEVs is the battery cost (Faria, Moura, Delgado, & de Almeida, 2012). Large battery manufacturing factories can try to cut costs slightly, but researchers calculate that the saving of cost with respect to high-volume manufacturing are almost fatigued at the production volumes. So, our purpose is now to attain knowledge of purchasing inspirations of initial PHEVs adopters, which might provide evidence on the way towards incentivizing the PHEVs adoption. The hypothetical study presents that there lies a widespread range of influences motivating the adoption of hybrids, containing concern in new types of technical as well as financial benefits, environmental values and policy-related benefits (Faria *et al.*, 2012). Whereas, they further highlight the two strong influences such as attitude and lifestyle on the decisions of purchasing the PHEVs. Moreover, the symbolic image carried by driving a hybrid has been proved to be an important factor in adoption (Carley, Krause, Lane, & Graham, 2013), which can make a perception or ideology that hybrid-vehicle ownership reflects a particular community's values and norms. Additional research is required to decouple behavior of consumer from the social norms of identity and status (Kalghatgi, 2014) surrounding ICE-vehicle ownership, and incentivize PHEVs adoption.

Technological Diffusion Perspective

Innovation diffusion is influenced by behavioral and technological factors. Innovations spread through social networks, and technologies improve over time. Individuals learn of innovations from previous adopters, which can positively influence further adoption (Faria et al., 2012). Improved technological performance can increase returns to adoption and accelerate diffusion (Tran, 2012). Energy-technology diffusion is typically assessed with learning curves, which is the relationship between cost, c, and the cumulative growth in stock, y, empirically observed to be a power law of form $c(y) \propto y-\alpha$ where the exponent, α is the rate of improvement called the progress ratio, $2-\alpha$, which is the factor by which costs decrease with each doubling of cumulative production. Therefore, that relationship has been observed for different energy technologies (ethanol fuels, installed wind capacity, photovoltaic cell) (Botkin, Keller, & Rosenthal, 2012). The learning curve reduces the diffusion process to cumulative stock and price effects. Although this is appropriate for supply-side technology (Botkin et al., 2012), growth in demand-side technology (PHEVs) will also be influenced by behavioral factors (preferences, attitudes, lifestyles and social norms). These factors are not typically accounted for the analysis of energy technology diffusion (Rahman et al., 2016). There is a need to better understand the feedbacks between how behavior can influence technological diffusion and how technology improvements can in turn influence adoption.

Policy and Implications Perspective

Under federal fuel economy standards, countries that mandate electric vehicle sales allow other countries to the modification of large-emitting vehicle fleets (Richardson, 2013). The result will be greater division in the types of vehicles bought in other countries without minimizing emissions or consumption of gasoline. So, a variety of factors that will affect adoption patterns for electrified vehicles (Faria et al., 2012). Moreover, mainstream consumers will need costs to come way down in order to produce a high level of production. However, the problem occurs with the limited residential parking suitable for electric vehicle charging may pose a long-term limit to mainstream adoption, and public charger investment is an expensive way to save gasoline (Rahman et al., 2016). Loss of vehicle range in extreme weather regions may also affect regional adoption, and adoption in some regions can lead to higher-polluting fleets in other regions. Recent Malaysian researchers also indicate that exposure to hybrids through social networks gave buyers confidence in the technology, which positively influenced adoption (Ozaki & Sevastyanova, 2011). Empirical and theoretical work on innovation diffusion and environmental behavior show that consumers are influenced by their social groups and willing to comply with their norms (Egbue & Long, 2012). These findings indicate that government and industrial need to more effectively communicate how PHEVs can address both the financial concerns and social aspirations of potential adopters (Rahman et al., 2016). There is scope for policy to be informed by new understanding of how information and innovations spread through social networks (Johansson & Mattsson, 2012) to identify potential adopters and increase exposure, familiarity, and knowledge about the benefits of PHEVs. A significant research within Malaysia suggests that exposure to hybrids technology through social networks provide the consumer an extra confidence in the technology, which positively influenced adoption. Technical as well as the theoretical work on innovation diffusion and environmental behavior suggests that consumers get motivated though their social groups and willing to comply with the same status. Findings point out that government and industry should adopt more effective and efficient approach to communicating how one can be beneficial both financially and socially aspirations. Social media viral information should be scale out with proper policy enforcement with an understanding of how beneficial and environment-friendly information and innovation spreads out to identify potential adopters of PHEVs (MANTUS, 2015).

A CASE STUDY ON FORECASTING THE ADOPTION OF PLUG-IN HYBRID ELECTRIC VEHICLES AMONG MALAYSIAN CONSUMERS

The need to reduce carbon emission has been sensed worldwide (Lehmann, 2007; Rahman et al., 2016). There are nations that are taking steps to control and reduce carbon emission (Pandey, Agrawal, & Pandey, 2011). The world transportation sector is a major contributor in carbon gas emission (Pongthanaisawan & Sorapipatana, 2013). Currently, it is estimated to be responsible for 23% emission but by the year 2030, this figure is expected to rise to 50%. In line with this policy, Malaysia too is now actively taking steps to reduce carbon emissions (Lippert, 2015; Susarla & Friedrich, 2013). Its energy consumption has shown a rapid rise, up 36.8% in 2012 using 1990 consumption as a base (Rahman et al., 2015a; Solís & Sheinbaum, 2013). This is the highest consumption level among all the sectors in the country. It is clear that fuel consumption is expected to rise given the increase in the number of vehicles that are coming on the road (F.-Y. Chen, 2013). Whereas, the increase is estimated at 8.7% (Johansson & Mattsson, 2012). This state of affairs makes the transportation sector as a challenging contributor to CO2 emission (Parshall et al., 2010). One of the reasons for the prevalence of this situation is the inadequate performance of the public transport system which has compelled commuters to seek personal mode of transportation (Parshall et al., 2010). The usage of public transportation is a mere 16%, lowest amongst other major Asian countries (Parshall et al., 2010). The reliance on fossil fuel leads to the uncertain situation (Golosov, Hassler, Krusell, & Tsyvinski, 2014). Additionally, Yang, Li, Sun, and Chen (2014) stated that the expenditure on imported oil weighs heavily on a country's finances. Furthermore, Giles (2014) specified that the security element that a country has to consider to ensure uninterrupted supplies. Whereas, hang, Ji, and Fan (2013) indicated that the concerns that make sense to adopt a technology which at least reduces fossil fuel consumption. Barbarossa, Beckmann, De Pelsmacker, Moons, and Gwozdz (2015) highlighted the point that throughout the world the attempts are being made to control and to reduce carbon emission. The United Kingdom plans to reduce emission by 45% by 2020 (Bateman et al., 2013). European Union countries have set the target as 20% by the end of 2020 (Nugent & Rhinard, 2015). The Malaysian Government pledged to reduce emission by 40% by 2020, using 2005 emission level as the base (Parshall et al., 2010). This pledge was made during United Nations Climate Conference in Copenhagen-2009. Vehicles using alternative fuel to petrol are attracting attention worldwide (Masum et al., 2013). The alternative is electrically powered vehicles technology which is available in relatively simple form (Masum et al., 2013). It is now important to generate consumer acceptance of such electrically driven vehicles based on EVs (Parshall et al., 2010). Such vehicles use batteries which require being charged frequently. Vehicles using alternative fuel to petrol are attracting attention worldwide (Wang, Fan, Zhao, Yang, & Fu, 2016). He further explains that the performance of battery improves. As Fischer et al. (2012) seen that more time and effort, as well as finances, are being spent to improve battery performances and some progress has also been reported. A number of car manufacturers are engaged in trying to develop a car which would not only be viable but also be easily acceptable in the quest to reduce carbon emission (Bergek, Berggren, Magnusson, & Hobday, 2013; Lee & Ofori-Boateng, 2013).

An electric vehicle which uses both electrical and internal combustion engines for propulsion purposes appears to be a very promising prospect (Millo et al., 2014). Sharaf and Orhan (2014) stated that the advantage of the electric vehicles is that it does not have to charge its batteries. Hence, this sort of vehicle offers an advantage in the mission to reduce carbon emission by as much as 30-50 percent and able to attain 40-60 percent improvement in terms of fuel efficiency although these figures are provided by the manufacturers. Though, he further stated that in actual fact, they are going to be somewhat on the lower side. On the other hand, Rahman et al. (2015b) stated that plug-in vehicles are better as there is no CO2 emission. Schuitema, Anable, Skippon, and Kinnear (2013) argued that the disadvantage is that the batteries cannot offer the same mileage that electric vehicles would it can easily drain off. Furthermore, Hosseini, Badri, and Parvania (2012) claimed that there are very few plug-in facilities that such vehicles may need. In order to achieve the main goal of this study we need to identify and resolve the shortcomings i.e. limited mileage offered by batteries as well as the inability to charge the batteries with the frequency required, that hindered the acceptability of EVs (Chang, Probstl, Goswami, Zamani, & Chakraborty, 2015). However, Johansson et al., (2012) itemizing the adoption of plug-in hybrid electric vehicles will increase popularity and acceptability. Because of PHEVs being more practicable they are becoming more popular in the U.S., Japan and Europe (Fotouhi, Auger, Propp, Longo, & Wild, 2016). With keen consideration, popularity and performance Malaysian government also took drastic measures to promote the usage and adaptability of electric vehicles (Luo et al., 2012). The Malaysian higher authority has fixed the goal of 500,000 PHEVs playing on Malaysian roads at the end of 2015 and around five million by the year 2020 (The National Council of Malaysia, 2012). In order to promote the usage of PHEVs, the government has initiated a number of policies, including subsidizing the sale of PHEVs. The government has also paid special consideration on the advancement and manufacture of hybrid electric vehicles in the eleventh 5 yearlong Plan. The government also planned to invest RMB 100 billion ($ 16 billion) for the improvement of technologies in the twelfth 5 yearlong planning (Sang & Bekhet, 2015; Zhang et al., 2013). The government did indicate in 2009 a 10 cities thousand Vehicles initiative to give a boost to the growth of PHEVs and to popularize their use. However, the consumer reaction fell short of expectations (Richardson, 2013; Sang & Bekhet, 2015). According to Malaysian Associations of Automobile Manufacturers Association, the cumulative sales were 27,400 PHEVs in 2012. Of these, 23,000 were acquired by the govern agency and the community service sector while around 4,400 were bought by individuals. It was seen that the ordinary Malaysian considered performance of the conventional vehicle to be superior to the PHEVs (Zhang et al., 2013). The consumer did show his preference to have a PHEVs as a second vehicle (Sang & Bekhet, 2015). Currently, it is estimated that 13% of households have a second car. This figure may rise as the economy continues to expand. Very likely the PHEVs technology may improve also and the consumer may prefer the new innovations (Li & Loo, 2014). In any case, there are bright prospects of PHEVs gaining popularity in Malaysia. Figure 7 illustrates the adoption of Plug-in Hybrid Electric Vehicles.

The introduction of PHEVs into the Malaysian market has led the automotive industry to a whole new echelon in zero fuel dependency and increased fuel efficiency (Sang & Bekhet, 2015). Although Falvo, Martirano, Sbordone, and Bocci (2013) declared that PHEVs may reduce the tailpipe emission from the vehicle, the advantages in term of total emission are rather marginal if coal is still used to power the electricity generation. Therefore, the government has intensively promoted the wider use of renewable energy such as biomass and solar to reduce dependency on coal besides to have a better mix of electricity generation within the country (Rahman et al., 2014). While the usages of greener and cleaner vehicles, such as PHEVs, are well supported by government policies and programs, little information

Figure 7. Adoption of plug-in hybrid electric vehicles
Source: MANTUS, 2015.

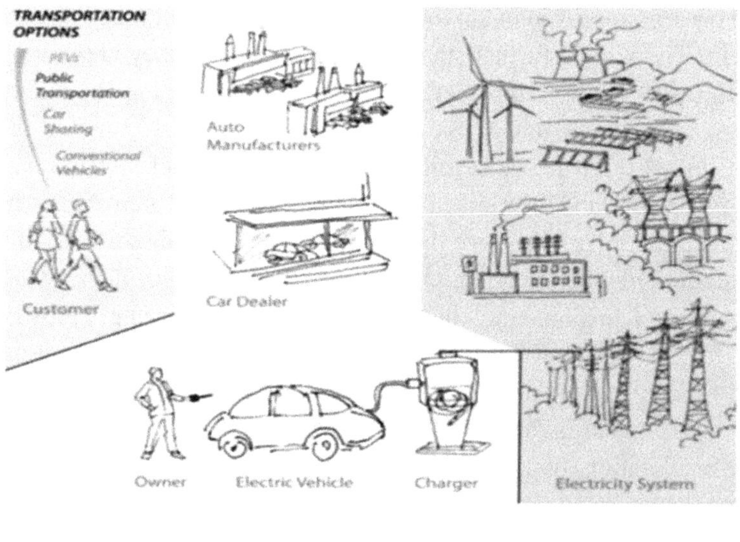

Figure 8. The conceptual framework

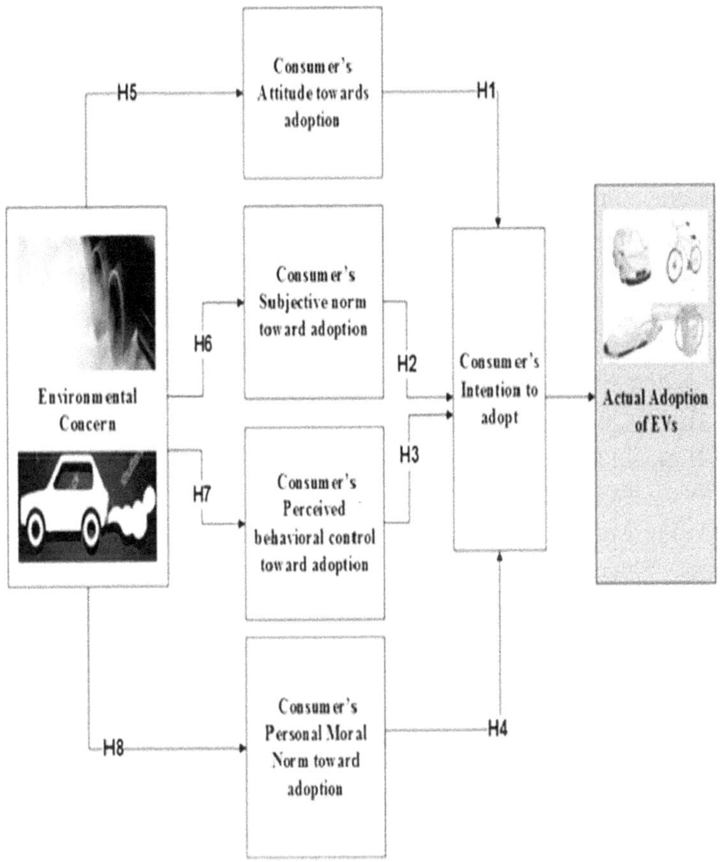

is divulged about the public acceptance of PHEVs from the social perspective (Danial, Lee, Lee, Yeo, & Ang, 2013). As the introduction of PHEVs is relatively new in Malaysia, there is no prior study or investigation that was carried out on Malaysian drivers to gauge the public acceptance levels and usage intentions of this new vehicle technology (Sang & Bekhet, 2015). As a matter of fact, public acceptance can emerge as a powerful impediment for market diffusion and can hinder the development of PHEV adoption in Malaysia. Plug-in Hybrid electric vehicles require the funding from different governmental agencies for successful market penetration, although the customers' target for buying PHEVs is also vital to point (Chua & Oh, 2011). Many researchers have studied the intention of customer considering their purchase of environment-friendly cars (Coad et al. 2009). For example, authors (2011) discovered the affecting factors for the adoption behavior among PPHEVs consumer community. As Schuitema *et al.* (2013) explored the effect of EVs adoption intention due to private vehicle owners' perception of EVs qualities. Hang *et al.* (2013) presented a review to examine intention of consumers to accept PHEVs as well as noticed some vital factors influencing adoption intention of consumers such as performance features, economic benefits, environmental consciousness and the psychological requirements. On the base of obtained evidence and the planned behavior extended theory Ajzen (1991) performed a questionnaire study. The purpose of that questionnaire study is to examine consumers' intention to accept plug-in hybrid EVs, and also offers some recommendations for the authorities and car vendors to encourage adoption intention.

REEXAMINE THE PAST WORK

The behavioral intention and the behavior are widely defined in the Theory of Planned Behavior (TPB) (Ajzen, 1991) which is extension model of Theory of Reasoned Action (Ajzen, 2011, 2015; Fishbein & Ajzen, 1975). This model, defined by the behavioral intention actual behavior is determined. After that, the behavioral intention is controlled by its 3 elements: attitude toward the behavior, subjective norm, and perceived behavioral control (Ajzen, 1991) .Now researchers have also utilized the TPB structure to discover eco-friendly consumer behavior. For example, by using TPB model by (C.-Y. Chen, Yang, Chen, Chen, & Chen, 2010) extract consumers' behavioral intention towards waste recycling and define consumer recycling intention. Whereas, the following researchers (Macintosh & Lockshin, 1997; Sigurdardottir, Kaplan, Møller, & Teasdale, 2013) utilized the TPB to expect the purposes of teenagers to convert by car or bicycle. M.-F. Chen and Tung (2014), worked on the TPB model by most psychological factors, such as attitudes and norms, have a major effect on the acceptance of clean cars. By these research comes to conclude that TPB model is an appropriate concept to predict eco-friendly communication, increase the overall explanatory power of TPB; by adding some variables like moral beliefs by (Kautonen, Gelderen, & Fink, 2015).For example, Beck and Ajzen (1991) and (M.-F. Chen & Tung, 2014) specified that TBP's explanatory power has been increased by personal approaches of moral accountability or individual moral ethics when inspecting intention of individual to behave in eco-friendly and note that one's moral norms are possible way to find the behavioral intention. Kroshus, Baugh, Daneshvar, and Viswanath (2014), states that German buyers are well known for climate change adopters and they want to adopt green vehicles by paying the significant amount and fulfill their moral norms and responsibility. By these research, we come to conclude that variable of personal moral norms plays a significant role on behavioral intention. TPB which previously having 3 primary elements i.e. attitude, subjective norms and perceived behavioral may convert into extended TPB model by adding personal norms in the TPB model (M.-F. Chen & Tung, 2014; Jalilvand & Samiei, 2012). Mentioned that consumer is now more concerned with the environment from last decades due to dreadful condition of the environment. Many researches defined the link between green concerns as well as definite ecofriendly behavior and have worried the environmental concerns in predicating that behavior. For example Kahn (2007) observed that environmentalists are usually more buying PHEV than non-environmentalists. Fedor et al. (2015) observed that environmental concern is a most important and dominant factor in the purchase of PHEVs and those consumer who pay highly concerned toward environment will be more willing to buy PHEVs as they show their concerned towards environment by means of their purchase. Ziegler (2012) showed in his research that buyer who show concerned towards environment have a greater stated preference for green vehicles (Jensen, Cherchi, & de Dios Ortúzar, 2014). Bateman et al. (2013) used the defined data and statistic on both decision to purchase vehicle and concerns to environmental to study consumer preferences towards green technologies and consumer will pay more for low emission vehicle as they highly concerned to environment. Bamberg 2003 defined the role of environmental concern and considered as an important element of the extended TPB model. This research study shows that by performing an all-inclusive study and to comprehend consumers' intention towards adoption of PHEVs, individual ethical norm and environmental concern were included into TPB model to change into an extended TPB model. This research established the appropriateness of the extended TPB model and confirmed that the extended TPB model has good explanatory power in predicting consumers' intention to adopt PHEVs.

CONCEPTUAL FRAMEWORK AND HYPOTHETICAL RELATIONSHIP

According to Davis (1989) observation in the TPB model, behavioral intention, as well as actual behavior, have the similar factors, although behavioral intention is usually more powerfully forecasted than the actual behavior. Moreover, Ajzen (1991) observed behavioral intention as an immediate determinant of actual behavior, and when a suitable measure of intention is attained, this will result from most accurate prediction of behavior. This indicates that intention towards adoption is may be more strongly connected to the determinants than actual adoption. Schuitema et al. (2013), also defined that the measurement of a level of actual adoption is slightly difficult to achieve. In the meanwhile HEV is in beginning mode in Malaysia and a large number of the consumer are taking a decision on whether to adopt PHEVs. Thus, this chapter covered that measuring adoption intention is more applicable than actual adoption. Han and Kim (2010), noted that the elements present in the extended theory of planned behavior in the TPB, attitude directs the complete evaluation of the specific behavior.in the perspective of consumer intention towards the adoption of PHEVs, and attitude is a term that is defined as a positive or negative assessment of the adoption behavior. Han and Kim (2010), observed that in many studies attitude is an important variable (anterior) of behavioral intention. For example,Klöckner, Nayum, and Mehmetoglu (2013) surveyed on national base to find out consumer intention towards the purchase of green vehicles and he found that consumer having the positive attitude towards environmental concerns are more willing to adopt green vehicles. Ajzen (1991) stated that the consumer who have more positive attitude, their intention will be stronger to perform a certain behavior. He further defined that subjective norms that is an individual's receive social pressure from groups of peoples or other people that are important in his/her life and wish him/her to show in a specific manner. Additionally, a number of researchers likewise, (Bockarjova & Steg, 2014; M.-F. Chen & Tung, 2014) observed that it is proved in last researches that subjective norms affect behavioral intention in a positive manner. However, he further elaborates that people considering that they should perform a specific behavior, they will have more intention to perform due to the higher degree of social pressure (M.-F. Chen & Tung, 2014). In the TPB Perceived, behavioral control is the last predictor of intention (Ajzen, 1991). While Ajzen (1991) also defined perceived behavioral control (PBC) is the degree of ease and difficulty perceived by an individual with respect to conducting behavior. In the recent scenario, perceived behavioral control consist of perception of technology, price, availability or knowledge to use the PHEV and the capability to perform the adoption behavior. López-Mosquera and Sánchez (2012), stated that the more the ability of the consumer to control these elements, the more behavioral intention will be developed. However, Ajzen (1991) defined that personal moral norm i.e. an extended element defined in TPB indicates that people senses for performing a specific moral behavior and makes his/her findings depend on his/her responsibility or principle. There is very much difference between the personal moral norm and subjective norm. Subjective norms cover external social pressure while personal moral norm can be differentiated by the internalized moral rules or values (Kautonen et al., 2015). Internalization is the main feature of the personal moral norm. In this research, we explain the personal moral norm through which consumer will decide either to adopt PHEVs or not based on his/her personal responsibility or moral principle rather than social pressure or social norms. Rezvani, Jansson, and Bodin (2015) stated that if the consumer has a higher degree of the personal moral norm than he/she will have more willing to adopt PHEVs. By thoroughly literature review mentioned above, the hypotheses are proposed as follows:

H1: Consumer's attitude will have a significant effect on consumer's intention to adopt PHEVs.
H2: Consumer's subjective norm will have a significant effect on consumer's intention to adopt PHEVs.
H3: Consumer's perceived behavioral control will have a significant effect on consumer's intention to adopt PHEVs.
H4: Consumer personal moral norm will have a significant effect on consumer's intention to adopt PHEVs.

EXTENDED THEORY OF PLANNED BEHAVIOR MODEL BASED ON ENVIRONMENTAL CONCERN

According to Schuitema et al. (2013) where researcher states that environmental concern is a term defined the considerate and awareness of environmental issues. Therefore, Richardson (2013) defined an important factor related to environmental concern is that help for individual to deviate from their present behavior to a more environmental-friendly behavior. Moreover, (Ajzen, 1991) mentioned in their research that environmental concerns do not impact directly specific environmental behavior rather than by some different variables indirectly. Hines, Hungerford, and Tomera (1987) has done a meta-analysis and find the correlation between environmental concern and environmentally friendly behavior and note that the reading between 0.23 and 0.35 this is called to .average correlation coefficient of environmental concern and behavior. This result shows that environmental concern does not depend on behavior which confirmed a result of (Ajzen, 1991; Taylor & Todd, 1995). Bamberg (2003) proposed that environmental issues put forth impact on individual's behavioral intention by norms, beliefs and attitudes. So we can conclude that environmental concern is an indirect factor of behavioral intention and a frontal factor of the elements of the extended TPB model. By these study, assumed that consumers' attitude, subjective norm, and personal moral norm and perceived behavioral will be used to control the adoption of PHEVs; are affected positively. The research framework is illustrated in Figure 8. Depend on the analysis done by above, the hypotheses are proposed as follows:

H5: Consumer's environment concern will have a significant effect on consumer's attitude toward adopting PHEVs.
H6: Consumer's environment concern will have a significant effect on consumer's subjective norm toward adopting PHEVs.
H7: Consumer's environment concern will have a significant effect on consumer's perceived behavioral control toward adopting PHEVs.
H8: Consumer's environment concern will have a significant effect on consumer's personal moral norm toward adopting PHEVs.

IMPLICATIONS

In the transport sector, reduction of carbon dioxide emissions keep in view, PHEVs has been considering as best alternative. The research for extended TPB model was used to find consumer intentions towards the adoption of PHEVs. We have also observed that individual ethical norm of the consumer has a progressive sign of their behavior intention towards adoption. But the comparison with past researchers (Arts, Frambach, & Bijmolt, 2011; Kaiser, Doka, Hofstetter, & Ranney, 2003; Long, Grow, Majoris,

& Hines, 2011) the addition of the personal moral norms has upgraded the explained variance which is less than the expected one. In this research; the impact of personal moral norms was minimum than measured values in international studies. This is not amazing in Malaysia the main reason is that communism is leading on numerous sides of day-to-day life (Furnham & Telford, 2012), and societal stress plays an important role in changing behavior of people. The role of subjective norm leads personal moral norms and effect of environmental concern on the elements of the extended TPB structure and intention towards the adoption is further explained.

It is defined that the intention towards adoption is affected by environmental concern indirectly and its effect is positively related to attitude, subjective norm, perceived behavioral control, and personal moral norm. The extended TPB model elements in part arbitrate the effects of consumer's environmental concern on intention towards adoption. It is vital to highlight that environmental concern and adoption intention is not directly proportional. In fact intention of adoption depends on upon effects of environmental concern and the four elements of the extended TPB model. Furthermore, we must aware that 50% of those attended in theoretical assessment is declined. The respondents are more motivated to purchase PHEVs than who refused to involve in assessment. This analysis is not only useful in literature but also finding relevant information for government and vehicle dealer. By the research concluded that consumer attitude towards adopting PHEVs is positive, impact by environmental concerns. In other words, if the consumer has more concern towards environment they will have more attraction towards adopting PHEVs. In general with respect to marketing angle, Vehicle seller shows and launched PHEVs by this they enhance the popularity of brand as well as consumer's environmental concern and emphasize the awareness of eco-friendly environmental benefits towards the adoption of PHEVs. Consumers give importance to social pressure or pressure inserted by other people or early adopters are one of the most significant factors of their intention towards adoption. By supporting the research, we will stand a chance of developing this further with theoretical frameworks of emotions in psychology, consumer behavior, and ethics. Whereas there is need of proper communication memoranda. Instruction and strategies can generate explicit intellectual and emotive replies in consumers and therefore, affect their choices and behaviors. Accepting the reasoning and emotional reactions can assist marketing authorities and lawful agencies in conniving their communication, instruction, and strategies to probably overcome more or less few obstacles toward the adoption of electric vehicles. The assessment of PHEVs of these participants and initial adopters bear a vital impact on customer's adoption intention. So that Government sector and sellers give high attention to enhancing the early adopters' evaluation of PHEVs. PHEVs Clubs and Word-of-Mouth (WOM) marketing strategy may be two effective and dominant methods to increase the subjective norm that consumers observed. Hence, this study tries to fill the gap by proposing a conceptual framework by tailoring the sustainability environment concern that leads towards the attitude, subjective norm, perceived behavior control and personal norm which leads in the direction of intention which direct towards actual adoption. The proposed conceptual framework theorized the significant relationship among the variable towards the proper adoption of PHEVs as well as environmental sustainability and opens a new path for future research to empirically prove the hypothetical relationship among the variables.

FUTURE RESEARCH DIRECTIONS

Although our study has some exciting outcomes and applications, it is vital to highlight the shortcomings of the current research. This study has a substantial future prospects in the domain of behavioral economics which informs us that consumers are motivated by the short-term more highly than the longer term, so in the outcome, if the up-front cost remains higher the total cost over three years would need to be significantly lower to be valued the same by people.

Preliminary, this research concentrated on consumers' adoption intention towards PHEVs. Yet, behavioral economics is the immediate element of consumer's actual behavior, and when an appropriate measure of intention is achieved, it will provide the most accurate prediction of behavior (Ajzen 1991). There is a gap between adoption intention and actual adoption behavior (Ajzen et al., 2011). A consumer's actual adoption behavior may not always equivalent to adoption intention. Consequently, to develop the suppositions, researchers should further investigate these respondents' actual adoption behavior by using interview and sampling methods in the following studies. Secondly, the participants in the research all come from the 10 pilot cities in Malaysia. Thus, we do expect that future study will be conducted with sample data from different cities in Malaysia. As we know, there are cultural differences between Malaysia and foreign developed countries in adopting PHEVs. For example, Malaysian consumers are more likely to adopt a conventional vehicle as the first vehicle and intend to adopt a PHEV as a second vehicle while in foreign developed countries consumers do not care about this matters. Higher income consumers in Malaysia prefer to adopt traditional larger vehicles since these vehicles are a symbol of identity and status, while consumers in foreign developed countries consider more about the performance and attributes of the vehicles. Upcoming studies can accomplish empirical studies to enhance the present research findings.

CONCLUSION

Sustainable policy enforcement, long-term industrial venture and basic changes in the behavior of consumer are the key factors required to decarbonize current mode of transportation and adoption of PHEVs. Although this chapter emphasized the significance of modern world connections between the technology and behavior through the magnitude of scales as well as their impact on market diffusion. Vital changes are required to integrate the approach of de-carbonization which will proportionally depend on technical as well as behavioral sciences. Another latest survey confirms the necessity of standardization, enforcement of the policy, consumer incentives, technology impacts, social constraints, advancements, and inter-market competition for PHEVs diffusion. Considering a win-win situation and assuming that PHEVs will provide a niche market over the next 20 years in general. A careful support will always be a handy option for a niche market during the early phases of diffusion. Another key factor i.e. Policy will assist niche market by providing free charging using renewable energies with a feasible option to avail, however, financial investors require a long-term planning and anticipation for under-utilization of charging infrastructure until the market gets stable and mature. Industrial investments could possibly make an important impact by exploring new business models such as vehicle leasing, which already makes up a share of US and Malaysia vehicle markets. At recent days, PHEVs getting sold as a complete purchase, battery leasing and vehicle purchasing along with combined lease of vehicle and battery. Other methods acquired from telecommunication industry such as shared ownership or pay-as-you-go schemes which are available for consumers. An additional study must need to be conducted for a potential market of small and short-range city PHEVs, to overcome the anxiety of range through public charging points or battery-swapping stations. Moreover, at any given time, 90% of the PHEVs are theoretically available that allow the consumer to earn revenue by selling the excess power of their vehicle. The costs provisioning of low-speed leased PHEVs for local city usage is far lesser than adopting the current ownership model of an all-purpose long-range ICE vehicle. The majority of this literature assumes that the market is homogenous. On the other hand, industrial manufacturers of a car gets lucky in demonstrating a huge heterogeneity in the market with their market capturing trends. With this saturation within an embryonic market, we need to get ourselves educated with modern diffusion procedures, the behavioral approach of early adopters, and how efficiently potential buyers and leasers can be identified and incentivized.

ACKNOWLEDGMENT

The authors would like to acknowledge Universiti Teknologi PETRONAS (UTP), Department of Management and Humanities to facilitate this research study. The authors would also like to thank the reviewers for their valuable suggestion in order enhance the chapter.

REFERENCES

Ajzen, I. (1991). The theory of planned behavior. *Organizational Behavior and Human Decision Processes*, *50*(2), 179–211. doi:10.1016/0749-5978(91)90020-T

Ajzen, I. (2011). The theory of planned behaviour: Reactions and reflections. *Psychology & Health*, *26*(9), 1113–1127. doi:10.1080/08870446.2011.613995 PMID:21929476

Ajzen, I. (2015). The theory of planned behaviour is alive and well, and not ready to retire: A commentary on Sniehotta, Presseau, and Araújo-Soares. *Health Psychology Review*, *9*(2), 131–137. doi:10.1080/17437199.2014.883474 PMID:26209198

Al-Alawi, B. M., & Bradley, T. H. (2013). Review of hybrid, plug-in hybrid, and electric vehicle market modeling studies. *Renewable & Sustainable Energy Reviews*, *21*, 190–203. doi:10.1016/j.rser.2012.12.048

Arts, J. W., Frambach, R. T., & Bijmolt, T. H. (2011). Generalizations on consumer innovation adoption: A meta-analysis on drivers of intention and behavior. *International Journal of Research in Marketing*, *28*(2), 134–144. doi:10.1016/j.ijresmar.2010.11.002

Barbarossa, C., Beckmann, S. C., De Pelsmacker, P., Moons, I., & Gwozdz, W. (2015). A self-identity based model of electric car adoption intention: A cross-cultural comparative study. *Journal of Environmental Psychology*, *42*, 149–160. doi:10.1016/j.jenvp.2015.04.001

Bateman, I. J., Harwood, A. R., Mace, G. M., Watson, R. T., Abson, D. J., Andrews, B. . . . Dugdale, S. (2013). Bringing ecosystem services into economic decision-making: land use in the United Kingdom. *Science, 341*(6141), 45-50.

Becker, T. A., Sidhu, I., & Tenderich, B. (2009). *Electric vehicles in the United States: a new model with forecasts to 2030*. Oakland, CA: University of California Berkeley.

Bergek, A., Berggren, C., Magnusson, T., & Hobday, M. (2013). Technological discontinuities and the challenge for incumbent firms: Destruction, disruption or creative accumulation? *Research Policy*, *42*(6), 1210–1224. doi:10.1016/j.respol.2013.02.009

Bockarjova, M., & Steg, L. (2014). Can Protection Motivation Theory predict pro-environmental behavior? Explaining the adoption of electric vehicles in the Netherlands. *Global Environmental Change*, *28*, 276–288. doi:10.1016/j.gloenvcha.2014.06.010

Borba, B. S. M., Szklo, A., & Schaeffer, R. (2012). Plug-in hybrid electric vehicles as a way to maximize the integration of variable renewable energy in power systems: The case of wind generation in northeastern Brazil. *Energy*, *37*(1), 469–481. doi:10.1016/j.energy.2011.11.008

Botkin, D. B., Keller, E. A., & Rosenthal, D. B. (2012). *Environmental science*. New York, NY: Wiley.

Carley, S., Krause, R. M., Lane, B. W., & Graham, J. D. (2013). Intent to purchase a plug-in electric vehicle: A survey of early impressions in large US cites. *Transportation Research Part D, Transport and Environment*, *18*, 39–45. doi:10.1016/j.trd.2012.09.007

Chang, W., Probstl, A., Goswami, D., Zamani, M., & Chakraborty, S. (2015). *Reliable CPS Design for Mitigating Semiconductor and Battery Aging in Electric Vehicles*. Paper presented at the Cyber-Physical Systems, Networks, and Applications (CPSNA), 2015 IEEE 3rd International Conference on. doi:10.1109/CPSNA.2015.16

Chen, C.-Y., Yang, Y.-F., Chen, C.-W., Chen, L.-T., & Chen, T.-H. (2010). Linking the balanced scorecard (BSC) to business management performance: A preliminary concept of fit theory for navigation science and management. *Int. J. Phys. Sci*, *5*(8), 1296–1305.

Chen, F.-Y. (2013). Managers' views on environmental management: An examination of the Taiwanese airline industry. *Journal of Sustainable Development*, *6*(1), 65.

Chen, M.-F., & Tung, P.-J. (2014). Developing an extended theory of planned behavior model to predict consumers intention to visit green hotels. *International Journal of Hospitality Management*, *36*, 221–230. doi:10.1016/j.ijhm.2013.09.006

Chua, S. C., & Oh, T. H. (2011). Green progress and prospect in Malaysia. *Renewable & Sustainable Energy Reviews*, *15*(6), 2850–2861. doi:10.1016/j.rser.2011.03.008

Contestabile, M., Offer, G. J., Slade, R., Jaeger, F., & Thoennes, M. (2011). Battery electric vehicles, hydrogen fuel cells and biofuels. Which will be the winner? *Energy & Environmental Science*, *4*(10), 3754–3772. doi:10.1039/c1ee01804c

Danial, S., Lee, C., Lee, G. S., Yeo, W. B., & Ang, C. Q. (2013). *Development of unmanned aerial vehicle (uav) using alternative sources of fuel bee*. Avion.

Dulac, J. (2012). *Global transport outlook to 2050 Energy Analyst, Energy Technology Policy Division International Energy Agency Targets and scenarios for a low-carbon transport sector*. Retrieved from https://www.iea.org/media/workshops/2013/egrdmobility/DULAC_23052013.pdf

Egbue, O., & Long, S. (2012). Barriers to widespread adoption of electric vehicles: An analysis of consumer attitudes and perceptions. *Energy Policy*, *48*, 717–729. doi:10.1016/j.enpol.2012.06.009

Ellabban, O., Abu-Rub, H., & Blaabjerg, F. (2014). Renewable energy resources: Current status, future prospects and their enabling technology. *Renewable & Sustainable Energy Reviews*, *39*, 748–764. doi:10.1016/j.rser.2014.07.113

Falvo, M. C., Martirano, L., Sbordone, D., & Bocci, E. (2013). *Technologies for Smart Grids: a brief review.* Paper presented at the Environment and Electrical Engineering (EEEIC), 2013 12th International Conference on. doi:10.1109/EEEIC.2013.6549544

Faria, R., Moura, P., Delgado, J., & de Almeida, A. T. (2012). A sustainability assessment of electric vehicles as a personal mobility system. *Energy Conversion and Management*, *61*, 19–30. doi:10.1016/j.enconman.2012.02.023

Fischer, A. R., Beers, P. J., van Latesteijn, H., Andeweg, K., Jacobsen, E., Mommaas, H., . . . Veldkamp, A. T. (2012). Transforum system innovation towards sustainable food: A review. *Agronomy for Sustainable Development, 32*(2), 595-608.

Fishbein, M., & Ajzen, I. (1975). *Belief, attitudes, intention, and behavior. An introduction to theory and research.* Addison-Wesley.

Fotouhi, A., Auger, D. J., Propp, K., Longo, S., & Wild, M. (2016). A review on electric vehicle battery modelling: From Lithium-ion toward Lithium–Sulphur. *Renewable & Sustainable Energy Reviews*, *56*, 1008–1021. doi:10.1016/j.rser.2015.12.009

Furnham, A., & Telford, K. (2012). *Public attitudes, lay theories and mental health literacy: The understanding of mental health.* INTECH Open Access Publisher.

Giles, C. (2014). Winners and losers of oil price plunge. *Financial Times*. Retrieved from http://www.ft.com/cms/s/2/3f5e491484901 1e4ba4f00144feab dc0.html#axzz3U51zg3iv

Golosov, M., Hassler, J., Krusell, P., & Tsyvinski, A. (2014). Optimal taxes on fossil fuel in general equilibrium. *Econometrica*, *82*(1), 41–88. doi:10.3982/ECTA10217

Graham-Rowe, E., Gardner, B., Abraham, C., Skippon, S., Dittmar, H., Hutchins, R., & Stannard, J. (2012). Mainstream consumers driving plug-in battery-electric and plug-in hybrid electric cars: A qualitative analysis of responses and evaluations. *Transportation Research Part A, Policy and Practice*, *46*(1), 140–153. doi:10.1016/j.tra.2011.09.008

Han, H., & Kim, Y. (2010). An investigation of green hotel customers decision formation: Developing an extended model of the theory of planned behavior. *International Journal of Hospitality Management*, *29*(4), 659–668. doi:10.1016/j.ijhm.2010.01.001

Hines, J. M., Hungerford, H. R., & Tomera, A. N. (1987). Analysis and synthesis of research on responsible environmental behavior: A meta-analysis. *The Journal of Environmental Education*, *18*(2), 1–8. doi:10.1080/00958964.1987.9943482

Hori, Y. (2012). *Novel EV society based on motor/capacitor/wireless—Application of electric motor, supercapacitors, and wireless power transfer to enhance operation of future vehicles.* Paper presented at the Microwave Workshop Series on Innovative Wireless Power Transmission: Technologies, Systems, and Applications (IMWS), 2012 IEEE MTT-S International.

Hosseini, S. S., Badri, A., & Parvania, M. (2012). *The plug-in electric vehicles for power system applications: The vehicle to grid (V2G) concept.* Paper presented at the Energy Conference and Exhibition (ENERGYCON), 2012 IEEE International.

Howey, D. A. (2012). Policy: A challenging future for cars. *Nature Climate Change, 2*(1), 28-29.

Hu, Y., Sun, J., Li, W., & Pan, Y. (2014). A scientometric study of global electric vehicle research. *Scientometrics, 98*(2), 1269–1282. doi:10.1007/s11192-013-1067-8

Jain, S. K., & Ahuja, I. S. (2013). Strategies and success factors for overcoming challenges in ISO 9000 implementation in Indian manufacturing industry. International Journal of Technology. *Policy and Management, 13*(2), 121–139.

Jalilvand, M. R., & Samiei, N. (2012). The impact of electronic word of mouth on a tourism destination choice: Testing the theory of planned behavior (TPB). *Internet Research: Electronic Networking Applications and Policy, 22*(5), 591–612. doi:10.1108/10662241211271563

Jensen, A. F., Cherchi, E., & de Dios Ortúzar, J. (2014). A long panel survey to elicit variation in preferences and attitudes in the choice of electric vehicles. *Transportation, 41*(5), 973–993. doi:10.1007/s11116-014-9517-6

Johansson, B., & Mattsson, L.-G. (2012). *Road pricing: Theory, empirical assessment and policy.* Springer Science & Business Media.

Kaiser, F. G., Doka, G., Hofstetter, P., & Ranney, M. A. (2003). Ecological behavior and its environmental consequences: A life cycle assessment of a self-report measure. *Journal of Environmental Psychology, 23*(1), 11–20. doi:10.1016/S0272-4944(02)00075-0

Kalghatgi, G. T. (2014). The outlook for fuels for internal combustion engines. *International Journal of Engine Research.*

Kautonen, T., Gelderen, M., & Fink, M. (2015). Robustness of the theory of planned behavior in predicting entrepreneurial intentions and actions. *Entrepreneurship Theory and Practice, 39*(3), 655–674. doi:10.1111/etap.12056

Khondaker, A. N., Hasan, M. A., Rahman, S. M., Malik, K., Shafiullah, M., & Muhyedeen, M. A. (2016). Greenhouse gas emissions from energy sector in the United Arab Emirates – An overview. *Renewable & Sustainable Energy Reviews, 59*, 1317–1325. doi:10.1016/j.rser.2016.01.027

Klass, A. B. (2016). Future-Proofing Energy Transport Law. *Washington University Law Review*, 16–11.

Klöckner, C. A., Nayum, A., & Mehmetoglu, M. (2013). Positive and negative spillover effects from electric car purchase to car use. *Transportation Research Part D, Transport and Environment, 21*, 32–38. doi:10.1016/j.trd.2013.02.007

Kroshus, E., Baugh, C. M., Daneshvar, D. H., & Viswanath, K. (2014). Understanding concussion reporting using a model based on the theory of planned behavior. *Journal of Adolescent Health, 54*(3), 269-274.

Lee, K. T., & Ofori-Boateng, C. (2013). *Biofuels: Production Technologies, Global Profile, and Market Potentials Sustainability of Biofuel Production from Oil Palm Biomass*. Springer. doi:10.1007/978-981-4451-70-3_2

Lehmann, J. (2007). A handful of carbon. *Nature, 447*(7141), 143–144. doi:10.1038/447143a PMID:17495905

Li, L., & Loo, B. P. (2014). Alternative and transitional energy sources for urban transportation. *Current Sustainable/Renewable Energy Reports, 1*(1), 19-26.

Lippert, I. (2015). Environment as datascape: Enacting emission realities in corporate carbon accounting. *Geoforum, 66*, 126–135. doi:10.1016/j.geoforum.2014.09.009

Long, W. C., Grow, J. N., Majoris, J. E., & Hines, A. H. (2011). Effects of anthropogenic shoreline hardening and invasion by Phragmites australis on habitat quality for juvenile blue crabs (Callinectes sapidus). *Journal of Experimental Marine Biology and Ecology, 409*(1), 215–222. doi:10.1016/j.jembe.2011.08.024

López-Mosquera, N., & Sánchez, M. (2012). Theory of Planned Behavior and the Value-Belief-Norm Theory explaining willingness to pay for a suburban park. *Journal of Environmental Management, 113*, 251–262. doi:10.1016/j.jenvman.2012.08.029 PMID:23041517

Luo, R., Liu, B., Xie, Y., Li, Z., Huang, W., Yuan, J., & Liu, Y. et al. (2012). SOAPdenovo2: An empirically improved memory-efficient short-read de novo assembler. *GigaScience, 1*(1), 1–6. doi:10.1186/2047-217X-1-18 PMID:23587118

Macintosh, G., & Lockshin, L. S. (1997). Retail relationships and store loyalty: A multi-level perspective. *International Journal of Research in Marketing, 14*(5), 487–497. doi:10.1016/S0167-8116(97)00030-X

Mantus, E. K. (2015). *Overcoming Barriers to Deployment of Plug-in Electric Vehicles*. Retrieved from http://www.nap.edu/catalog/21725/overcoming-barriers-to-deployment-of-plug-in-electric-vehicles

Masum, B., Masjuki, H., Kalam, M., Fattah, I. R., Palash, S., & Abedin, M. (2013). Effect of ethanol–gasoline blend on NOx emission in SI engine. *Renewable & Sustainable Energy Reviews, 24*, 209–222. doi:10.1016/j.rser.2013.03.046

Millo, F., Rolando, L., Fuso, R., & Mallamo, F. (2014). Real CO 2 emissions benefits and end users operating costs of a plug-in hybrid electric vehicle. *Applied Energy, 114*, 563–571. doi:10.1016/j.apenergy.2013.09.014

Nugent, N., & Rhinard, M. (2015). *The European Commission*. Palgrave Macmillan.

Ozaki, R., & Sevastyanova, K. (2011). Going hybrid: An analysis of consumer purchase motivations. *Energy Policy, 39*(5), 2217–2227. doi:10.1016/j.enpol.2010.04.024

Pandey, D., Agrawal, M., & Pandey, J. S. (2011). Carbon footprint: Current methods of estimation. *Environmental Monitoring and Assessment, 178*(1-4), 135–160. doi:10.1007/s10661-010-1678-y PMID:20848311

Parshall, L., Gurney, K., Hammer, S. A., Mendoza, D., Zhou, Y., & Geethakumar, S. (2010). Modeling energy consumption and CO 2 emissions at the urban scale: Methodological challenges and insights from the United States. *Energy Policy*, *38*(9), 4765–4782. doi:10.1016/j.enpol.2009.07.006

Pongthanaisawan, J., & Sorapipatana, C. (2013). Greenhouse gas emissions from Thailands transport sector: Trends and mitigation options. *Applied Energy*, *101*, 288–298. doi:10.1016/j.apenergy.2011.09.026

Rahman, I., Vasant, P., Singh, B. S. M., & Abdullah-Al-Wadud, M. (2015a). Swarm intelligence-based optimization for PHEV charging stations.Handbook of Research on Swarm Intelligence in Engineering, 374. doi:10.4018/978-1-4666-8291-7.ch012

Rahman, I., Vasant, P. M., Singh, B. S. M., & Abdullah-Al-Wadud, M. (2015b). *On the performance of accelerated particle swarm optimization for charging plug-in hybrid electric vehicles. Alexandria Engineering Journal.*

Rahman, I., Vasant, P. M., Singh, B. S. M., Abdullah-Al-Wadud, M., & Adnan, N. (2016). Review of recent trends in optimization techniques for plug-in hybrid, and electric vehicle charging infrastructures. *Renewable & Sustainable Energy Reviews*, *58*, 1039–1047. doi:10.1016/j.rser.2015.12.353

Rezvani, Z., Jansson, J., & Bodin, J. (2015). Advances in consumer electric vehicle adoption research: A review and research agenda. *Transportation Research Part D, Transport and Environment*, *34*, 122–136. doi:10.1016/j.trd.2014.10.010

Richardson, D. B. (2013). Electric vehicles and the electric grid: A review of modeling approaches, Impacts, and renewable energy integration. *Renewable & Sustainable Energy Reviews*, *19*, 247–254. doi:10.1016/j.rser.2012.11.042

Sang, Y.-N., & Bekhet, H. A. (2015). Modelling electric vehicle usage intentions: An empirical study in Malaysia. *Journal of Cleaner Production*, *92*, 75–83. doi:10.1016/j.jclepro.2014.12.045

Schuitema, G., Anable, J., Skippon, S., & Kinnear, N. (2013). The role of instrumental, hedonic and symbolic attributes in the intention to adopt electric vehicles. *Transportation Research Part A, Policy and Practice*, *48*, 39–49. doi:10.1016/j.tra.2012.10.004

Seixas, J., Simões, S., Dias, L., Kanudia, A., Fortes, P., & Gargiulo, M. (2015). Assessing the cost-effectiveness of electric vehicles in European countries using integrated modeling. *Energy Policy*, *80*, 165–176. doi:10.1016/j.enpol.2015.01.032

Sharaf, O. Z., & Orhan, M. F. (2014). An overview of fuel cell technology: Fundamentals and applications. *Renewable & Sustainable Energy Reviews*, *32*, 810–853. doi:10.1016/j.rser.2014.01.012

Sigurdardottir, S. B., Kaplan, S., Møller, M., & Teasdale, T. W. (2013). Understanding adolescents intentions to commute by car or bicycle as adults. *Transportation Research Part D, Transport and Environment*, *24*, 1–9. doi:10.1016/j.trd.2013.04.008

Solís, J. C., & Sheinbaum, C. (2013). Energy consumption and greenhouse gas emission trends in Mexican road transport. *Energy for Sustainable Development*, *17*(3), 280–287. doi:10.1016/j.esd.2012.12.001

Susarla, S., & Friedrich, E. (2013). The solar power policies and markets of Asia and Europe. *Asia Europe Journal*, *11*(3), 339–354. doi:10.1007/s10308-013-0353-7

Taylor, S., & Todd, P. (1995). Decomposition and crossover effects in the theory of planned behavior: A study of consumer adoption intentions. *International Journal of Research in Marketing*, *12*(2), 137–155. doi:10.1016/0167-8116(94)00019-K

Tong, F., Jaramillo, P., & Azevedo, I. M. (2015). Comparison of Life Cycle Greenhouse Gases from Natural Gas Pathways for Light-Duty Vehicles. *Energy & Fuels*, *29*(9), 6008–6018. doi:10.1021/acs.energyfuels.5b01063

Tran, M. (2012). Technology-behavioural modelling of energy innovation diffusion in the UK. *Applied Energy*, *95*, 1–11. doi:10.1016/j.apenergy.2012.01.018

Tran, M., Banister, D., Bishop, J. D., & McCulloch, M. D. (2012). Realizing the electric-vehicle revolution. *Nature Climate Change, 2*(5), 328-333.

Turton, H., & Moura, F. (2008). Vehicle-to-grid systems for sustainable development: An integrated energy analysis. *Technological Forecasting and Social Change*, *75*(8), 1091–1108. doi:10.1016/j.techfore.2007.11.013

Wang, S., Fan, J., Zhao, D., Yang, S., & Fu, Y. (2016). Predicting consumers intention to adopt hybrid electric vehicles: Using an extended version of the theory of planned behavior model. *Transportation*, *43*(1), 123–143. doi:10.1007/s11116-014-9567-9

Yang, Y., Li, J., Sun, X., & Chen, J. (2014). Measuring external oil supply risk: A modified diversification index with country risk and potential oil exports. *Energy*, *68*, 930–938. doi:10.1016/j.energy.2014.02.091

Yilmaz, M., & Krein, P. T. (2013). Review of battery charger topologies, charging power levels, and infrastructure for plug-in electric and hybrid vehicles. Power Electronics. *IEEE Transactions on*, *28*(5), 2151–2169.

Yuan, F., & Miyazaki, K. (2013). *Mapping Technological Dynamics as Keyword Co-occurrence Clusters: A Study on the Electrified Vehicles Research*. Academic Press.

Zhang, H.-Y., Ji, Q., & Fan, Y. (2013). An evaluation framework for oil import security based on the supply chain with a case study focused on China. *Energy Economics*, *38*, 87–95. doi:10.1016/j.eneco.2013.03.014

ADDITIONAL READING

Boulanger, A. G., Chu, A. C., Maxx, S., & Waltz, D. L. (2011). Vehicle electrification: Status and issues. *Proceedings of the IEEE*, *99*(6), 1116–1138. doi:10.1109/JPROC.2011.2112750

Contestabile, M. et al.. (2011). Battery electric vehicles, hydrogen fuel cells and biofuels. Which will be the winner? Energy. *Environmental Sciences*, *10*, 3754–3772.

Eberle, U., & von Helmolt, R. (2010). Sustainable transportation based on electric vehicle concepts: A brief overview. Energy. *Environmental Sciences*, *3*, 689–699.

Huetnik, F. J., van der Vooren, A., & Alkemade, F. (2009). Initial infrastructure development strategies for the transition to sustainable mobility. *Technol.Forecast. Soc.*, *77*(8), 1270–1281. doi:10.1016/j.techfore.2010.03.012

Khayyam, H., Ranjbarzadeh, H., & Marano, V. (2012). Intelligent control of vehicle to grid power. *Journal of Power Sources*, *201*, 1–9. doi:10.1016/j.jpowsour.2011.11.010

McNerney, J., Farmer, J. D., Redner, S., & Trancik, J. E. (2011). Role of design complexity in technology improvement. *Proceedings of the National Academy of Sciences of the United States of America*, *108*(22), 9008–9013. doi:10.1073/pnas.1017298108 PMID:21576499

Offer, G. J., Contestabile, M., Howey, D. A., Clague, R., & Brandon, N. P. (2011). Techno-economic and behavioral analysis of battery electric, hydrogen fuel cell and hybrid vehicles in a future sustainable road transport system in the UK. *Energy Policy*, *39*(4), 1939–1950. doi:10.1016/j.enpol.2011.01.006

KEY TERMS AND DEFINITIONS

Consumer Behavior: The study of consumer behavior is related to individuals, groups, or organizations and the processes they use to select, secure, practice, and dispose of products, services, experiences, or ideas to satisfy needs and the influences that these processes have on the consumer and society.

Electric Vehicle: An electric vehicle (EV), also discussed as an electric drive vehicle (EDV), needs one or more electric motors or traction motors for the purpose of propulsion. An electric vehicle is normally power-driven through a collector system by electricity from off-vehicle sources, or may be self-contained with a battery or generator to convert fuel to electricity.

Environmental Concern: Environmental concern deals with the harmful consequences of human action on the biophysical surroundings. Environmentalism, an environmental and social movement, reports environmental issues via promotion, education and activism.

Plug-in Hybrid Electric Vehicles: Plug-in Hybrid Electric Vehicles (PHEVs) are being made with relatively large sized batteries that can be charged during off-peak hours, and permit the vehicle owner to use exclusively electric made for 30 – 60 miles of driving as well as switching into traditional gasoline for longer trips. PHEVs offer customers the opportunity for fuel at gasoline-equivalent prices of less than $1.00 per gallon. For a given size battery bank, the range of a PHEV can be prolonged significantly before batteries need recharging by turning on the engine or fuel cell whenever the vehicle power demand exceeds some threshold.

APPENDIX: NOMENCLATURE

EVs: Electric vehicles
PHEVs: Plug-in hybrid electric vehicles
ICE: Internal combustion engine
EPRI: Electric power research institute
V2G: Vehicle-to-grid
SoC: State-of-charge
ICEV: Internal combustion engine vehicles
AEVs: All-electric vehicles
HEVs: Hybrid electric vehicles
AER: All-electric-range
TPB: Theory of planned behavior

Compilation of References

Adams, C. (1993). *For Good or Evil: The Impact of Taxes on the Course of Civilization*. London: Madison Books.

Agosto, D. E. (2002). Bounded rationality and satisficing in young peoples web-based decision making. *Journal of the American Society for Information Science and Technology*, *53*(1), 16–27. doi:10.1002/asi.10024

Ainslie, G. (2001). *Breakdown of will*. Cambridge, UK: Cambridge University Press. doi:10.1017/CBO9781139164191

Ainslie, G., & Herrnstein, R. J. (1981). Preference reversal and delayed reinforcement. *Animal Learning & Behavior*, *9*(4), 476–482. doi:10.3758/BF03209777

Ajzen, I. (1991). The theory of planned behavior. *Organizational Behavior and Human Decision Processes*, *50*(2), 179–211. doi:10.1016/0749-5978(91)90020-T

Ajzen, I. (2011). The theory of planned behaviour: Reactions and reflections. *Psychology & Health*, *26*(9), 1113–1127. doi:10.1080/08870446.2011.613995 PMID:21929476

Ajzen, I. (2015). The theory of planned behaviour is alive and well, and not ready to retire: A commentary on Sniehotta, Presseau, and Araújo-Soares. *Health Psychology Review*, *9*(2), 131–137. doi:10.1080/17437199.2014.883474 PMID:26209198

Aker, A. T., Onen, P., & Karakilic, H. (2007). Psychological Trauma: Research and Practice in Turkey. *International Journal of Mental Health*, *36*(3), 38–57. doi:10.2753/IMH0020-7411360306

Al-Alawi, B. M., & Bradley, T. H. (2013). Review of hybrid, plug-in hybrid, and electric vehicle market modeling studies. *Renewable & Sustainable Energy Reviews*, *21*, 190–203. doi:10.1016/j.rser.2012.12.048

Allingham, M. G., & Sandmo, A. (1972). Income Tax evasion: A Theoretical Analysis. *Journal of Public Economics*, *1*(3-4), 323–338. doi:10.1016/0047-2727(72)90010-2

Alm, J. J., Martinez-Vazquez, & Torgler, B. (2010). Developing Alternative Frameworks for Explaining Tax Compliance. In J. Alm, J. Martinez-Vazquez, & B. Torgler (Eds.), Developing Alternative Frameworks for Explaining Tax Compliance (pp. 3-12). London: Routledge.

Almedon, A. (2008). Resilience Research and Policy, Practice Discourse in Health, Social, Behavioral and Environmental Sciences Over the Past Ten Years. *African Health Sciences*, 5–13.

Alm, J., & Torgler, B. (2006). Culture differences and tax morale in the United States and in Europe. *Journal of Economic Psychology*, *27*(2), 224–246. doi:10.1016/j.joep.2005.09.002

Alos-Ferrer, C. (2006). A simple characterization of approval voting. *Social Choice and Welfare*, *27*(3), 621–625. doi:10.1007/s00355-006-0145-8

Al-Subhi Al-Harbi, K. M. (1998). Sharing fractions in cost-plus incentive-fee contracts. *International Journal of Project Management*, *16*(2), 73–80. doi:10.1016/S0263-7863(97)00013-6

Anastasopoulos, P., Anastasopoulos, Ch., McCullouch, B. G., Gkritza, K., Mannering, F. L., & Sinha, K. C. (2010). Cost savings analysis of performance-based contracts for highway maintenance operations. *Journal of Infrastructure Systems*, *16*(4), 251–263. doi:10.1061/(ASCE)IS.1943-555X.0000012

Angeletos, G. M., Laibson, D., Repetto, A., Tobacman, J., & Weinberg, S. (2001). The hyperbolic consumption model: Calibration, simulation, and empirical evaluation. *The Journal of Economic Perspectives*, *15*(3), 47–68. doi:10.1257/jep.15.3.47

Antoniou, F., Aretoulis, G. N., Konstantinidis, D., & Kalfakakou, G. P. (2012). Selection criteria used for the choice of contract type for major highway construction projects. *Procedia - Social and Behavioral Sciences Journal, 48*, 3508–3517.

Antoniou, F., Aretoulis, G. N., Konstantinidis, D., & Kalfakakou, G. P. (2013). Engineers perception and assessment of contract types for highway construction projects. *International Journal of Applied Behavioral Economics*, *2*(4), 1–24. doi:10.4018/ijabe.2013100101

Arditi, D., Khisty, J., & Yasamis, F. (1997). Incentive/disincentive provisions in highway contracts. *Journal of Construction Engineering and Management*, *123*(3), 302–307. doi:10.1061/(ASCE)0733-9364(1997)123:3(302)

Arditi, D., & Yasamis, F. (1998). Incentive/Disincentive contracts: Perceptions of owners & contractors. *Journal of Construction Engineering and Management*, *124*(5), 361–373. doi:10.1061/(ASCE)0733-9364(1998)124:5(361)

Aretoulis, G. N., Angelides, D. C., Kalfakakou, G. P., Fotiadis, G. S., & Anastasiadis, K. I. (2006). A prototype system for the prediction of final cost in construction projects. *International Journal of Operational Research, Special Issue*, *6*(3), 423–432.

Arnsten, A. (2009). Stress Signaling Pathways that Impair Prefrontal Cortex Structure and Function. *National Review of Neuroscience*, 410-422.

Arrow, K. J. (1982). Risk Perception In Psychology And Economics. *Economic Inquiry*, *20*(1), 1–9. doi:10.1111/j.1465-7295.1982.tb01138.x

Arsel, Z. (2016). Assembling markets and value. In R. Canniford & D. Bajde (Eds.), *Assembling consumption. Researching actors, networks and markets* (pp. 32–41). London, UK: Routledge.

Arts, J. W., Frambach, R. T., & Bijmolt, T. H. (2011). Generalizations on consumer innovation adoption: A meta-analysis on drivers of intention and behavior. *International Journal of Research in Marketing*, *28*(2), 134–144. doi:10.1016/j.ijresmar.2010.11.002

Ashraf, Q., Gershman, B., & Howitt, P. (2013). How Inflation Affects Macroeconomic Performance: An Agent-Based Computational Investigation. *Macroeconomic Dynamics*, 1-24.

Atkinson, P., Martin, C., & Rankin, J. (2009). Resilience revisited. *Journal of Psychiatric and Mental Health Nursing*, *16*(2), 137–145. doi:10.1111/j.1365-2850.2008.01341.x PMID:19281544

Austen-Smith, D., & Banks, J. S. (1998). Social Choice Theory, Game Theory, and Positive Political Theory. *Annual Review of Political Science*, *1*(1), 259–287. doi:10.1146/annurev.polisci.1.1.259

Ausubel, L. M. (1991). The failure of competition in the credit card market. *The American Economic Review*, *81*(1), 50–81.

Axelrod, R. (2006). *The Evolution of Cooperation*. Basic Books.

Baccarini, D. (1996). The concept of project complexity a review. *International Journal of Project Management*, *14*(4), 201–204. doi:10.1016/0263-7863(95)00093-3

Badenfelt, U. (2011). Fixing the contract after the contract is fixed: A study of incomplete contracts in IT and construction projects. *International Journal of Project Management*, *29*(5), 568–576. doi:10.1016/j.ijproman.2010.04.003

Balinski, M., & Laraki, R. (2010). *Majority Judgement*. Cambridge, MA: MIT Press.

Balliet, D., Parks, C., & Joreman, J. (2009). Social value orientation and cooperation in social dilemmas: A meta-analysis. *Group Processes & Intergroup Relations*, *12*(4), 533–547. doi:10.1177/1368430209105040

Barbarossa, C., Beckmann, S. C., De Pelsmacker, P., Moons, I., & Gwozdz, W. (2015). A self-identity based model of electric car adoption intention: A cross-cultural comparative study. *Journal of Environmental Psychology*, *42*, 149–160. doi:10.1016/j.jenvp.2015.04.001

Bar-Gill, O. (2004). Seduction by Plastic. *Northwestern University Law Review*, *98*(4), 1373–1434.

Baron, S., Harris, K., & Harris, R. (2001). Retail theater. The intended effect of the performance. *Journal of Service Research*, *4*(2), 102–117. doi:10.1177/109467050142003

Baston, C. D. (1991). *The altruism question: Towards a social-psychological answer*. Hillsdale, NJ: Lawrence Erlbaum Associates.

Baston, C. D., Ahmad, N., & Stocks, E. L. (2011). Four forms of prosocial motivation: Egoism, altruism, collectivism, and principlism. In D. Dunning (Ed.), *Social motivation*. New York, NY: Psychology Press.

Bateman, I. J., Harwood, A. R., Mace, G. M., Watson, R. T., Abson, D. J., Andrews, B. . . . Dugdale, S. (2013). Bringing ecosystem services into economic decision-making: land use in the United Kingdom. *Science, 341*(6141), 45-50.

Bathory, D. (2015b). Personality, Relationships, and Decision Making with Relational Dynamics. *International Journal of Applied Beahvioral Economics*, 52-74.

Bathory, D. S. (1993, July). *Psychological, Neurobiological and Developmental Consequences of Trauma in Children* (Unpublished Doctoral Dissertation). Forest Institute of Professional Psychology, Honolulu, HI.

Bathory, D. S. (2012). Entrepreneurial Characteristics and Relational Dynamics. In *Proceedings of CReBUS 9th International Conference on Higher Education and Entrepreneurship*. Bucharest, Romania: EU & CReBUS.

Bathory, D. S. (2013a). Applied Psychological Trauma Theory and its Reflection in Architecture: Wounds and Memorials. In A. Кадујевић (Ed.), Простори Памћења Spaces of Memory Volume 1 Architecture (pp. 375-394). Belgrade, Serbia: Faculty of Philosophy University of Belgrade & Museum of Applied Art.

Bathory, D. S. (2014). The Mugs of Reflection & Relational Dynamics. *5th Global Conference on Trauma*. Prague, Czech Republic: Interdisciplinary Net.

Bathory, D. S. (2016a). *Interdisciplinary Perspectives with Relational Dynamics*. IGI Global. Retrieved from http://www.igi-global.com

Bathory, D. S. (2016b, May 20). Design and Decision Making. In *Design and Decision Making*. Belgrade, Serbia: University of Belgrade.

Bathory, D., & Celik, F. (2014). Intergenerational Trauma & Relational Dynamics. In *Proceedings of the 5th Global Conference on Trauma*. Prague: Interdisciplinary Net.

Bathory, D., & Lajbenšperger, N. (2014). The Collective Mind in Design and Relational Dynamics. *Зборник Матице Српске за Ликовне Уметхости*, 209-223.

Bathory, D. (2012). The Preservation of a Cultural Psyche: A Comparison of the Hawaiian Islands and the Balkan Peninsula.*Hawaii University International Conference of Arts and Humanities* (pp. 1-21).

Bathory, D. (2014). Healing Worldwide Wounds- Applied Trauma Theory and Relational Dynamics. *International Journal of Applied Behavioral Economics*, *3*(2), 1–14. doi:10.4018/ijabe.2014040101

Bathory, D. (2015a). Behavioral Health and Relational Dynamics. *International Journal of Applied Behavioral Economics*, *4*(2), 36–52. doi:10.4018/ijabe.2015040103

Bathory, D. S. (2013b). Economics and Practical Applications for Applied Trauma Theory: Sustainable Engery and Rural Tourism. *International Journal of Applied Behavioral Economics*, *2*(2), 41–55. doi:10.4018/ijabe.2013040103

Bathory, D. S. (2015). The Proof for Evolution and Coming Out of Prison with Relational Dynamics. *International Journal of Applied Behavioral Economics*, *4*(1), 58–69. doi:10.4018/ijabe.2015010104

Bathory, D. S. (in press). Stress Decision Making and Relational Dynamics. *International Journal of Applied Behavioral Economics*.

Baujard, A., Gavrel, F., Igersheim, H., Laslier, J.-F., & Lebon, I. (2015). *How voters use grade scales in evaluative voting*. Academic Press.

Baujard, A., Igersheim, H., Lebon, I., Gavrel, F., & Laslier, J.-F. (2014, June). Whos favored by evaluative voting? An experiment conducted during the 2012 French presidential election. *Journal of Electoral Studies*, *34*, 131–145. doi:10.1016/j.electstud.2013.11.003

Baumeister, R. F., & Leary, M. R. R. (1995). The need to belong: Desire for interpersonal attachments as a fundamental human motivation. *Psychological Bulletin*, *117*(3), 497–529. doi:10.1037/0033-2909.117.3.497 PMID:7777651

Baumeister, R. F., Vohs, K. D., Aaker, J. L., & Garbinsky, E. N. (2013). Some key differences between a happy life and a meaningful life. *The Journal of Positive Psychology*, *8*(6), 505–516. doi:10.1080/17439760.2013.830764

Becker, G. (1968). Crime and Punishment: An Economic Approach. *Journal of Political Economy*, *76*(2), 169–217. doi:10.1086/259394

Becker, G. S., & Mulligan, C. B. (1997). The endogenous determination of time preference. *The Quarterly Journal of Economics*, *112*(3), 729–758. doi:10.1162/003355397555334

Becker, T. A., Sidhu, I., & Tenderich, B. (2009). *Electric vehicles in the United States: a new model with forecasts to 2030*. Oakland, CA: University of California Berkeley.

Belk, R. W. (2013). Extended self in a digital world. *The Journal of Consumer Research*, *40*(3), 477–500. doi:10.1086/671052

Belk, R. W., Ger, G., & Askegaard, S. (2003). The fire of desire: A multisited inquiry into consumer passion. *The Journal of Consumer Research*, *30*(3), 326–351. doi:10.1086/378613

Bellenger, D. N., & Korgaonkar, P. K. (1980). Profiling the recreational shopper. *Journal of Retailing*, *56*(3), 77–92.

Benabou, R., & Tirole, J. (2000). *Self-confidence: Intrapersonal strategies* (No. 209). Woodrow Wilson School Working Paper. Princeton University Press

Benzion, U., Rapoport, A., & Yagil, J. (1989). Discount rates inferred from decisions: An experimental study. *Management Science*, *35*(3), 270–284. doi:10.1287/mnsc.35.3.270

Berends, T. C. (2000). Cost plus incentive fee contracting - experiences & structuring. *International Journal of Project Management*, *18*(3), 165–171. doi:10.1016/S0263-7863(99)00076-9

Bergek, A., Berggren, C., Magnusson, T., & Hobday, M. (2013). Technological discontinuities and the challenge for incumbent firms: Destruction, disruption or creative accumulation? *Research Policy*, *42*(6), 1210–1224. doi:10.1016/j.respol.2013.02.009

Berns, G. S., Laibson, D., & Loewenstein, G. (2007). Intertemporal choice–toward an integrative framework. *Trends in Cognitive Sciences*, *11*(11), 482–488. doi:10.1016/j.tics.2007.08.011 PMID:17980645

Betancourt, R. R. (2016). Distribution services, technological change and the evolution of retailing and distribution in the twenty-first century. In E. Basker (Ed.), *Handbook on the economics of retailing and distribution* (pp. 73–94). Cheltenham, UK: Edward Elgar. doi:10.4337/9781783477388.00012

Birch, D. L. (1979). *The Job Generation Process* (Unpublished report). Washington, DC: MIT Program on Neighborhood and Regional Change for the Economic Development Administration, U.S. Department of Commerce.

Birch, D. L. (1981). Who Creates Jobs? *The Public Interest*, *65*(3), 3–14.

Birch, D. L. (1987). *Job Creation in America: How Our Smallest Companies Put the Most People to Work*. New York: Free Press.

Bird, E. J., Hagstrom, P. A., & Wild, R. (1997). *Credit cards and the poor (1148-97)*. University of Wisconsin-Madison: Institute for Research on Poverty.

Biro, M., Mihić, V., Milan, P., & Logar, S. (2002). Did Socio-Political Changes in Serbia Changed the Level of Authoritariansm and Ethnocentrism of Citizens? *Psihologija*, 37-47.

Blanchflower, D. G. (2000). Self-employment in OECD Countries. *Labour Economics*, *7*(5), 471–505. doi:10.1016/S0927-5371(00)00011-7

Blum, W. J., & Kalven, H. Jr. (1953). *The Uneasy Case for Progressive Taxation*. Chicago: University of Chicago Press.

Bockarjova, M., & Steg, L. (2014). Can Protection Motivation Theory predict pro-environmental behavior? Explaining the adoption of electric vehicles in the Netherlands. *Global Environmental Change*, *28*, 276–288. doi:10.1016/j.gloenvcha.2014.06.010

Boeri, T., & Garibaldi, P. (2002). *Shadow activity and unemployment in a depressed labour market*. CEPR Discussion paper, DP3433.

Bogaert, S., Boone, C., & Declerck, C. (2008). Social value orientation and cooperation in social dilemmas: A review and conceptual model. *The British Journal of Social Psychology*, *47*(3), 453–480. doi:10.1348/014466607X244970 PMID:17915044

Boone, C., De Brabander, B., & van Witteloostuijn, A. (1999). The impact of personality on behavior in five Prisoners Dilemma games. *Journal of Economic Psychology*, *20*(3), 343–377. doi:10.1016/S0167-4870(99)00012-4

Boortz, N., & Linder, J. (2005). *The Fair Tax Book: Saying Goodbye to the Income Tax and the I.R.S.* New York: HarperCollins.

Borba, B. S. M., Szklo, A., & Schaeffer, R. (2012). Plug-in hybrid electric vehicles as a way to maximize the integration of variable renewable energy in power systems: The case of wind generation in northeastern Brazil. *Energy*, *37*(1), 469–481. doi:10.1016/j.energy.2011.11.008

Borghans, L., Duckworth, A. L., Heckman, J. J., & ter Weel, B. (2008). The economics and psychology of personality traits. *The Journal of Human Resources*, *43*(4), 972–1059. doi:10.3368/jhr.43.4.972

Bosch-Rekveldt, M., Jongkind, Y., Mooia, H., Bakker, H., & Verbraeck, A. (2011). Grasping project complexity in large engineering projects: The TOE (Technical, Organizational and Environmental) framework. *International Journal of Project Management*, *29*(6), 728–739. doi:10.1016/j.ijproman.2010.07.008

Botkin, D. B., Keller, E. A., & Rosenthal, D. B. (2012). *Environmental science*. New York, NY: Wiley.

Boukendour, S. (2007). Preventing post-contractual opportunism by an option to switch from one contract to another. *Construction Management and Economics*, *25*(7), 723–727. doi:10.1080/01446190701392994

Boukendour, S., & Bah, R. (2001). The guaranteed maximum price contract as call option. *Construction Management and Economics*, *19*(6), 563–567. doi:10.1080/01446190110049848

Bower, D., Ashby, G., Gerald, K., & Smyk, W. (2002). Incentive Mechanisms for Project Success. *Journal of Management Engineering*, *18*(1), 37–43. doi:10.1061/(ASCE)0742-597X(2002)18:1(37)

Brams, S. J. (1980, September). Approval Voting in Multi Candidate Elections. *Policy Studies Journal: the Journal of the Policy Studies Organization*, *9*(1), 102–108. doi:10.1111/j.1541-0072.1980.tb00928.x

Brams, S. J., & Fishburn, P. C. (2005). Going from theory to practice: The mixed succes of approval voting. *Social Choice and Welfare*, *25*(2-3), 457–474. doi:10.1007/s00355-005-0013-y

Bröchner, J., & Badenfelt, U. (2011). Changes and change management in construction and IT projects. *Journal of Automation in Construction*, *20*(7), 767–775. doi:10.1016/j.autcon.2011.01.001

Broome, J., & Perry, J. (2002). How practitioners set share fractions in target cost contracts. *International Journal of Project Management*, *20*(1), 59–66. doi:10.1016/S0263-7863(00)00035-1

Browning, M., & Crossley, T. F. (2001). The life-cycle model of consumption and saving. *The Journal of Economic Perspectives*, *15*(3), 3–22. doi:10.1257/jep.15.3.3

Brown, S., Taylor, K., & Price, S. W. (2005). Debt and distress: Evaluating the psychological cost of credit. *Journal of Economic Psychology*, *26*(5), 642–663. doi:10.1016/j.joep.2005.01.002

Brown, T., & Plache, L. (2006). Paying with plastic: Maybe not so crazy. *The University of Chicago Law Review. University of Chicago. Law School, 73*, 63–86.

Bruce, D., & Mohsin, M. (2003). *Tax Policy and Entrepreneurship: New Time Series Evidence*. Working Paper, University of Tennessee-Knoxville.

Bruce, D. (2000). Effects of the United States Tax System on Transitions into Self-Employment. *Labour Economics, 7*(5), 545–574. doi:10.1016/S0927-5371(00)00013-0

Brucks, W. M., & Van Lange, P. A. M. (2007). When prosocials act like proselfs in a commons dilemma. *Personality and Social Psychology Bulletin, 33*(5), 750–758. doi:10.1177/0146167206298569 PMID:17440204

Brusdal, R., & Lavik, R. (2008). Just shopping? A closer look at youth and shopping in Norway. *Young. Nordic Journal of Youth Research, 16*(4), 393–408. doi:10.1177/110330880801600403

Bryman, A. (2004). *The Disneyization of society*. London, UK: Sage Publications Ltd.

Bubshait, A. A. (2003). Incentive/disincentive contracts and its effects on industrial projects. *International Journal of Project Management, 21*(1), 63–70. doi:10.1016/S0263-7863(01)00078-3

Burns, A. (2000). Emotion and urban experience: Implications for design. *Design Issues, 16*(3), 67–79. doi:10.1162/07479360052053333

Camerer, C. F., & Lowenstein, G. (2004). Behavioral economics: Past, present, future. In Advances in Behavioral Economics, (pp. 3-51). Academic Press.

Camerer, C. F., Dreber, A., Forsell, E., Ho, T. H., Huber, J., Johannesson, M., & Heikensten, E. et al. (2016). Evaluating replicability of laboratory experiments in economics. *Science, 351*(6280), 1433–1436. doi:10.1126/science.aaf0918 PMID:26940865

Camerer, C. F., & Loewenstein, G. (2004). Behavioral Economics: Past, Present, Future. In C. F. Camerer, G. Loewenstein, & M. Rabin (Eds.), *Advances in Behavioral Economics* (pp. 1–52). Princeton, NJ: Princeton University Press.

Camerer, C. F., & Loewenstein, G. (2004). Behavioral economics: Past, present, future. In C. F. Camerer, G. Loewenstein, & M. Rabin (Eds.), *Advances in Behavioral Economics* (pp. 3–51). Princeton, NJ: Princeton University Press.

Canner, G. B., & Cyrnak, A. W. (1985). Recent developments in credit card holding and use patterns among US families. *Journal of Retail Banking, 7*(3), 63–74.

Cannon, W. B. (1914). The Emergency Function of the Adrenal Medullla in Pain and the Major Emotions. *The American Journal of Physiology*, 356–372.

Capgemini. (2015). *Rethinking the value chain. New realities in collaborative business*. Retrieved from: https://www.capgemini.com/

Carley, S., Krause, R. M., Lane, B. W., & Graham, J. D. (2013). Intent to purchase a plug-in electric vehicle: A survey of early impressions in large US cites. *Transportation Research Part D, Transport and Environment, 18*, 39–45. doi:10.1016/j.trd.2012.09.007

Carrillo, J. D. (1998). *Self-control, moderate consumption and craving*. CEPR Discuss Paper.

Carrillo, J. D., & Mariotti, T. (2000). Strategic ignorance as a self-disciplining device. *The Review of Economic Studies*, *67*(3), 529–544. doi:10.1111/1467-937X.00142

Carter, R. M., Meyer, J. R., & Huettel, S. A. (2010). Functional neuroimaging of intertemporal choice models: A review. *Journal of Neuroscience, Psychology, and Economics*, *3*(1), 27–45. doi:10.1037/a0018046

Carty, G. J. (1995). Construction. *Journal of Construction Engineering and Management*, *121*(3), 319–328. doi:10.1061/(ASCE)0733-9364(1995)121:3(319)

Chan, D. W. M., Chan, A. P. C., Lam, P. T. I., Yeung, J. F. Y., & Chan, J. H. L. (2011b). Risk ranking and analysis in target cost contracts: Empirical evidence from the construction industry. *International Journal of Project Management*, *29*(6), 751–763. doi:10.1016/j.ijproman.2010.08.003

Chan, D. W., Chan, A. P., Lam, P. T., & Wong, J. M. (2011a). An empirical survey of the motives and benefits of adopting guaranteed maximum price and target cost contracts in construction. *International Journal of Project Management*, *29*(5), 577–590. doi:10.1016/j.ijproman.2010.04.002

Chang, W., Probstl, A., Goswami, D., Zamani, M., & Chakraborty, S. (2015). *Reliable CPS Design for Mitigating Semiconductor and Battery Aging in Electric Vehicles.* Paper presented at the Cyber-Physical Systems, Networks, and Applications (CPSNA), 2015 IEEE 3rd International Conference on. doi:10.1109/CPSNA.2015.16

Chapman, G. B. (1996). Temporal discounting and utility for health and money. *Journal of Experimental Psychology. Learning, Memory, and Cognition*, *22*(3), 771–791. doi:10.1037/0278-7393.22.3.771 PMID:8656156

Chapman, G. B., & Elstein, A. S. (1995). Valuing the future temporal discounting of health and money. *Medical Decision Making*, *15*(4), 373–386. doi:10.1177/0272989X9501500408 PMID:8544681

Chapman, G. B., & Weber, B. J. (2006). Decision biases in intertemporal choice and choice under uncertainty: Testing a common account. *Memory & Cognition*, *34*(3), 589–602. doi:10.3758/BF03193582 PMID:16933768

Chen, C.-Y., Yang, Y.-F., Chen, C.-W., Chen, L.-T., & Chen, T.-H. (2010). Linking the balanced scorecard (BSC) to business management performance: A preliminary concept of fit theory for navigation science and management. *Int. J. Phys. Sci*, *5*(8), 1296–1305.

Chen, F.-Y. (2013). Managers' views on environmental management: An examination of the Taiwanese airline industry. *Journal of Sustainable Development*, *6*(1), 65.

Chen, M.-F., & Tung, P.-J. (2014). Developing an extended theory of planned behavior model to predict consumers intention to visit green hotels. *International Journal of Hospitality Management*, *36*, 221–230. doi:10.1016/j.ijhm.2013.09.006

Cheung, S. O., Yiu, T. W., & Chiu, O. K. (2009). The aggressive–cooperative drivers of construction contracting. *International Journal of Project Management*, *27*(7), 727–735. doi:10.1016/j.ijproman.2008.09.001

Chua, S. C., & Oh, T. H. (2011). Green progress and prospect in Malaysia. *Renewable & Sustainable Energy Reviews*, *15*(6), 2850–2861. doi:10.1016/j.rser.2011.03.008

Chung, S. H., & Herrnstein, R. J. (1967). Choice and delay of reinforcement1. *Journal of the Experimental Analysis of Behavior*, *10*(1), 67–74. doi:10.1901/jeab.1967.10-67 PMID:16811307

Cincotti, S., Raberto, M., & Teglio, A. (2012). The Eurace macroeconomic model and simulator. In Agent-based Dynamics, Norms, and Corporate Governance. In *Proceedings of the 16th World Congress of the International Economic Association*. Palgrave.

Colander, D., Howitt, P., Kirman, A., Leijonhufvud, A., & Mehrling, P. (2008). Beyond DSGE models: Toward an empirically based macroeconomics. *The American Economic Review*, *98*(2), 236–240. doi:10.1257/aer.98.2.236

Coller, M., Harrison, G. W., & Rutström, E. E. (2005). *Does Everyone Have Quasi-Hyperbolic Preferences*? University of Central Florida Department of Economics, Working Paper.

Contestabile, M., Offer, G. J., Slade, R., Jaeger, F., & Thoennes, M. (2011). Battery electric vehicles, hydrogen fuel cells and biofuels. Which will be the winner? *Energy & Environmental Science*, *4*(10), 3754–3772. doi:10.1039/c1ee01804c

Cox, D., & Jappelli, T. (1993). The effect of borrowing constraints on consumer liabilities. *Journal of Money, Credit and Banking*, *25*(2), 197–213. doi:10.2307/2077836

Cubitt, R. P., Munro, A., & Starmer, C. (2004, July). Testing Explanations of Preference Reversal. *The Economic Journal*, *114*(497), 709–726. doi:10.1111/j.1468-0297.2004.00238.x

Cullen, J. B., & Gordon, R. H. (2002). *Taxes and Entrepreneurial Activity: Theory and Evidence for the U.S.* NBER Working Paper 9015.

Cushman & Wakefield. (2016). *European shopping centre development report*. Available: http://www.cushmanwakefield.com/en/research-and-insight/2016/european-shopping-centre-development-report-april-2016/

Danial, S., Lee, C., Lee, G. S., Yeo, W. B., & Ang, C. Q. (2013). *Development of unmanned aerial vehicle (uav) using alternative sources of fuel bee*. Avion.

Darwin, C. (1859). *The Origin of the Species*. London: Penguin Books. (reprinted 1982)

Davies, E., & Lea, S. E. (1995). Student attitudes to student debt. *Journal of Economic Psychology*, *16*(4), 663–679. doi:10.1016/0167-4870(96)80014-6

Davis, J., Smith, T., & Mardsen, P. (2005). *General Social Survey, 1972–2004: Cumulative codebook*. Chicago, IL: National Opinion Research Centers.

Davis, S. J., Haltiwanger, J., & Schuh, S. (1996). Small Business and Job Creation: Dissecting the Myth and Reassessing the Facts. *Small Business Economics*, *8*(4), 297–315. doi:10.1007/BF00393278

Dawes, R. M., & Messick, D. M. (2000). Social Dilemmas. *International Journal of Psychology*, *35*(2), 111–116. doi:10.1080/002075900399402

Dawkins, R. (1989). *The Selfish Gene*. Oxford Press.

De Zulueta, C. (2007). Mass Violence and Mental Health: Attachment and Trauma. *International Review of Psychiatry (Abingdon, England)*, *19*(3), 221–233. doi:10.1080/09540260701349464 PMID:17566900

Deissenberg, C., Van der Hoog, S., & Dawid, H. (2010). EURACE: A massively parallel agent-based model of the European economy. *Applied Mathematics and Computation*, *204*(2), 541–552. doi:10.1016/j.amc.2008.05.116

Diener, E. (2009). The science of well-being: The collected works of Ed Diener. Champaign, IL: Springer Science & Business Media.

Diener, E., & Seligman, M. E. (2004). Beyond money toward an economy of well-being. *Psychological Science in the Public Interest*, *5*(1), 1–31. doi:10.1111/j.0963-7214.2004.00501001.x PMID:26158992

Dolan, P., & White, M. P. (2007). How can measures of subjective well-being be used to inform public policy? *Perspectives on Psychological Science*, *2*(1), 71–85. doi:10.1111/j.1745-6916.2007.00030.x PMID:26151920

Doloi, H. K. (2011). Understanding stakeholders perspective of cost estimation in project management. *International Journal of Project Management*, *29*(5), 622–636. doi:10.1016/j.ijproman.2010.06.001

Donoghue, O, T., & Rabin, M. (2005). Optimal taxes for sin goods. *Swedish Economic Policy Review*, *12*(2), 7.

Đorđevic, J. (2003). Jedan Pokušaj Klasifikacije Teorijskih Rasmatranja Nacionalnog Identiteta. *Psihologija*, 125-140.

Đorđević, J. (2007). Primordialistic Concept of National Identity in Serbia. *Psihologija*, 385-397.

Douhan, R. (2009). *Compulsory Education and Jack of all trades Entrepreneurs!* Working Paper Series 797. Research Institute of Industrial Economics, Stockholm, Sweden.

Dovidio, J. F., Piliavin, J. A., Schoeder, D. A., & Penner, L. A. (2006). *The social psychology of prosocial behavior*. New York, NY: Taylor and Francis Group.

Drentea, P. (2000). Age, debt and anxiety. *Journal of Health and Social Behavior*, *41*(4), 437–450. doi:10.2307/2676296 PMID:11198567

Drentea, P., & Lavrakas, P. J. (2000). Over the limit: The association among health, race and debt. *Social Science & Medicine*, *50*(4), 517–529. doi:10.1016/S0277-9536(99)00298-1 PMID:10641804

Dulac, J. (2012). *Global transport outlook to 2050 Energy Analyst, Energy Technology Policy Division International Energy Agency Targets and scenarios for a low-carbon transport sector*. Retrieved from https://www.iea.org/media/workshops/2013/egrdmobility/DULAC_23052013.pdf

Dunning, D., & Fetchenhauer, D. (1991). Understanding the psychology of trust. In D. Dunning (Ed.), *Social motivation* (pp. 103–126). New York, NY: Psychology Press.

Duverger, M. (1963). *Political Parties: The Organization and Activity in the Modern State*. New York: Wiley. (Original work published 1951)

Edwards, C., & Mitchell, D. J. (2008). *Global Tax Revolution: The Rise of Tax Competition and the Battle to Defend It*. Washington, DC: Cato Institute.

Egbue, O., & Long, S. (2012). Barriers to widespread adoption of electric vehicles: An analysis of consumer attitudes and perceptions. *Energy Policy*, *48*, 717–729. doi:10.1016/j.enpol.2012.06.009

Eigsti, I. M., Zayas, V., Mischel, W., Shoda, Y., Ayduk, O., Dadlani, M. B., & Casey, B. J. (2006). Predicting cognitive control from preschool to late adolescence and young adulthood. *Psychological Science*, *17*(6), 478–484. doi:10.1111/j.1467-9280.2006.01732.x PMID:16771797

Ellabban, O., Abu-Rub, H., & Blaabjerg, F. (2014). Renewable energy resources: Current status, future prospects and their enabling technology. *Renewable & Sustainable Energy Reviews*, *39*, 748–764. doi:10.1016/j.rser.2014.07.113

Elster, J. (1979). *Ulysses and the Sirens: Studies in Rationality and Irrationality*. Cambridge, UK: Cambridge University Press.

Erkison, E. (1963). *Childhood and Society*. New York: Norton.

Esbjerg, L., & Bech-Larsen, T. (2009). The brand architecture of grocery retailers: Setting material and symbolic boundaries for consumer choice. *Journal of Retailing and Consumer Services*, *16*(5), 414–423. doi:10.1016/j.jretconser.2009.06.002

Etzioni, A. (2011). Behavioral economics: Towards a new paradigm. *The American Behavioral Scientist*, *55*(8), 1099–1119. doi:10.1177/0002764211412355

Evans, D., & Jovanovic, B. (1989). An estimated model of entrepreneurial choice under liquidity constraints. *Journal of Political Economy*, *97*(4), 808–827. doi:10.1086/261629

Evans, D., & Leighton, L. (1989). Some empirical aspects of entrepreneurship. *The American Economic Review*, *79*, 519–535.

Fagerstrøm, A., Foxall, G. R., & Arntzen, E. (2010). Implications of motivating operations for the functional analysis of consumer choice. *Journal of Organizational Behavior Management*, *30*(2), 110–126. doi:10.1080/01608061003756331

Fagerstrøm, A., & Hantula, D. A. (2013). Buy it now and pay for it later: An experimental study of student credit card use. *The Psychological Record*, *63*(2), 323–332. doi:10.11133/j.tpr.2013.63.2.007

Falk, A., Becker, A., Dohmen, T., Enke, B., Sunde, U., & Huffman, D. (2015). *The nature of human preferences: Global evidence*. Working Paper.

Falvo, M. C., Martirano, L., Sbordone, D., & Bocci, E. (2013). *Technologies for Smart Grids: a brief review*. Paper presented at the Environment and Electrical Engineering (EEEIC), 2013 12th International Conference on. doi:10.1109/EEEIC.2013.6549544

Fan, W., & White, M. J. (2003). Personal Bankruptcy and the Level of Entrepreneurial Activity. *The Journal of Law & Economics*, *46*(2), 543–567. doi:10.1086/382602

Faria, R., Moura, P., Delgado, J., & de Almeida, A. T. (2012). A sustainability assessment of electric vehicles as a personal mobility system. *Energy Conversion and Management*, *61*, 19–30. doi:10.1016/j.enconman.2012.02.023

Fehr, E. (2002). Behavioural science: The economics of impatience. *Nature*, *415*(6869), 269–272. doi:10.1038/415269a PMID:11796988

Fehr, E., & Fischbacher, U. (2004). Social norms and human cooperation. *Trends in Cognitive Sciences*, *8*(4), 187–190. doi:10.1016/j.tics.2004.02.007 PMID:15050515

Fehr, E., & Rockenbach, B. (2004). Human altruism: Economic, neural, and evolutionary perspectives. *Current Opinion in Neurobiology*, *14*(6), 784–790. doi:10.1016/j.conb.2004.10.007 PMID:15582384

Feige, E. L. (1989). *The Underground Economies: Tax Evasion and Information Distortion*. Cambridge University Press. doi:10.1017/CBO9780511571749

Feinberg, R. A. (1986). Credit cards as spending facilitating stimuli: A conditioning interpretation. *The Journal of Consumer Research*, *13*(3), 348–356. doi:10.1086/209074

Felsenthal, D. S., Maoz, Z., & Rapoport, A. (1993, January). An Empirical Evaluation of Six Voting Procedure: Do They Really Make Any Difference? *British Journal of Political Science*, *23*(1), 1–27. doi:10.1017/S0007123400006542

Field, A. (2009). *Discovering Statistics using SPSS* (3rd ed.). SAGE Publications Inc.

Firat, A. F., & Dholakia, N. (2006). Theoretical and philosophical implications of postmodern debates: Some challenges to modern marketing. *Marketing Theory*, *6*(2), 123–162. doi:10.1177/1470593106063981

Fischer, A. R., Beers, P. J., van Latesteijn, H., Andeweg, K., Jacobsen, E., Mommaas, H., . . . Veldkamp, A. T. (2012). Transforum system innovation towards sustainable food: A review. *Agronomy for Sustainable Development, 32*(2), 595-608.

Fischer, C. (2001). Read this paper later: Procrastination with time-consistent preferences. *Journal of Economic Behavior & Organization*, *46*(3), 249–269. doi:10.1016/S0167-2681(01)00160-3

Fishbein, M., & Ajzen, I. (1975). *Belief, attitudes, intention, and behavior. An introduction to theory and research.* Addison-Wesley.

Fishburn, P. (1973). *The Theory of Social Choice*. Princeton, NJ: Princeton University Press.

Fishburn, P. C. (1978). Axioms for Approval Voting: Direct Proof. *Journal of Economic Theory*, *19*(1), 180–185. doi:10.1016/0022-0531(78)90062-5

Fisher, I. (1930). *The theory of interest*. New York: The Macmillan Company.

Flyvbjerg, B., Holm, M. S., & Buhl, S. (2002). Underestimating costs in public works Projects. Error or lie? *Journal of the American Planning Association*, *68*(3), 279–295. doi:10.1080/01944360208976273

Fomotor, B., & Paradi-Dolgos, A. (2015). The Possible Effects of Inter-temporal Choice Models on Consumer Loan Agreements. *Regional and Business Studies*, *7*(1), 9–17.

Ford, C., Phillips, D., & Williams, J. (2009). The Time Course of Dopamine Transmission in the Ventral Tegmental Area. *The Journal of Neuroscience*, 133344–133352. PMID:19846722

Forgas, J. P., Williams, K. D., & Laham, S. M. (2005). *Social motivation: Conscious and unconscious processes*. New York, NY: Cambridge University Press.

Fortat, V., Denant-Boemont, L., & Funaki, Y. (2012). *Coordination and cooperation in an assurance game: A cross-cultural experiment.* Unpublished manuscript, Economics Department, University of Rennes, Rennes, France.

Foster, K., Meijer, E., Schuh, S., & Zabek, M. A. (2010). The 2008 Survey of Consumer Payment Choice (Paper No. 09-10). Boston: Federal Reserve Bank of Boston.

Fotouhi, A., Auger, D. J., Propp, K., Longo, S., & Wild, M. (2016). A review on electric vehicle battery modelling: From Lithium-ion toward Lithium–Sulphur. *Renewable & Sustainable Energy Reviews*, *56*, 1008–1021. doi:10.1016/j.rser.2015.12.009

Frankel, V. (1963). *Man's Search for Meaning*. New York: Pocket Books.

Frederick, S., Loewenstein, G., & ODonoghue, T. (2002). Time discounting and time preference: A critical review. *Journal of Economic Literature*, *40*(2), 351–401. doi:10.1257/jel.40.2.351

Freud, S. (1962). Three Essays on the Theory of Sexuality. Basic Books.

Frey, B. S., & Pommerehne, W. W. (1982). Measuring the Hidden Economy: Though this be Madness, there is Method in it. In The Underground Economy in the United States and Abroad. D.C Heath and Co.

Frimer, J. A., Schaefer, N. K., & Oakes, H. (2014). Moral actor, selfish agent. *Journal of Personality and Social Psychology*, *106*(5), 790–802. doi:10.1037/a0036040 PMID:24749822

Furnham, A., & Telford, K. (2012). *Public attitudes, lay theories and mental health literacy: The understanding of mental health*. INTECH Open Access Publisher.

Gatti, D. D., Gaffeo, E., & Gallegati, M. (2010). Complex agent-based macroeconomics: A manifesto for a new paradigm. *Journal of Economic Interaction and Coordination*, *5*(2), 111–135. doi:10.1007/s11403-010-0064-8

Gentry, W. M., & Hubbard, R. G. (2000). Tax Policy and Entrepreneurial Entry. *The American Economic Review*, *90*(2), 283–287. doi:10.1257/aer.90.2.283

Giles, C. (2014). Winners and losers of oil price plunge. *Financial Times*. Retrieved from http://www.ft.com/cms/s/2/3f5e4914849011e4ba4f00144feab dc0.html#axzz3U51zg3iv

Gintis, H., Bowles, S., Boyd, R., & Fehr, E. (2003). Explaining altruistic behavior in humans. *Evolution and Human Behavior*, *24*(3), 153–172. doi:10.1016/S1090-5138(02)00157-5

Giri, F., Riccetti, L., Russo, A., & Gallegati, M. (2016). *Monetary Policy and Large Crises in a Financial Accelerator Agent-Based Model*. MPRA Paper No. 70371.

Gleick, J. (1987). *Chaos: Making a New Science*. Penguin Books.

Goldman, S. M. (1979). Intertemporally inconsistent preferences and the rate of consumption. *Econometrica*, *47*(3), 621–626. doi:10.2307/1910409

Goldman, S. M. (1980). Consistent plans. *The Review of Economic Studies*, *47*(3), 533–537. doi:10.2307/2297304

Golledge, R. G., & Stimson, R. J. (1990). *Analytical behavioral geography*. London, UK: Routledge.

Golosov, M., Hassler, J., Krusell, P., & Tsyvinski, A. (2014). Optimal taxes on fossil fuel in general equilibrium. *Econometrica*, *82*(1), 41–88. doi:10.3982/ECTA10217

Goodrum, P. M., Wan, Y., & Fenouil, P. C. (2009). A decision-making system for accelerating roadway construction. *Journal of Engineering. Construction and Architectural Management*, *16*(2), 116–135. doi:10.1108/09699980910938000

Gordon, R. J. (1990). U.S. Inflation, Labor's Share, and the Natural Rate of Unemployment. In *Economics of Wage Determination*. Springer-Verlag. doi:10.1007/978-3-642-84134-7_1

Gouldner, A. W. (1960). The norm of reciprocity: A preliminary statement. *American Sociological Review*, *25*(2), 161–178. doi:10.2307/2092623

Graetz, M., & Wilde, L. L. (1985). The Economics of Tax Compliance: Fact and Fantasy. *National Tax Journal*, *38*(3), 355–363.

Graham-Rowe, E., Gardner, B., Abraham, C., Skippon, S., Dittmar, H., Hutchins, R., & Stannard, J. (2012). Mainstream consumers driving plug-in battery-electric and plug-in hybrid electric cars: A qualitative analysis of responses and evaluations. *Transportation Research Part A, Policy and Practice*, *46*(1), 140–153. doi:10.1016/j.tra.2011.09.008

Green, L., Fisher, E. B., Perlow, S., & Sherman, L. (1981). Preference reversal and self-control: Choice as a function of reward amount and delay. *Behaviour Analysis Letters*, *12*(1), 43-51.

Green, L., Fristoe, N., & Myerson, J. (1994). Temporal discounting and preference reversals in choice between delayed outcomes. *Psychonomic Bulletin & Review*, *1*(3), 383–389. doi:10.3758/BF03213979 PMID:24203522

Green, L., & Myerson, J. (1996). Exponential versus hyperbolic discounting of delayed outcomes: Risk and waiting time. *American Zoologist*, *36*(4), 496–505. doi:10.1093/icb/36.4.496

Green, L., & Myerson, J. (2004). A discounting framework for choice with delayed and probabilistic rewards. *Psychological Bulletin*, *130*(5), 769–792. doi:10.1037/0033-2909.130.5.769 PMID:15367080

Greenwood, S. (2007). *10 Excellent Reasons not to Hate Taxes*. New York: The New Press.

Gregory, M.A.G. (1998). Taxation: Catholic Social Thought and Classical Liberalism. *I J. Acct. Ethics & Pub. Pol'y,* 91-100.

Greiner, B. (2003). *An Online Recruitment System for Economic Experiments*. Academic Press.

Grether, D. M., & Plott, C. R. (1979, September). Economic Theory of Choice and the Preference Reversal Phenomenon. *The American Economic Review*, *69*(4), 623–638.

Gruber, J., & Koszegi, B. (2001). Is addiction "rational"? Theory and evidence. *The Quarterly Journal of Economics*, *116*(4), 1261–1303. doi:10.1162/003355301753265570

Gruneberg, S., Hughes, W., & Ancell, D. (2007). Risk under performance-based contracting in the UK construction sector. *Construction Management and Economics*, *25*(7), 691–699. doi:10.1080/01446190601164097

Gualdi, S., Tarzia, M., Zamponi, F., & Bouchaud, J. P. (2015). *Monetary Policy and Dark Corners in a stylized Agent-Based Model.* arXiv e-prints.

Haeseveoets, T., Folmer, C. R., & Van Hiel, A. (2015). Cooperation in mixed-motive games: The role of individual differences in selfish and social orientation. *European Journal of Personality*, *29*(4), 445–458. doi:10.1002/per.1992

Hall, R. E., & Rabushka, A. (1985). *The Flat Tax*. Stanford, CA: Hoover Institution Press.

Halpin, D. W., & Senior, B. A. (2011). *Construction Management* (4th ed.). John Wiley & Sons, Inc.

Hamilton, J. D. (2003). What is an oil shock? *Journal of Econometrics*, *113*(2), 363–398. doi:10.1016/S0304-4076(02)00207-5

Hamm, R. M. (1984). *The Conditions of Occurrence of the Preference Reversal Phenomenon*. Institute of Cognitive Science.

Han, H., & Kim, Y. (2010). An investigation of green hotel customers decision formation: Developing an extended model of the theory of planned behavior. *International Journal of Hospitality Management*, *29*(4), 659–668. doi:10.1016/j.ijhm.2010.01.001

Harting, P. (2015). *Stabilization policies and long term growth: Policy implications from an agent-based macroeconomic model*. Technical Report 6. Bielefeld Working Papers in Economics and Management.

Heidhues, P., & Kőszegi, B. (2008). Competition and price variation when consumers are loss averse. *The American Economic Review*, *98*(4), 1245–1268. doi:10.1257/aer.98.4.1245

Helpern, S. D., Ubel, P. A., & Asch, D. A. (2007). Harnessing the Power of Default Options to Improve Health Care. *The New England Journal of Medicine*, *357*(13), 1340–1344. doi:10.1056/NEJMsb071595 PMID:17898105

Henrich, J., Boyd, R., Bowles, S., Camerer, C., Fehr, E., Gintis, H., & McElreath, R. (2001). In Search of Homo Economicus: Behavioral Experiments in 15 Small-Scale Societies. The American Economic Review, (2), 73.

Henrich, J., Heine, S. J., & Norenzayan, A. (2010). The weirdest people in the world? *Behavioral and Brain Sciences*, *33*(2-3), 61–83. doi:10.1017/S0140525X0999152X PMID:20550733

Herbsman, Z. J., & Glagola, C. R. (1998). Lane rental - innovative way to reduce road construction time. *Journal of Construction Engineering and Management*, *124*(5), 411–417. doi:10.1061/(ASCE)0733-9364(1998)124:5(411)

Herbsman, Z. J., Tong Chen, W., & Epstein, W. C. (1995). Time is money: Innovative contracting methods in highway construction. *Journal of Construction Engineering and Management*, *121*(3), 273–281. doi:10.1061/(ASCE)0733-9364(1995)121:3(273)

Hernandez, T., & Jones, K. (2005). Downtown in transition. Emerging business improvement are strategies. *International Journal of Retail & Distribution Management*, *33*(11), 789–805. doi:10.1108/09590550510629392

Herten, H. J., & Peeters, W. A. R. (1986). Incentive contracting as a project management tool. *International Journal of Project Management*, *4*(1), 34–39. doi:10.1016/0263-7863(86)90060-8

Hines, J. M., Hungerford, H. R., & Tomera, A. N. (1987). Analysis and synthesis of research on responsible environmental behavior: A meta-analysis. *The Journal of Environmental Education*, *18*(2), 1–8. doi:10.1080/00958964.1987.9943482

Hinton, P. R., Brownlow, C., McMurray, I., & Cozens, B. (2004). *SPSS Explained*. New York: Routledge, Taylor and Francis Group.

Hippocrates, . (2009). *The Corpus*. New York: Basic Books.

Hirsch, J. B., & Peterson, J. B. (2009). Extraversion, neuroticism, and the prisoners dilemma. *Personality and Individual Differences*, *46*(2), 254–256. doi:10.1016/j.paid.2008.10.006

Hoge, E. A., & Pollack, M. (2007). Resilience: Research Evidence and Conceptual Considerations for Post-traumtic Stress Disorder. *Depression and Anxiety*, *24*(2), 139–152. doi:10.1002/da.20175 PMID:16892420

Holbrook, M. B. (1999). Introduction to consumer value. In M. B. Holbrook (Ed.), *Consumer value. A framework for analysis and research* (pp. 1–28). London, UK: Routledge. doi:10.4324/9780203010679.ch0

Holbrook, M. B., & Hirschman, E. C. (1982). The experiential aspects of consumption: Consumer fantasies, feelings, and fun. *The Journal of Consumer Research*, *9*(2), 132–140. doi:10.1086/208906

Hori, Y. (2012). *Novel EV society based on motor/capacitor/wireless—Application of electric motor, supercapacitors, and wireless power transfer to enhance operation of future vehicles*. Paper presented at the Microwave Workshop Series on Innovative Wireless Power Transmission: Technologies, Systems, and Applications (IMWS), 2012 IEEE MTT-S International.

Hortacsu, A., & Syverson, C. (2015). The ongoing evolution of US retail: A format tug-of-war. *The Journal of Economic Perspectives*, *29*(4), 89–112. doi:10.1257/jep.29.4.89

Hosseini, S. S., Badri, A., & Parvania, M. (2012). *The plug-in electric vehicles for power system applications: The vehicle to grid (V2G) concept*. Paper presented at the Energy Conference and Exhibition (ENERGYCON), 2012 IEEE International.

Hough, D. (2013). *Irrationality in Health Care*. Palo Alto, CA: Stanford University Press.

Howard, W. E., Bell, L. C., & McCormick, R. E. (1997). Economic principles of contractor compensation. *Journal of Management Engineering*, *13*(5), 81–89. doi:10.1061/(ASCE)0742-597X(1997)13:5(81)

Howey, D. A. (2012). Policy: A challenging future for cars. *Nature Climate Change, 2*(1), 28-29.

Huang, J. Y., & Bargh, J. A. (n.d.). The Selfish Goal: Autonomously operating motivational structures as the proximate cause of human judgment and behavior. *Behavioral and Brain Sciences*, *37*(2), 121–135. PMID:24775120

Hultberg, N. (1996). *Why We Must Abolish the Income Tax and the IRS: A Special Report on the National Sales Tax*. Dallas, TX: AFR Publications.

Hunter. (2013). Physical activity loyalty cards for behavior change: a quasi-experimental study. *American Journal of Preventative Medicine*.

Huppert, F. A., & Willoughby, A. (2010). *The big flourishing society*. Government Briefing document.

Huppert, F. A. (2009). Psychological well-being: Evidence regarding its causes and consequences. *Applied Psychology: Health and Well-being*, *1*(2), 137–164.

Huppert, F. A., Baylis, N., & Keverne, B. (2005). *The Science of Well-being*. Oxford, UK: Oxford Press. doi:10.1093/acprof:oso/9780198567523.001.0001

Hu, Y., Sun, J., Li, W., & Pan, Y. (2014). A scientometric study of global electric vehicle research. *Scientometrics*, *98*(2), 1269–1282. doi:10.1007/s11192-013-1067-8

Igersheim, H., Baujard, A., Gavrel, F., Laslier, J.-F., & Lebon, I. (2015). *Individual Behavior under Evaluative Voting: A Comparison between Laboratory and In Situ Experiments*. Academic Press.

Inman, J. J., Winer, R. S., & Ferraro, R. (2009). The interplay among category characteristics, customer characteristics, and customer activities on in-store decision making. *Journal of Marketing*, *73*(5), 19–29. doi:10.1509/jmkg.73.5.19

Irfan, M., Khurshid, M. B., Anastasopoulos, P., Labi, S., & Moavenzadeh, F. (2011). Planning-stage estimation of highway project duration on the basis of anticipated project cost, project type, and contract type. *International Journal of Project Management*, *29*(1), 78–92. doi:10.1016/j.ijproman.2010.01.001

Isaacs, R. (2000). The urban picturesque: An aesthetic experience of urban pedestrian places. *Journal of Urban Design*, *5*(2), 145–180. doi:10.1080/713683961

Israel, T. (2003). *Some place like home. Using design psychology to create ideal places*. Chichester, UK: John Wiley & Sons.

ITA Working Group 3. (2011) *Contractual Practices*. International Tunneling and Underground Space Association. Retrieved from http://www.ita-aites.org/fileadmin/filemounts/general/pdf/ItaAssociation/ProductAndPublication/WorkingGroupsPublication/WG3/ITA_Report_N6_WG3_P.pdf

ITA Working Group. (1996). ITA position paper on types of contract. *Tunneling & Underground Space Technology, 11*(4), 411-429.

Jaafari, A. (1996). Twinning time & cost in incentive-based contracts. *Journal of Management Engineering*, *12*(4), 62–72. doi:10.1061/(ASCE)0742-597X(1996)12:4(62)

Jackowski, A., de Araujo, C., de Lacerda, A., & Mari, J. (2009). Neurostructural imaging findings in chidlren with post-traumatic stress disorder: Brief Review. *Psychiatry and Clinical Neurosciences*, *63*(1), 1–8. doi:10.1111/j.1440-1819.2008.01906.x PMID:19154207

Jackson, P., & Thrift, N. (1996). Geographies of consumption. In D. Miller (Ed.), *Acknowledging consumption. A review of new studies* (pp. 204–237). London, UK: Routledge.

Jain, S. K., & Ahuja, I. S. (2013). Strategies and success factors for overcoming challenges in ISO 9000 implementation in Indian manufacturing industry. International Journal of Technology. *Policy and Management*, *13*(2), 121–139.

Jalilvand, M. R., & Samiei, N. (2012). The impact of electronic word of mouth on a tourism destination choice: Testing the theory of planned behavior (TPB). *Internet Research: Electronic Networking Applications and Policy*, *22*(5), 591–612. doi:10.1108/10662241211271563

Janet, P. (1925). *Psychological Healing: A historical and clinical study*. New York: MacMillan.

Jappelli, T. (1990). Who is credit constrained in the US economy? *The Quarterly Journal of Economics*, *105*(1), 219–234. doi:10.2307/2937826

Jaraiedi, M., Plummer, R. W., & Aber, M. S. (1995). Incentive/disincentive guidelines for highway construction contracts. *Journal of Construction Engineering and Management*, *121*(1), 112–120. doi:10.1061/(ASCE)0733-9364(1995)121:1(112)

Jefferson, T. (1776). *The unanimous Declaration of the thirteen united States of America*. Washington, DC: United States Congress, National Archives and Records Administration.

Jensen, A. F., Cherchi, E., & de Dios Ortúzar, J. (2014). A long panel survey to elicit variation in preferences and attitudes in the choice of electric vehicles. *Transportation*, *41*(5), 973–993. doi:10.1007/s11116-014-9517-6

Johansson, B., & Mattsson, L.-G. (2012). *Road pricing: Theory, empirical assessment and policy*. Springer Science & Business Media.

Johnson, E. J., & Goldstein, D. (2003, November). Do Defaults Save Lives? *Science*, *302*(5649), 1338–1339. doi:10.1126/science.1091721 PMID:14631022

Johnson, E. J., Hershey, J., Meszaros, J., & Kunreuther, H. (1993). Making Decisions about Liability and Insurance. *Journal of Risk and Uncertainty*, *7*(1), 35–52. doi:10.1007/BF01065313

Johnson, E. J., Shu, S. B., Dellaert, B. G., Fox, C., Goldstein, D. G., Häubl, G., & Wansink, B. et al. (2012). Beyond nudges: Tools of a choice architecture. *Marketing Letters*, *23*(2), 487–504. doi:10.1007/s11002-012-9186-1

Joulfaian, D., & Rider, M. (1998). Differential Taxation and Tax Evasion by Small Business. *National Tax Journal*, *51*(4), 675–687.

Joyce, M., Miles, D., Scott, A., & Vayanos, D. (2012). Quantitative Easing and unconvencional monetary policy – an introduction. *The Economic Journal*, *122*(564), 271–288. doi:10.1111/j.1468-0297.2012.02551.x

Jung, C. (1916). *Psychology of the Unconscious*. Dover-Mineola, NY: Yard and Company. (reprinted 2002)

Kahneman, D. (2003). Theories of Decision Making in Economics. *The American Economic Review*, 1449–1475. doi:10.1257/000282803322655392

Kahneman, D., Krueger, A. B., Schkade, D. A., Schwarz, N., & Stone, A. A. (2004). A survey method for characterizing daily life experience: The day reconstruction method. *Science*, *304*(5702), 1776–1780. doi:10.1126/science.1103572 PMID:15576620

Kahneman, D., Slovic, P., & Tversky, A. (1982). *Judegement under Uncertainty: Heuristics and Biases*. Cambridge, UK: Cambridge University. doi:10.1017/CBO9780511809477

Kahneman, D., & Tversky, A. (1974). Judgement under uncertainty: Heuristics and Biases. *Science*, 1124–1131.

Kahneman, D., & Tversky, A. (1979, March). Prospect Theory: An Analysis of Decision under Risk. *Econometrica*, *47*(2), 263–292. doi:10.2307/1914185

Kahneman, D., & Tversky, A. (1984). Choices, values, and frames. *The American Psychologist*, *39*(4), 341–350. doi:10.1037/0003-066X.39.4.341

Kaiser, F. G., Doka, G., Hofstetter, P., & Ranney, M. A. (2003). Ecological behavior and its environmental consequences: A life cycle assessment of a self-report measure. *Journal of Environmental Psychology*, *23*(1), 11–20. doi:10.1016/S0272-4944(02)00075-0

Kaitz, M., Levy, M., Ebstein, R., Faraone, S., & Mankuta, D. (2009). The Intergenerational Effects of Traums from Terror: A Real Possiblity. *Infant Mental Health Journal*, *30*(2), 158–179. doi:10.1002/imhj.20209

Kalghatgi, G. T. (2014). The outlook for fuels for internal combustion engines. *International Journal of Engine Research*.

Kaopua, L., Braun, K., Browne, C., Mokuau, N., & Park, C. (2011). Why Are Native Hawaiians Under-represented in Hawai(i)s Older Adult Population? Exploring Social and Behavioral Factor of Longevity. *Journal of Aging Research*, *2011*, 1–8. doi:10.4061/2011/701232 PMID:21966592

Kaszowska, J., & Santos, J. L. (2014). The Role of Risk Perception in the Systemic Risk Generation and Amplification: Agent-Based Approach. *ACRN Journal of Finance and Risk Perspectives*, *3*(4), 146–170.

Kautonen, T., Gelderen, M., & Fink, M. (2015). Robustness of the theory of planned behavior in predicting entrepreneurial intentions and actions. *Entrepreneurship Theory and Practice*, *39*(3), 655–674. doi:10.1111/etap.12056

Kennickell, A. B., Starr-McCluer, M., & Surette, B. J. (2000). Recent changes in US family finances: Results from the 1998 Survey of Consumer Finances. *Federal. Reserve Bulletin,* (83), 1-24

Kenrick, D. T., Griskevicius, V., Neuberg, S. L., & Schaller, M. (2010). Renovating the pyramid of needs: Contemporary extensions built upon ancient foundations. *Perspectives on Psychological Science, 5*(3), 292–314. doi:10.1177/1745691610369469

Khondaker, A. N., Hasan, M. A., Rahman, S. M., Malik, K., Shafiullah, M., & Muhyedeen, M. A. (2016). Greenhouse gas emissions from energy sector in the United Arab Emirates – An overview. *Renewable & Sustainable Energy Reviews*, *59*, 1317–1325. doi:10.1016/j.rser.2016.01.027

Kim, H., & DeVaney, S. A. (2001). The determinants of outstanding balances among credit card revolvers. *Journal of Financial Counseling and Planning*, *12*(1), 67.

Kimmel, S. E., Chen, Z., Price, M., Parker, C. S., Metlay, J. P., Christie, J. D., & Gross, R. et al. (2007). The influence of patient adherence on anticoagulation control with warfarin: Results from the International Normalized Ratio Adherence and Genetics (IN-RANGE) study. *Archives of Internal Medicine*, *167*(3), 229–235.

Kirby, K. N. (1997). Bidding on the future: Evidence against normative discounting of delayed rewards. *Journal of Experimental Psychology. General*, *126*(1), 54–70. doi:10.1037/0096-3445.126.1.54

Kirby, K. N., & Maraković, N. N. (1995). Modeling myopic decisions: Evidence for hyperbolic delay-discounting within subjects and amounts. *Organizational Behavior and Human Decision Processes*, *64*(1), 22–30. doi:10.1006/obhd.1995.1086

Klass, A. B. (2016). Future-Proofing Energy Transport Law. *Washington University Law Review*, 16–11.

Klayman, J., & Brown, K. (1993). Debias the environment instead of the judge: An alternative approach to reducing error in diagnostic (and other) judgment. *Cognition*, *49*(1), 97–122. doi:10.1016/0010-0277(93)90037-V PMID:8287676

Klöckner, C. A., Nayum, A., & Mehmetoglu, M. (2013). Positive and negative spillover effects from electric car purchase to car use. *Transportation Research Part D, Transport and Environment*, *21*, 32–38. doi:10.1016/j.trd.2013.02.007

Klügl, F. (2008). A validation methodology for agent-based simulations. In *Proceedings of the 2008 ACM symposium on Applied computing* (pp. 39-43). ACM. doi:10.1145/1363686.1363696

Knox, P. L. (2005). Creating ordinary places: Slow cities in a fast world. *Journal of Urban Design*, *10*(1), 1–11. doi:10.1080/13574800500062221

Kolm, A.S., & Birthe, L. (2003). *Does tax evasion affect unemployment and educational choice?* Economics Working Paper No: 22. Retrieved from papers.ssrn.com

Koole, S. L., Jager, W., van den Berg, A. E., Vlek, C. A. J., & Hofstee, W. K. B. (2001). On the Social Nature of Personality: Effects of Extraversion, Agreeableness, and Feedback about Collective Resource Use on Cooperation in a Resource Dilemma. *Personality and Social Psychology Bulletin*, *27*(3), 289–301. doi:10.1177/0146167201273003

Kozinets, R. V. (2008). Brands in space: New thinking about experiential retail. In T. M. Lowrey (Ed.), *Brick & mortar shopping in the 21st century* (pp. 3–15). Mahwah, NJ: Lawrence Erlbaum.

Kressel, L. M., & Chapman, G. B. (2007). The Default Effect in End-of-Life Medical Treatment Preferences. *Medical Decision Making*, *27*(3), 299–310. doi:10.1177/0272989X07300608 PMID:17545499

Kroshus, E., Baugh, C. M., Daneshvar, D. H., & Viswanath, K. (2014). Understanding concussion reporting using a model based on the theory of planned behavior. *Journal of Adolescent Health, 54*(3), 269-274.

Kunreuther, H., & Slovic, P. (1978). Economics, Psychology, and Protective Behavior. *The American Economic Review*, *68*(2), 64–69.

La Barbera, F., Cariota Ferrara, P., & Boza, M. (2014). Where are we coming from versus who we will become: The effect of priming different contents of European identity on cooperation. *International Journal of Psychology*, *49*(6), 480–487. doi:10.1002/ijop.12073 PMID:25355671

Laibson, D., Repetto, A., & Tobacman, J. (2003). A Debt Puzzle. In P. Aghion, R. Frydman, J. Stiglitz, & M. Woodford (Eds.), Knowledge, Information and Expectations in Modern Economics: In Honor of Edmund S. Phelps (pp. 228–266). Princeton, NJ: Princeton University Press.

Laibson, D. (1997). Golden eggs and hyperbolic discounting. *The Quarterly Journal of Economics*, *112*(2), 443–477. doi:10.1162/003355397555253

Lai, I. K. W., & Lam, F. K. S. (2010). Perception of various performance criteria by stakeholders in the construction sector in Hong Kong. *Construction Management and Economics*, *28*(4), 377–391. doi:10.1080/01446190903521515

Lambropoulos, S. (2007). The use of time & cost utility for construction contract award under European Union Legislation. *Building and Environment*, *42*(1), 452–463. doi:10.1016/j.buildenv.2005.08.002

Lancaster, P. J., Plotkin, E. S., Lerner, J. N., & Morris, M. D. (2001). *Construction in Cities Social, Environmental, Political, and Economic Concerns*. New York: CRC Press LLC.

Landau, S., & Everitt, B. S. (2004). *A Handbook of Statistical Analyses using SPSS*. Chapman & Hall/CRC Press LLC.

Lange, C., & Byrd, M. (1998). The relationship between perceptions of financial distress and feelings of psychological well-being in New Zealand university students. *International Journal of Adolescence and Youth*, *7*(3), 193–209. doi:10.1080/02673843.1998.9747824

Lanne, M., Luoto, J., & Nyberg, H. (2014). *Is the Quantity Theory of Money Useful in Forecasting US Inflation?* Working Paper No. 2014-26. School of Economics and Management, University of Aarhus.

Larrick, R. P. (2004). Debiasing. In D. J. Koehler & N. Harvey (Eds.), *Blackwell Handbook of Judgment and Decision Making*. Malden, MA: Blackwell. doi:10.1002/9780470752937.ch16

Laslier, J. F., & Van der Straten, K. (2008). A live experiment on approval voting. *Experimental Economics*, *11*(1), 97–105. doi:10.1007/s10683-006-9149-6

Laslier, J.-F., & Sanver, R. M. (2010). *Handbook on Approval Voting*. London: Springer. doi:10.1007/978-3-642-02839-7

Lasser, K. J., & Bathory, D. S. (1997). Reciprocal Causality and Childhood Trauma: An Application of Chaos Theory. In *The Psychological Meaning of Chaos* (pp. 147–176). Washington, DC: American Psychological Association. doi:10.1037/10240-006

Lea, S. E., Webley, P., & Walker, C. M. (1995). Psychological factors in consumer debt: Money management, economic socialization, and credit use. *Journal of Economic Psychology*, *16*(4), 681–701. doi:10.1016/0167-4870(95)00013-4

Lee, K. T., & Ofori-Boateng, C. (2013). *Biofuels: Production Technologies, Global Profile, and Market Potentials Sustainability of Biofuel Production from Oil Palm Biomass*. Springer. doi:10.1007/978-981-4451-70-3_2

Lehmann, J. (2007). A handful of carbon. *Nature*, *447*(7141), 143–144. doi:10.1038/447143a PMID:17495905

Levin, J., & Nalebuff, B. (1995). An Introduction to Vote-Counting Schemes. *The Journal of Economic Perspectives*, *9*(1), 3–26. doi:10.1257/jep.9.1.3

Levitt, S. D., & List, J. A. (2007). What Do Laboratory Experiments Measuring Social Preferences Reveal about the Real World? *The Journal of Economic Perspectives*, *21*(2), 153–174. doi:10.1257/jep.21.2.153

Levitt, S., & Dubner, S. (2005). *Freakonomics. A Rogue Economist Explores the Hidden Side of Everything*. New York, NY: William Morrow & Co.

Levy, B. R., Slade, M. D., Kunkel, S. R., & Kasl, S. V. (2002). Longevity increased by positive self-perceptions of aging. *Journal of Personality and Social Psychology*, *83*(2), 261–270. doi:10.1037/0022-3514.83.2.261 PMID:12150226

Lewis, A., & van Venrooij, M. (1995). A note on the perceptions of loan duration and repayment. *Journal of Economic Psychology*, *16*(1), 161–168. doi:10.1016/0167-4870(95)00002-6

Li, L., & Loo, B. P. (2014). Alternative and transitional energy sources for urban transportation. *Current Sustainable/Renewable Energy Reports, 1*(1), 19-26.

Lindley, J. T., Rudolph, P., & Selby, E. B. Jr. (1989). Credit card possession and use: Changes over time. *Journal of Economics and Business*, *41*(2), 127–142. doi:10.1016/0148-6195(89)90012-X

Lippert, I. (2015). Environment as datascape: Enacting emission realities in corporate carbon accounting. *Geoforum*, *66*, 126–135. doi:10.1016/j.geoforum.2014.09.009

Liu, L., Wang, X., & Sheng, Z. (2012). Achieving ambidexterity in large, complex engineering projects: A case study of the Sutong Bridge project. *Journal of Construction Management and Economics*, *30*(5), 399–409. doi:10.1080/01446193.2012.679948

Livingstone, S. M., & Lunt, P. K. (1992). Predicting personal debt and debt repayment: Psychological, social and economic determinants. *Journal of Economic Psychology*, *13*(1), 111–134. doi:10.1016/0167-4870(92)90055-C

Loewenstein, G. (2007). *Exotic Preferences. Behavioral Economics and Human Motivation*. Oxford, UK: Oxford University Press.

Loewenstein, G., & O'Donoghue, T. (2006). We can do this the easy way or the hard way: Negative emotions, self-regulation, and the law. *The University of Chicago Law Review. University of Chicago. Law School*, *73*(1), 183–206.

Loewenstein, G., & Prelec, D. (1992). Anomalies in intertemporal choice: Evidence and an interpretation. *The Quarterly Journal of Economics*, *107*(2), 573–597. doi:10.2307/2118482

Loewy, A. (1986). *Central Regulation of Autonomic Functions*. New York: Oxford University Press.

Löfgren, O. (2014). Urban atmospheres as brandscapes and lived experiences. *Place Branding and Public Diplomacy*, *10*(4), 255–266. doi:10.1057/pb.2014.26

Long, J. E. (1982). The Income Tax and Self-Employment. *National Tax Journal*, *35*(1), 31–42.

Long, W. C., Grow, J. N., Majoris, J. E., & Hines, A. H. (2011). Effects of anthropogenic shoreline hardening and invasion by Phragmites australis on habitat quality for juvenile blue crabs (Callinectes sapidus). *Journal of Experimental Marine Biology and Ecology*, *409*(1), 215–222. doi:10.1016/j.jembe.2011.08.024

López-Mosquera, N., & Sánchez, M. (2012). Theory of Planned Behavior and the Value-Belief-Norm Theory explaining willingness to pay for a suburban park. *Journal of Environmental Management*, *113*, 251–262. doi:10.1016/j.jenvman.2012.08.029 PMID:23041517

Lozada, M., D'Adamo, P., & Fuentes, M. A. (2011). Beneficial effects of human altruism. *Journal of Theoretical Biology*, *28912-16*. doi:10.1016/j.jtbi.2011.08.016 PMID:21872608

Luo, R., Liu, B., Xie, Y., Li, Z., Huang, W., Yuan, J., & Liu, Y. et al. (2012). SOAPdenovo2: An empirically improved memory-efficient short-read de novo assembler. *GigaScience*, *1*(1), 1–6. doi:10.1186/2047-217X-1-18 PMID:23587118

Luther, S., Cicchetti, D., & Becker, B. (2000). The Construct of Resilience: A Critical Evaluation and Guidelines for Future Work. *Child Devleopment*, 543-562.

Macintosh, G., & Lockshin, L. S. (1997). Retail relationships and store loyalty: A multi-level perspective. *International Journal of Research in Marketing*, *14*(5), 487–497. doi:10.1016/S0167-8116(97)00030-X

Madrian, B. C., & Shea, D. F. (2001). The Power of Suggestion: Inertia in 401(k) Participation and Savings Behavior. *The Quarterly Journal of Economics*, *116*(4), 1149–1187. doi:10.1162/003355301753265543

Maier, S., & Seligman, M. (1976). Learned Helplessness: Theory and Evidence. *Journal of Experimental Psychology. General*, *105*(1), 3–46. doi:10.1037/0096-3445.105.1.3

Mantus, E. K. (2015). *Overcoming Barriers to Deployment of Plug-in Electric Vehicles*. Retrieved from http://www.nap.edu/catalog/21725/overcoming-barriers-to-deployment-of-plug-in-electric-vehicles

Maslow, A. (1943). A Theory of Human Motivation. *Psychological Review*, *50*(4), 370–396. doi:10.1037/h0054346

Masum, B., Masjuki, H., Kalam, M., Fattah, I. R., Palash, S., & Abedin, M. (2013). Effect of ethanol–gasoline blend on NOx emission in SI engine. *Renewable & Sustainable Energy Reviews*, *24*, 209–222. doi:10.1016/j.rser.2013.03.046

Mayer, K. J., & Argyres, N. S. (2004). Learning to contract: Evidence from the personal computer industry. *Organization Science*, *15*(4), 394–410. doi:10.1287/orsc.1040.0074

May, K. O. (1952, October). A Set of Independnet and Necessary and Sufficient Conditions for Simple Majority Decision. *Econometrica*, *20*(4), 680–684. doi:10.2307/1907651

Mazur, J. E. (1987). An adjusting procedure for studying delayed reinforcement. In M. L. Commons, J. E. Mazur, J. A. Nevin, & H. Rachlin (Eds.), Quantitative analysis of behavior: The effect of delay and of intervening events on reinforcement value (vol. 5, pp. 55–73). Hillsdale, NJ: Erlbaum.

McCleery, J., & Harvey, A. (2004). Integration of Psychological and Biological Approaches to Trauma Memory: Implications for Pharmacological Prevention of PTSD. *Journal of Traumatic Stress*, *17*(6), 485–496. doi:10.1007/s10960-004-5797-5 PMID:15730067

McClure, S. M., Laibson, D. I., Loewenstein, G., & Cohen, J. D. (2004). Separate neural systems value immediate and delayed monetary rewards. *Science*, *306*(5695), 503–507. doi:10.1126/science.1100907 PMID:15486304

McEwen, B. (2000). Allostasis and Allostatic Load: Implications for Neuropsychopharmacology. *Neuropsychopharmacology*, *22*(2), 108–124. doi:10.1016/S0893-133X(99)00129-3 PMID:10649824

McGee, R. W. (2006). Three Views on the Ethics of Tax Evasion. *Journal of Business Ethics*, *67*(1), 15–35. doi:10.1007/s10551-006-9002-z

McGee, R. W. (Ed.). (2012). *The Ethics of Tax Evasion in Theory and Practice*. New York: Springer. doi:10.1007/978-1-4614-1287-8

McNeil, B. J., Pauker, S. G., Sox, H. C. Jr, & Tversky, A. (1982). On the elicitation of preferences for alternative therapies. *The New England Journal of Medicine*, *306*(21), 1259–1262. doi:10.1056/NEJM198205273062103 PMID:7070445

Meier, S., & Sprenger, C. (2007). *Impatience and credit behavior: evidence from a field experiment (No 07-3)*. Boston: Federal Reserve Bank of Boston.

Meier, S., & Sprenger, C. (2010). Present-biased preferences and credit card borrowing. *American Economic Journal. Applied Economics*, *2*(1), 193–210. doi:10.1257/app.2.1.193

Mendelson, A. L., & Papacharissi, Z. (2011). Look at us. Collective narcissism in college student facebook photo galleries. In Z. Papacharissi (Ed.), *A networked self. Identity, community, and culture on social network sites* (pp. 252–273). New York, NY: Routledge.

Meng, X., & Gallagher, B. (2012). The impact of incentive mechanisms on project performance. *International Journal of Project Management*, *30*(3), 352–362. doi:10.1016/j.ijproman.2011.08.006

Michaelson, J., Abdallah, S., Steuer, N., Thompson, S., & Marks, N. (2009). *National accounts of well-being: Bringing real wealth onto the balance sheet*. London, UK: New Economics Foundation.

Millar, A., & Navarick, D. J. (1984). Self-control and choice in humans: Effects of video game playing as a positive reinforcer. *Learning and Motivation*, *15*(2), 203–218. doi:10.1016/0023-9690(84)90030-4

Millo, F., Rolando, L., Fuso, R., & Mallamo, F. (2014). Real CO 2 emissions benefits and end users operating costs of a plug-in hybrid electric vehicle. *Applied Energy*, *114*, 563–571. doi:10.1016/j.apenergy.2013.09.014

Miroiu, A. (2004). Charachterizing Majority Rule: From profiles to societies. *Economics Letters*, *85*(3), 359–363. doi:10.1016/j.econlet.2004.05.003

Mischel, W., Shoda, Y., & Rodriguez, M. I. (1989). Delay of gratification in children. *Science*, *244*(4907), 933–938. doi:10.1126/science.2658056 PMID:2658056

Missbauer, H., & Hauber, W. (2006). Bid calculation for construction projects: Regulations and incentive effects of unit price contracts. *European Journal of Operational Research*, *171*(3), 1005–1019. doi:10.1016/j.ejor.2005.01.014

Mitrut, C., Serban, D., & Vasilache, S. (2013). Indicators of Social Trust in Romania – A Quantitative Analysis. *Economic Computation and Economic Cybernetics Studies and Research*, *47*(1), 27–40.

Mooi, E., & Sarstedt, M. (2011). *A Concise Guide to Market Research. The Process, Data, and Methods Using IBM SPSS Statistics*. Berlin: Springer-Verlag.

Morales, A. (1998). Income Tax Compliance and Alternative Views of Ethics and Human Nature. *Journal of Accounting, Ethics &. Public Policy*, *1*(3), 380–399.

Mtra, R., & Sapolsky, R. (2008). Acute corticosterone treatment is sufficent to induce anxiety and amygdloid dendritic hypertrophy.*Proceedings of the National Academy of Science*, 5573-8.

Myerson, J., & Green, L. (1995). Discounting of delayed rewards: Models of individual choice. *Journal of the Experimental Analysis of Behavior*, *64*(3), 263–276. doi:10.1901/jeab.1995.64-263 PMID:16812772

Nagel, J. H. (2007, February). The Burr Dilemma in Approval Voting. *The Journal of Politics*, *69*(1), 43–58. doi:10.1111/j.1468-2508.2007.00493.x

Nash, J. (1950). *Non-cooperative Games* (Unpublished Doctoral Dissertation). Princeton University, Princeton, NJ.

Neumark, D., Wall, B., & Zhang, J. (2011). Do small businesses create more jobs? New evidence for the united states from the national establishment time series. *The Review of Economics and Statistics*, *93*(1), 16–29. doi:10.1162/REST_a_00060

Ng, S. T., & Skitmore, R. M. (2001). Contractor Selection Criteria: A Cost–Benefit Analysis. *IEEE Transactions on Engineering Management*, *48*(1), 96–106. doi:10.1109/17.913169

Nisbett, R. E. (1992). *Rules for reasoning*. Hillsdale, NJ: Lawrence Erlbaum.

Nitschke, J., Sarinopoulous, I., Oathes, D., Johnstone, T., Whalen, P., Davidson, R., & Kalin, N. (2009). Anticipatory Activationn in the Amydala and Anterior Cingilate in Generalized Anxiety Disorder and Prediction of Treatment Response. *The American Journal of Psychiatry*, 1–10. PMID:19122007

Norvilitis, J. M., & MacLean, M. G. (2010). The role of parents in college students financial behaviors and attitudes. *Journal of Economic Psychology*, *31*(1), 55–63. doi:10.1016/j.joep.2009.10.003

Norvilitis, J. M., Merwin, M. M., Osberg, T. M., Roehling, P. V., Young, P., & Kamas, M. M. (2006). Personality factors, money attitudes, financial knowledge, and credit-card debt in college students1. *Journal of Applied Social Psychology*, *36*(6), 1395–1413. doi:10.1111/j.0021-9029.2006.00065.x

Norvilitis, J. M., Szablicki, P. B., & Wilson, S. D. (2003). Factors Influencing Levels of Credit-Card Debt in College Students1. *Journal of Applied Social Psychology*, *33*(5), 935–947. doi:10.1111/j.1559-1816.2003.tb01932.x

Noval, L. J. (2016). On the misguided pursuit of happiness and ethical decision making: The roles of focalism and the impact bias in unethical and selfish behavior. *Organizational Behavior and Human Decision Processes*, 1331–16. doi:10.1016/j.obhdp.2015.12.004

Nowak, M. (2011). *Super Cooperators: Altruism, Evolution, and Why We Need Each Other to Survive*. Free Press.

Nugent, N., & Rhinard, M. (2015). *The European Commission*. Palgrave Macmillan.

O'Shaughnessy, J. (1987). *Why people buy*. New York, NY: Oxford University Press.

Ockenfels, A., & Werner, P. (2014). Scale manipulation in dictator games. *Journal of Economic Behavior & Organization*, *97*, 138–142. doi:10.1016/j.jebo.2013.11.002

ODonoghue, T., & Rabin, M. (1999). Doing it now or later. *The American Economic Review*, *89*(1), 103–124. doi:10.1257/aer.89.1.103

ODonoghue, T., & Rabin, M. (2000). The economics of immediate gratification. *Journal of Behavioral Decision Making*, *13*(2), 233–250. doi:10.1002/(SICI)1099-0771(200004/06)13:2<233::AID-BDM325>3.0.CO;2-U

ODonoghue, T., & Rabin, M. (2001). Choice and procrastination. *The Quarterly Journal of Economics*, *116*(1), 121–160. doi:10.1162/003355301556365

Ojo, S. O., Aina, O., & Adeyemi, A. Y. (2011). A comparative analysis of the performance of traditional contracting and design-build procurements on client objectives in Nigeria. *Journal of Civil Engineering and Management*, *17*(2), 227–233. doi:10.3846/13923730.2011.574449

Oldenburg, R., & Brissett, D. (1982). The third place. *Qualitative Sociology*, *5*(4), 265–284. doi:10.1007/BF00986754

Olsen, T. E., & Osmundsen, P. (2005). Sharing of endogenous risk in construction. *Journal of Economic Behavior & Organization*, *58*(4), 511–526. doi:10.1016/j.jebo.2003.09.019

Osborne, M. J. (2004). *An introduction to game theory*. New York, NY: Oxford University Press.

Ozaki, R., & Sevastyanova, K. (2011). Going hybrid: An analysis of consumer purchase motivations. *Energy Policy*, *39*(5), 2217–2227. doi:10.1016/j.enpol.2010.04.024

Pablo-Marti, F., Garcia-Tabuenca, A., Santos, J. L., Gallo, M. T., del Val, M. T., & Mancha, T. (2014). Macroeconomic Forecasting with Agent-Based Models: Prediction and Simulation of the Impact of Public Policies on SMEs. In Advances in Computational Social Science (pp. 139-155). Springer Japan.

Pablo-Martí, F., García-Tabuenca, A., Gallo, M. T., Santos, J. L., del Val, M. T., & Mancha, T. (2013). MOSIPS Agent-based model for predicting and simulating the impact of public policies on SMEs. In *Proceedings of the European Conference on Complex Systems 2012* (pp. 399-413). Springer International Publishing. doi:10.1007/978-3-319-00395-5_50

Pablo-Martí, F., Santos, J. L., & Kaszowska, J. (2015). An agent-based model of population dynamics for the European regions. Emergence. *Complexity and Organization*, *17*(2), C1.

Padhi, S. S., & Mohapatra, P. K. J. (2009). Centralized bid evaluation for awarding of construction projects – A case of India government. *International Journal of Project Management*, *28*(3), 275–284. doi:10.1016/j.ijproman.2009.06.001

Pandey, D., Agrawal, M., & Pandey, J. S. (2011). Carbon footprint: Current methods of estimation. *Environmental Monitoring and Assessment*, *178*(1-4), 135–160. doi:10.1007/s10661-010-1678-y PMID:20848311

Parks, C. D. (2015). Determinants of cooperation in social dilemmas. In D. A. Schoeder & W. G. Graziano (Eds.), *The Oxford handbook of prosocial behavior (pp. 524 – 547)*. New York, NY: Oxford University Press.

Parshall, L., Gurney, K., Hammer, S. A., Mendoza, D., Zhou, Y., & Geethakumar, S. (2010). Modeling energy consumption and CO 2 emissions at the urban scale: Methodological challenges and insights from the United States. *Energy Policy*, *38*(9), 4765–4782. doi:10.1016/j.enpol.2009.07.006

Paul, A., & Gutierrez, G. (2005). Simple probability models for project contracting. *European Journal of Operational Research*, *165*(2), 329–338. doi:10.1016/j.ejor.2004.04.005

Pauwels, L. (2010). Visual sociology reframed: An analytical synthesis and discussion of visual methods in social and cultural research. *Sociological Methods & Research*, *38*(4), 545–581. doi:10.1177/0049124110366233

Pavlov, I. (1927). *Conditioned reflexes: An investigation of the Physiological Activity of the Cerebral Cortex*. New York: Dover.

Pender, J. L. (1996). Discount rates and credit markets: Theory and evidence from rural India. *Journal of Development Economics*, *50*(2), 257–296. doi:10.1016/S0304-3878(96)00400-2

Pennock, R. T. (1998). Death and Taxes: On the Justice of Conscientious War Tax Resistance.*1 J. Acct. Ethics & Pub. Pol'y*, *58*, 58–76.

Peres, F. M., Nasello, A., & Moores, K. (2008). Traumatic memories: bridging the gap between functional neuroimgaging and psychotherapy. *Australian and New Zealand Journal of Psychiatry*, 478-488.

Permanent International Association of Road Congresses' (PIARC). (2003). *Procurement of works, goods and services by road administrations*. PIARC Technical Committee, C15 Report.

Perry, B. (1993). Neuro-development and the Neurophysiology of Trauma I: Conceptual Consideration for Clinical Work with Maltreated Children. *The Advisor*, 14-18.

Pesendorfer, W. (2006). Behavioral economics comes of age: A review essay on advances in behavioral economics. *Journal of Economic Literature*, *44*(3), 712–721. doi:10.1257/jel.44.3.712

Pestieau, P., & Possen, U. M. (1991). Tax Evasion and Occupational Choice. *Journal of Public Economics*, *45*(1), 107–125. doi:10.1016/0047-2727(91)90050-C

Phelps, E. S., & Pollak, R. A. (1968). On second-best national saving and game-equilibrium growth. *The Review of Economic Studies*, *35*(2), 185–199. doi:10.2307/2296547

Pine, B. J., & Gilmore, J. H. (1999). *The experience economy: Work is theatre & every business a stage*. Boston, MA: Harvard Business School Press.

Pink, S. (2012). *Situating everyday life*. London, UK: Sage Publications Ltd.

Pollak, R. A. (1968). Consistent planning. *The Review of Economic Studies*, *35*(2), 201–208. doi:10.2307/2296548

Pommerehne, W. W., Schneider, F., & Zweifel, P. (1982, June). Economic Theory of Choice and the Preference Reversal Phenomenon: A Reexamination. *The American Economic Review*, *72*(3), 569–574.

Pongthanaisawan, J., & Sorapipatana, C. (2013). Greenhouse gas emissions from Thailands transport sector: Trends and mitigation options. *Applied Energy*, *101*, 288–298. doi:10.1016/j.apenergy.2011.09.026

Popoyan, L., Napoletano, M., & Roventini, A. (2016). *Taming Macroeconomic Instability: Monetary and Macro Prudential Policy Interactions in an Agent-Based Model.* Working Paper 6/2015. ISI Growth.

Pramangioulis, P. (2008). *Guide to data analysis using SPSS*. Athens: Athens University of Economics and Business. Department of Statistics.

Prelec, D., & Loewenstein, G. (1991). Decision making over time and under uncertainty: A common approach. *Management Science*, *37*(7), 770–786. doi:10.1287/mnsc.37.7.770

Prelec, D., & Loewenstein, G. (1998). The red and the black: Mental accounting of savings and debt. *Marketing Science*, *17*(1), 4–28. doi:10.1287/mksc.17.1.4

Prelec, D., & Simester, D. (2001). Always leave home without it: A further investigation of the credit-card effect on willingness to pay. *Marketing Letters*, *12*(1), 5–12. doi:10.1023/A:1008196717017

Puhalo, S. (2003). Etnička distanca građana Repubike Srpske i Feeracije BiH prema narodima bivše. *Psihologija*, 141-156.

Pyyry, N. (2016). Participation by being: Teenage girls hanging out at the shopping mall as ´dwelling with´. *Emotion, Space and Society*, *18*, 9–16. doi:10.1016/j.emospa.2016.01.006

Rabin, M. (1998, March). Psychology and Economics. *Journal of Economic Literature*, *36*, 11–46.

Rachlin, H., Raineri, A., & Cross, D. (1991). Subjective probability and delay. *Journal of the Experimental Analysis of Behavior*, *55*(2), 233–244. doi:10.1901/jeab.1991.55-233 PMID:2037827

Rahman, I., Vasant, P., Singh, B. S. M., & Abdullah-Al-Wadud, M. (2015a). Swarm intelligence-based optimization for PHEV charging stations.Handbook of Research on Swarm Intelligence in Engineering, 374. doi:10.4018/978-1-4666-8291-7.ch012

Rahman, I., Vasant, P. M., Singh, B. S. M., & Abdullah-Al-Wadud, M. (2015b). *On the performance of accelerated particle swarm optimization for charging plug-in hybrid electric vehicles. Alexandria Engineering Journal.*

Rahman, I, Vasant, P. M., Singh, B. S. M., Abdullah-Al-Wadud, M., & Adnan, N. (2016). Review of recent trends in optimization techniques for plug-in hybrid, and electric vehicle charging infrastructures. *Renewable & Sustainable Energy Reviews*, *58*, 1039–1047. doi:10.1016/j.rser.2015.12.353

Redelmeier, D. A., & Heller, D. N. (1993). Time preference in medical decision making and cost-effectiveness analysis. *Medical Decision Making*, *13*(3), 212–217. doi:10.1177/0272989X9301300306 PMID:8412549

Reilly, R. J. (1982, June). Preference Reversal: Further Evidence and Some Suggested Modifications in ExperimentalDesign. *The American Economic Review*, *72*(3), 576–584.

Reisch, L. A., & Sunstein, C. R. (2016). *Do Europeans like nudges?*. Available at SSRN 2739118.

Rezvani, Z., Jansson, J., & Bodin, J. (2015). Advances in consumer electric vehicle adoption research: A review and research agenda. *Transportation Research Part D, Transport and Environment*, *34*, 122–136. doi:10.1016/j.trd.2014.10.010

Richardson, D. B. (2013). Electric vehicles and the electric grid: A review of modeling approaches, Impacts, and renewable energy integration. *Renewable & Sustainable Energy Reviews*, *19*, 247–254. doi:10.1016/j.rser.2012.11.042

Rieskamp, J., Busemeyer, J. R., & Mellers, B. A. (2006). Extending the bounds of rationality: Evidence and theories of preferential choice. *Journal of Economic Literature*, *44*(3), 631–661. doi:10.1257/jel.44.3.631

Robb, C. A., & Sharpe, D. L. (2009). Effect of personal financial knowledge on college students' credit card behavior. *Journal of Financial Counseling and Planning*, *20*(1), 25–43.

Roberts, R., Golding, J., & Towell, T. (1998). Student finance and mental health. *The Psychologist*, *11*, 481–491.

Roberts, R., Golding, J., Towell, T., & Weinreb, I. (1999). The effects of economic circumstances on British students mental and physical health. *Journal of American College Health*, *48*(3), 103–109. doi:10.1080/07448489909595681 PMID:10584444

Rose, T., & Manley, K. (2011). Motivation toward financial incentive goals on construction projects. *Journal of Business Research*, *64*(7), 765–773. doi:10.1016/j.jbusres.2010.07.003

Rosser, J. B. Jr, & Rosser, M. V. (2015). Complexity and behavioral economics. *Nonlinear Dynamics Psychology and Life Sciences*, *19*(2), 201–226. PMID:25783044

Rutter, M., Tuma, A., & Lann, I. (1988). *Assessment and Diagnosis in Child Psychopathology*. Guilford Press.

Salle, I., Senegas, M. A., & Yildizoglu, M. (2013). *How transparent about its inflation target should a Central Bank be? An Agent-Based Model Assessment.* Working paper No. 2013-24. Groupe de Recherche en Economie Théorique et Appliquée.

Samuelson, P. A. (1937). A note on measurement of utility. *The Review of Economic Studies*, *4*(2), 155–161. doi:10.2307/2967612

Samuelson, W., & Zeckhauser, R. (1988). Status Qvo Bias in Decision Making. *Journal of Risk and Uncertainty*, *1*(1), 7–59. doi:10.1007/BF00055564

Sang, Y.-N., & Bekhet, H. A. (2015). Modelling electric vehicle usage intentions: An empirical study in Malaysia. *Journal of Cleaner Production*, *92*, 75–83. doi:10.1016/j.jclepro.2014.12.045

Schlaes, A. (1999). *The Greedy Hand: How Taxes Drive Americans Crazy and What To Do about It.* New York: Random House.

Schmitt, B. (1999). Experiential marketing. *Journal of Marketing Management*, *15*(1-3), 53–67. doi:10.1362/026725799784870496

Schuetze, H. J. (2000). Taxes, Economic Conditions and Recent Trends in Male Self-Employment: A Canada-U.S. Comparison. *Labour Economics*, *7*(5), 507–544. doi:10.1016/S0927-5371(00)00012-9

Schuitema, G., Anable, J., Skippon, S., & Kinnear, N. (2013). The role of instrumental, hedonic and symbolic attributes in the intention to adopt electric vehicles. *Transportation Research Part A, Policy and Practice*, *48*, 39–49. doi:10.1016/j.tra.2012.10.004

Seaward, H. G., & Kemp, S. (2000). Optimism bias and student debt. *New Zealand Journal of Psychology*, *29*(1), 17.

Seixas, J., Simões, S., Dias, L., Kanudia, A., Fortes, P., & Gargiulo, M. (2015). Assessing the cost-effectiveness of electric vehicles in European countries using integrated modeling. *Energy Policy*, *80*, 165–176. doi:10.1016/j.enpol.2015.01.032

Seligman, M. (2011). *Flourish*. New York: Nicholas Brealey Publishing.

Selten, R. (2002). What Is Bounded Rationality? In *Bounded rationality, the adaptive toolbox* (pp. 13–36). Cambridge, MA: MIT Press.

Shackman, A., McManamin, B., Maxwell, J., Greischar, L., & Davidson, R. (2009). Right Dorsolateral Prefrontal Cortical Activity and Behavioral Inhibition. *Psychological Science*, *20*(12), 1500–1506. doi:10.1111/j.1467-9280.2009.02476.x PMID:19906125

Sharaf, O. Z., & Orhan, M. F. (2014). An overview of fuel cell technology: Fundamentals and applications. *Renewable & Sustainable Energy Reviews*, *32*, 810–853. doi:10.1016/j.rser.2014.01.012

Sharp, T. (2012, November 27). *livescience*. Retrieved from www.livescience.com

Shefrin, H. M., & Thaler, R. H. (1988). The behavioral life-cycle hypothesis. *Economic Inquiry*, *26*(4), 609–643. doi:10.1111/j.1465-7295.1988.tb01520.x

Shields, R. (1992). Spaces for the subject of consumption. In R. Shields (Ed.), *Lifestyle shopping. The subject of consumption* (pp. 1–20). London, UK: Routledge.

Shr, J. F., & Chen, W. T. (2003). A method to determine minimum contract bids for incentive highway projects. *International Journal of Project Management*, *21*(8), 593–599. doi:10.1016/S0263-7863(02)00056-X

Shr, J. F., & Chen, W. T. (2004). Setting Maximum Incentive for Incentive/Disincentive contracts for Highway Projects. *Journal of Construction Engineering and Management*, *130*(1), 84–93. doi:10.1061/(ASCE)0733-9364(2004)130:1(84)

Sigurdardottir, S. B., Kaplan, S., Møller, M., & Teasdale, T. W. (2013). Understanding adolescents intentions to commute by car or bicycle as adults. *Transportation Research Part D, Transport and Environment*, *24*, 1–9. doi:10.1016/j.trd.2013.04.008

Simon, H. (1955). A Behavioral Model of Rational Choice. *The Quarterly Journal of Economics*, *69*(1), 99–118. doi:10.2307/1884852

Simon, H. (1959). Theories of Decision Making in Economics and Behavioral Science. *The American Economic Review*, 253–283.

Sito-Sucic, D., & Djurica, M. (2014, May 19). *Floods affect over 1 million in Balkans, destruction terrifying*. Retrieved from Reuters: www.moblie.reuters.com

Skinner, B. F. (1969). *Contingencies of Reinforcement: A Theoretical Analysis*. New York, NY: Appleton-Century-Crofts.

Slemrod, J. (2007). Cheating Ourselves: The Economics of Tax Evasion. *Journal of Economic Perspectives*, *21*(1), 25–48.

Slemrod, J., Blumenthal, M., & Christian, C. (2001). Taxpayer Response to an Increased Probability of Audit: Evidence from a Controlled Experiment in Minnesota. *Journal of Public Economics*, *79*(3), 455–483. doi:10.1016/S0047-2727(99)00107-3

Slovic, P., & Lichtenstein, S. (1983, Sep.). Preference Reversals: A Broader Perspective. *Preference Reversals: A Broader Perspective*, *73*(4), 596-605.

Smart, A., & Smart, J. (2003). Urbanization and the global perspective. *Annual Review of Anthropology*, *1*(32), 263–285. doi:10.1146/annurev.anthro.32.061002.093445

Solís, J. C., & Sheinbaum, C. (2013). Energy consumption and greenhouse gas emission trends in Mexican road transport. *Energy for Sustainable Development*, *17*(3), 280–287. doi:10.1016/j.esd.2012.12.001

Solnick, J. V., Kannenberg, C. H., Eckerman, D. A., & Waller, M. B. (1980). An experimental analysis of impulsivity and impulse control in humans. *Learning and Motivation*, *11*(1), 61–77. doi:10.1016/0023-9690(80)90021-1

Solomon, M. R. (2002). *Consumer behavior: Buying, having, and being*. Upper Saddle River, NJ: Prentice-Hall.

Soman, D. (2001). Effects of payment mechanism on spending behavior: The role of rehearsal and immediacy of payments. *The Journal of Consumer Research*, *27*(4), 460–474. doi:10.1086/319621

Soman, D., & Cheema, A. (2002). The effect of credit on spending decisions: The role of the credit limit and credibility. *Marketing Science*, *21*(1), 32–53. doi:10.1287/mksc.21.1.32.155

Sotero, M. (2006). A Conceptual Modela of Hisotrical Trauma: Implications for Public Health Practice and Research. *Journal of Health Disparities Research and Practice*, 93-108.

Sroufe, L., & Rutter, M. (1984). The Domain of Psychopathology. *Child Development*, *55*(1), 17–29. doi:10.2307/1129832 PMID:6705619

Steffen, A. (2011). *World Changing: A User's Guide for the 21st Century*. New York: Abrams.

Stewart, N. (2009). The cost of anchoring on credit-card minimum repayments. *Psychological Science*, *20*(1), 39–41. doi:10.1111/j.1467-9280.2008.02255.x PMID:19152539

Stone, C. (2012, November 2). *US News and World Report*. Retrieved from www.usnews.com

Strotz, R. H. (1955). Myopia and inconsistency in dynamic utility maximization. *The Review of Economic Studies*, *23*(3), 165–180. doi:10.2307/2295722

Susarla, S., & Friedrich, E. (2013). The solar power policies and markets of Asia and Europe. *Asia Europe Journal*, *11*(3), 339–354. doi:10.1007/s10308-013-0353-7

Tang, W., Qiang, M., Duffield, C. F., Young, D. M., & Lu, Y. (2008). Incentives in the Chinese Construction Industry. *Journal of Construction Engineering and Management*, *134*(7), 457–467. doi:10.1061/(ASCE)0733-9364(2008)134:7(457)

Taylor, S., & Todd, P. (1995). Decomposition and crossover effects in the theory of planned behavior: A study of consumer adoption intentions. *International Journal of Research in Marketing*, *12*(2), 137–155. doi:10.1016/0167-8116(94)00019-K

Tetlock, P. E., & Mellers, B. A. (2002, January). The Great Rationality Debate. *Psychological Science*, *13*(1), 94–99. doi:10.1111/1467-9280.00418

Thaler, R. (1980). Toward a positive theory of consumer choice. *Journal of Economic Behavior & Organization*, *1*(1), 39–60. doi:10.1016/0167-2681(80)90051-7

Thaler, R. H. (1981). Some Empirical Evidence on Dynamic Inconsistency. *Quasi Rational Economics*, *8*(3), 127–136.

Thaler, R. H. (2015). *Misbehaving. The Making of Behavioral Economics*. New York: W.W. Norton & Company.

Thaler, R. H., & Benartzi, S. (2004). Save more tomorrow™: Using behavioral economics to increase employee saving. *Journal of Political Economy*, *112*(S1), S164–S187. doi:10.1086/380085

Thaler, R. H., & Shefrin, H. M. (1981). An economic theory of self-control. *Journal of Political Economy*, *89*(2), 392–406. doi:10.1086/260971

Thaler, R. H., & Sunstein, C. R. (2008). *Nudge. Improving Decisions About Health, Wealth, and Happieness*. New Haven, CT: Yale University Press.

Thaler, R. H., & Sunstein, C. R. (2008). *Nudge: Improving decisions about health, wealth, and happiness*. New Haven, CT: Yale University Press.

The Boston Consulting Group. (2014). *The digital future. A game plan for consumer packaged goods*. Available: https://www.bcgperspectives.com/

Thorndike, J. J., & Ventry, D. J. Jr. (2002). *The Ongoing Debate on Tax Justice*. Washington, DC: The Urban Institute Press.

Tong, F., Jaramillo, P., & Azevedo, I. M. (2015). Comparison of Life Cycle Greenhouse Gases from Natural Gas Pathways for Light-Duty Vehicles. *Energy & Fuels*, *29*(9), 6008–6018. doi:10.1021/acs.energyfuels.5b01063

Torgler, B. (2002). Speaking to Theorists and Searching for Facts: Tax Morale and Tax Compliance in Experiments. *Journal of Economic Surveys*, *16*(5), 657–683. doi:10.1111/1467-6419.00185

Torgler, B. (2006). The Importance of Faith: Tax Morale and Religiosity. *Journal of Economic Behavior & Organization*, *61*(1), 81–109. doi:10.1016/j.jebo.2004.10.007

Torgler, B. (2008). What Do We Know about Tax Fraud? An Overview of Recent Developments. *Social Research*, *75*(4), 1239–1270.

Tran, M., Banister, D., Bishop, J. D., & McCulloch, M. D. (2012). Realizing the electric-vehicle revolution. *Nature Climate Change, 2*(5), 328-333.

Tran, M. (2012). Technology-behavioural modelling of energy innovation diffusion in the UK. *Applied Energy*, *95*, 1–11. doi:10.1016/j.apenergy.2012.01.018

Tuan, Y.-F. (2003). *Space and Place. The perspective of experience*. Minneapolis, MN: University of Minnesota Press.

Turner, J. R., & Simister, S. J. (2001). Project contract management and a theory of organization. *International Journal of Project Management*, *19*(8), 457–464. doi:10.1016/S0263-7863(01)00051-5

Turton, H., & Moura, F. (2008). Vehicle-to-grid systems for sustainable development: An integrated energy analysis. *Technological Forecasting and Social Change*, *75*(8), 1091–1108. doi:10.1016/j.techfore.2007.11.013

Tversky, A., & Kahneman, D. (1981, January30). The framing of decisions and the psychology of choice, *Science. New Series*, *211*(4481), 453–458.

Tversky, A., & Kahneman, D. (1989). *Rational choice and the framing of decisions.* Berlin: Springer. doi:10.1007/978-3-642-74919-3_4

U. S. Department of the Treasury. (2005b). *Understanding the Tax Gap. FS-2005-14.* Washington, DC: Author.

U.S. Department of the Treasury. (2005a). *Internal Revenue Service.* Tax Gap Facts and Figures.

U.S. General Accounting Office. (2012). *Tax Gap: Sources of Noncompliance and Strategies to Reduce It.* GAO-12-651T. Retrieved from http://gao.gov

Ungern-Sternberg, T. (1994). Quality incentives in auctions for construction contracts. *International Journal of Industrial Organization*, *12*(1), 89–104. doi:10.1016/0167-7187(94)90029-9

Urminsky, O., & Zauberman, G. (2015). The Psychology of Intertemporal Preferences. In G. Keren & G. Wu (Eds.), The Wiley Blackwell Handbook of Judgment and Decision-making (pp. 1-50). West Sussex, UK: Blackwell Publishing. doi:10.1002/9781118468333.ch5

Vâlsan, C., Druică, E., & Ianole, R. (2015). Social Capital, Sustainability, and a History of Transitions in Romania: From Communism to Free Markets. In O. Schwarz-Herion & A. Omran (Eds.), *Strategies towards the New Sustainability Paradigm: Finding the Balance between Global Anarchy and Global Dictatorship* (pp. 35–48). Springer International Publishing.

van der Kolk, B. (1987). *Psychological Trauma.* Washington, DC: American Psychiatric Press.

van der Kolk, B., Roth, S., Pelcovitz, D., Sunday, S., & Spinazzola, J. (2005). Disorders of Extreme Stress: The Empirical Foundation of a Complex Adaption to Trauma. *Journal of Traumatic Stress*, *18*(5), 389–399. doi:10.1002/jts.20047 PMID:16281237

Van Lange, P. A. M., Balliet, D., Parks, C. D., & Van Vugt, M. (2014). *Social dilemmas: The psychology of human cooperation.* New York, NY: Oxford University Press.

Veld, J., & Peeters, W. A. (1989). Keeping large projects under control: The importance of contract type selection. *International Journal of Project Management*, *7*(3), 155–162. doi:10.1016/0263-7863(89)90034-3

Velupillai, K. V., & Zambelli, S. (2015). Simulation, computation and dynamics in economics. *Journal of Economic Methodology*, *22*(1), 1–27. doi:10.1080/1350178X.2015.1004933

Vidal, L.-A., Marle, F., & Bocquet, J.-C. (2011). Measuring project complexity using the Analytic Hierarchy Process. *International Journal of Project Management*, *29*(6), 718–727. doi:10.1016/j.ijproman.2010.07.005

Vittersø, J., Biswas-Diener, R., & Diener, E. (2005). The divergent meanings of life satisfaction: Item response modeling of the satisfaction with life scale in Greenland and Norway. *Social Indicators Research*, *74*(2), 327–348. doi:10.1007/s11205-004-4644-7

Vlăducu, A., & Guțu, D. (2013). Un experiment privind regulile de vot la alegerile locale din Chișinău – Republica Moldova. In A. Miroiu, & Ș. Cerchez (Eds.), *Competiția Politică în România* (pp. 190-224). Iași: Polirom.

Vlăducu, A., & Guțu, D. (2011, December). Un experiment asupra regulilor de vot. *Perspectives on Politics*, *4*(1), 99–111.

Volpp, K. G., Loewenstein, G., Troxel, A. B., Doshi, J., Price, M., Laskin, M., & Kimmel, S. E. (2008). A test of financial incentives to improve warfarin adherence. *BMC Health Services Research*, *8*(1), 272. doi:10.1186/1472-6963-8-272 PMID:19102784

Volpp, , Troxel, A. B., Pauly, M. V., Glick, H. A., Puig, A., Asch, D. A., & Audrain-McGovern, J. et al. (2009). A randomized, controlled trial of financial incentives for smoking cessation. *The New England Journal of Medicine*, *360*(7), 699–709. doi:10.1056/NEJMsa0806819 PMID:19213683

Waber, R. L., Shiv, B., Carmon, Z., & Ariely, D. (2008). Commercial features of placebo and therapeutic. *Journal of the American Medical Association*, *299*(9), 1016–1017. doi:10.1001/jama.299.9.1016 PMID:18319411

Wang, E. T. G., Ju, P.-H., Jiang, J. J., & Klein, G. (2008). The effects of change control and management review on software flexibility and project performance. *Information & Management*, *45*(7), 438–443. doi:10.1016/j.im.2008.05.003

Wang, S., Fan, J., Zhao, D., Yang, S., & Fu, Y. (2016). Predicting consumers intention to adopt hybrid electric vehicles: Using an extended version of the theory of planned behavior model. *Transportation*, *43*(1), 123–143. doi:10.1007/s11116-014-9567-9

Wang, W. C., Wang, H. H., Lai, Y. T., & Li, J. C. C. (2006). Unit-price-based model for evaluating competitive bids. *International Journal of Project Management*, *24*(2), 15–166. doi:10.1016/j.ijproman.2005.06.002

Ward, S. C., & Chapman, C. B. (1995). Evaluating fixed price incentive contracts. *Omega*, *23*(1), 49–62. doi:10.1016/0305-0483(94)00047-E

Ward, S., & Chapman, C. (1994). Choosing contractor payment terms. *International Journal of Project Management*, *12*(4), 216–221. doi:10.1016/0263-7863(94)90045-0

Wärneryd, K. E. (1999). *The Psychology of Saving: A Study on Economic Psychology*. Cheltenham, UK: Edward Elgar Publishing.

Warren, E. (1998). The Bankruptcy Crisis. *Indiana Law Journal (Indianapolis, Ind.)*, *73*(4), 1079–1110.

Warwick, J., & Mansfield, P. (2000). Credit card consumers: College students knowledge and attitude. *Journal of Consumer Marketing*, *17*(7), 617–626. doi:10.1108/07363760010357813

Webber, C., & Wildavsky, A. (1986). *A History of Taxation and Expenditure in the Western World*. New York: Simon & Schuster.

Weber, J. M., Kopelman, S., & Messick, D. M. (2004). A conceptual review of decision making in social dilemmas: Applying a logic of appropriateness. *Personality and Social Psychology Review*, *8*(3), 281–307. doi:10.1207/s15327957pspr0803_4 PMID:15454350

Weich, S., & Lewis, G. (1998). Material standard of living, social class, and the prevalence of the common mental disorders in Great Britain. *Journal of Epidemiology and Community Health, 52*(1), 8–14. doi:10.1136/jech.52.1.8 PMID:9604035

White, M. P., & Dolan, P. (2009). Accounting for the richness of daily activities. *Psychological Science, 20*(8), 1000–1008. doi:10.1111/j.1467-9280.2009.02392.x PMID:19549079

Wilmot, C. G., & Cheng, G. (2003). Estimating Future Highway Construction Costs. *Journal of Construction Engineering and Management, 129*(3), 272–279. doi:10.1061/(ASCE)0733-9364(2003)129:3(272)

Wolf, S., Bouchaud, J. P., Cecconi, F., Cincotti, S., Dawid, D., Gintis, H., . . . Paroussos, L. (2011) Describing economic agent-based models, Dahlem ABM documentation guidelines. In *Proceedings of the 100th Dahlem conference on new approaches in economics after the financial crisis.*

Wong, H., & Bitran, R. (1999). Designing a benefits package. Prepared for the flagship course on Health Sector Reform and sustainable financing. World Bank Institute.

Woolley, H., & Johns, R. (2001). Skateboarding: The city as a playground. *Journal of Urban Studies, 6*(2), 211–230. doi:10.1080/13574800120057845

Woolley, H., Dunn, J., Spencer, C., Short, T., & Rowley, G. (1999). Children describe their experiences of the city centre: A qualitative study of the fears and concerns which may limit their full participation. *Landscape Research, 24*(3), 287–301. doi:10.1080/01426399908706564

Xu, Y., & Zhong, Z. (2009). Single profile of preferences with variable societies: A characterization of simple majority rule. *Economics Letters*, 1–3.

Yamagishi, T., & Cook, K. S. (1993). Generalized Exchange and Social Dilemmas. *Social Psychology Quarterly, 56*(4), 235. doi:10.2307/2786661

Yang, Y., Li, J., Sun, X., & Chen, J. (2014). Measuring external oil supply risk: A modified diversification index with country risk and potential oil exports. *Energy, 68*, 930–938. doi:10.1016/j.energy.2014.02.091

Yannis, G. (2006). Entrepreneurship and the Policy Environment. *Federal Reserve Bank of St. Louis Review.*

Yilmaz, M., & Krein, P. T. (2013). Review of battery charger topologies, charging power levels, and infrastructure for plug-in electric and hybrid vehicles. Power Electronics. *IEEE Transactions on, 28*(5), 2151–2169.

Yitzhaki, S. (1974). A Note on Income Tax Evasion: A Theoretical Analysis. *Journal of Public Economics, 3*(3), 201–202. doi:10.1016/0047-2727(74)90037-1

Yoo, P. S. (1998, January). Still charging: The growth of credit card debt between 1992 and 1995. *Federal Reserve Bank of St. Louis Review*, 19-27.

Young, H. P. (1974). An axiomatization of Bordas rule. *Journal of Economic Theory, 9*(1), 43–52. doi:10.1016/0022-0531(74)90073-8

Yuan, F., & Miyazaki, K. (2013). *Mapping Technological Dynamics as Keyword Co-occurrence Clusters: A Study on the Electrified Vehicles Research.* Academic Press.

Zamfirescu, D. (2008). *Nevroză balcanică.* Editura Trei.

Závacká, J. (2015) Monetary policy during the business cycle. In *Proc. 11th International Conference on Strategic Management and its Support by Information Systems 2015*, (pp. 329–338).

Zettle, R. D., & Hayes, S. C. (1982). Rule governed behavior: A potential theoretical framework for cognitive behavior therapy. In P. C. Kendall (Ed.), Advances in cognitive behavioral research and therapy (pp. 73-118). New York, NY: Academic Press. doi:10.1016/B978-0-12-010601-1.50008-5

Zhang, H.-Y., Ji, Q., & Fan, Y. (2013). An evaluation framework for oil import security based on the supply chain with a case study focused on China. *Energy Economics*, *38*, 87–95. doi:10.1016/j.eneco.2013.03.014

Zunjić, S. (1999). An Introduction to the Study of Serbian Philosophy. *Gledšita*, 5-77.

About the Contributors

Rodica Ianole is Associate Professor at the Faculty of Business and Administration, University of Bucharest, Romania. She holds a PhD in Behavioral Economics, a master degree in Economic Cybernetics and Quantitative Economics and a bachelor degree in Business Administration.

* * *

Nadia Adnan received her Bachelor in Business Administration (Honors) from Jinnah University for Women, Karachi, Pakistan. MBA in (Marketing) from Jinnah University for Women, Karachi, Pakistan and CEMBA in (Persuasive Marketing) from Institution of Business Administration (IBA), Karachi, Pakistan. Currently she is pursuing Doctor of philosophy from the Department of Management and Humanities, Universiti Teknologi PETRONAS, Malaysia. Her Research interest are Behavior Marketing which is based on Decision making, Attitudes and persuasion, Social influence, Motivation Cognition, Culture, Nonconscious behavior influences and Consumer behavioral approach. Her research is based on Quantitative Marketing Analaysis Investigating consumer choices and purchase behavior. Examining product, pricing, advertising, and promotion strategies of firms. Analyzing competition in a wide range of domains.

Fani Antoniou holds a BEng in Civil Engineering, an MSc in Concrete Structures from the Imperial College, London and a PhD from the Aristotle University of Thessaloniki. She is a Certified IPMA-Level D: PM Associate. She has been employed at Egnatia Odos S.A., a client organisation responsible for the design, construction, operation and maintenance of the Egnatia Motorway in Northern Greece since 1997, where she has held the position of Project Manager since 2006. She is currently a National representative in the Technical Committee 'Performance of Transport Administrations' of the World Road Association.

Georgios N. Aretoulis is an Assistant Professor since 2015, at the Civil Engineering Department of the Aristotle University of Thessaloniki, Greece. He holds a Diploma, an MSc in Environmental Protection and Sustainable Development, as well as a PhD from the Aristotle University of Thessaloniki.

David S. Bathory, Psy.D., has owned and operated his own private research and consulting firm since 2010. He has extensive experience in behavioral health, development and management, both clinical and academic. His research interests and publications involve exploring the basis of relationships (Relational Dynamics), decision making, and applications of these in areas, such as, Behavioral Economics, Art and Architectural Design, and discovering viable solutions for complex issues such as aiding in the recovery process for large populations exposed to psychological trauma.

Vasanthakumar N. Bhat received his Ph.D from the Yale University. He is the author of three books on environmental management and medical malpractice. He has widely published on a variety of topics including management science, healthcare management, and environmental management.

Gabriela Carrasco has a Ph.D. in Experimental Psychology from Texas Tech University in 2007. Has worked at the University of North Alabama for 9 years.

Elena Druică is full professor of Statistics for Business, Applied Econometrics and Data Analysis with the University of Bucharest. She was formally trained in Mathematics, completing her PhD in 2003. During her PhD she studied genetic algorithms and optimization processes, developing a new classification of objective functions that converge to the optimum in polynomial time. During her second doctoral work she studied Economics with a particular focus on risk assessment, and she now applies her skills in the area of saving behavior, implementing agent based modeling to explain the peer pressure influence on economic rationality. Elena is interested in agent based modeling and uses Net Logo to simulate various social and economic phenomena and is also skilled in using statistical and econometric methods to deal with real data for both descriptive, and predictive purposes. She is trained in R programming language.

Ari Huuhka is University Lecturer at the University of Vaasa, Department of Marketing. His research interests are in the area of retailing and consumer behavior. They include theories of retail change, retail marketing, international retailing, cross-cultural aspects of consumer behavior, and consumer inferences. He has carried out numerous national and international research projects. He has worked as a visiting researcher in Japanese universities. He has published works for example in European Retail Research and Journal of East-West Business.

Glykeria Kalfakakou is a Professor of Investments Appraisal and the Director of the Laboratory of Construction Equipment and Management at the Department of Civil Engineering at the Aristotle University of Thessaloniki in Greece. She is also the Director of the post graduate programme under the title "Technical Projects Management", which is offered at the same department. Professor Kalfakakou has a significant professional experience on planning of construction works and infrastructure. She is teaching the following courses of the undergraduate programme: "Project Management and Planning", "Construction Business Management and Organization", "Investments Appraisal", "Optimization of Technical Projects Production", "Project Management". Furthermore, she is teaching the following courses of the postgraduate programme: "Operational Research", "Decision and Risk Analysis". She also gives invited lectures to training seminars in the field of investments appraisal and construction management.

Jagoda Kaszowska is Master in Financial Mathematics at theJagiellonian University, BA in Economics at the University of Alcalá. She is currently doing her doctoral thesis at CracowUniversity of Economics and she is working in the Central Bank of Poland.

Dimitrios K. Konstantinidis holds a Diploma in Civil Engineering from the Aristotle University of Thessaloniki and an MSc as well as a PhD from the Imperial College, London. He has been a Professor at the Alexander Technological Educational Institute in Greece since 2006 and was Dean of the School of Technological Applications until 2014. Currently he is Head of the Department of Civil Engineering. For the last 18 years, he has been involved in the design of bridges. Since 2003, he has held the position of National Representative in the Technical Committee 'Road Bridges' of the World Road Association.

Martti Laaksonen is Professor of Marketing at the University of Vaasa. His key research areas include consumer behavior, retail marketing and development of product concepts. He has published for example in Advances in Business Marketing, Journal of Business Research (monograph), Journal of Economic Psychology, International Journal of Research in Marketing, and Psychology & Marketing.

Pirjo Laaksonen is Professor of Marketing at the University of Vaasa. Her main research areas are connected to consumption and consumer behavior, marketing of consumer goods, and marketing communication. She has published extensively about involvement, for example a book in English and in Japanese. Examples of publishing forums in the area of marketing are such as International Journal of Research in Marketing, in the area of consumer behavior such as Psychology & Marketing and Journal of Consumer Culture and in the area of application of marketing such as Place Branding and Journal of Product & Brand Management. Pirjo Laaksonen has been the president of the multidisciplinary Finnish Association of Consumer Research.

Tomás Mancha Navarro is Ph. D. in Economics (University of Malaga). Professor of Economic Policy (University of Alcala). Director of the Institute of Economic and Social Analysis (IAES) of the University of Alcala. His main focus is in Regional Economics, Spanish Economy Policy, fields where he has several national and international publications. In the last years his main scope is connected to model complex systems. He has been adviser in Regional Development Planning for Spanish Public Administrations, Inter American Development Bank and European Commission.

Amir Noor has completed his Bachelor from Department of Computer Science, London Metropolitan University, 166-220 Holloway Rd, Holloway, London N7 8DB, United Kingdom. He is currently associated with software development firm.

Shahrina Md Nordin has an academic experience in the fields of language and communication. She obtained her B.HSc in Language and Literature from International Islamic university Malaysia. Her Master's degree was in Education from Universiti Teknologi Malaysia where her project was on technical communication in the engineering industry. Her PhD thesis was on second language writing in technical communication in Universiti Sains Malaysia. She is currently Head of Centre of Social Innovation (CoSI) and Director of Project Management Office, Universiti Teknologi PETRONAS (UTP). She has taught undergraduate and postgraduate programs in the area of Academic Writing, Technical and Professional Writing, Professional Communication Skills, Research Methodology, Business Communication, and Corporate Communication. Her current research areas are in communications for innovation diffusion, CSR communications for community empowerment and organizational communications. She has published many papers, two books and has received a number of awards including Most Commendable Paper by Emerald. She is currently an advocate of Social Innovation that draws upon the strength of multidisciplinary effort in impacting the communities.

Imran Rahman received BSc. Engineering from Department of Electrical and Electronic Engineering, Islamic University of Technology (IUT), Bangladesh in the year 2011 and MSc. (research) from Department of Fundamental and Applied Sciences, Universiti Teknologi PETRONAS (UTP), Bandar Seri Iskandar, Malaysia in the year 2016.

Juan Luis Santos received a Master in Systems Engineering (Universidad Rey Juan Carlos) and a Master in Applied Economic Analysis (Universidad Complutenses de Madrid and Universidad de Alcala). He participated in Mosips model (7th framework programme of the European Commission) and 'Analysis of systemic risk in EU countries: Implications for Poland' funded by the National Science Centre (NCN). Currenty he is finishing his Ph.D 'Big data in multiagent systems: market design solutions' under the supervision of Tomás Mancha Navarro.

Shruti Surachita completed her M. Sc. Programme in Behavioral and Economic Sciences, with distinction from the University of Warwick, UK. Prior to her post graduate education, she passed her Bachelor's degree in 2014 with Economics (Honors) from Utkal University, India. She did a Research Project on "Understanding the effect of Subjective Wellbeing on Cooperation Levels in Social Situations", as a partial fulfillment of the MSc. Degree from the University of Warwick. She participated in the International Conference on 'Anthropological Perspectives and Local Approaches: Indigenous Application in Management and Marketing' at Eastern China University of Science and Technology, Shanghai, China in 2013 and presented a paper on 'Wellbeing and Cooperation' at Warwick Economics Exchange in 2015. Currently she is working as a research intern in the Marketing Area at XLRI-Xavier School of Management, Jamshedpur, India.

Pandian Vasant is a senior lecturer at Department of Fundamental and Applied Sciences, Universiti Teknologi PETRONAS in Malaysia. His research interests include Soft Computing, Hybrid Optimization, Holistic Optimization and Applications. He has co-authored research papers and articles in national journals, international journals, conference proceedings, conference paper presentation, and special issues lead guest editor, lead guest editor for book chapters' project, conference abstracts, edited books and book chapters. In the year 2009, P. Vasant was awarded top reviewer for the journal Applied Soft Computing (Elsevier). Currently he is Editor-in-Chief of IJCO and IJEOE and Editor of GJTO. H-Index SCOPUS = 30, H-Index Google Scholar = 21.

Andrei Vlăducu is a doctor in political science at the Political Science at National School of Political Science and Public Administration where he focused his research on social choice rules and behavioral economics. He works as an associate professor at the Faculty of Political Science where he teaches seminars of behavioral social sciences, experiments in political science and European policy. He led a series of field and laboratory experiments, having research experience in this areas. His research interests are behavioral economics, the power of habit, emotions and human decision making theories.

Index

www.ingramcontent.com/pod-product-compliance
Lightning Source LLC
LaVergne TN
LVHW062147200926
848484LV00007B/1875